China & America's Emerging Partnership

A Realistic New Perspective

JOHN MILLIGAN-WHYTE
DAI MIN

New York

Specialist Press International books can be purchased for educational, business or sales promotional use. For ordering details, please contact:
Special Markets Department
Specialist Press International – SPI Books
99 Spring Street • New York, NY 10012
(212) 431-5011 • sales@spibooks.com

For further information, contact:

New York

S.P.I. Books
99 Spring Street, 3rd Floor
New York, NY 10012
(212) 431-5011 • Fax: (212) 431-8646
E-mail: publicity@spibooks.com
www.spibooks.com

10 9 8 7 6 5 4 3 2 1

First Edition

Library of Congress cataloging-in-publication data available.

ISBN (13): 978-1-56171-202-1
ISBN: 1-56171-202-7

Also by John Milligan-Whyte and Dai Min
NEW CHINA BUSINESS STRATEGIES:
CHINESE AND AMERICAN COMPANIES AS GLOBAL PARTNERS
(Specialist Press International Books — S.P.I. Books)

Table of Contents

CHINA & AMERICA'S EMERGING PARTNERSHIP: A REALISTIC NEW PERSPECTIVE

Acknowledgements

This book about partnerships of human beings in countries and companies could not have been created without the wisdom, courage, and support, for a quarter of a century, of Orlando Smith, the Managing Partner of Milligan-Whyte & Smith.

The tireless support of Lei Valli Thompson, Amani Flood, Dora Baker and staff of Milligan-Whyte & Smith, Doris Goodman of Reporting and Transcription Services, and David McCormick of the University of Toronto were also essential, as were the contributions of Robert Levin of Transclick, Ian Shapolsky of Specialist Press International SPI Books, and Wilder Knight and Robert Stein of Pryor Cashman.

We are grateful for the encouragement of Ambassador Richard Swett of APCO Worldwide; the late Representative Tom Lantos, Chairman of the U.S. House Foreign Affairs Committee; Representative John Conyers, Jr., Chairman of the House Judiciary Committee, Representative Carolyn Maloney; Chair of the House Financial Institutions and Consumer Credit Subcommittee, and Representative Lester Wolff, (Ret.), former Chair of the House Asian Affairs Subcommittee; former UN Under-secretary General Maurice Strong; Seymour Topping of the Council on Foreign Relations and former managing editor, and editorial director (Editor) of the New York Times; Maurice Johnson, Editor of China Business Wire; Cyril Rance of XL Capital; Mary Grace of E-Smart Technologies; The Honorable Judge Melvin Schweitzer; Jytte Marstrand; Zhang Liyong, President of China General Chamber of Commerce; Dr. Chen Wenshen; Jin Juanping, Dr. Deng Ya, Hu Jun, Prof. Li Shixin; Xie Na and Dr. Geng Xiefeng of Peking University; Chen Xialou, Ji Sanmeg, Liu Fan and Dr. Zhao Gangzhu of Renmin University.

Jerry St. Paer, the former CFO of XL Capital and Honorary Chairman of the China Bermuda Society, Virginia Kampsky of Kampsky & Associates and the China Institute provided significant impetus for the book.

We also thank the over 1.6 billion Americans and Chinese who inspired and for whom the book was written.

Foreword ———
by Ambassador Richard Swett, FAIA

At a time when serious students of international affairs are bombarded with sobering scenarios that predict a future of growing economic and military confrontation between the United States and a rising Asia, it has been hard to be optimistic about what lies ahead. We have all heard the assertion that the 21st Century will be "China's Century." The implication is that America has passed its zenith and faces inevitable decline.

Through this fog of dire predictions shines a beacon of hope that offers a compelling case for a robust and successful next century for *both* the United States and China. In two new companion books on geopolitical and business strategy, the authors have illuminated a unique new roadmap to how and why the world's leading Superpower and the fastest rising New-Power must turn their dangerous global competition in a cooperative direction. Such a shift will only yield enormous economic benefits for both. More importantly, it will go a long way toward creating a more governable, safer, and prosperous world.

The first book, *China & America's Emerging Partnership: A Realistic New Perspective* by John Milligan-Whyte and co-author Dai Min, presents a new perspective on the causes and consequences of China's meteoric economic rise, and points the way to a resolution of the adversarial competition between the two economies. It begins by helping the reader understand how capitalism with Chinese characteristics diverge and intersects with capitalism with American characteristics.

The authors then illustrate how these two great capitalist powers currently find themselves on a dangerous collision course. The work of internationally acclaimed economists and analysts are referenced in support of the authors' arguments, and the picture that initially emerges is not a pretty one. The authors make it clear that without a significant course correction, China and the United States face a looming crisis. Fortunately, John Milligan-Whyte and Dai Min explain how the needed course correction can be achieved. Using insights from game theory, the authors construct a compelling alternative strategy and scenario for America and China's successful shared future. They demonstrate convincingly that the current self-defeating cut-throat competition is not in the economic or national security interests of either country, and that it is possible to shift to a "win-win" geopolitical and economic relationship by employing *realistic, mutually beneficial and enforceable* strategies of cooperation.

The companion book, *New China Business Strategies: Chinese and American Companies as Global Partners* by John Milligan-Whyte and co-authors Dai Min, Professor Mannie Liu, and Howard H. Jiang, uses actual case studies to illustrate what works and what doesn't. From the disastrous 2005 battle of American and Chinese companies over the acquisition of Unocal, to the path-breaking cooperative venture between IBM and Legend that resulted in the creation of Lenovo, the authors offer concrete examples of the failures of a zero-sum game approach as contrasted with the competitive advantages and successes of a more collaborative model. They suggest advanced strategies for how American and Chinese companies can work together in arenas with enormous and essentially untapped mutual benefits.

These books are the first of their kind to look at the huge potential to be found in combining the strengths of America and China to advance their respective prospects and ameliorate the potential dangers each is striving to avoid. In doing so, the authors see beyond the fear of China's growing power to a sustainable future of mutual advantage.

The authors are realistic in their assessment of the obstacles, ethnic, political, and cultural, that must be navigated to build the collaborative strategic partnership that the United States and China's national security and economic interests require in the dangerous circumstances of the 21st century. They offer a credible blueprint for building a strong new framework for the relationship between these two countries.

This refreshing perspective and new analysis of the entwined futures of China and America could not have come at a better time. A new kind of leadership, a leadership of inclusion and cooperation, is necessary to build the peaceful, prosperous 21st Century we all want. In applying the new perspectives and strategic approaches in these two unique new books, American and Chinese political and business leaders will have, in their hands, the roadmap to a more hopeful, stable future for all of us.

Ambassador Richard Swett, FAIA
Senior Counselor at APCO Worldwide
Former Member of Congress and U.S Ambassador to Denmark
Author of *Leadership by Design: Creating an Architecture of Trust*

Summary

This book and its companion book, *New China Business Strategies: Chinese and American Companies as Global Partners*, present the case for why and how America and China, and American and Chinese companies, must prosper together as committed global partners. This is the only alternative to America and China remaining zero-sum-game competitors that can slip into trade war, Cold War, armed conflict, and ecological catastrophe. The two books present a new perspective and "mindset" essential to understanding China, and new business structures and strategies required for America and American companies to align themselves with and prosper from China's growing economic power.

Game theory is useful in clarifying America and China's complex relationship. From a game theory perspective, in "The China Game," the world's most powerful developed and developing nations are in an ongoing interaction. Serious economic decline or social collapse (losing) is unacceptable to either and will lead to armed conflict and ecological catastrophe in which neither can win (both losing). The case for America and China using win-win instead of zero-sum-game strategies is compelling because neither nation can sustainably prosper if the other does not also prosper. In game theory, an approach called a "Generous Tit-for-Tat Strategy" has been found most likely to result in sustained win-win outcomes for both players in such an ongoing interaction.

Our thesis is that America and China will both lose if either pursues zero-sum strategies that result in either one or the other nation losing. Neither can succeed unless both can profitably and sustainably collaborate.

There has been said to be three main perspectives[1] in the debate about the future of China, and ultimately about the future of America and China: China will collapse[2]; inevitably become democratic[3]; or remain resiliently authoritarian[4] and stagnate.[5] Recently, other perspectives have emerged: China will not collapse, and should, before it gets any stronger, be confronted with a policy focused on demands that it move to an American-style democracy[6]; China must adopt the values of the European Enlightment if there is to be peace and a partnership between China and America[7]; China's internal politics and problems could derail China's peaceful rise[8] and China as an opportunity and threat for America, depending on the policy choices each makes, and American policy should try to shape China's future in ways that reinforce Americans' lives, long-term security, prosperity, and peace.[9] These perspectives are related to a view that armed conflict between America and China may be or is inevitable.[10] All these perspectives are based on the false assumption that China *can and should be* like America. *China & America's Emerging Partnership: A Realistic New Perspective* presents a perspective that is based on the reality that China's political, social, economic, and legal systems and business culture *cannot and will not be* like America's anytime soon. Nonetheless, China and America now share a passion for the prosperity that successful capitalism produces, and are playing the game of 21st century capitalism and making up new rules as they go. We call this new perspective the "win-win perspective."

The new perspective accepts the reality that China's 50-century-old-civilization has created a new model of "capitalism with Chinese characteristics." It accepts the reality that more and more Mainland Chinese are thriving in China's cultural, political, social, economic, and legal systems, that are different than America's.

The new perspective accepts the reality that China will not collapse, remain resiliently authoritarian, or stagnate, and that armed conflict between America and China can and must be prevented.

The new "win-win perspective" provides vital opportunities for America that the other perspectives do not. It explains why and how America can thrive in spite of the reality that China's economy will be larger, stronger, and more innovative than America's, sooner than many Americans expect or can accept. It explains why and how China's hoped-for peaceful development can be peacefully accepted by America. It provides a basis for the genuine global partnership of America and China that is essential for their shared prosperity, and for making the world safe from "unrestricted warfare" and ecological collapse. It explains why and how American and Chinese companies must design and operate sustainably successful genuine global joint ventures, and why and how American capitalism and capitalism with Chinese characteristics must accommodate each other. It provides a "succeed with China" alternative to the "fear China" genre of media coverage.

The Chinese government and people's shift from a communist to a capitalist economy, and China's resulting economic success, constitutes a paradigm shift between the 20th and 21st centuries. Americans urgently require a corresponding new perspective that explains and accommodates China's cultureal and capitalism's economic success. The established and other perspectives do not. They ignore, deny, and underestimate China's successful use of capitalism with Chinese characteristics, the success to date of China's one-party political system, and the success of China's pre-rule of law legal system in managing economic development and reform. The new perspective and mindset changes presented in *China & America's Emerging Partnership: A Realistic New Perspective* and *New China Business*

Strategies: Chinese and American Companies as Global Partners answer the urgent questions of why and how America and China's styles of capitalism *can and must* accommodate each other's continued success.

The reality is that America and China will inevitably fail as civilizations if they do not successfully collaborate to make the world more governable and ecologically safer. The speed, unpredictability, and destructiveness of 21st century "unrestricted warfare" make the sustained success of America and China's collaboration essential. The attack on the World Trade Center, by a small number of individuals rather than a state power, is the best-known example to date of "unrestricted warfare". The "unrestricted warfare" of the 21st century will present new forms and scales of attack beyond even the nuclear, biological, and other weapons of mass destruction invented and used in the 20th century. In addition, the ecological damage threatening human life, which America and China are world leaders in causing, can only be addressed through successful collaboration, and the leadership, innovation, and example to other nations in ameliorating man-made ecological damage.

The relationship between America and China involves the interaction of common and conflicting interests. The classical theory of trade holds that America and China are better off by trading and that it is healthy to have some economic competitors. But it is comforting to America if its competitors are weaker. The reality is that in less than 30 years of reopened trade relations, using only 30% of China's population, China's developing economy is growing three times faster than America's developed economy, and will soon be larger than America's, and continue to grow for decades. The reality is that America, the world's only current economic, geopolitical, and military superpower, is increasingly having difficulty competing economically with China. That reality is difficult for Americans to accept or accommodate.

Nonetheless, the reality is that for all but the past 2 of 50 centuries of Chinese civilization, China has been the wealthiest, most innovative and largest economy in the world. The past 2 centuries have been an anomaly in world history in that respect. Today, China has more than four times the population, or "human capital," of America. China's adoption of capitalism is redefining the wealth and competitiveness of nations in the 21st century, and creating increasing conflict with America over vital resources and geopolitical and economic power. Most American political leaders perceive China as an economic, geopolitical, and military threat. Forty-four percent of Americans reportedly believe that America has not been "tough enough" in dealings with China.[11]

America has used zero-sum-game strategies that attempted unsuccessfully to contain China. In 2005, the American government's blocking of NYSE-listed, partly Chinese-government owned China National Offshore Oil Company's acquisition of a publicly traded American company put in place a template for failure in the China Game.

In response, China is pragmatically now reducing its economic dependence on America, while still seeking a win-win strategic partnership with America. The outcome of America's zero-sum approach is that America is losing. Therefore, China is also losing the China Game. But the game is not over yet.

In 2005, the first global joint venture or combination between major American and Chinese companies established a win-win strategic template for success. That template must be improved upon, creating what is seen in both China and America as a successful and sustainable *genuine global* joint venture template, and must proliferate successfully.

Our main theme is the critical leadership challenge of sustaining peace and prosperity facing America and China's political and business leaders. *China & America's Emerging Partnership: A Realistic New Perspective* and *New China Business Strategies: Chinese and American Companies as Global Partners* are being published in America and China, in English and Mandarin, in order to put in the hands of America and China's political and business leaders in 2008 a shared new win-win mindset, blueprint, and strategy for committed global partnerships between America and China, American and Chinese companies, and American and Chinese styles of capitalism. The status quo of ad hoc problem-solving using zero-sum-game mindsets and strategies in countless daily geopolitical and corporate contests will inevitably result in catastrophe for America and China. For either nation to "win," America and China's political and business leaders *must do whatever it takes* to make geopolitical and business collaboration work in order to avoid the economic decline of both nations.

Our second key theme is that to make such a win-win collaboration work and ensure that neither superpower loses, a new geopolitical, economic, and military framework of a *committed, genuine* partnership of America and China is essential and must be adopted by America's and China's political parties in order to provide the required framework for both nations' successive political leaders to identify, negotiate, and implement domestic and foreign policies that avoid either nation losing.

Our third key theme is that a win-win mindset change and alignment between America and China's political leaders are essential for the new framework to avoid trade war, Cold War, and armed conflict. Win-win mindset change and alignment among American and Chinese business leaders also offers shared competitive advantages to Chinese companies "going global," and American companies seeking to profit on a sustained basis from China's rapidly evolving economic power. China has combined a capitalist mindset change with its vast human, financial and other resources, and competitive advantages in the 21st century, with China's evolving one party political system and 50 century-old culture. China's resulting emergence from poverty necessitates a similarly profound mindset change for America and American companies, which must align themselves profitably on a sustainable basis with China's economic success.

Our fourth key theme is that China is likely to be the world's richest nation sooner than Americans anticipate or wish. China's 22% of the world's population has enormous competitive advantages in the 21st century's "Knowledge Revolution". China's rates of macroeconomic and economic competitiveness growth will accelerate and compound. Being realistic about China's profound competitive advantages is critical to understanding why America and American companies must align their strategies rather than seek to contain China's economic growth and Chinese companies' "going global".

Our fifth key theme is a deep concern about the future of democracy in both America and in China. The real issue American and Chinese leaders face is not how fast democratic institutions and decision-making emerge in China. It is whether democratic institutions and decision-making are sustainable in either America or China in the circumstances of the 21st century. American expectations or demands for China to adopt American-style majority-rule democracy are unrealistic, premature, and endanger America and China's economic and national security. Many Americans, who are proud of America's history of success with majority-rule democracy, believe that what works for them is essential for everyone. There is an influential assumption among Americans that nations that are majority-rule democracies will not go to war with other majority-rule democracies. The assumption is that China and America's interests would not be in conflict if China adopted American-style majority-rule democratic institutions and processes. This "democratic peace theory" has been viewed with skepticism by China experts. It is amazing that this fallacious theory and its assumptions play such major roles in American policy towards China. Its genesis was in the idealism that created America, and it played a dominant role in the Cold War conflict between communist and capitalist ideology in the 20th century, which is outdated now that China has embraced capitalism. The democratic peace theory has resilience, even after the end of the Cold War, because Americans instinctively fear living in an undemocratic world. That fear in the American mindset perhaps explains why the democratic peace theory makes sense to many Americans even though it and its assumption overlook many realities.

Here are three examples of the types of realities the democratic peace theory ignores. In Europe, after World War I, democracy was imposed on Germany, which did not have a spontaneous history of democracy like America's. Hitler received 2.6% and 37% of votes in the 1928 and 1932 elections, before being appointed Chancellor. He then abolished elections and attacked democratic and undemocratic countries.[12] In China, with the collapse of the Qing Dynasty in 1911, the commander of the Beijing Army, Yuan Shikai, negotiated the abdication of the emperor. The widely recognized leader of the new republic, Sun Yat-sen, yielded the Presidency to Yuan Shikai while an election was held. A provisional assembly was elected in 1912. The Guomindang, or Nationalist Party, led by Sun Yat-sen, gained the most seats, but Yuan Shikai refused to relinquish power to the elected government, dissolved the assembly, and tried to make himself emperor. This precipitated yet another unstable period in China, dominated by warlords, as the nascent democracy failed to sustain itself in China. Many countries will be unstable and go to war if they become American-style majority-rule democracies. For example, China would be more nationalistic and susceptible to an anti-American party or parties capturing power than it currently is as a stable one-party state. Perhaps the greatest fallacy of the democratic peace theory is that America is a majority-rule democracy, but America has attacked democratic and undemocratic countries, sometimes without even a majority view among Americans that a particular war is wise or sustainable.

It is unrealistic for Americans, with less than 3 centuries of experimentation and experience with democracy in which the right to vote was gradually extended over many generations, to ignore 50 centuries of China's different historical experience, cultural traditions, and political experimentation.[13] The reality is that China will naturally use its indigenous consensus-based social and political culture in its incrementally evolving political system and capitalism with Chinese characteristics that have succeeded in meeting China's needs for stable government, rapid economic growth, and incremental-but-major reform since 1978. If America continues to use the fallacious democratic peace theory and its assumptions as the core of its policy towards China, it will impede rather than accelerate the evolution of Chinese-style democratic institutions and decision-making in China.

Without effective political and economic collaboration between America and China, China's economic growth and competitive advantages' impact on America will put great strains on the stability and sustainability of American-style majority-rule democracy in America. It is in neither country's national security or economic interests for American-style majority-rule democracy to be born prematurely in China or wither away in America.

The purpose of this and our related business strategy book is to establish widespread understanding of and support in both nations for win-win frameworks and strategies for managing America and China's common and conflicting interests. To achieve the books' objectives, we must address very different audiences simultaneously, which include America and China's political and business leaders, other business and politically-oriented readers, experts, and students, and American and Mainland Chinese readers. These two books are designed to be a common point of reference for all those audiences, who need to consider simultaneously the required win-win mindset, blueprint and strategies in a new 21st century framework.

Mindset change is hard to achieve. For some people, it is impossible. Many feel there are compelling reasons why it is unrealistic or impossible for America and China, and American and Chinese companies, to become successful committed, genuine, global partners. One of the most serious challenges in the world we live in is that those with zero-sum-game mindsets only have those assumptions, experiences, and thought processes to use in evaluating the realism and pragmatism of a win-win mindset and strategies. This formidable reality affects the process of selecting political leaders, their cognitive and decision-making processes, and resulting public policy choices, and puts America's national and economic security and democratic institutions at risk, which puts China's peaceful development at risk.[14]

Human beings are fallible. Whether you believe in original sin or Godel's Theorem Of Incompleteness,[15] or whatever you believe in, it is impossible to persuasively argue that human beings are infallible.

Logic (and therefore game theory) is less compelling in the real world than how people *feel* emotionally about ideas and facts. The logic and validity of our theses are compelling to people with win-win mindsets. We do not know whether we will persuade people with zero-sum-game mindsets. In the real world, when zero-sum mindsets and strategies do not produce the desired results, it does not stop people with zero-sum mindsets from using them again. Nonetheless, we believe that the ideas, facts, and new win-win perspective will come to be *felt* by a critical mass among America and China's political and business leaders, and then *felt* by a sustaining critical mass of Americans and Chinese to be obvious, true, and compelling.

The basis of our belief is not an assumption that human beings are rational. People are mysteries even to themselves. We each have finite minds grappling with the infinities we find within and around us. People are not rational because of the role of our unconscious minds on behavior. Nonetheless, it is our *belief* that a critical mass of Americans and Chinese *will* do what we need to do to survive in The Age Of Species Lethal Weapons. We believe that human nature and intelligence can solve the potentially species lethal problems they create.

John Milligan-Whyte
America-China Partnership Foundation
New York
May 2008

Reader's Guide

China & America's Emerging Partnership: A Realistic New Perspective examines the political, economic, and national security strategy aspects of our game-theory thesis and the five key themes set out in the Summary.

It examines what we term "The China Game," the case for a committed, genuine economic and geopolitical partnership between America and China, and a new mindset about China's nation-building and "Socialist Market Economy Capitalism."

New China Business Strategies: American And Chinese Companies As Global Partners examines the mindset changes and new Genuine Global Joint Venture Model and advanced win-win strategies and structures, and the structures, strategies, and best practices that foreign companies have used with China. The advantages of the new Genuine Global Joint Venture Model and of American companies aligning their China strategies with the needs and goals of China's economic development, and Chinese companies going global, are examined.

In the real world, politics, economics, and national security are played out in business and vice versa. Resolving political and business problems requires the successful interaction and alignment of political and business strategies. Readers interested in geopolitics, political economy, macroeconomic growth, or competitiveness and defense strategy may focus on the first book, but the second will help in understanding the business dynamics combining zero-sum-game and win-win strategies that drive or damage the relationship of America and China. Business-oriented readers may focus on the second book, but the first will help in understanding the mindset changes about doing business with China and win-win structures and strategies required for them to have powerful competitive advantages in the 21st century.

China & America's Emerging Partnership: A Realistic New Perspective is presented in 17 chapters, and *New China Business Strategies: American And Chinese Companies As Global Partners* is presented in 13 chapters. The overviews at the beginning of each chapter are designed to provide a concise summary and enable readers to find the discussions of topics of interest to them.

Detailed information is presented in the 30 chapters examining our thesis and key themes that is excessive for some readers' needs, but useful for others new to or very familiar with China's development. The overview that begins each chapter will enable readers that wish to skim or skip its subject, or the detailed information in it, to see what each chapter's focus and main points are. The headings throughout each chapter are also designed to facilitate selective reading.

In *China & America's Emerging Partnership: A Realistic New Perspective*, Chapter 1 examines the need for elite accomodation between America and China. Chapter 2 examines why America and China will fail or succeed together. Chapter 3 examines the American policy choices of containment or collaboration and five key questions facing America's political and business leaders. Chapter 4 examines China's capitalism, that is redefining the competitiveness and wealth of nations in the 21st century. Chapter 5 examines China's success as what we refer to as a "Permission Society," a "Consensus Democracy," and "Pre-Rule of Law Society" in which 22% of humanity is increasingly thriving. Chapter 6 examines the genius of the Chinese government, people, and culture in so rapidly emerging from the economic wreckage of the Cultural Revolution.

Chapter 7 examines whether America can peacefully accept China's peaceful development. Chapter 8 examines the leadership challenges in coping with American's resentment and fear of China. Chapter 9 examines the need for collaboration between America and China as elite capitalist superpowers. Chapters 10 and 11 examine how a committed, genuine global partnership between America and China would ameliorate the trade deficit, job losses, and other issues that the current relationship based on ad hoc, zero-sum-game strategies will fail to do. Chapter 12 examines win-win and zero-sum-game approaches and game theory relevant to their interaction's success. Chapter 13 examines China's past and future scientific and technological contributions to America. Chapter 14 examines the very similar evolution of the concept of intellectual property rights and their similar piracy and enforcement in America in the 19th and 20th centuries and in China in the 21st century.

Chapter 15 examines how America and China's partnership can be established and sustained in the 21st century. Chapter 16 examines whether America and China will choose together to succeed or fail as civilizations. Chapter 17 examines why a committed, genuine partnership of the world's current and emerging superpowers is essential for both America and China to consistently produce leaders in the 21st century able to sustain their shared peace and prosperity.

In *New China Business Strategies: Chinese and American Companies As Global Partners,* Part 1 provides a visual synopsis of both books and of An American Executive's Mindset Change Regarding China. Part 2's chapters 1 through 6 examine best practices in traditional China business strategies and new win-win strategies and structures designed to align American companies' strategies with the Chinese government's strategies for economic development and the needs of Chinese state-owned and private companies "going global." Chapter 1 examines the competitive advantages for American companies of a win-win mindset, value propositions, strategies, and rewards.

Chapter 2 examines how American companies can sustainably profit from China's economic growth.

Chapter 3 examines advanced strategies aligning American companies with Chinese companies "going global". Chapter 4 examines an advanced structure for American and Chinese companies as global partners. Chapter 5 examines case studies of traditional structures, strategies, and best practices used by American companies' joint ventures or in investing in China. Chapter 6 examines further case studies of traditional structures and strategies and the advantages of the Genuine Global Joint Venture Model. Chapter 7 examines China's commitments as a member of the World Trade Organization and some observers' expectations about them in the context of the evolution of China's Permission Society.

In Part 3, Chapters 8 through 12 examine alignment opportunities for American companies with the goals and needs of China's evolving financial services sector. Chapter 8 examines the current mindset among many Americans that unrealistically assumes China's evolving financial services sector must copy foreign models. Chapters 9 through 12 then examine in more detail China's evolving banking, insurance and reinsurance, stock market, and venture capital sectors, and alignment opportunities for American companies. Chapter 13 examines China's education and regional disparity challenges, and alignment opportunities for American companies.

It is useful in creating a new mindset and framework to present in these two books the views of many observers, in their own words, from many sources, that readers would otherwise never see together. Long quotes enable readers to see ideas and facts expressed in the words that diverse observers have used, and reveal important attitudes and assumptions that a summary of their views cannot easily or objectively do.

PART 1

Capitalism with American or Chinese Characteristics

1

Elite Accommodation of America and China

Overview

America and China, as the current and emerging elite superpowers, must accommodate each other's economic and political needs and collaborate as partners in "win-win" strategies that successfully geopolitically and economically manage the world.

The Elite Accommodation[1] of America and China

America's policy toward China of "containment" is a euphemism for "hostility." Nonetheless, China, through its own problem-identification and problem-solving processes, has achieved an average annual Gross Domestic Product (GDP) growth rate between 1979 and 2005 of 9.5% and become the fastest growing economy set in the largest and most populous country in the world. Given the long history of America's policy of containment towards China, an overt declaration of a collaborative genuine partnership between America and China is required to serve as a "paradigm shift,"[2] as well as a mindset change in which one conceptual worldview is replaced by another.

China and America are the elite of the developing and developed global economies. Many problems in their relationship, if collaborated on by America and China's political leaders, contain potential direct or indirect solutions. Such solutions are not always recognized in zero-sum-game confrontations that can rapidly escalate into trade war or armed conflict.

America and China's foreign policies must be based on an overt commitment to work together to solve shared economic challenges to each country's economic growth and stability. The framework of a committed genuine partnership is essential to create a stable domestic and foreign policy framework in which the two countries can reduce the blunders in dealing with a myriad of problems currently being addressed on an ad hoc basis. Dealing with problems ad hoc encourages zero-sum-game strategies inconsistent with win-win outcomes. America and China's political leaders must also eschew rhetoric and actions which are inconsistent with sustaining trust and collaboration among partners.

Creating the Framework of the Partnership of America and China in the 21st Century

It will be easier for the Chinese government to "sell" the paradigm and mindset shift of collaborating with America to the Chinese people than it will be for American political leaders to "sell" a collaborative approach to China's economic development to various interest groups in America. But, it is possible for America's political and business leaders to do so, if they can accept the paradigm shift that is occurring, and the mindset change that is necessary. The case for doing so is obviously compelling, but it has not been presented by a critical mass of America's political and business leaders to the American people. The obvious problems that China's economic achievements pose to American economic wellbeing have created a national debate about what to do about China. Many respected American political and business leaders are advising that containment will not work.

The various interest groups most immediately affected by China's competitive economic advantages, such as the labor unions and manufacturing associations and some business and political groups, etc., are seeking containment-driven American public policy decisions that are misguided. Containment policies will not solve the problems they are concerned with, but will cause problems their supporters are not sufficiently concerned with. Interest groups pushing for "containment" are looking for solutions to problems that containment may obviously, or not so obviously, lack.

Unless a majority of Americans can only deal with issues on an ad hoc zero-sum-game basis, the option of an overtly declared collaborative partnership between America and China is still open. Containment will not work because other countries will eagerly do business with China even if America slipped into a trade war with China. Every nation in the world wants to do business with China. An America policy of containment will exacerbate the erosion of America's economic lead, and leadership globally.

As time goes on, ad hoc confrontations with China, together with American interest group activism, will degrade the ability of the Chinese government to nourish a partnership with America. There is currently a window of opportunity to develop a collaborative policy and to solidify that new approach in a committed, stable partnership between China and America. As the relationship between the two nations deteriorates, collaboration will become politically, economically, and militarily more difficult.

America and Soviet Union Elite Accommodation in the Solution to the Cuban Missile Crisis

One of the lessons of the Cuban Missile Crisis in 1962 was that President Kennedy rose above much of the advice he was given. Nuclear war with the former Soviet Union was suddenly imminent, and was clearly a potential catastrophe for both nations as well as mankind. President Kennedy chose what many of his advisors saw as the more dangerous response—a naval blockade of Cuba. America's president saw that the option of an air strike to destroy Soviet missiles in Cuba, possibly followed by an invasion of Cuba by America, entailed the likely consequence of conventional armed conflict rapidly escalating into inevitably using nuclear weapons.

President Kennedy was unwilling to voluntarily select a course of action that was likely to lead to nuclear war. Focusing on the outcome that made sense, rather than the problem, he chose the blockade option although it potentially allowed the Soviet missiles already in Cuba to become operational and strike America. President Kennedy was also careful to try to find a solution to the Soviet Union's leader's problem of how to extract the missiles from Cuba while protecting Cuba from American invasion. In successfully solving Secretary Khrushchev's problem of how to extract the missiles while not abandoning Cuba, Kennedy solved his own problem of how to remove the missiles while avoiding nuclear war. His attention to the necessity of providing a solution to Secretary Khrushchev's problems enabled the Soviet Union's leader to provide a solution to President Kennedy's problems.[3]

Time Is of the Essence

The Chinese believe any success depends on "Tian shi, Di li, Ren He," meaning favorable timing, appropriate place, and homogeneous relationships among people. This is required for the success of a win-win strategy for America and China.

China's (and India's) drive to escape from poverty means that the future for America and the developed and developing world is not what it used to be. Equally important, the future is now. The Chinese government is taking the lead in seeking a win-win relationship with America. Can America respond positively given that it is a "Majority-Rule Democracy" in which less than 50.01% of American voters can impose their policy choices, or perceived self-interest, on more than 49.99% of Americans?

China has pragmatically chosen to succeed. Whether America chooses to succeed or fail is a fascinating test of the genius of American democracy, America's leadership, and ultimately, of the character of the American people.

2

America and China on the Road to Success or Failure Together

Overview

This chapter introduces the case for a committed partnership between America and China, and global joint ventures by American and Chinese companies.

The Reality That America and China Must Be Good Partners for Either to "Win" in the 21st Century

Robert Frost's poem "The Road Not Taken" celebrates how the choices we make change our lives. The "China strategies" of many foreign companies from 1979 to 2006, even when they have been profitable, have not been as successful as "China's strategy" for economic development.

China's strategy is to protect China's sovereignty and increase the standard of living of people by combining its own and foreign intellectual and financial capital to sustain the world's highest rate of economic development. China's strategy is so successful that China's "Socialist Market Economy" is poised to dwarf America's economy.

The Road Not Taken

Two roads diverged in a yellow wood,
And sorry I could not travel both
And be one traveler, long I stood
And looked down one as far as I could
To where it bent in the undergrowth;

Then took the other, just as fair,
And having perhaps the better claim,
Because it was grassy and wanted wear;
Though as for that the passing there
Had worn them really about the same,

And both that morning equally lay
In leaves no step had trodden black.
Oh, I keep the first for another day!
Yet knowing how way leads on to way,
I doubted if I should ever come back.

I shall be telling this with a sigh
Somewhere ages and ages hence:
Two roads diverged in a wood, and I—
I took the one less traveled by,
And that has made all the difference.

—Robert Frost

America's traditional geopolitical and business strategies seeking to contain China are strategies for America's failure. Most Americans do not recognize the far-reaching disaster for America that occurred when the U.S. government blocked China's National Offshore Oil Company's acquisition bid for Unocal. In 2005 and 2006 America's hostility towards China's economic competitiveness and power in the 21st century had begun damaging American companies' ability to do business in China, and American companies' global competitiveness.

The reality is that American companies without sustainably-profitable "China strategies" will find it increasingly difficult to remain profitable at all. American companies face both competition from companies from many other countries and the necessity and difficulties in doing business with China. Beginning in 2002, Chinese companies have been moving into positions to emerge as "mega-multinationals" and displace or acquire Fortune 1000 companies sooner than many had anticipated.

How can American companies profit from China's growing global economic power? China is what we will refer to as a "Permission Society," because it does not have the well-defined, reliable legal and regulatory system, democratic leadership or decision-making of what we will refer to as a "Rights Society" like America. A mindset change focusing on the sustained usefulness of a foreign company's value propositions and creative win-win strategies in fulfilling the needs and goals of the Chinese government and Chinese trading partners are competitive advantages in dealing profitably with a "Permission Society" achieving global economic power. American companies should focus on how their "China strategy" can be aligned with and enhance "China's strategy." That alignment should seek quick and sustained profitability and never get past the apex of the curve of gratitude of American companies' Chinese trading partners and the Chinese government.

Such alignment is an essential competitive advantage for America and American companies seeking to prosper in the 21st century.

Zero-sum-game strategies developed and used successfully in a "Rights Society" may be intrinsically unsuccessful when used in business dealings in a "Permission Society." "Genuine Global Joint Ventures" and other strategies operating both outside and inside China between Chinese and American companies that are based on "win-win" value propositions and "Generous Tit-For-Tat" strategies,[14] offer competitive advantages in profitably dealing with the growing economic power of China's "Permission Society." In game theory, a "Generous Tit-For-Tat Strategy" uses a cooperative response and then always repeats the opposing player's previous move.

Why Should China Be America's Good Partner?

The Chinese government, people, culture, and their way of doing things were able to produce rapid economic growth, incremental reform, and social stability between 1979 and 2006 in large part because the Chinese possess a one party state and strong entrepreneurial spirit. The Chinese government's succession mechanism in this period gave ultimate leadership to Deng Xiaoping, then to Jiang Zemin, and now to Hu Jintao. China's economic achievements under three leaders constitute success in the largest management challenge on the planet. China's leadership, people, and culture must be admired for their demonstrated management and entrepreneurial abilities. That respect is one key to the "win-win" success of America and China.

In 1976 China had a moribund economy with a national gross domestic product of US$64 billion. The Chinese government and people made a series of extraordinary economic reform decisions, which were profound mindset and social changes, after Mao Zedong's death in 1976. As a result, the Chinese government and people are winning "The China Game." To continue the successful economic growth and "peaceful rise of China,"[15] the Chinese government must ensure that America wins also. The Chinese government cannot feed the Chinese people's stomachs, minds, and hopes without far-seeing empathy for the impact China's success has on America. That is a key trait that the leadership generated from among the Chinese people and culture needs to have. Jiang Zemin, China's leader in 2000, proposed a "strategic partnership" between America and China. The Chinese government seeks a "cooperative partnership" with America.[16]

Why Should America Be China's Good Partner?

Why should America, the world's richest country with a US$10 trillion annual GDP in 2004,[17] form a comitted global partnership with China? Why should American companies create and strive to sustain genuine global joint ventures with Chinese companies? China only had a US$1.6 trillion annual GDP in 2004,[18] and has an annual per capita income that is about 12% of America's. The Chinese government is only projecting China having a US$4 trillion annual GDP by 2020. The reasons are compelling, but not enough Americans have thought them through and accepted them yet.

America won its Cold War with communism. China has embraced capitalism. China's economic development is challenging America with capitalism, not communism. Chinese capitalism has demonstrated its ability to grow three times faster than American capitalism, and can continue to do so for decades. America has the choice of embracing 1.3 billion emerging Chinese capitalists, or doing what it can, if anything, to prevent them from escaping poverty. The prospect of China overtaking America economically necessitates that American foreign policy towards China change from containment to collaboration.

The simple arithmetic of China's 1.3 billion people compared to America's 300 million suggests that China's economy will be larger than America's. One recent estimate of the world GDP notes that in 2004 China and America's economies were 4% and 28% respectively of the world's GDP and suggests that by 2025 China and America's economies will be 15% and 26% respectively, and by 2050 will be 28% and 26% respectively.[19] A containment policy will undermine the competitiveness of American companies and the American economy globally. In the final analysis, collaboration is the only smart and realistic choice for America.

America's genius as a nation with a uniquely inspiring idealism and economic, political, and military history of world leadership is challenged by the rise of China from poverty to prosperity. China's unexpected and extraordinary transformation is a new and interesting challenge to the ideals of American democracy and the "realism" of American power. The magnitude of the political, economic, and social changes China has achieved from 1978 to 2006 challenges America to change similarly. America's policy of "containment" of China has not worked in the 20th century and will not work in the 21st century. Will the American way of doing things be as pragmatic, flexible, and successful as the Chinese way of doing things in the 21st century?

3

How America and China Can Win Together

Overview

This chapter examines the concepts of The China Game, The Human Experiment, the Age Of Species Lethal Weapons, and the key question of how America and China can understand each other well enough to coexist in shared prosperity and peace. That question, at its heart, is much simpler: How can people who are different understand each other and prosper together? Billions of people do that every day. We believe that successfully answering that question in the real world of America and China's geopolitical, economic, and business relationships is not beyond the ability of human ingenuity, goodwill, and collaboration. But successfully answering that question requires the leaders and people of both America and China to better understand each other and to have "the right spirit" and mutual respect from which, in time, emerges trust and affection.

This book raises four other related key questions:

1. Will China and America produce leaders able to balance the demands of China's economic growth and sovereignty with the needs of America's economic growth and prosperity?

2. Will America's political and business leaders confront or collaborate with China's accelerating economic growth and Chinese companies "going global," and China's different institutions, customs, and hunger for economic development and sovereignty?

3. How will America's democracy cope if the growth of China's economic power demonstrates that China's institutions, customs, and way of doing business can economically outperform America's democratic institutions, system of government and law, and way of doing business?

4. Realistically, how quickly will China's 50-century-old civilization that sought to ignore foreigners until 28 years ago evolve from a "Permission Society" with a Pre-Rule of Law system into a "Rights Society" with a Rule of Law system that immigrants on a pristine continent incrementally built in America in the past three centuries?

The China Game

These five key questions are the leadership challenge of what we will term "The China Game." The only possible outcomes in The China Game are for America and China to share prosperity or catastrophe. Our thesis is that the China Game can only be won on a "win-win" basis because it is not winnable by either China or America on a zero-sum-game basis. These five questions and our thesis require careful analysis, candid debate, and successful action in America and China, and in American and Chinese companies, because they must become win-win global partners soon or remain zero-sum-game competitors in the 21st century.

America and China are at opposite ends of a spectrum of attitudes, social norms and governance systems. Only a tiny portion of the 300 million Americans and 1.3 billion Chinese interact with each other in person. After 28 years of political and trade relations, Americans and Mainland Chinese remain strangers to each other. Strangers misunderstand and distrust each other. Throughout mankind's long evolution, we have learned to instinctively view strangers as aggressors or victims. China's sudden economic competitiveness and wealth bring two very different, proud, and accomplished civilizations into accelerating political, economic, and business competition.

We define China's culture and traditions as being a "Permission Society" rather than a "Rights Society," a "Consensus Democracy" rather than a "Majority-Rule Democracy," and a "Pre-Rule of Law" rather than a "Rule of Law" society. We invite others to improve on our examination of these and other concepts, such as "the right spirit" needed in a good partnership between nations and companies, and to debate the significance of these concepts in shaping the fate of the global village we share. Such an international debate is essential because many of the important decisions about the future success or failure of America and China and mankind will be made by very small groups of leaders.

America and China now share a passion for the wealth creation that capitalism generates. Their relationship is at the cutting or "melding" edge of human evolution. With their recently re-established trade relationships and different ways of doing things, they need to evoke "the right spirit" in each other to prosper and live in peace. The "right spirit" is the resourcefulness, loyalty, and wisdom owed among family and friends. The "wrong spirit" is the selfishness, untrustworthiness, and deceit of both civilized and uncivilized barbarians.

When strangers meet, they must decide, based on assessments of each other's character and capabilities, whether they will become friends or barbarians. The American and Chinese people will become partners with "the right spirit" in the Family of Man[1] or barbarians.[2]

"What goes around comes around" is a proverb in most human societies. In America it is known as "Do unto others as you would have them do unto you." In Mandarin it is "Yin guo bao ying." We will examine the proverb's application in the context of America and China's relationship.

The Human Experiment and the Age Of Species Lethal Weapons

We live in what we will term "the Age Of Species Lethal Weapons,"[3] which is defined by the reality that nuclear and biological weapons of mass destruction enable nations and even an individual human being to destroy our species. After the countless conflicts that produced what the human species is today, this new power demands new wisdom and ways of dealing with conflict and competition.

We live in a fragile world in which conflict can destroy what we will refer to as "the Human Experiment," in which our survival or extinction as a life form is tested. In the Human Experiment we will learn whether, in our lifetimes, human nature and intelligence can solve the problems human intelligence and nature creates. Will America and China produce leaders able to prevent the failure of the Human Experiment?

The Chinese government and people's hunger for economic development and their achievements in the first 28 years of their participation in the global economy indicates that China has the capability to continue to progress. The rise of China's power challenges America's power, standards of living, and pride. The Chinese government has stated that China's rise will be peaceful. Some historians believe that no great civilization has grown and supplanted others without armed conflict.[4]

Many Americans are wondering whether America has the capability to continue to progress. Some see America sliding into barbarism.[5] Some see American democracy mutating into a dangerous populism that increasingly does not respect the right of self-determination of nations or the opinions and rights of others, which are required for a democracy to sustain itself.[6] Some see the defining character and moral authority of America being lost because American foreign policy abandoned the ideals of tolerance and respecting and championing the rights of others. Some see America's inspiring historic ideals and moral authority as its greatest power in a world that is increasingly ungovernerable and hostile to America.[7] Many Americans are proud that their nation's foreign policy is championing the implantation of America's brand "democracy" or beliefs and goals abroad. Others see a record revealing that America backs democracy abroad only if it is consistent with America's own perceived national interests. Some see American democracy and its backbone and nervous system, the rule of law, being weakened in it's War on Terror.[8] Some fear that America is dangerously overextending its power.[9]

In the midst of these and other real or imagined dangers, America's leaders and people are deciding how to respond to the emergence of China from poverty, and China's leaders and people, day by day, are working out what China's relationship with America can be.

We believe that with careful stewardship by China and America's political and business leaders, China's emergence from poverty may not destabilize America economically and politically. America and China's leaders share the challenges of their own and each other's potential hubris and innate fallibility.

In the final analysis, in the real-world, are America and China's shared prosperity and peace possible? The answer has to be "yes." No other answer is acceptable in the Age of Species Lethal Weapons. Therefore, the urgent, real world question we present an answer to is: *how* will shared peace and prosperity be achieved?

How America and China Can Win the China Game

We believe that after internal debate and discussions with each other, America and China's political and business leaders will agree that a collaborative alignment of China's strategy of economic development and America's China strategy is achievable and essential for either nation to enjoy peace and prosperity.

How America and China can understand each other well enough to prosper and coexist without trade war and armed conflict in the next 25 years is explored in this book and in our inter-related business strategy book in 30 chapters. As an introduction, consider the following points:

1. America is and will continue to be very rapidly changed in the years ahead by the emergence of China from poverty.

2. China is and will be gradually changed in the decades ahead by its economic and social reforms and increasing wealth.

3. Neither America nor China can enjoy prosperity in the 21st century if they engage in trade war and armed conflict.

4. A 21st century armed conflict, which has been called "unrestricted war," between America and China is not "winnable" by either.

5. Therefore, armed conflict must be avoided by incremental policy choices by China and America's leaders.

6. China and America must become partners with "the right spirit" in the 21st century and prosper together.

7. America and China's political and business leaders must design and implement a successful global partnership of America and China in reciprocally enriching and stabilizing political, economic, and military cooperation.

8. Although America will initially pursue a zero-sum-game strategy that could lead to trade war, Cold War, and armed

conflict, the Chinese government will look beyond provocations and ensure that America and American companies "win" in the China Game.

9. China's leaders recognize that as China becomes the more advantaged nation in the 21st century's "Knowledge Economy," China can only win in the China Game if America wins also.

10. "Do unto others as you would have them do unto you" is an American maxim. The Chinese version translates as "Don't do unto others what you would not want to have done to yourself." This maxim is the key to how America and China can work and prosper together.

11. America has codified "Do unto others as you would have them do unto you" in laws. China has made the maxim a systemic moral principle *within* the relationships that define Chinese society.

12. The People's Republic of China had not worked or done business with foreigners until 28 years ago. In the encounters that China has had with foreigners over the centuries, China found that many foreigners, but not all, do not live by the maxim, "Do unto others as you would have them do unto you" in business or military matters. China has found foreigners to be "corrupt" and "immoral" as China's civilization defines these concepts.

13. Since many foreigners have shown themselves *not* to be trustworthy, China treats foreigners warily and does unto foreigners what foreigners in many instances do unto the Chinese. When the Chinese do so, Americans feel China is "corrupt" and "immoral" as American civilization defines these concepts.

14. China and America's concepts of what is "corrupt" and "immoral" need to be understood in their respective historical

contexts before they can be gradually synchronized or integrated in some way.

15. The 1.3 billion Chinese and the 300 million Americans, for all their foibles, cultural pride, and xenophobia, are good and kind people. The good qualities Americans and Chinese share, which the Chinese call having "the right spirit," if reciprocally insisted on in practice, can enable America and China to work and prosper together.

16. China and America's political and business leaders must ensure that American companies seeking profitable "China strategies" collaborate with Chinese companies seeking to become multinationals. This book's companion business strategy book, *New China Business Strategies: Chinese and American Companies as Global Partners*, presents advanced strategies and structures that seek to align American companies' China strategies with China's strategies for economic development.

17. Collaborative global strategies by American and Chinese companies are essential to the successful collaboration of America and China.

18. American companies' profitability will be affected sooner than some expect if they do not find ways to sustainably collaborate profitably with Chinese companies doing business both inside and outside China.

19. China's development into the most competitive global economy in the first 25 years of the 21st century challenges key assumptions in America and the Western democracies regarding how nations must be organized and governed in order to be competitive economically.

20. China's evolving "Socialist Market Economy Capitalism" or "capitalism with Chinese characteristics" is a successful new phenomenon in economic theory and practice.

China's capitalism is a unique and legitimate new set of tools the Chinese government is using to enable the people of China to emerge from poverty.

21. China's one-party state economic capitalism is a successful alternate model to America's two-party state political and economic capitalism.

22. China is sustaining economic growth, radical reform, and social stability using its own culture and traditions.

23. Americans believe that China must accept the same type of democratic institutions and decision-making processes that have been the foundation of America's growth and stability. In the long term, that assumption may be correct.

24. How China governs itself is for the Chinese to decide, based on their traditions and needs.

25. Perhaps, for longer than many American observers hope or expect, China will continue to thrive economically and enjoy the growth, reform, and stability produced by China's own culture and traditions, and capitalism with Chinese characteristics.

26. China's way of managing conflict and building consensus is a successful and useful alternative model to America's majority rule model.

27. The Chinese way of doing things has much to contribute to and learn from Americans' understanding of cross-cultural "morality" and problem-solving thought processes and behavior.

28. The challenges Americans and Chinese face in the China Game are man-made and, therefore, can be solved by man.

29. By respecting their different ways of doing things and avoiding hypocrisy, China and America can be partners working and prospering together.

30. By ignoring each other's legitimate rights, interests, and positions, both countries will fail as civilizations.

Small personal decisions and actions of political leaders reflect big decisions between nations. For example, after China's successful Communist Revolution in 1949, China's Premier Zhou Enlai's offer to shake hands was turned down by American Secretary of State John Foster Dulles. It took decades and the suffering of the Korean and Vietnam Wars to move beyond that rebuff until President Nixon shook hands with China's leaders. In the Age of Species Lethal Weapons, a more sophisticated and mature way of America and China dealing with each other is essential to successfully handling geopolitical, economic and business realities.

The China Game's Controversial Realities and Fallacies

Americans and Mainland Chinese can only develop the mutual understanding and respect required for shared prosperity and peace if they can accept 21st century realities and recognize false assumptions. This book examines factual and logical assertions about many realities and fallacies.

Many readers and others will find our game-theory-based thesis is wrong, naïve, or controversial. But from a real-world perspective, for example, if American domestic and foreign policies of containment seek to or make China lose, then American corporations' competitiveness and ability to do business with China will be negatively affected. American business leaders have a vital role in ensuring that domestic and foreign policies move from zero-sum-game strategies of containment to win-win collaboration so that American companies can find sustainable ways to remain competitive and profit from China's economic growth.

Tom Friedman, in *The World Is Flat, A Brief History Of The 21st Century*,[10] focused on how, in what he refers to as "Globalization

3.0," it is possible for individuals to collaborate and compete globally.[11] In Friedman's conceptual framework:

> "Globalization 1.0" lasted from 1492 when Columbus opened trade between the Old World and the New World, until about 1800. In "Globalization 1.0" countries and governments knitted the world together. "Globalization 2.0" lasted roughly from 1800 to 2000 in which the driving force was multinational companies. Beginning with the Dutch and English joint-stock companies and powered by the Industrial Revolution, the European and then American worlds embraced. In that era, it was possible to arbitrage products and services which multinationals did. In 1992 e-mail was relatively an unused and unknown phenomenon but by 2000 was a rapidly expanding global revolution that was creating "Globalization 3.0" in which the driving force is the newfound power of individuals to collaborate and compete globally.[12]

Friedman views the world as "flat" because individuals can compete with countries and corporations in Globalization 3.0.

New ideas and facts can be threatening, confusing, or provocative when they challenge our confidence in our beliefs and well-being. However, ignoring new ideas and facts reduces our opportunities to deal with reality successfully. There are many "new facts" and "emerging new realities" in The China Game:

1. The economic competitiveness of China's 1.3 billion people will soon surpass America's 300 million people in the "Knowledge Revolution" and Globalization 3.0.

2. China's economy will be larger than America's sooner than many observers expect.

3. China's economy will continue to grow long after it is larger than America's.

4. China is producing its sustained, unprecedented rate of economic growth in less than 30 years since embarking on

its modern reforms, so far, using only 30% of its huge population.

5. Economic growth is both higher in some parts and lower in other parts of China than the accelerating national average GDP growth per year of 10.3% in the first half of 2006, up from 9.9% in 2005, and 9.5% in 2004.

6. China's annual economic growth rate in some areas is above 20% and very low in others.

7. The cumulative benefits of economic growth and ongoing reforms will continue to accelerate China's economic development.

8. The Chinese government and state-owned and private companies are focused on enhancing China's successful "factory of the world economy" strategy with a rapidly emerging "innovative economy of the world" strategy.

9. Chinese companies "going global" will acquire or put out of business many current Fortune 1000 companies sooner than many expect.

10. The Chinese government knows it must and will bring more of the other 70% of its population, 800 million plus people, into participation in the global economy.[13]

11. It is widely recognized that the growing global power and productivity of capitalism in China challenges America's power. But it must also be recognized that the competitive success of capitalism in China impacts also the sustainability of democratic processes and institutions in America.

Although it is difficult for Americans to recognize or accept, a realistic new mindset requires that current American demands for American-style democracy in China be recognized as premature, counter-productive, and a danger to America and China's national interests and security.

"Nonsense!" many will say. But realistically, in America, a hundred years of passionate local struggles and a five-year national civil war were required, even after the writing and implementation of one of mankind's greatest achievements, the U.S. Constitution in 1791, for the essential details of American-style democracy to be worked out and shown to be sustainable in America. America is a land of immigrants fleeing oppression over the past 400 years. China is not a land of immigrants and has a culture developed over 5000 years. Realism requires that Americans recognize that China is as unlikely to simply or quickly copy America as America is to simply or quickly copy China.

How will American politics and business be impacted if China's different way of doing things with what we term its "Permission Society," "Consensus Democracy," "Pre-Rule of Law" legal system, and "Socialist Market Economy Capitalism" is far more economically successful than American capitalism and democratic processes? In pursuing peace and economic success, American political and business leaders will benefit from a mindset change that recognizes the limited speed at which China can stably evolve politically. This is examined next in Chapters 4, 5, and 6.

A new realistic mindset also recognizes that China's economic growth, stability, and sovereignty are fostered and protected by China not being, at this time of China's nation building and entering the global economy, a "Rights Society," and "Majority-Rule Democracy" with a "Rule of Law" system. With the stability and mutual benefits of economic collaboration between America and China, in time, democracy with Chinese characteristics will emerge. However, in the real world, China's democracy will reflect it's right of self-determination and 50 centuries of cultural evolution interacting with China's integration into the global economy.

A realistic assessment recognizes that America's relatively short and China's long histories and their cultures and mindsets are different. Some observers do not acknowledge the ramifications of these facts in the real world. They find it hard to accept that China needs time for the nation building required for democracy to be sustainable in China. They may find it hard to accept ideologically or in the real world that, in the meantime, both America and the world's economy may change as profoundly as China changes, and probably much more quickly. An unrealistic mindset about America and China in the emerging realities of the 21st century cannot lead to peace and shared prosperity.

What future do America and China's leaders and people want? How can America and China's shared prosperity and peace be realized? Can America and China's political systems produce leaders able to provide prosperity and peace in the 21st century? Supporters of the containment approach win many elections in America's Majority-Rule Democracy. The American people may elect political leaders who favor both "containment" and prosperity and peace. But the containment approach has a zero-sum-game mindset and strategies that lead America and China away from prosperity and peace.

To understand 21st century China so that a partnership can grow stronger, American's must understand how in a single generation, China's "Socialist Market Economy" is competing so effectively with American capitalism? What is China's "Socialist Market Economy"? How can China be so economcally competitive without American-style "Majority-Rule Democracy" and the Rule of Law? We examine these questions next. Understanding the answers is necessary to find the answer to how what we will refer to as "China's Socialist Market Economy Capitalism" can co-exist prosperously and peacefully with American capitalism.

4

China's Capitalism Is Redefining the Competitiveness and Wealth of Nations

Overview

This chapter examines the existing and emerging realities that necessitate a mindset change among America's political and business leaders and the American people, and global partnerships between America and China and American and Chinese companies:

1. China's economic growth and Socialist Market Economy Capitalism is redefining the competitiveness and wealth of nations in the 21st century.

2. China's economic growth rate will accelerate faster than many observers expect.

3. China's economy will be more scientifically and technologically advanced than America's sooner than many observers expect.

4. America's strategies for dealing with these existing and emerging realities are critical to sustaining the vigor ofAmerica's economy and democratic institutions and processes.

The Reality that China Is Already Outperforming All Other Economies' Growth Rates Using Merely 30% it's Population

China's already formidable success in the first 28 years of its reentering the global economy was produced by merely 30% of China's human and intellectual capital, constituting approximately 400 to 500 million of the 1.3 billion people living in its coastal areas who had an average annual per capita income in 2003 of a mere US$3000.[1] Other estimates put China's annual per capita income in 2005 at US$1500.[2] The Chinese government must economically develop its inland regions to ease regional tensions, control migration to the coastal regions, and fulfill the Chinese people's needs and aspirations. As it does, the other 70% of China's human capital of 800 or 900 million people with an average per capita income of US$800 in 2003[3] will "come on line" also. Other per capita income estimates in 2004 were US$5000 in coastal regions and US$1000 or less elsewhere.[4]

The Chinese government recognizes how essential ameliorating regional and income disparities are to preserving China's social stability and the Chinese Communist Party's leadership role. The tools available to the government in China's Socialist Market Economy and the Knowledge Revolution can make the growth curve of China's economic power steeper and faster than some observers expect.

The Chinese government strategy of economic development oversaw 9.5% average GDP rates at comparable prices in 1979–2004.[5] In 2005, the rate of growth accelerated to 9.9%. The 2004 annual GDP growth 9.5% rate is a national average made up of some regions where the GDP growth rate is 13% to 15% or as high as 32% per year and others where it is much lower.[6] As the poor regions develop economically, the GDP growth rate could accelerate locally and nationally. China's national annual growth rate has continued to accelerate in 2005[7] in spite of the Chinese government trying to slow it down. From 1982 through 2003, America's annual GDP growth rate oscillated between 2% and 4% and averaged 3%.[8] China's strategy has been so effective that it could become the world's largest economy sooner than many expect. For example, America has approximately 16 cities with more than a one million population. China created 146 new cities with populations greater than one million between 1990 and 2000.[9]

The Chinese government's investment in cities is accelerating. Fixed income investments rose 30.3% year on year in the first five months of 2006. Chinese banks expanded credit availability 16% year on year, lending US$26.2 billion in the first five months of 2006. China is planning new cities for 500 million people in the next ten years.[11]

[10]

Chinese Cities Over a Million People

Population in Millions	Number of Cities	
	1990	2000
1–3	17	156
3–5	3	4
>5	0	6
Total	20	166

Source: Chinese Statistics on Population, 2001.

The Reality That China's New Capitalism and Emergence from Poverty Is a Paradigm Shift

Many observers insist on comparing the American and Chinese ways of running an economy. For example, *The Wall Street Journal* commented:

> China—like the U.S.—is wrestling with incipient signs of inflation. Yet while interest rates are the main policy tool for the Federal Reserve Board, China's financial system is less developed and traditionally less sensitive to rate changes

alone. As a result, authorities are trying to rein in the economy with a number of other levers, too, including the currency exchange rate and hard-knuckle rhetoric.[12]

The insistence on assuming that the Chinese economy must operate as the American economy does is so strong that it obscures the success of the Chinese government even when the facts are overwhelming. In examining this lack of realism, we will consider the Chinese government's way of administering the thriving economy of China. Many observers insist on comparing the Chinese economy with America's, and think that because America and China's ways of managing their economies are different, they fail to see the effectiveness of the Chinese government's system of economic regulation. An example of the underestimation of the capabilities of the administrative style of management of China's economy can be seen in the following comments in *The Financial Times*:

> Government officials have again served notice that China's economy is growing too fast for comfort. Their assessment is flawless. Fixed asset investment in towns and cities is growing by 30 percent. If banks continue lending at the pace set in the first four months [of 2006] they will meet the annual target for new loans in a few more weeks. The trade surplus is on course for another record this month, after hitting US$13 billion in May.
>
> Beijing's solution is less judicious. Rather than raise interest rates or allow meaningful appreciation of the currency—which it fears would encourage more capital inflows—the government is again falling back on administrative measures. That means raising banks' reserve requirements and ordering them to lend less, thereby slowing the relentless construction of factories and plants. History shows this method is pretty ineffective. China is awash with money and there are few investment avenues: the rapid rise in property prices is testament to this. As a result, investors denied bank capital can usually access "kerb" funding.

Worse administrative measures do nothing to reduce the central bank's mounting foreign reserves, now the largest in the world. Inflation is still relatively benign, but the scale of required sterilization is large and growing. Total issuance of sterilization bonds now stands at US$345 billion, or 15% of gross domestic product.

For now, the People's Bank of China is sitting pretty: it receives around 4 percent on foreign reserves and pays 2–2.5 percent to sterilize at home. But the bonds have an average maturity of just six months, so any demands by purchasing banks for higher rates would rapidly erode the spread. Stuffing commercial banks with low-yield bonds should prove a harder sell now that foreign investors own a chunk of the banks. Bering's so called administrative "fine tuning" is an increasingly clumsy tool.[13]

However, for example, China's monthly industrial output grew 17.9% in May 2006.[14] China's foreign reserves, including gold, exceeded US$1 Trillion in October 2006.[15] Foreign inflows into American markets fell to their lowest level in a year in April 2006.[16] The U.S. dollar loses ground if inflows of funds into America weaken in spite of rising interest rate expectations, which appear to lose their ability to support the U.S. dollar. The U.S. Treasury reported that net inflows into U.S. assets of more than one-year duration totaled only US$46.7 billion in April 2006, the lowest monthly figure for a year, and was insufficient to cover America's monthly trade deficit in April 2006 of US$63.4 billion.[17]

How can China's economy be so underdeveloped yet so strong relative to the American economy? Putting the type of facts just examined in a realistic context requires a major mindset change among many economic analysts. The rules of economics govern both China and America. But what are those rules? What if the rules of economics are different because China's model of capitalism is more powerful than America's or because the impact of the laws of economics are different now and in the future than they were when China was not participating in the global economy? A realistic mindset also requires the recognition that the Chinese government's tools in the management of it's economy are profoundly effective, rather than "clumsy," compared to the tools available to the American government to manage their more developed economy.

China's New Model of Capitalism

The overwhelming reality is that China's Socialist Market Economy Capitalism presents a new, powerful component of 21st century capitalism or an alternate model of capitalism. Capitalism with Chinese characteristics is redefining the global economy.

The Mainland Chinese have passionately embraced capitalism since 1978, as America does. But, as one should expect, it is capitalism with Chinese characteristics, not just a copy of capitalism with American characteristics. Some may object to our adding "Capitalism" to "Socialist Market Economy" in order to help explain what China's additional component of 21st century capitalism or alternate, powerful model of capitalism is. In order for Americans to better understand and accept China's economic success, it is necessary to accept the successful capitalistic features in China's Socialist Market Economy. In America, capitalism is both an economic and political phenomena. In China, capitalism is an economic phenomena, but not a political phenomena. Nonetheless, now both America and China are enjoying the rewards of capitalism.

A new mindset is needed to recognize and respond successfully to the key question many observers are not addressing: What if China sustains its Socialist Market Economy Capitalism Model or "capitalism with Chinese characteristics" rather than copying a market economy on the American model? A new mindset is necessary for some observers to consider whether it is possible or inevitable that the global economy and American economy may be reshaped by China's huge competitive advantages in the new and different 21st century in which we live.

We ask American readers to consider a mindset change regarding "capitalism with Chinese characteristics." This change is necessary because of the paradigm shift caused by the integration into the global economy of China, comprising 22% of the human race, which did not participate in Globalization 1.0 and 2.0. The mindset change must recognize that "capitalism with Chinese characteristics" is being shaped daily by China's legitimate focus on ameliorating poverty, as America has done, preserving and protecting its economic sovereignty, as America has done, and by emerging successfully from China's "century of humiliation," as America emerged from its early colonial history after the American Revolution.

We ask Chinese readers to consider the implications of China being so successful as a global economic competitor that America's standard of living degenerates and, in that process, China is denied, by trade war and armed conflict, the prosperity and stability it seeks.

It is hard to present a realistic scenario where either China or America will accept economic decline caused by the other nation. But the prevailing mindset is that America should pursue a zero-sum-game strategic approach to China's growing success. We believe that it is therefore essential and realistic to ask: Can a "win-win" strategy be developed through collaboration between America and China and American and Chinese companies in the 21st century? Can a "win-win" strategy work? These are critical questions because China's economic development, competitive advantages, and wealth accumulation will accelerate.

China's Economic Development Is Rapid with Unexpected Leaps Forward

A proactive feature of the Chinese government's economic reform strategy from 1979 to 2006 was it's causing economic growth with direct foreign investment while restricting Mainland Chinese entrepreneurs' and companies' access to debt and equity capital. The Chinese government also selectively took advantage of some spontaneous reforms initiated by China's people. This combination of top-down-driven reforms and restricting the emergence of Mainland Chinese domestic entrepreneurs but accepting some bottom-up-driven reforms has gradually reformed China's economy and society. The Chinese government has sustained high rates of economic growth and maintained a stable political system under the control of the Chinese Communist Party. Economic growth and political and social stability are reciprocally dependent. China cannot have one without the other in repairing the economic failure of the planned economy by creating a Socialist Market Economy and "capitalism with Chinese characteristics." The economic base and reforms created from 1979 to 2006 will generate dividends for the Chinese government and people. In the 2005–2030 stage, China is well positioned to leverage its human capital in a knowledge-driven 21st century global economy.

As the full human and intellectual capital of China's overwhelming number of talented, hard-working people participate in the 21st century's global economy, China's competitive advantages and rate of economic growth may continue to surprise many observers.

Business Week reported[19] that at the end of the Cultural Revolution, 60% of China's people were literate, and that by 2003, 90.9% were. In 2003, 92.7%, 43.8%, and 17% had access to

China and India are racing ahead of the U.S. in   18
numbers of young professionals

Finance and Accounting

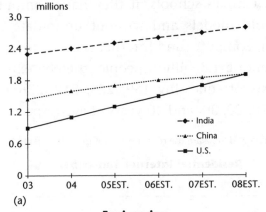

(a)

Engineering

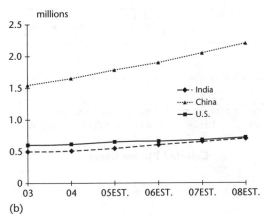

(b)

Life Sciences

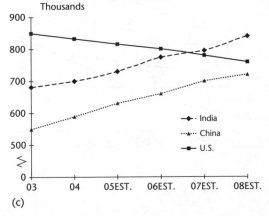

(c)

Data: McKinsey Global Institute

elementary, secondary, and university education respectively. But only 5% of homes had access to personal computers[20] and 3.4% to the Internet. China's schools, if they have computers at all, typically have old models and without up-to-date software.[21] These education, computer and Internet access rates are going to climb quickly among 1.3 billion people, thereby expediting the drop in the costs of educating 159, 228, 212, 236 millions of Chinese under 10, 20, 30, and 40 years of age respectively.[22]

China and India are the most important growth markets 23

Residential Internet Subscribes

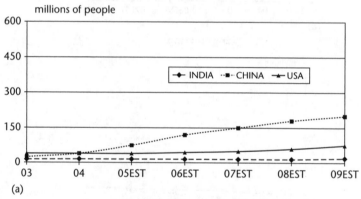

(a)

Cellular Phone Users

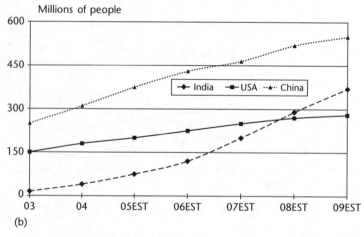

(b)

Data: Gartner Dataquest

As Economic Reforms Come Online, China's Rate of GDP Growth May Increase

Another factor that can increase China's rate of economic growth is the cumulative effect of the economic and other reforms the Chinese government and people created from 1979 to 2004. What will China's rate of economic growth be when those reforms, plus the further WTO-driven economic reforms, are in place? China's extraordinary economic growth rate is succeeding even with the currently incomplete competitive reforms in place. This success is occurring in large part because of the combination of spontaneous capitalism among the Chinese people, the effectiveness of China's one party "undemocratic" political system in managing economic growth, and the Chinese government and people's commitment to economic development. China's leadership and people, of one mind after the turmoil of the Cultural Revolution, created China's unexpected and awesome rapid economic development.[24]

The Chinese Communist Party leadership has pulled an estimated 350 million people out of poverty since reforms began in the 1980s.[25] The Chinese middle class may number over 500 million people by 2020. China has not seen such a materially and emotionally fulfilling era in the past 500 years. Even those in China who are not yet the beneficiaries of this golden era have the hope of being, or of their descendants being, beneficiaries. China's GDP growth rates, in many locations, compound and may accelerate.

China's Socialist Market Economy Capitalism Is Not Predicted, Explained, or Accommodated by Existing Theories and Models of the Causes of Wealth and Competitiveness of Nations

Assumptions, theories, and models of economics and strategic planning developed in the 20th century by Michael Porter and other Western scholars of competitiveness, and used by the World

Economic Forum and American multinational companies (among others), need to be reconsidered because they do not predict or accurately assess the competitiveness of Chinese companies and competitive advantages of China's economy in the 21st century. A search of the literature indicated that Michael Porter has not written extensively on China or updated his classic *The Competitive Advantages Of Nations*,[26] which does not focus on China.

At least three major features of the real world are not captured or recognized in these leading 20th century Western economic and competitiveness rubrics' assumptions and conclusions:

1. The combination of the work ethic of the Chinese, China's poverty, and per capita income that is 1/12 of America's, and resulting lower costs of labor and materials, together with the Chinese government's brilliant economic development strategies from 1979 to date, make "capitalism with Chinese characteristics" much more competitive in the globalized economy than the wealth, higher per capita income, and economic strategies of successive American governments.

2. Traditional 20th century economic theories do not adequately recognize, explain or predict the realities of the rapidly and profoundly changing 21st century global economy.

3. Western strategic planning theory and practice do not adequately recognize, explain, predict, or work well in the context of the economic success of "capitalism with Chinese characteristics" or the way Chinese businesses operate.

Point 1 helps explain why China's annual GDP growth rates are so much higher than America's, why China's economic competitiveness is so high relative to America's, and why China's annual trade surpluses with America are so high. Point

1 also helps explain why China's GDP has grown at an average of 9.5% annually for the past 28 years, while the American economy, which attracted far more foreign direct investment than China did from 1978 until recently, has grown at an average of 2% to 4% per year in the same period. With America's average of 3% per year in GDP growth, China's "growth competitiveness" and "macroeconomic competitiveness" has grown at an average of 300% over the American rate of growth each year for 28 years.

Examining points 2 and 3 will make it easier to understand point 1 because:

1. If the economic theories American political and business leaders use are defective guides in the context of "capitalism with Chinese characteristics" or in understanding Chinese companies, then those defects are profoundly important to correct;

2. If American companies' strategic planning theories and practices in the globalized economy of the 21st century are defective, that is profoundly important to correct; and

3. If China's different and evolving economic theories and strategies are working very successfully;

4. Then American economic and strategic thinking has a lot to learn from the unprecedented GDP growth rate and competitiveness of China's economic development and Chinese companies going global in updating and correcting American economic and strategic thinking.

In any event, even if all of the points enumerated above are incorrect, the sustained 300% faster GDP growth of China's emerging "capitalism with Chinese characteristics" is a phenomenon that American political and business leaders and other observers must study, understand, and deal with in planning future strategies.

The competitive capabilities and deficiencies of American companies and Chinese companies can be viewed and responded to as either problems or opportunities. Obviously, they are both. Perhaps the capabilities of each nation's companies can remedy the deficiencies of the other nation's companies. How that can be achieved is examined in *New China Business Strategies: Chinese and American Companies as Global Partners*.

The Fallacy That Economic Theories and Models Developed Before China's Socialist Market Economy Capitalism Can Explain the Global Economy

A new mindset is required to recognize the true, compelling, and unfamiliar reality that China's participation in the global economy is redefining the competitiveness and wealth of nations.

Kenichi Ohmae offers a new mindset in making fundamental criticisms of all existing strategic planning and economic models:

> The economic realities in which economists such as Smith, Ricardo, and Keynes lived are distant worlds away from the one we inhabit at the beginning of the twenty-first century. No one could have possibly imagined the impact that technology would have on information or the business world. After all, perhaps the greatest examples of "new" technology known to Ricardo was Rothschild's use of carrier pigeons to bring the news of Wellington's victory at Waterloo back to London in 1815.
>
> Technology has also transformed work. It has changed perceptions of the world we inhabit. Thirty years ago, Americans viewed Europe or Japan as places on the other side of the world. Letters took more than a week to move between them. Communications were possible but expensive. Today, documents can be sent to the "other side of the world" within the space of the time taken to click "Send" on a screen.

Greater use of Voice over IP (VoIP) telephony allows friends and family members to chat casually and frequently....

But most important of all is the way technology has transformed geopolitics, turning old-style nation-states into anachronisms. The global economy has also generated or raised the profiles of new business elements that were unthinkable before, such as multiples and derivatives. The role played by multiples or price per earning ratios in today's business world is a deliberate challenge to traditional ways of looking at companies. These are also a defiance of time. They seem to rely on non-statistical elements, often non-rational or even irrational. One of these is euphoria. During the heady days of the technology-inspired new economy in the late 1990s, most people felt positive about the U.S. economy. It was on the right road and it was growing apace, so, not surprisingly, multiples grew exponentially.[27]

...the global economy is a reality—it is not a theory. But so many of those who should know better, especially those whom people expect to know better, seem to be still asleep. The majority of the world's economists remain cocooned in a pleasant dream....

The economy is no longer closed in a country, nor is the world an assembly of autonomous and independent nation-states, a model most of them have assumed as the underlying structure of the economy. Instead, the world consists of interdependent units of nations and regions. Some regions have a population of hundreds of millions. The legacy they have left behind is so strong that the economists today, including most of the recent Nobel Prize laureates, are working on a variation of their old masters' themes. The economists are not looking straight at the economy itself, but are trying to interpret the economy through the lenses of the old masters, by modifying the antiquated equations and developing mathematical models that explain only a part of the global economy....

There is no model to describe the global economy as such because we are dealing with so many parameters and variables, and so many 'units of economy.' These can be strongly interlinked, as with currency exchange rates, or loosely interlinked, as with real estate investment trusts (REITS) and tax rates. Cross-border investment decisions are made to take advantage of the differences in these and many other factors.

Furthermore, advances in IT have made inventories significantly less necessary. Companies such as Toyota, Dell, and Inditex have demonstrated that they can make their products "just in time" and in response to orders. So, the grand theories of adjusting interest rate downward to expect the business to stockpile inventories is no longer that effective. They know that cash is the best form of inventory as it is tangible and exchangeable for other goods at a moments notice.

Another complication is that the cyber economy is growing fast and the cross-border exchange of goods, services, and even financial instruments is taking place in areas unbeknown to the economist, let alone the government.

Finally, though this may not [be] the final item by enlightened students of the global economy, there is an increase—or even explosion—of funny money. Bonds and Treasury bills are funny monies from the point of view of the traditional economists because they are not exactly money, but they act as money, with liabilities for taxpayers to pay later. The trouble is that the buyers of these public liabilities are no longer the residents of an issuing country. For example, over the past 20 years, Japan has financed about a third of the entire U.S. Treasury deficits. At the end of March 2004, the IMF published statistics revealing that Japan had a foreign reserve of $817 billion, while China had $432 billion, the European Union had $230 billion, and Taiwan had $227 billion....

So overall, the effectiveness of any government's fiscal policy is at the mercy of not only what businesses and consumers do at home, but also what other governments and the individual companies and consumers in the rest of the world do....

At this stage, we simply have to acknowledge that in today's interlinked global economy, the money sitting on one side of the globe could be deployed with huge multiples, halfway around the world, either to accelerate the prosperity of a region or to destroy a nation's economy. There is no formal or effective mechanism globally to govern the super liquidity produced as a result of an individual government's political situation, even though the collective effect is globally serious and sometimes destructive. Likewise, no economic model can begin to address this issue and the previously described issues.

I do not believe that we are at the stage of being able to establish a mathematical economic model. Too many variables and other forces are at work, many of which are not even discernible or documented with credible statistics. However, this should not deter us from exploring the new global economy. In the end, there may never be a suitable mathematical methodology to describe the twenty-first century economy. But there may be an approach possible through a different model, such as theory of complexity, to begin to address the issue in totality. This may be decades away, but we can begin to gather the evidence of global and cyber economics as fundamentally different from—and many times opposite of—twentieth century economics."[28]

Ohmae compares this application of old theories that are "defective" being applied to a relationship that is "akin to a jigsaw puzzle that has maybe two-thirds of its pieces missing."[29]

The World Economic Forum's Global Competitiveness Report

In the 2002 *World Economic Forum's Global Competitiveness Report*, China rose from being ranked 43rd to 38th in terms of macroeconomic competitiveness, and from 39th to 33rd in terms of growth competitiveness, which forecasts medium to long-term potential among the 80 economies ranked. (In later years China's ranking was lower.) The rankings were based on an executive survey of over 4,800 business people plus available data on a range of competitive inputs.[30] However, one must question the efficacy, assumptions, and criteria used in the World Economic Forum's global competitiveness model. For example, why is China, which has received more than US$650 million direct foreign investment since 1978 and displaced America in 2003 as the leading recipient nation for direct foreign investment globally, ranked 38th in macroeconomic competitiveness and 33rd in growth competitiveness out of 80 countries ranked?

Why is China's "Socialist Market Economy" and "capitalism with Chinese characteristics" so rapidly and sustainably out-performing the nations, such as America, that are ranked as so much more competitive than China in the current leading models of competitiveness? Why are established, traditional competitiveness theories, assumptions, criteria, and models not fully recognizing China's economic competitiveness?

The Fallacies of "Rights Society" Biases in Assessing China's "Permission Society"

A key reason is that it is a common fallacy for Western observers, press, and media to assume that China must be like the Western democracies. Such observers, seeing that China is dissimilar to the Western democracies, assume that therefore, China is going to become like the Western democracies or fail.[31]

There is another, subtler theme in much of the Western commentaries, press and media coverage. That subtler theme is a zero-sum-game mindset. This mindset also seems imbued with assumptions, such as: Western companies *must* win, therefore, China *must* fail or *must* be like Western countries, so Western companies *can* win in China, and that China *should* adopt Western democratic institutions and decision-making processes and rules so that Western companies *can win* in China.

In contrast to such observers, we suggest that China is writing new chapters in economic theory and practice by achieving and thereby validating what has never been envisioned or seen before. The Chinese government has combined proactive reforms begun in 1979 with gradual, very selective shifts of property rights from the state to individuals. In doing so, in contrast to and in spite of China's macroeconomic competitiveness or growth-competitiveness rankings in *The World Economic Forum's Global Competitiveness Reports*, the Chinese government has attracted high rates of foreign direct investment (FDI) throughout the 1979 to 2006 period. This success is partly the result of the overall attractiveness of China's economic rate of growth, social stability, low costs, huge market, and massive potential market. Notwithstanding China's competitiveness rankings, the Chinese government has attracted FDI inflows, which have provided the money for China to become the highly competitive economy that is redefining the global and American economies now. The Chinese government is also *selectively* taking advantage (in a typically "Permission Society", rather than "Rights Society," way) of the spontaneously manifested capitalist talents of China's people.

The reality of the unprecedented and sustained growth of China's economy in the real world since 1978, and the macroeconomic competitiveness and growth competitiveness of China's economy in 2002, do not correspond to ranking 38th in macroeconomic competitiveness and 33rd in growth competitiveness among 80 nations. It seems more likely that China should rank 1st or 2nd in competitiveness. The definitions of macroeconomic competitiveness and growth competitiveness that *The World Economic Forum Global Competitiveness Report* uses do not capture or predict the already established facts of China's macroeconomic and growth competitiveness relative to, for example, America. The chart of "Growth Competitiveness Ranking 2003" on page 48 was sourced from The World Economic Forum. The pie chart #33, which appeared in *Business Week* in 2005, show China's GDP's percentage of World GDP as being 4% in 2004, with estimates that it will be 15% in 2025, and 28% in 2050. It shows America's percentage in 2004 as 28%, and estimates America's to be 27% in 2025, and 26% in 2050. At a minimum, the *Business Week* estimates suggest that the trends of China's macroeconomic growth and economic competi-

Growth Competitiveness Ranking 2003		IMD World Competitiveness Scoreboard 2004		32
1	Finland	1	United States	
2	United States	2	Singapore	
3	Sweden	3	Canada	
4	Denmark	4	Australia	
5	Taiwan	5	Iceland	
6	Singapore	6	Hong Kong	
7	Switzerland	7	Denmark	
8	Iceland	8	Finland	
9	Norway	9	Luxembourg	
10	Australia	10	Ireland	
11	Japan	11	Sweden	
12	Canada			
13	Netherlands	22	United Kingdom	
14	Germany	23	Japan	
15	New Zealand	24	China	
Source: World Economic Forum.		Source: IMD.		

Competitiveness rankings.

tiveness in the next 20 and 45 years will accelerate and America's will stagnate and decline.

The membership of the World Economic Forum is heavily made up of well-established European and American multinational corporations seeking to better understand and exploit global economic, political, and other trends. If the definitions used are influenced by that particular audience's interests, values, and assumptions rather than, in China's case, the realities of the macroeconomic and growth competitiveness of China as a nation, then it is possible that the World Economic Forum's rankings could be inaccurate and need updating.

Perhaps, in China's case, the rankings and survey results reflect the pre-rise of China assumptions of multinational corporations and the models used to prepare the rankings.

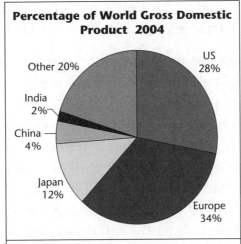

Percentage of World Gross Domestic Product 2004

Other 20%
US 28%
India 2%
China 4%
Japan 12%
Europe 34%

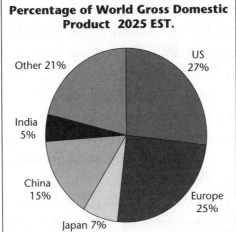

Percentage of World Gross Domestic Product 2025 EST.

Other 21%
US 27%
India 5%
China 15%
Japan 7%
Europe 25%

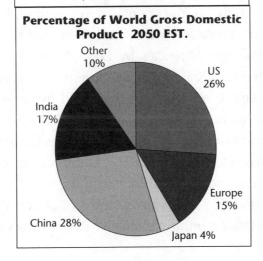

Percentage of World Gross Domestic Product 2050 EST.

Other 10%
US 26%
India 17%
China 28%
Japan 4%
Europe 15%

Existing Econometric Models Cannot Identify or Compute All Variables in China's Economic Growth

Existing econometric models cannot identify or compute all the variables in the Chinese unprecedented economic growth equation[34] as China transforms itself from a State-Owned Enterprise (SOE) based economy to a joint stock Socialist Market Economy (SME) which we have termed "Socialist Market Economy Capitalism." However, if current trends continue, and the evidence to date is that they will, China's economic development in the first 50 years after opening diplomatic and trade relations with America in 1978 will dwarf America and Europe's economic achievements in the more than 200 years since their 17th Century Industrial Revolution began to free their people's productivity from the limitations of subsistence agriculture.

Since China's GDP and market grew three times faster per year than America's in 1979–2003[35] and, to date, China has emerged as the world's most competitive and fastest growing economy, and a vast and growing provider of massive cost reductions, and as a potentially growing market for American products and services in these first 25 years.[36]

Measured in a purchasing-power-parity basis in 2003, China was the second-largest economy in the world after the American economy, although in per capita terms China is still poor.[37] Goldman Sachs predicted that China's economy will overtake Japan's by 2015 and America's by 2039.[38] The World Economic Forum indicated in 2003 that at its current rate of growth, China would be the largest economy in the world by about 2023.[49] The World Bank predicts that China's annual GDP will be larger than Italy, France, and Britain's, and nearly as large as Germany's by 2008, and will surpass America's by 2020.[40] China's economic growth is poised to continue compounding, becoming more and more competitive economically, innovative, and out-performing America's long after America's economy is smaller than China's economy.

Although econometric models currently cannot estimate China's rate of continued economic growth, it is clear that it's participation, after millennia of trying to ignore foreigners, is redefining both China's world view and the realities of foreigners' worlds. For example, China's economy was estimated to be the sixth largest in the world in 2004.[41] Japan's economy is the second largest in the world.[42] The human capital of Japan is 90 million people. The human capital of China is over 1400 percent larger. However, describing China's emerging global economic power as "economic dominance" is disturbing to foreigners' worldviews. It is comforting for human beings to underestimate, deny, or attack things that disturb them. But the reality is that China's development is a "paradigm shift"[43] that America must deal with successfully.

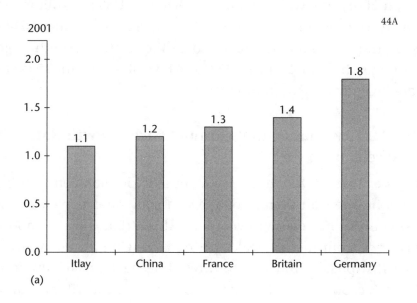

(a)

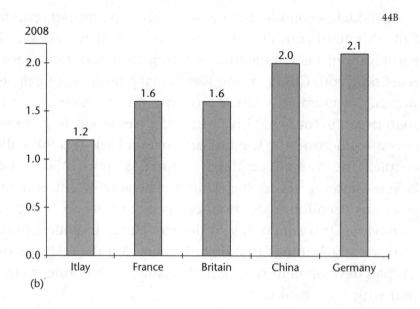

(b)

In 2003, the world economy's GDP was US$36.4 trillion, and America's economy, the world's largest, had an annual GDP of $10.6 trillion. China, estimated to be the world's seventh largest economy, had an annual GDP of $1.4 trillion. China's seventh ranking may have been too low.[45]

The Reality That China's Annual GDP Growth Rate Is Accelerating

In the 1979-2004 phase of economic development, China's economy grew an average of 9.5% annually and tripled in size. No country has ever grown that fast for that long in modern history[46] from such a weak starting base. China's economy, in that first phase, grew two to three times faster than America's. China's economy in the next phase, in which it will be reaping the benefits of the first phase, will accelerate it's economic growth. At the same time, America's economy may slow from its 2%–4%-per-year growth rate in the 1979 to 2006 period.[47]

China's annual rate of GDP growth in 2005 was expected to be 9.2%[48] in spite of the Chinese government's attempts to slow the rate of growth, but it was actually 9.9%. China's economic rate of growth accelerated at its fastest rate in more than a decade in the second quarter of 2006, due to a trade surplus and rapid expansion in investment. The annual rate of GDP growth in the first quarter of 2006 was 10.2%.[49] The annual rate rose to 10.9% in the second quarter of 2006, during a period where the Chinese government was again seeking to slow GDP growth.[50]

As we have recognized, the rate of GDP growth in the coastal regions of China is higher than the national rate of GDP growth. In other words, the rate of China's GDP growth in the 30% of China participating in China's economic miracle is much higher than 9.2% or 10.2%. The annual per capita income in the coastal regions is many times that of the inland regions that have not yet fully been the beneficiaries of China's economic growth strategy.

Mark Thirlwell has noted, "The table below sets out the positions of China in the world economy in terms of GDP and population as of 2004, and compares this with two other economies, the United States and India."

Comparisons: GDP and Population [51]

(2004)	China	US	India
GDP (market exchange rate)	US$1,649.3b	US$11,667.5b	US$691.9b
% of world total (rank)	4.0% (#7)	28.5% (#1)	1.7% (#10)
GDP (PPP)	$7,123.7b	$11,628.1b	$3,362.9b
% of world total (rank)	12.7% (#2)	20.8% (#1)	6.0% (#4)
Population	1,296.5m	293.5m	1,079.7m
% of world total (rank)	20.4% (#1)	4.6% (#3)	17.0% (#2)
GNI per capita (MER)	US$1,290	US$41,400 (#5)	US$620
GNI per capita (PPP)	$5,530	$39,710 (#3)	$3,100

Sources: World Bank on line indicators. Rank reported for top 20 economies only.

Thirlwell comments:

> This set of comparisons raises (at least) two questions. First, what is the appropriate metric for comparing output across countries? The choice clearly matters: in 2004 China was either the seventh largest economy in the world (when output is measured using market exchange rates, or MERs) or it was the second largest economy (output measured using Purchasing Power Parity or PPP rates). In either comparison China is a significant player in the world economy (it is also the world's largest economy by population).... But China's relative importance differs markedly in the two comparisons: the PPP-based measure cited here implies that China is a much more significant player in the world economy than does the MER based one: on the former basis, the US economy is a little more than one and a half times bigger than the Chinese one, for example, while on the latter it is about seven times larger.
>
> Which comparison better captures the underlying reality? We don't seem to have a consensus on this. For example, in a recent IMF survey on the global implications of Chinese growth, the authors argue that when the focus is on China's impact on other countries, then since that impact arises mainly through trade and other flows that are conducted at market exchange rates, MER based comparisons are more appropriate. In contrast, Ian Castles and David Henderson have recently made a strong case that the *only* appropriate way to compare GDP across countries is to use PPP rates.
>
> The second question relates to the choice of appropriate comparator economies. On PPP-based measures of *total* GDP, for example, it makes sense to compare the world's second largest economy with its largest, the United States. But a look at gross national income (GNI) per capita reminds us that China is still a relatively poor economy (ranked 116th in the world using PPP rates) and hence the relative comparator may be other developing economies....[52]

But the fundamental reality is that China's human capital and competitive advantages in the 21st century can enable its economy to continue to grow at rapid rates for decades after it is larger than America's. In 2003, America had the highest income per capita among large countries.[53] China's per capita income was 12% of America's in 2003. If its per capita income doubles, China would still be a poor country, with a per capita income only 25% of America's. Nonetheless, if China's per capita income were 25% of America's, it's economy would be 100% larger than America's. If China's per capita income grows to 50% of America's, it's economy would be 250% larger than America's.[54] Even while it's per capita income remains lower than America's, China's economy will get relentlessly larger if China's economic growth rates continue at the highest levels in the world.

Lester Thurow has argued that:

> Economic power...depends upon per capita GDP—not absolute GDP. *Leading edge products are sold to leading edge consumers, and leading edge consumers have to be high-income consumers.* In 2000, China's per capita GDP was $847 using exchange rates to convert yuan to dollars. America's was $36,868. Economic change starts in America precisely because America has those high-income consumers. China may become an important economic power in the future, but that future is distant.
>
> To demonstrate this latter point to yourself, take out your hand calculator and key in both China's per capita GDP and America's per capita GDP. Then key in the speed at which you expect the United States to grow over the next century, (in the last century per capita GDP grew at 2%) and the growth rate you expect from China over the next century. *Remember that no country has every averaged more than 3 percent per year per capita over a full century.* Then calculate what China's per capita GDP will be in the year 2100 relative to that of the United States.
>
> Unless you key in something quite unlikely for China's growth rate over the next century, you will find that in 2100

China will still have a per capita GDP far below that of the
United States. Since China has more than four times as many
people as the United States, its absolute GDP will probably be
above that of the United States in 2100, but that fact is
irrelevant. Per capita GDP is the name of the game. There may
be a Chinese economic century, but if there is, it will be the
22nd and not the 21st century.[55] (*Emphasis added*)

If the first italicized sentences above are not empirically
accurate, then per capita GDP and absolute GDP will be higher
than Thurow projects. Kodak recently assumed that Chinese
consumers would buy its traditional film rather than switch to
digital. Kodak was wrong. If the second italized sentence is
empirically incorrect, i.e., the growth of China's annual GDP
remains at or above 8% (the number needed to have China's
economy grow sufficiently to produce enough employment to
prevent social instability), then the conclusion Thurow draws
about the time it will take China to be an "economic power," as
he defined the term, will be wrong.

Thurow makes other assumptions that are perhaps empirically wrong. He assumes that per capita GDP will grow slowly in
the future, as it did in the past, because it took over a century for
America to reach its current per capita GDP levels.[56] He assumes
that China will not become an "economic power" in the 21st
century. But, in China's case, with its competitive advantages in
the Knowledge Revolution and other competitive advantages, a
much greater than 3% per year growth rate may be sustainable.
As Kodak found out, Chinese consumers may opt for the latest
technology even though the average of the low and higher per
capita incomes in China are below the American levels.
Thurow's two assumptions, which are italized in the quote, are
noteworthy. It can be argued that it is precisely because of
China's population size and the introduction of capitalism that
China's absolute GDP and per capita GDP rates of growth can
continue at "unlikely" growth rates.

One 2005 assessment and estimate of the economic development relationship of China, India and America published in *Business Week* set out in the following graphs:

China and India have radically different economic models. But give   57
their relative advantages and flaws, both are expected to deliver ve
high growth for decades

China will remain the manufacturing giant...

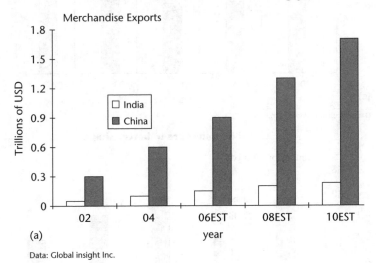

(a)

Data: Global insight Inc.

...While India soars in tech and services

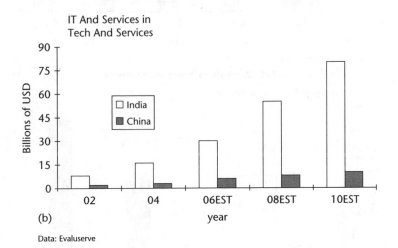

(b)

Data: Evaluserve

India's companies are more profitable...

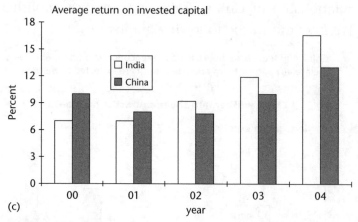

Average return on invested capital

(c)

Data: Standard & Poor's compustat

...and its banks are in better shape ...

Nonperforming Loans

(d)

Data: International monetary fund

...But China lures more investment   58

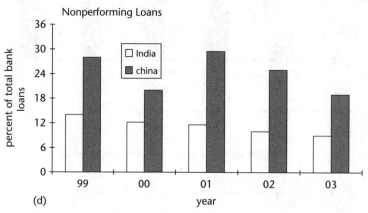

Foreign Direct investment

(a)

China has surged ahead of India...

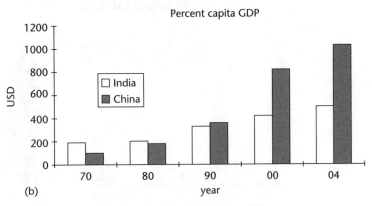

(b)

...but India's younger workforce...

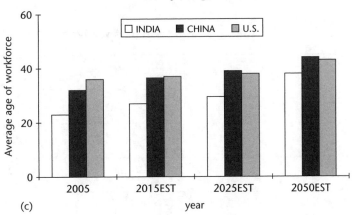

(c)

...and swelling population...

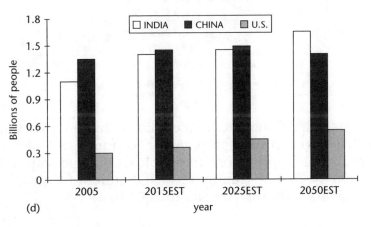

(d)

...will help it catch up

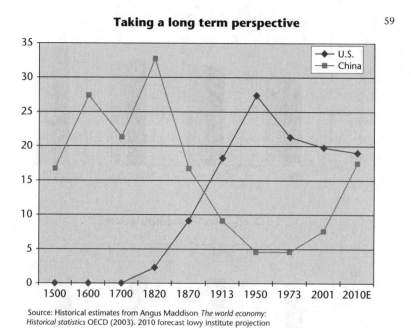

(e)

Taking a long term perspective   59

Source: Historical estimates from Angus Maddison *The world economy:*
Historical statistics OECD (2003). 2010 forecast lowy institute projection

The Central Committee of the China Communist Party approved
on October 11, 2005, a proposal for economic and social development including provisions to double China's per capita income
in 2000 by 2010.[60] Huang Ju, Vice-Premier of China, indicated
at the World Economic Forum in 2005 that:

In the next decade, we will ... concentrate on building a moderately prosperous society, so that in 2020 China's GDP will reach US$4 trillion ... and per capita GDP will reach US$3000.

That developmental target is to increase GDP by 400% and per capita GDP by 300% over year 2000 levels. It also would increase the per capita GDP of approximately 800 million Chinese not enjoying in 2005 the per capita GDP of US$3000 to at least the current level of the coastal areas of China.

The World Economic Forum's summary of Huang Ju's speech noted:

Huang stressed that hitting per capita GDP growth targets will entail a "period of profound changes in socio-economic structure", and warned that unless China's leadership follows "right strategies and policies", the country could experience polarization between the rich and the poor, a high unemployment rate, a widening regional and urban-rural gap, acute social problems and ecological degradation, resulting in stagnation and social disturbances and setback.[61]

The Chinese government is focusing on the social equality and regional disparity issues and, by addressing them and seeking a US$3000 national average GDP, the Chinese government may, as a corollary, substantially increase China's GDP growth rates.

It has been estimated that by 2010 nearly 50% of all Chinese will live in urban areas and become potential consumers constituting a consumer market with a population of roughly 700 million, which is about the size of America, Europe, and Japan's consumer markets combined.[62] The Chinese who currently earn approximately 12% of what Americans earn save a national average of more than 30% of their incomes. If the Chinese have more money to spend, they may spend it more. If so, that may accelerate China's economic growth rate.

The Acceleration Effects of the Knowledge Revolution, Internet Economy, and Globalization 3.0 on China's Economic Growth Rates

There are other current and emerging indications that China's economic growth rates will accelerate, which many observers do not yet fully take into account. However, some observers do see that China's economic growth rates are likely to accelerate. For example, James Murdoch, Chairman and CEO of STAR TV, News Corporation's Asian satellite television and multi-media service recognizes that:

> ...a Chinese economic powerhouse today is going to be very different than it might have been twenty, or even ten, years ago. Technology does change things, and markedly in China. Internet usage growth creates a positive environment for economic growth as well as international economic integration. Indeed, it is this growth in connectivity on a mass scale that has seeded the ground for an unprecedented acceleration of development, an acceleration that is necessary in a country as large and diverse as China.[63]

Case Study: Instant Language Translation Technology and the Amelioration of Language Barriers

The Knowledge Revolution must be factored into China's increasing rate of economic development. For example, technology will become ubiquitous, providing real-time translation of voice, e-mail, and data communication between different languages with accuracy. What will be the impact of eliminating language barriers on the productivity, learning curves, and economic development of China? A Chinese CEO who speaks only Chinese will be able to speak in Mandarin and be understood by, and understand others who do not speak Mandarin. Change is accelerating. In 1992 most people in the developed and developing worlds had never heard of e-mail. The concept of a "global village" is a reality. The ability of language to separate knowledge and communications will disappear for many day-to-day purposes.

What will happen in China as cell phones, wireless networking and personal computer and laptop Internet, voice recognition and instant voice and data translation among the world's languages, and other new technologies converge? The effects of convergence on productivity in China may combine with the competitive reality that China, with its increasing competitive advantages, is where much of the world's cell phones, personal computers, and laptop computers are manufactured. Leading manufacturers such as the Taiwanese, in fact, manufacture in Mainland China.

China's Competitive Advantage as a Developing Nation

Many other precedent-shattering technologies will emerge and assist China's economic performance and growth rates in the second 25-year period. What effect will such new technologies have on China's rate of providing fuller education opportunities among 1.3 billion people and China's intellectual and scientific capabilities? Currently China has low percentages of use, relative to America, of personal computers, Internet access and distant learning access. What effect will the increase of these capabilities have on China's rate of economic growth? China has the competitive advantage of not having the same degree of deployed legacy systems, as developed countries have, which impede the widescale and rapid adoption of the most advanced technology. China is hungry to use and create state of the art systems, and has become a testing field for many new technologies due to the lack of resistance by vested interests.

Cell phone use is one illustration. China can skip hard wiring and fiber-optic cabling of much of its population and 1G and 2G

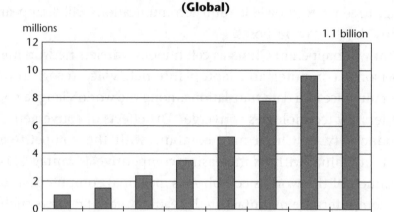

Mobile Phone Subscribers (Global)

Source: ITV, Ministry of global affairs (japan)

(a)

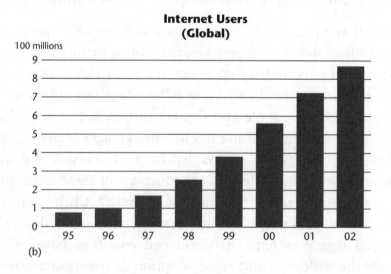

Internet Users (Global)

(b)

technology. The standard of 3G or 4G technologies that China adopts, with economies of scale in its huge, hungry market, may determine the viability of future technologies. The graphs above and across show the growth of mobile phone and Internet use in

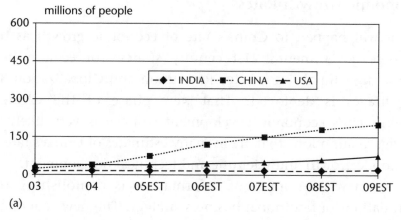

Residential internet subscribers

(a)

Data: Gartner Dataquest

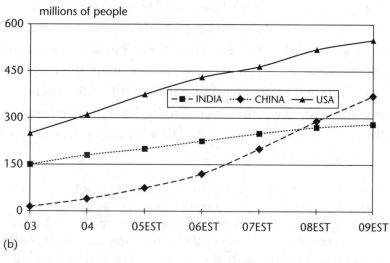

Cellular phone users

(b)

Data: Gartner Dataquest

the world and the roles of China and India as the most important growth markets for mobile phones and Internet access in the world.

The Information Economy's Acceleration of China's Economic Growth Rates

What will happen to China's rate of economic growth as the Chinese government's 21st century strategy of economically exploiting China's Knowledge Revolution and Globalization 3.0 advantages is deployed? That new phase of the Chinese government's economic development strategy is very likely to change assumptions that are in many estimates of China's rate of economic growth and scientific and technical development.

The new economics of information is demolishing the foundations of traditional business strategy. The new economics of information are at work in ways that some observers, looking at China's developmental needs and goals from the Western perspective, do not see yet. Many Western observers believe China currently lacks scientific and technological creativity and capabilities relative to the West, and will continue to do so for some time. New technologies being developed will radically change current estimations of the speed that connectivity and, therefore, productivity leaps in the Knowledge Revolution in Globalization 3.0. These changes will accelerate China's economic development:

> The impact of wireless on the Internet and for mobile Internet access (m-commerce) is already being felt and...will likely dominate wire line connections as the way to access the Net....
> China has not been slow off the mark either.... Combining this new technology with the mobile phone of the future, a hybrid phone, IA/PDA and new voice recognition systems, will foster the birth of yet another generation of applications. This is of particular relevance to China, which will be freed from the inconvenient and laborious task of inputting Chinese characters through an unsuitable, input device—the keyboard.... The wireless world is integral to the evolution of the Internet and m-commerce and is expected to deliver on the long-hyped

prediction that the way we work, rest, and play is going to radically change. China is poised as a leading adopter of these new devices and techniques—described as 'the boom technology of tomorrow'—for connecting its citizens to each other and the rest of the world in the process of fundamentally changing its society in ways unimaginable now.[66]

Models of China's economic growth rate based on assumptions that do not accurately predict personal computer and telecommunication penetration and use by China's 1.3 billion people, will have to be raised if China's use of new state-of-the-art computing and communications devices move China rapidly from an analog to a digital, "on line" economy.

The New York Times reported in 2005 that:

> One of the more interesting technology sessions at Davos, Switzerland, this year was Nicholas Negroponte's presentation of a $100 laptop computer intended for developing countries.... Quanta Computer would be manufacturing the device, based on a chip from Advanced Micro Devices, and the Linux operating system. Quanta, a Taiwan company, makes about 30 percent of the world's laptops, so its involvement lends considerable credibility to the project.... Despite the technological ingenuity of the device, it engendered considerable skepticism. One audience member asked what good a $100 laptop was when network connections cost at least $25 a month. Mr. Negroponte responded that the laptops would send and receive Internet data only when higher-paying commercial data was not being transmitted, leading to lower networking costs.
>
> Microsoft's vice president and chief technology officer, Craig J. Mundie argued that a cellphone-like device would make more sense than a laptop computer in developing countries, because the demand for wireless communications services is strong and growing....
>
> In the discussion after his presentation Mr. Negroponte emphasized the educational value of laptops, while

Mr. Mundie and others focused on the business models enabled by cell phones.[67]

China's competitive advantages can be expected to multiply repeatedly because technological, scientific, educational, and economic development will act as catalysts to each other. China's economic growth and technological and scientific development reinforce each other and may develop more rapidly than some observers currently expect.

The Reality of China's Dominant or Co-dominant Role in Globalization 3.0

In *The World Is Flat, A Brief History Of The 21st Century,*[68] Tom Friedman argues that the world is "flat" because individuals can compete with countries and corporations in "Globalization 3.0". Friedman points out that in Globalization 1.0, from 1492 to 1800, countries and governments knitted the world together. Friedman notes that in 1800, China had the biggest economy in the world.[69] China, instead of focusing on global expansion in the 18th, 19th and 20th centuries as Europe and America did, remained, with some profoundly memorable humiliations for the Chinese people, a world unto itself. All that changed in 1978 when China decided to open up.

In Globalization 2.0, from 1800 to 2000, multinational companies were the driving force. In Globalization 3.0, the rapid penetration Indian outsourcing was achieved since 1997 as it offered cost savings of about 80% and other efficiencies. In classical economics, work moves to where it can be done most effectively and efficiently. Friedman quotes the director of one of the largest homegrown software firms in Dalian, China: "I've taken a lot of American people to Dalian and they are amazed at how fast the China economy is growing in the high-tech area.

Americans don't realize the challenge to the extent that they should."[70]

Friedman quotes the Mayor of Dalian:

> "The Japanese enterprises originally started some data processing industries here and with this base they have now moved into R & D and software development.... In the past one or two years, the software companies of the U.S. are also making some attempts to move outsourcing of software from the U.S. to our city.... We are approaching and we are catching up with the Indians. Exports of software products [from Dalian] have been increasing by 50 percent annually and China is now becoming the country that develops the largest number of university graduates. Though in general our English is not as competent as that of the Indian people, we have a bigger population [so] we can pick out the most intelligent students who can speak the best English.... My personal feeling is that Chinese youngsters are more ambitious than Japanese or American youngsters in recent years, but I do not think they are ambitious enough, because they are not as ambitious as my generation."[71]

There is more talent being educated in China than America. China will produce 3.1 million college graduates in 2005 and America 1.3 million.[72] Dalian's mayor commented:

> The rule of the market economy is that if somewhere has the richest human resources and the cheapest labor, of course, the enterprises and the business will naturally go there.... Chinese people first were the employees and working for the big foreign manufactures, and after several years, after we have learned all the processes and steps, we can start our own firms. Software will go down the same road ... first, we will have our young people employed by the foreigners, and then we will start our own companies. It is like building a building. Today, in the U.S., you are the designers, the architects and the developing countries are the bricklayers for the buildings. But one day I hope we will be the architects.[73]

China's Socialist Market Economy Capitalism Model

Leading models of competitiveness and the competitive advantages of nations do not address the reality of what China has achieved in less than 30 years' effort, with only nascent individual property rights,[74] and without an American-style Majority Rule Democracy and Rule of Law system, which before China's economic success, have been regarded in the West important requirements for economic development.[75]

The Knowledge Revolution, Internet Economy, Globalization 3.0 and many other phenomena are redefining the causes, patterns, and results of competitiveness in the real world.

Billions of observers are suddenly realizing that China is the most economically competitive nation in the world. It will become increasingly evident that China has the most competitive advantages in the 21st century, as it did in the centuries before 1800. Unless trade war and armed conflict shatter both China and America's prosperity, China's competitive advantages and economic growth are likely to rapidly grow for decades. China's sustained highest economic growth rates during the 1979 to 2005 phase of the Chinese government and people's economic development efforts position China's economic success to continue in the 2005 to 2030 second phase and for decades beyond.

The Paradigm Shift of Successfully Combining Socialist and Capitalist Concepts in Socialist Market Economy Capitalism

The rate of China's growth and macroeconomic competitiveness will increase because of China's development of "Socialist Market Economy Capitalism." Successfully combining the powers of a socialist state and a capitalist market economy in a one-party-governed state is new in economic theory and practice. No country has successfully done so except China. Such a seemingly theoretically impossible combination is in practice redefining China's, and the world's, economy.

By successfully combining socialist and capitalist concepts and practices in uniquely Chinese ways, China is redefining the competitiveness and wealth of nations.

In the 19th and 20th centuries, Communism, was a theory that became practice in a large part of the world and involved an aggressive ideological competition with capitalism. Communism lost that competition late in the 20th century. In the 21st century, China's combination of socialism and capitalism is not ideologically aggressive or an ideologically driven innovation. It is a pragmatic innovation. The necessity in China of economic development, social stability, and direct foreign investment was the mother of invention, not Western economic theory.

The economic failure of Communist economic theory and practice under Mao Zedong led the Chinese government under the leadership of Deng Xiaoping and then Jiang Zemin and now Hu Jintao to combine socialist and capitalist theories and practices in a process that has been very successful and is continuing to be designed and deployed in China.

Only as recently as 1992, Deng Xiaoping declared that a market economy was possible in a socialist system and that the ultimate goal of reform in China was to build a "socialist market economy." In 1992, the Chinese Communist Party implemented a "Socialist Market Economy" concept among the reforms replacing China's "planned economic approach". The Chinese government's reforms seek to create more Western-style markets in China, which are sufficient, at least, to be compatible with Western and World Trade Organization (WTO) capitalist norms. However, China's processes for developing and implementing such reforms benefit from the political, social, and economic governance system run by the Chinese Communist Party, which is the only institution powerful enough to provide the leadership and social stability required for China's economic growth and emergence from poverty.

Income per Capitia in 2002
(PPP-adjusted, in current $)

76

■ Below $2,000
$2,000-$4,000
$4,000-$20,000
■ Above $20,000
No Data

Source: Data from World Bank (2004).

The Chinese Communist Party and the Chinese government's "politics of command" oversee the reforms required for economic growth. China's "politics of command," which we refer to as a "Permission Society" without a fully developed Rule of Law system, are reciprocally safeguarding China's economic sovereignty, economic progress, and the Communist Party's leadership. The Chinese government's "politics of command" were able, from 1979 to-date to combine top-down initiated reforms and take advantage of bottom up reforms that spontaneously occurred. At the same time, the Chinese government's reform program also attracted and used an estimated US$ 650 billion in direct foreign investment and foreign intellectual capital and technologies. In the process, many

SOEs were closed or revitalized or otherwise reformed to varying degrees in a process that is ongoing and is now also driven by the reform momentum of China's WTO membership.

What Is China's "Socialist Market Economy Capitalism"?

The Chinese government describes their new economic approach as a "Socialist Market Economy" and "capitalism with Chinese characteristics." It may also be described as China's "Socialist Market Economy Capitalism." By any name, it is a powerful new form of state-controlled and partially state-owned capitalism. However described, the economic development that the Chinese government has overseen since 1978 is self-evidently redefining the competitiveness and wealth of nations. Among the questions examined in this chapter and in Chapters 5 and 6 are:

1. How can China's "Permission Society" now be the leading recipient of direct foreign investment in the world?

2. Doesn't a nation have to be a "Rights Society", multi-party, and "Majority-Rule Democracy" with free elections with universal adult suffrage and a Rule of Law system to be the most economically competitive nation in the world?

3. How has a nation with a low per capita income, that is a "Permission Society," a one-party state, with a "Consensus Democracy," and without a "Rule Of Law"-based legal system become one of the most competitive nations and increasingly had the most competitive advantages in our 21st century world?

These three questions reflect paradigm-shifting realities that many Western strategic planners and leading 20th century models of competitiveness fail to address.

China's "Socialist Market Economy Capitalism" paradigm-shifting phenomenon has never before been seen for two major reasons, among others. First, leading models of competitiveness and the competitive advantages of nations do not predict or explain the overwhelming competitive advantages of China's Socialist Market Economy Capitalism. Secondly, China's Socialist Market Economy Capitalism is writing new 21st century chapters in economic theory and practice, that require a rethinking of 17th to 20th century economic theory and practice.

The question of what is China's Socialist Market Economy Capitalism is misunderstood, complex, and evolving, like many issues presented by China's emergence from poverty.

China's Socialist Market Economy can be viewed as one of the most extreme capitalist experiments in history. It can be viewed as representing wild market forces with an authoritarian framework superimposed. In some ways, early Chinese capitalism is like early American capitalism, which has been characterized as an era of robber barons. Such similarities are ironic. America cannot expect China to do in a few years what America struggled to achieve over a hundred years or more.

Some observers assert that China is no longer a socialist country except in name. In their view, the "socialist" character of China may be viewed as being lost in China's transitioning from a planned to a market economy. They highlight that there is a lack of policies and a legal framework of social welfare protecting the weak. The social welfare system that operated in China when there were no private property rights was dominated by SOEs, which increasingly faltered financially in the 1980s and 1990s.

Chinese business is being increasingly privatized, the communist "iron rice bowl" social security is being dismantled, and the new social welfare system being developed. In such a massive reengineering that was necessitated by the failure of the unreformed SOE system, dislocation and suffering is unavoidable.

Kenichi Ohmae has stated that:

> China today contains the most brutal, inhumane, and unsentimental capitalism imaginable.... China exhibits capitalism in the rawest form.... this is the purest, most unadulterated form of capitalism on the planet today. It is a world taken from the pages of Charles Dickens or Theodore Dreiser. It is a primitive form of industrialization, not to be found in today's Japan or the United Kingdom or the United States.[77]

Ironically, judged by the standard of China a generation ago, this is an amazing improvement in the lives and hopes of 1.3 billion people. China is industrializing at an unprecedented speed. In that context, if China's "raw capitalism" is criticized by foreigners, they must take into account that America was no better at a comparable stage of its development, and that America took much longer to progress than the rate at which China is building a new economic and social system. To compare America and China today is less appropriate than to compare America in 1840 and China in 2005. Critics must acknowledge that China is a developing nation, in the midst of a massive transition from a communist to a capitalist economic system, and that they are judging by the standards of developed nations. Is that a fair comparison? The economic growth and reform that the Chinese government, people, and culture is achieving in moving from an annual GDP of $64 billion in 1978 to $1.6 trillion in 2004 is pulling hundreds of millions of Chinese out of poverty and enabling more to anticipate such relief from suffering.

Top 10 Countries in the World by GDP

78

GDP Ranking in 1990			GDP Ranking in 2003		
Rank	Country	GDP (Trillion$)	Rank	Country	GDP (Trillion$)
1	U.S.	5.8	1	U.S.	11.0
2	Japan	3.0	2	Japan	4.3
3	Germany	1.5	3	Germany	2.4
4	France	1.2	4	U.K.	1.8
5	Italy	1.1	5	France	1.8
6	U.K.	1.0	6	Italy	1.5
7	Canada	0.6	7	China	1.4
8	Spain	0.5	8	Canada	0.9
9	Brazil	0.5	9	Spain	0.8
10	China	0.4	10	Mexico	0.6

* Assuming that China keeps growing at 8% p.a., it will:
- catch up with the U.K. in 2007
- catch up with Germany in 2008

* Assuming strengthening of RMB by a factor of two after its float in 2005–05, its GDP will:
- double in dollar terms
- catch up with Japan in 2008
- become the number 2 economy in the world by 2010

The graph above shows the World Bank's GDP rankings of the top ten countries in the world in 1990 and 2003. China's leap is enormous in many respects.

Hank Greenberg has pointed out: "…for those who criticize China's human rights policies, if they go back, look at China in 1975, and then look again at China today, the progress including in the field of human rights, has been enormous. When you feed and clothe and shelter 1,300 million people, that is human rights, compared to what it was before."[79]

As highlighted in the Summary, the established perspectives on China's future (i.e., collapse, inevitable democracy, or authoritarian stagnation)[80] do not explain why China is making so much money, so fast, on such a sustained basis since embracing capitalist-oriented reforms. They also do not explain how America and American companies can secure peace and prosperity, given the consequences for the wealth of nations with Deng

Xiaoping declaring that the prosperity capitalism produced was not a bad thing.

Some observers emphasize the social unrest that often occurs and is firmly repressed by the Chinese government, such as mining disasters and neglected and marginalized populations, regional disparity, increasing disparities in income, and pollution that cause protests or violent riots. Nonetheless, change is occurring on an unprecedented scale, and hundreds of millions in China are enjoying much-improved standards of living that are encouraging for the Chinese who are already enjoying it and those who hope to.

Other observers would point to Jiang Zemin's "Three Representations" and the Chinese government's increased focus now in the second 25 years of China's economic development on income and regional disparities. Such observers point to the ability of China's Communist Party to successfully address and ameliorate such threats to social stability and the continued high rate of economic development in order to preserve its leadership of China.

China's "Socialist Market Economy Capitalism" is a pragmatic and evolving work in progress that will only be accurately defined by the passage of time. But it is possible to begin to identify features of "socialist," "market," and "capitalism" in the pragmatic way of doing things that the Chinese government and people are creating.

China's Evolving Socialist Market Economy Capitalism's Socialist Features

Many features could be asserted to give a "socialist" twist to "capitalism with Chinese characteristics:" The government alone manages the building of the nation; It is without universal adult suffrage; One party has control of all of the society's functions; Social, economic and political chaos is strongly disliked in the society generally; Upgrading standards of living is universally desired; and national economic planning, directed by the national government in incremental steps, without a full private property ownership system and state ownership of successful companies is encouraged, while private firms are discouraged. Private firms' excellence is tolerated, then championed. Foreign firms provide capital, expertise and competition, while the state retains whole or part ownership of major companies, and regulates rule-making and policies. The state is a major customer, and provides access to capital. In a Permission Society with a rule by law system rather than a rule of law system.

The Chinese government emphasizes social harmony and amelioration of poverty, and addresseses regional disparities and educational needs, etc.

China's Evolving Socialist Market Economy's Capitalist "Market" Features

The "Market" features include:

1. The governing party and Chinese government now accept that the "communist" centrally-planned economy was not working;

2. The governing party and Chinese government has retreated to planning economic development without directly operating all companies;

3. The Chinese government is permitting foreign investment to identify and develop economic opportunities in China;

4. The Chinese adoption of a steady, rapid and incremental economic, social and political reform process that has attracted foreign investment; and

5. The building a "market oriented economy" to alter and augment the 1949–1978 era's communist planned economy;

6. Upgrading its banking, insurance and reinsurance, stock exchanges and venture capital sectors, among many other industries, to support an increasingly market oriented economy;

7. Accepts that many uncompetitive, unprofitable SOEs go out of business;

8. Permits economic, social and political experiments in special economic zones;

9. Accepts that competition will spur and direct competitive forces in China;

10. The Chinese government is letting market needs play a larger, but controlled role, in helping to allocate resources;

11. Accepts capitalist philosophy;

12. Accepts capitalists as members of the ruling party; and

13. Etc.

China's Socialist Market Economy's "Capitalist" Features

The "capitalist" features in both America and China's economics are not absolute, in as much as in a pure "capitalist" system there might be no rules. To the degree that capitalism requires rules (in

America, the rule of law; and in China "rule by law") neither country is a "pure capitalist" system. The point here is that the same criteria should be used to define America as a "capitalist" system as are used to assert that China is not "capitalist."

Capitalism has been described as an unraveling mystery by Hernando de Soto.[81] He finds the origin of the word "capitalism" in Medieval Latin, where "capital" denoted cattle or livestock, from which additional wealth (more cattle) and "surplus value" including milk, hides, wool, meat, and fuel set up other industries. He then refers to the theories of economists such as Adam Smith and Karl Marx. Smith believed "the wealth of nations" was caused by economic specialization, i.e., the division of labor and subsequent exchange of products in markets, which create increased productivity. Smith traced the origins of the word "capital" to mankind's progression from agricultural to commercial societies in which mutual interdependence, specialization, and trade increased productivity enormously. The debate about what capitalism is not, is our main focus here, other than to note that it evolved over time and what it is remains subject to debate.[83]

Hernando de Soto asserts that "capital" has now become confused with "money." What there is no doubt about is that China is making money. The issue is what should America and American companies do about China and Chinese companies making so much money, so fast, for so long?

China's Socialist Market Economy Capitalism Combines State and Private Enterprise Capitalism

China's Socialist Market Economy Capitalism differs from American capitalism, but is capitalism nonetheless. One of the most important respects in which it differs from American capitalism is that the Chinese government and entities favored by it remain owner and in control of and able to assist many major Chinese companies in ways that American companies have not seen or had to cope with before. The financial cost of capital and structure of NYSE-listed CNOOC's bid for Unocal examined in Chapters 8 and 9 exhibited very significant competitive advantages that Chinese companies have in China's new economic model and processes.

Many more Chinese companies, including both partially and non-government-owned companies, will, in the 2005 to 2030 period, become global corporations. Many such Chinese emerging multinational companies will be involved in securing the resources China needs for its economic development, improving their profit-oriented business capabilities and earning foreign currency. The type of financing advantages that such Chinese companies have, as exhibited in the CNOOC bid for Unocal, is a profound feature of China's Socialist Market Economy Capitalism. Such Chinese multinationals have different agendas, criteria, and resources than American companies. But American companies perform the same functions for America.

The Chinese government is combining the advantages of China's socialist one-party government system, which we term a "Permission Society," with the advantages and practices of capitalism. This is another feature of China's innovations in economic theory and practice with which America and American companies, among others, must come to terms. China's embracing of capitalism reveals advantages of capitalism that American and other companies have not seen before, such as having the government of the fastest growing economy in the world as a major shareholder and stakeholder in companies' competition in global capitalism. The table on page 82 lists some major Chinese companies becoming multinationals that are wholly or partly Chinese government owned.

There are advantages and disadvantages to such companies arising from state ownership.[84] State ownership can involve the advantages of Chinese government operational and financing benefits, and disadvantages that can include interference in operations and American government resistance such as that we

Chinese companies are starting to make their mark outside the mainland, but most of the leaders remain largely in state hands

Company	2004 Sales ($Billions)	Business	Share Owned by Goverment
Sinopec	73.6	Oil production and distribution	84%
PetroChina	70.4	Oil production and distribution	90
China Mobile	23.6	Cellular operator	75
First Auto Works (FAW)	14.0*	Auto maker	100
China Minmetals	12.1*	Mining	100
Shanghai Automotive (SAIC)	11.8*	Auto maker	100
China Life	8.1	Insurance	73
China Netcom	7.9	Fixed line phone operator	75
Baoshan Iron & Steel	7.1	Steel	61
CNOOC	6.8	Oil exploration	71
TCL	4.9	Consumer electronics	25
ZTE	4.1	Telecom networking equipment	53
Lenovo	2.7	Computers	50
China Merchants Bank	2.6	Bank	18
Haier	1.8	Appliances, consumer electronics	30
Konka	1.6	Consumer electronics	24
Sinochem	1.6	Petrochemicals	43
Changhong Electric	1.4	Consumer electronics, appliances	54
Dongfeng Automobile	0.7	Auto maker	70
Cosco	0.2	Shipping	52

Data: Business work company reports.
*2003 data.

will refer to as "CNOOC jingoism" in going global. For example. *Business Week* comments:

> The age of the Chinese multinational is upon us...if China's multinationals do emerge as power players, many of them will have the state to thank for their success. These companies have implicit or explicit backing from Beijing and can build on China's other strengths as well—low wages, vast internal markets, and rapid economic growth. ... A number of Chinese companies have carved out a smallish piece of their businesses—typically the most profitable chunks—and floated them either in Hong Kong or New York. But the listed company is usually majority-owned by its parent, which remains in state hands. ... State control can clearly give them business advantages at home. In the early 1990s, when China began embracing the market economy in earnest, state-owned companies in key industries were chosen to lead the country's development drive, landing lucrative contracts or receiving tariff protection, cheap land, easy credit from state banks, and preferential access to listing their shares. ... The government has steered foreign joint-venture partners to these national champions to ensure they have access to imported technology and management know-how.
>
> Abroad, though, those state ties can suddenly start looking less advantageous. Chinese companies, government links and their easy access to loans from state banks are likely to dog their foreign adventures ... CNOOC, for instance, is generally considered a well-run company and has been traded in Hong Kong since 2001. But U.S. lawmakers focused instead on its government ownership and access to cheap credit.[85]

In addition, American observers, such as Donald Sull, are recognizing that successful non-government-owned Chinese companies have survived little or sporadic access to capital, competition from multinationals, and shifting regulations, while other government- and non-government-owned Chinese companies failed because they responded quickly to change and competition.[86]

The Chinese Government's "Managed Marketization" of the Chinese Economy

To understand the capabilities of China's Socialist Market Economy one must examine how uniquely effective it has been in the past in dealing with internal and external economic crises: the failing SOE system of organizing the means of production, the urgent need for a wide range of banking and economic reforms, out-of-control inflation, the need for economic growth not faltering, and an external Asian financial crisis. It is in this context that the powerful macroeconomic management tools and competitive economic development advantages that China's "Permission Society" provides have enabled China to achieve sustained economic growth and social stability while protecting economic sovereignty. In the hands of the able and bold leaders that the Chinese governmental system produced and supported since 1978, these tools worked impressively during the Asian crisis that wreaked havoc elsewhere.

Laurence Brahm summarizes the "managed marketization of China's economy":

> From the moment he assumed the role of Vice Premier in 1992, through his term as State Council Premier (1992–1998), Zhu Rongji managed China's transformation into a market economy over the critical decade of the 1990s. Unabashedly combining the tools of command and market economics, Zhu has brought inflation down from 21.7% in 1994 to 1% in 2002, while maintaining an average 8% growth rate over this same period. He has streamlined and rationalized China's banking and financial systems, taking on and closing down the investment and trust companies, old bastions of an unregulated system in the early states of transition. He steered China

through the Asian financial crisis without devaluation of the Reminbi, strengthening the currency in the process. The reforms Zhu has overseen as Premier have involved reengineering the state-owned enterprises, cutting government bureaucracy by half, and replacing the 'iron rice-bowl' system with the framework of a modern social-security and insurance-based healthcare and pension system. Such reforms have involved more than structural changes and institutional capacity building. They have required the reengineering of Chinese society as a whole.

The execution of any International Monetary Fund (IMF) or World Bank reform measures in Russia, Eastern Europe, Central Asia, Mongolia, Indonesia, South Korea, or any other transitional economy has received praise from Washington D.C. and the predominantly pro-Western international media. However, one must ask honestly: how many of these reforms have been successful in carrying out economic structural capacity-building, raising lifestyles, invigorating those economies, and establishing social and political stability in those countries?

China has crossed the same period, as Deng Xiaoping put it, like crossing a river one step at a time, on the rocks. None of the fancy voodoo economic formulas rattled off by academic gurus from think tanks in Boston or Washington D.C. were applied. China's economy nevertheless grew at an average of 8% per annum during the 1990s, and, with the exception of a single critical period in 1993–94, witnessed low, and often negative inflation. ... It is hard to imagine the leader of any other country daring to take the political risks inherent in tackling economic and financial challenges on such a scale as China's. Yet, Zhu has done so and, arguably, succeeded. In doing so, he has ignored the formulas and sacrosanct IMF prescription for developing countries. Many of those who accepted the economic panacea proffered by Western academics have lived to regret it. Zhu, however, developed his own practical model suited to Chinese realities, his own theory of the 'managed marketization' of China's economy, and China's economy is all the stronger for it today.

The Asian financial crisis brought into focus the question of what kind of economic model China should adopt. Before the crisis, China was seeking to develop a Japanese-style market economy based on the success of Japan and South Korea during the 1980s. But this view was dropped after the meltdown of these models in 1997. Zhu Rongji's view was that the market should play the major role, with corporate governance under law taking a stronger, firmer position. China's state-owned enterprises could hardly be protected forever. Enterprise group mergers completed through administrative means could only be pursued so far. The lessons learned from the Asian financial crisis would become the inspiration for Zhu to push against domestic political opposition protecting certain industrial sectors in aggressively seeking entry into the World Trade Organization for China.

At the back of Zhu's mind were memories of the hardships of the 1950s and 1960s. But China had managed to pull through those times. Belt-tightening could work. It would be better to look inward than become an IMF colony and have to pay back Western debts forever. Although the decision not to devalue the currency was basically Zhu's, it received the repeated public backing of Jiang Zemin and the Politburo. Not to devalue the Reminbi was a move calculated to maintain 8% growth targets, to show capacity to support Hong Kong, to provide the psychological effect of financial stability and to demonstrate the government's willingness to enforce its decisions to maintain stability and serve in its own capacity as a rudder and model to the rest of Asia. This last factor most likely irritated the IMF and the so-called Washington Consensus the most.

In fact, China's successful handling of the crisis directly challenged the vision of the Washington Consensus. What would have been the cost of addressing the crisis if China had had a so-called American-style democracy like Taiwan or Japan can only be imagined. Because the government was being run like a tightly held family business, Zhu was able to make decisions quickly, react appropriately, and mobilize all resources toward one target. If a government is weak and cannot reach consensus, it cannot enforce policy. The unity within the Chinese Communist Party and the ability to mobilize unified action at all levels of the system enabled the leadership to implement its decisions and keep China on course."[87]

This ability of the Chinese system of one-party government and Socialist Market Economy Capitalism to deliver economic stability, growth, and sovereignty is essential for China's emergence from poverty. The effective governmental tools may last as long as China requires them because they work.

The Fallacy That Rule of Law and Property Rights Have Been Required for China's Capitalism

Hernando de Soto has argued that capitalism has not worked in societies in Latin America, Africa, and Asia, not because they lack entrepreneurship, intelligence or capital, but because property ownership rights are not adequately identifiable and enforced. He asserts that the lack of rule of law identifying and protecting property rights means that the rights to property are not adequately documented, and property cannot be readily turned into capital, nor traded outside of narrow circles where people know and trust each other, nor used as collateral for loans or advanced forms of investment. Third-world and former communist countries have houses but not titles, crops but not deeds, businesses but not statutes of incorporation: "It is the unavailability of these essential representations that explains why people who have adapted every other Western invention, from the paper clip to the nuclear reactor, have not been able to produce sufficient capital to make their domestic capitalism work." He calls that the "mystery of capitalism."[88]

However, China has been able to balance its national budgets, cut subsidies to many state-owned enterprises, and welcomed and attracted massive, sustained foreign investment. If China does not copy foreign democratic institutions and a foreign system rule of law as rapidly as some hope, consider the implications. We have focused on the question of "How will America's market economy capitalism coexist with a Socialist Market Economy capitalism that has performed so well in the first 28 years of its evolution and has increasing competitive advantages?" The success to date of China's Socialist Market Economy demonstrates that capitalism, state-ownership and the socialism, if not the failed communism economics, of China's past have been successfully combined in the real world.

The Reality of the Rule by Law Authority in China's Customary Law System

The *"rule by law,"* but not the *"rule of law,"* is at the core of China's Socialist Market Economy Capitalism. It has been assumed in the West that the rule of law was an essential ingredient in economic growth and competitiveness. But the rule of law has not been able to develop in China's feudal culture and communist experience. Some observers see chaos as an innate flaw and lack of basic moral bearing in China's business environment, because it operates with the rule of men rather than the rule of law. Most Western observers assert that the rule of law rather than the rule of men will have to play a larger role in China or it will malfunction due to corruption and chaos.

For China to integrate into the global system of economic and political interdependence, it has to design and deploy a "platform" on which its legal system can communicate with the laws and institutions of its trading partners. But, China cannot and therefore will not rigidly copy foreign democratic institutions and a foreign legal system. It will have to design and deploy a new set of domestic institutions based on the experience of developed countries, but with Chinese characteristics. China, over the generations to come, will steadily design, develop, test, and inculcate in its existing culture the acceptance in its new system of rule of law. China cannot copy foreign democratic institutions and a foreign legal system totally or as rapidly as some observers hope. China, in the process of increasingly participating in and being dependent upon its success in global markets, will develop its own evolving system combining China's rule-by-law, one-party political system, and culture with the foreign concept of rule of law. In doing so it will be affected by and draw on the experience of other capitalist countries. China is unlikely to conduct experiments that are vast gambles like the Cultural Revolution.

Accepting the Reality of a New Model of Capitalism: China's 21st Century Capitalism

Cognitive dissonance (or denial) can occur when a new reality (i.e., a new model of 21st century China and a new model of capitalism with Chinese characteristics) that people believe can't or shouldn't work does work. Observers of China who insist on comparing American capitalism to capitalism with Chinese characteristics are, as a result, not working with models that explain China's overwhelming and sustained economic success. Nonetheless, they assert that what China is doing, which has worked for 25 years in pulling hundreds of millions of people out of economic failure and poverty, is wrong and that the traditional models they are using are right.

Many observers need a different model of Chinese capitalism, rather than the American model of capitalism they now use, to explain what is occurring and to predict what will occur in the development of China's economy and capital markets. Many observers need a mindset change in order to cope with the paradigm shift that the interaction of Chinese economic capitalism and American political and economic capitalism presents today.

Consider, for example, an analysis published in 2006 by Minxin Pei,[89] who faults the Chinese government's model of capitalism although it "works." His perspective on China's future is that China will remain "resiliently authoritarian" and "stagnate:"

> The only thing rising faster than China is the hype about China. In January [2006], the People's Republic's gross domestic product (GDP) exceeded that of Britain and France, making China the world's fourth-largest economy. In December [2005] it was announced that China replaced the United States as the world's largest exporter of technology goods. Many experts predict that the Chinese economy will be second only to the United States by 2020, and possibly surpass it by 2050.
>
> *Western investors hail China's strong economic fundamentals— notably a high savings rate, huge labor pool, and powerful work ethic—and willingly gloss over its imperfections. Business people talk about China being simultaneously the world's greatest manufacturer and its greatest market. Private equity worlds are scouring the Middle Kingdom for acquisitions. Chinese Internet companies are fetching dot-com-era prices on the NASDAQ. Some of the worlds leading financial institutions, including the Bank of America, Citibank, and HSBC, have bet billions on the country's financial future by acquiring minority stakes in China's state-controlled banks, even though many of them are technically insolvent. Not to be left out, every global automobile giant has built or is planning new facilities in China, despite a flooded market and plunging profit margins.*
>
> And why shouldn't they believe the hype? The record of China's growth over the past two decades has proven pessimists wrong and optimists not optimistic enough. But before we all start learning Chinese and marveling at the accomplishments of the Chinese Communist Party, we might want to pause for a moment. Upon close examination, China's record loses some of its luster. China's economic performance since 1979, for example, is actually less impressive than that of its East Asian neighbors, such as Japan, South Korea and Taiwan, during comparable periods of growth. *Its banking system, which costs Beijing about 30 percent of annual GDP in bailouts, is saddled with nonperforming loans and is probably the most fragile in Asia.* The comparison with India is especially striking. In six major industrial sectors

(ranging from autos to telecom) from 1999 to 2003, Indian companies delivered rates of return on investment that were 80 to 200 percent higher than their Chinese counterparts. The often-breathless conventional wisdom on China's economic reform overlooks major flaws that render many predictions about China's trajectory misleading, if not downright hazardous.

Behind the glowing headlines are fundamental frailties rooted in the Chinese neo-Leninist state. *Unlike Maoism, neo-Leninism blends one-party rule and state control of key sectors of the economy with partial market reforms and an end to self-imposed isolation from the world economy.* The Maoist state preached egalitarianism and relied on the loyalty of workers and peasants. *The neo-Leninist state practices elitism, draws its support from technocrats, the military and the police, and co-opts new social elites (professionals and private entrepreneurs) and foreign capital—all vilified under Maoism. Neo-Leninism has rendered the ruling Chinese Communist Party more resilient but has also generated self-destructive forces.*

To most Western observers, China's economic success obscures the predatory characteristics of its neo-Leninist state. But Beijing's brand of authoritarian policies is spawning a dangerous mix of crony capitalism, rampant corruption, and widening inequality. Dreams that the country's economic liberalization will someday lead to political reform remain distant. Indeed, if current trends continue, China's political system is more likely to experience decay than democracy. *It's true that China's recent economic achievements have given the party a new vibrancy. Yet the very policies that the party adopted to generate high economic growth are compounding the political and social ills that threaten its long-term survival.*

...The Chinese state remains deeply entrenched in the economy. According to official data for 2003, the state directly accounted for 38 percent of the country's GDP and employed 85 million people (about one-third the urban workforce). For its part, the formal private sector in urban areas employed only 67 million people. A research report by the financial firm UBS argues that the private sector in China accounts for no more than 30 percent of the economy. These figures are startling even for Asia, where there is a tradition of heavy state involvement in the

economy. State owned enterprises in most Asian countries con-tribute about 5 percent of GDP. In India, traditionally considered a socialist economy, state owned firms generate less than 7 percent of GDP.

But China's tentacles are even more securely wrapped around the economy than these figures suggest. First, Beijing continues to own the bulk of capital. In 2003, the state controlled $1.2 trillion worth of capital stock, or 56 percent of the country's fixed industrial assets. Second, the state remains, as befits a quintessentially Leninist regime, securely in control of the "commanding heights" of the economy: it is either a monopolist or a dominant player in the most important sectors, including financial services, banking, telecommunications, energy, steel, automobiles, natural resources, and transportation. It protects its monopoly profits in these sectors by blocking private domestic firms and foreign companies from entering the market (although in a few sectors, such as steel, telecom, and automobiles, there is competition among state firms). Third, the government maintains tight control over most investment projects through the poser to issue long-term bank credit and grant land-use rights.

China's business cycle is therefore driven by Beijing. Private sector firms have very limited access to finance or new markets. The state even dominates many ostensibly deregulated sectors, such as the brewing industry, the retail sector, and textiles. Of the 66 publicly traded retailers in the country, only one is private. There are only 40 private firms among the 1,520 Chinese companies listed on domestic and foreign exchanges.

To many observers, Beijing's tight grip on the Chinese economy means only that its reform process is incomplete. As China continues to open itself, they predict state control will ease and market forces will clear away inefficient industries and clean up state institutions. The strong belief in gradual but inexorable economic liberalization often has a political corollary: that market forces will eventually produce civil liberties and political pluralism.

It is a comforting thought. Yet these optimistic visions tend to ignore the neo-Leninist regime's desperate need for unfet-tered access to economic spoils.... Today, Beijing oversees a vast patronage system that secures the loyalty of supporters and allocates privileges to favored groups. The party appoints 81 percent of the chief executives of state-owned enterprises and 56 percent of all senior corporate executives. The corporate reforms implemented since the late 1990s — designed to turn state-owned firms into shareholding companies—haven't made a dent in patronage. In large and medium-sized state enterprises (ostensibly converted into shareholding companies, some of which are even traded on overseas stock markets), the Communist Party secretaries and the chairmen of the board were the same person about half the time. In 70 percent of the 6,275 large and medium-sized state enterprises classified as 'corporatized' as of 2001, the members of the party committee were members of the board of directors. All told, 5.3 million party officials — about 8 percent of its total membership and 16 percent of its urban members—held executive positions in state enterprises in 2003, the last year for which figures were available.

The combination of authoritarian rule and the state's economic dominance has bred a virulent form of crony capitalism, as the ruling elites convert their political power into economic wealth and privilege at the expense of equity and efficiency....

State enterprises are also miserably unprofitable. In 2003, a boom year, their median rate of return on assets was a measly 1.5 percent. More than 35 percent of state enterprises lose money and 1 in 6 has more debts than assets. *China is the only country in history that has achieved record economic growth and a record number of non-performing bank loans.*

Party membership and business acumen do not often go together.... China at least, boasts genuine private entrepreneurs who have built prosperous companies.

Rapid economic growth has not yet produced China's much-anticipated political pluralism. Perhaps, some observers speculate, China is still too poor to afford democracy. But with a per capita income of nearly $1,500 ($4,500 if you consider people's purchasing power), China is richer than many poor democracies. It is not poverty that is holding up democracy; it's a neo-Leninist state and the crony capitalism it fosters.

In part, democracy itself has been a victim of the country's economic expansion. However flawed and mismanaged, the country's rapid growth has bolstered Beijing's legitimacy and reduced pressure on its ruling elites to liberalize. Democratic transitions in developing countries are often triggered by economic crisis blamed on the incompetence and mismanagement of the ancien regime. China hasn't yet experienced that crisis. Meanwhile, the riches available to the ruling class tend to drown any movement for democratic reform from within the elite. Political power has become more valuable because it can be converted into wealth and privilege unimaginable in the past. At the moment, China's economic growth is having a perverse effect on democratization....[90]

Accepting the Reality That China's Socialist Market Economy Capitalism and One Party System of Government Are Working

It is the differences (italized in the quote above) between American political and economic capitalism and Chinese economic capitalism that help, rather than hinder, Chinese capitalism and society to "work." American-style democracy and pluralism which Minxin Pei and Americans want for China would not have enabled China to achieve and sustain the emergence from poverty China is exhibiting.

That is the point. The instincts in many Americans to contain China and the aspirations to make China an American-style democracy complement each other. China would be weaker if it had American-style democracy and pluralism. China being weaker would benefit American interests. To date, American-style democracy has not been the path China has taken. But, since the death of Mao Zedong, China has moved along a continuum from neo-Leninism to capitalism or state-directed capitalism.

It is ironic that this analysis by Minxin Pei captures much of why and how economic capitalism in China "works" and how it will evolve, but fails to see, explain or emphasize how American capitalists should prudently align themselves with a "neo-Leninist" state that "works" and must continue to "work."

The Cold War era mindset and its "neo-Leninism" conceptual framework obscures for some observers the reality that China is powerfully committed to economic but not political capitalism. It is disturbing to observers like Minxin Pei that what he terms a "neo-Leninist" state and we term "capitalism with Chinese characteristics" works so well. China's ongoing emergence from poverty because of China's economic growth's impact on the global and American economies is disturbing to Americans.

Minxin Pei's analysis recognizes the Chinese Communist Party has been legitimizing and preserving its leadership by adopting policies that are producing economic development. He seems to almost state that in doing so, the party is changing its future nature as well as preserving its role. What this type of analysis does not accept is the reality that the Chinese Communist Party can be and is increasingly aptly described from an American perspective as the "Capitalist Party of China" and is trying to preserve some of its egalitarian legitimacy by pulling more and more Chinese out of poverty, while successfully managing rapid and sustained economic development.

What the Minxin Pei type of analysis does not see or accept is that China is operating an alternate model of economic capitalism and one party government that is being validated and legitimized by economic and social progress which the Mainland Chinese crave.

For Americans, the most important deficiency of Minxin Pei's type of analysis is that it does not emphasize that America and American companies must align themselves with China's economic prosperity in order to protect America's prosperity and peace.

Cognitive Dissonance Regarding China's Future Rate of Economic Growth

Six psychological factors, among others, affect Americans' perceptions about China:

1. Some things are true and compelling, but people have not thought of them before.

2. Human thought and behavior is driven by unconscious and conscious needs and wants.

3. Definitions of rationality that do not take into account the role of the unconscious mind are deficient.

4. Unconscious needs and wants affect our rationality—so just how rational are human beings really?

5. All human beings have finite minds that cannot perceive or process the infinite interactions of cause and effect that shape our fates.

6. What is called "cognitive dissonance" (denial) in our thought processes occurs because human beings do not see or accept things they do not like. China's success and emerging economic dominance creates cognitive dissonance and hostility in some observers.

These psychological factors play a role in America's political and business leaders' choice of containment strategies regarding China notwithstanding:

1. The need for a paradigm shift in Americans' worldview in the 21st century to accommodate China's Manifest Destiny.

2. The success of China's economic development and the new trend of Chinese companies becoming multinational competitors.

3. The "future shock" and "CNOOC jingoism" that is growing in America regarding China's economic growth and competitiveness.

4. The need for a shift from the existing zero-sum-game strategy mindset that many American political and business leaders have regarding China.

5. The need for a shift among Americans to a "win-win" game strategy and mindset in dealing with China's emergence from poverty.

With these psychological factors and problems in mind, we will return to questions: What is China's Socialist Market Capitalism? How can China's Socialist Market Economy Capitalism be so economically competitive without being a "Rights Society" and having American-style Majority-Rule Democracy and a Rule of Law system?

Or to put the question another way:

How can China's Socialist Market Economy Capitalism be so economically competitive as a "Permission Society" with one party rule, a "Consensus Democracy," and a "Pre-Rule of Law" system? Understanding these questions is important in the interaction of American and Chinese companies. For example, how can an American company used to operating in a "Rights Society" and a Chinese company used to operating in a "Permission Society" best work with and prosper together? With that question in mind, Chapters 5 and 6 examine the genesis of and why China's Socialist Market Economy Capitalism is doing so well.

5

China Is a Successful Permission Society, Consensus Democracy and Pre-Rule of Law System

Overview

This chapter examines how the Permission Society, Consensus Democracy and Pre-Rule of Law system in China is working with such sustained and unprecedented success. Seeing China as a uniquely successful one-party state Permission Society Model is essential for the mindset change that is required by non-Chinese observers seeking to understand and benefit from China's economic success. The Permission Society Model is a more realistic conceptual framework than the ubiquitous Western model of China quickly becoming a Rights Society, Majority Rule Democracy with a Rule of Law system. Observers using a Rights Society mindset to understand China have unrealistic assumptions regarding the rate at which China can, will, or should evolve. Observers expecting that China will collapse or stagnate are unable to accept and adapt to the reality that China is thriving.

The Reality that China Is a Permission Society

China has been a Permission Society for 5000 years. It is a "rule by law" society where law is an administrative tool, not a "rule of law" society in which law is used as an adjudicative and administrative tool. In a Permission Society, if you have permission to do something, you have the "privilege" to do it at the discretion of the relevant decision-makers of the day.

There are institutional and cultural dynamics suggesting that China will remain a Permission Society for the foreseeable future in order to sustain its sovereignty, dignity, political and social stability, and economic and social development. President Hu Jintao stated in 2004, "Western political systems would be a blind alley for China."[1]

Ever since the overthrow of the Qing Dynasty in 1911, generations of Chinese leaders have sought to reform and modernize China. Other than under Deng Xiaoping, Jiang Zemin, and Hu Jintao, it has not been possible to find the road to peaceful change. Change with stability is the road on which China's contemporary leaders must guide China. Positive change in China requires stability, and stability in China requires positive change. President Hu Jintao and the other leaders face that fascinating challenge after Deng Xiaoping and Jiang Zemin's capable initiation and management of the transformation of China's economy.

The reforms that were introduced by Deng Xiaoping, Jiang Zemin, and Hu Jintao are a welcome relief to China. The Nationalist Revolution in the early 1900s might have been necessary, but looking back, some Chinese feel that a constitutional monarchy might have been a better alternative to the Kuomintang Revolution that produced dictatorship, civil strife, and foreign invasion for the following hundred years.

China's system of government evolved under feudalism over most of these 5000 years and under communism after 1949. Despite efficiency from 1978 to date in directing and managing economic development, it is creating increasing demands from America for a transition to a Chinese version of a Rights Society. But, it is China's Permission Society characteristics and capabilities that enabled it to achieve economic reform and growth.

The Chinese government and people want China to become a developed economy. The achievement of that goal may, in time, encourage the government to fully develop a system of rule of law. But, designing and then inculcating a "rule of law" mindset in a society that has operated without one for 5000 years involves the challenge of gradually training 1.3 billion Chinese people to respect such new procedures. Some observers believe that as that transition occurs (which will take perhaps as long as seventy-five years) the Chinese government can gradually open up society to political pluralism and executive, legislative, and judicial processes that are not indigenous in China.

Some observers assert that China is analogous to a super computer operating on out-dated software. They assert that China has to borrow two sets of enabling software from its developed Western partners: the rule of law and more-open-but-stable pluralistic political institutions that can ameliorate the systemic rigidity evident in China in spite of rapid change. But in doing so, China has to do a better "installation" of such "enabling software" than other developing countries have.

It is true that the design and deployment of a rule-of-law system adapted to China's needs that successfully disciplines markets and regulates economic activity is needed. One of the Chinese Communist Party's challenges is to withdraw from microeconomic decision-making as it reformed and is continuing to reform the SOE-based economy.

Gradual reform of China's political institutions and decision-making processes will enhance it's prosperity. A steady, gradual approach is needed to prevent the emergence of radical politicians that could destabilize China and in so doing, destabilize the world. The Chinese Communist Party can choose between maintaining one-party authoritarian rule and gradually permitting the development of reasonable and responsible political parties. It is experimenting incrementally with power sharing, not merely within the party, but among different points of view in seeking the way forward for China. Such experiments may defuse political structural challenges and ease pressures such as those seen in the Tiananmen Square anti-corruption demonstrations.

The Fallacy that China Has to Have an American-Style Majority-Rule Democracy to Develop Economically

In past centuries, countries with majority-rule-democracy have outperformed China economically. As we have recognized, a key challenge in the 21st century is how these democracies will interact and cope with the emerging ability of a one-party-state consensus democracy to outperform them economically.

Majority-Rule Democracy vs. Consensus Democracy: Stability in The Age of Species Lethal Weapons

Perhaps Chinese-style democracy by consensus is a more stable system in the Age Of Species Lethal Weapons[2] than the American style of the majority making all decisions and seeking to impose its will on the minority. China might ask America, "Why should 51% be allowed to dictate to 49% when the support of the 49%, or a large amount of them, is required to implement the 51%'s will?"

Jiang Zemin commented on the differences in China and America's political systems:

> China's system of a National People's Congress involves a system of consultation under the leadership of the Communist Party together with other parties cooperating.

> Eight parties are participating. Some [U.S.] congressmen ask, who is the opposition party? Why do we need an opposition party? America wants to apply its concept of values to the whole world. They think that every region of the world will use the American political system. This is simply unintelligent. Every country's election system must be based on their own situation, historical traditions, culture, economic and development level, and education level.[3]

It is vital for Americans to understand that collective consultation underpins Chinese government decision-making. As a law is drafted in China, government departments may be involved in the process and add their opinions. Session after session of drafting and review will take place till the result is a reflection of the various opinions. This may be interpreted as a democratic consultative process among the parts of China's government, which will be responsible for law, policy, or regulations enforcement.

From a Chinese perspective, in a democratic vote in which 51% agree on an issue or political candidate, why should the other 49% have to suffer the result that they do not accept and are unwilling to uphold them?[4] China's people and leaders believe that democracy is unanimity in the collective pursuit of ideals and the achievement of goals selected in a process of internal consultation rather than a system in which 49% endure the decisions of 51%. China is a culture of Yin and Yang, which emphasizes harmony and balance. Interest groups fighting among themselves, leaving China without direction, is one of China's greatest fears with the enormous development challenges it faces. China's history has proven the value of its one-party system of leadership and government.[5]

This concept of consensus in China's 5000-year collective consciousness traces its roots to the villages, which in ancient times were often huge extended families. The concept and process of consensus can be seen operating at the highest level of China's government. Consensus is part of China's culture and historical development, which works for China. But it is often not understood or respected in America, where social conditions and historical development are different.[6]

China's history and concept of government involves leaders emerging and ruling till they misgovern to the point that the people overthrow them. In the process, a new leadership group emerges. The ability of the Communist Party to retain power depends upon its ability to provide China with sovereignty, economic development, and social stability.[7] China's political system cannot be like America's due to cultural, historical, social, and economic factors. China's leadership recognizes the need to absorb Western principles that are effective in other countries while adapting them to China's needs. China's one-party system of government under Mao Zedong, Deng Xiaoping, Jiang Zemin, and Hu Jintao, protected China's sovereignty and then advanced its economic development. The Communist Party is the strongest leadership group in China and the only existing indigenous mechanism that can provide the direction and organization that China requires.

The Reality of Consensus-Building and Stability in a One-Party System Government

Hard experience over the last 50 years, including the famines of the Great Leap Forward in the 1950s and the trauma of the Cultural Revolution in the late 1960s and 1970s, has made the Chinese government and people extremely concerned about consensus and stability. Even with the incremental introduction of greater rights to private property, the Chinese government and the Party's Socialist Market Economy will still need and wish to improve the lives of the socially and economically deprived.

The Chinese have witnessed what can happen when change occurs too quickly and with inadequate control. They will not permit the horrors experienced in Russia in recent years to be repeated in China. With 1.3 billion people to feed and care for, the risks are too great. Control is essential to stability and economic progress in China.

The Chinese government has, with a sustained amount of internal consensus-building, developed and implemented a gradual yet highly-effective evolution of major reforms in 25 years. While attracting increasing amounts of essential FDI over that sustained period, the government has protected China's economic sovereignty from both foreign domination and internal instability. To develop and implement such increases in FDI and China's standards of living and major reforms while preserving stability is an astounding feat.

Some observers attribute China's successful and sustained economic growth to the liberalization, decentralization, and greater freedom of decision-making that China experienced as the planned economy increasingly faltered and forced leaders to pursue economic development through reforms. Such observers do not acknowledge that the one-party government produced the causes of the extraordinary success of the Chinese government's economic management in the past 25 years.[8]

Under the Permission Society's planned economy, SOEs and households were assigned rights to and obligations for the pro-duction of fixed quantities of commodities at fixed prices. Rights and obligations were specific to individual SOEs and households and there were government sanctions if they failed to fulfill their obligations. In transforming the Permission Society's SOE economy into a gradually deploying joint stock ownership Socialist Market Economy, the Chinese government had to replace administrative allocation with market allocation, and administered prices with market prices. The government is using a "dual track" approach in which the planned amounts are enforced but output above them is determined by market forces and consumer demand.[9] The move to market pricing has been fostered by the rapid shift in ownership. In 1979, 97% of retail sales were by SOEs and collectively-owned enterprises. This was reduced to 37% by 1998.[10]

The capabilities of the Chinese government and the effectiveness of China's Permission Society culture are spectacularly demonstrated by the decision to limit Chinese population growth, which has been successfully implemented. This achievement is possible in a Permission Society, but not in a Rights Society.

The Chinese government announced the blueprint for a Socialist Market Economy in 1993 and considerable reform has been implemented. But much is still to be accomplished in improving the performance of SOEs, reforming the financial system, public finances, monetary policy, freeing markets, World Trade Organization membership reforms,[11] and developing legal and regulatory frameworks to empower but regulate it's economy. The speed of the reform of the SOE system emphasizes that in China, "gradual" does not mean "slow."[12] The fully deployed power of China's "Socialist Market Economy" has not yet been brought "on line." As it is, we believe China's rates of growth and economic performance may compound and accelerate in speed and significance, which some observers, while urging the Chinese government about the need for American style institutions and economic reform, may not fully appreciate. China's extraordinary economic growth has been accomplished in the context of a planned economy with still-incomplete economic reform of its SOE structures. In a country as large as China, making that transition while producing consistently increasing prosperity is an extraordinary achievement.

China's economic performance is the most successful in transitioning from an SOE-based economy.[13] China's Communist Party leadership began welcoming private entrepreneurs to Party membership in 2001, and in 2002 began emphasizing the importance of the non-state-owned sector in promoting economic growth, creating jobs, and invigorating markets.

The Communist Party's 2004 National Congress also began other reforms by permitting limited elections to fill certain grass roots Party posts in order to curb corruption, strengthen the Party's ability to manage economic and social progress, and safeguard the Party's leadership role in a "socialist market economy."[14] According to the Chinese Communist Party's 16th Congress, "Socialist Market Economy" is defined as market economy under the socialist macro-control and supervision.

The Party is evolving to protect its leadership of China. This will enhance the Party's already astute leadership selection process, and is the alternative selected by the Party to making China's legislature more democratic according to the American two-party model. There are many factors that suggest that China must and will keep its one-party decision-making structure as the key tool for ensuring its stability, sovereignty, dignity, rising living standards, and the happiness of China's people. Foreign companies should assume that the restructuring of the SOEs and other nationally vital economic and social reforms underway in China will occur within the safeguard of China's wealth and future remaining in China's one-party leadership's control. A Permission Society can protect itself from foreigners encroaching on its sovereignty more easily than a Rights Society can. For example, land in Mainland China is generally owned by the State and merely leased.[15]

Another example of the ability of the Chinese government to address problems which can be seen in their abrupt change from an initial ineffective response, using traditional denial and information control tactics, to other immediately-effective Permission Society tactics in dealing with the SARS crisis in 2003. Once the government recognized the SARS threat to ending China's rapid economic development, they used China's Permission Society and relatively highly-centralized political system's strength. China's leaders suspended the May Day national holiday week, and schools, businesses, hotels, restaurants, theatres, etc. were summarily closed in Beijing. The outbreak of SARS did not spread and China showed an amazing 9.1% GDP growth rate for the third quarter of 2003 immediately after the outbreak.

The Fallacy That China's Political System Has to Be Like America's to Be Successful

The emergence of democratic decision-making processes and institutions and well-defined legal and regulatory systems enforcing statutory, common law, and contractual rights and obligations in England and America empowered their economic dominance in the 19th and 20th centuries. But China's huge, rapid economic development has not, in the 1949 to 2006 period, required these "Rights Society" features.

The 1949 Communist Revolution and the 1978 Socialist Market Economy's "Capitalist Evolution" were pragmatic necessities that the strongest forces in China and China's people accepted. Mao Zedong used Communist ideology to motivate his followers, legitimize his leadership, and organize China for the protection of its sovereignty. George Washington and the leaders of the American Revolution used a form of new American democratic ideology to motivate their followers, legitimize their leadership, and organize America for the protection of its sovereignty. Democracy and Communism were each novel concepts in human history that worked in revolutions in America in 1776 and China in 1949. American democracy relied on rights for its legitimacy. Communism relied upon curtailed rights, in the interest of the common good, for its legitimacy. Historically, in empowering national sovereignty and economic and social development, a "Rights Society" has worked for America and a "Permission Society" has worked for China. China has not needed democratic institutions like America's to outperform America's economic productivity.

Nation building is very much still underway in China. There have not been 43 leaders of China since Mao Zedong as there has been of America since George Washington. China's leadership since 1949 knows only the inspiring and frightening challenge of nation building. China's leadership and people are not looking back on more than 200 years of sustained sovereignty and economic and social progress as America's leaders and people are. China today has the drive that Americans have, to some degree, lost in their success. This higher "Drive Quotient" is another key competitive advantage. In China, people live to work; in America, people work to live. The ethos of nation building is stronger in China 56 years after the Communist Revolution than Americans may understand more than 200 years after the American Revolution.

It is likely today that no single person, either American or Chinese, is intelligent, far-sighted, and persuasive enough to foresee, understand, and explain all the factors involved in correctly defining how China should not only successfully implement democratic reform, but more importantly, establish democratic institutions and decision-making processes that sustain themselves. It is likely that even Chinese leaders and people who cherish the evolution of American-style democratic institutions and decision-making in China do not yet fully understand how such institutions and decision-making could operate and sustain both themselves and China's economic and social development. It is important for both Americans and Chinese to recognize and respect this current reality.

It is also important to recognize and accept that the successful evolution of sustainable democratic institutions and decision-making in America and China is better served by collaboration than by conflict. Democracy is fragile. Creating and sustaining democratic institutions and decision-making is the work of many people over many years. America is profoundly fortunate that its commitment to democratic institutions established in its Constitution in the 18th century has stood the tests of over two hundred years to date. Will America's democratic institutions and decision-making processes successfully meet the tests of the future? The use of coercion or force by Americans, however noble or ignoble their intentions, may undermine their survival at home. That is a key danger that Americans who cherish democracy must ponder and accept. Democracy is about respecting the rights of persons with whom you do not agree.

China Has Competitive Advantages as a "Permission Society" and Pre-Rule of Law System

China has the competitive advantage, in economic development terms, of being a Permission Society rather than a Rights Society like India. China and India[16] compare in 2004 as follows: their per capita incomes were US$1300 and US$620[17]; their average annual GDP growth rates from 1993 to 2003 were 9.5% and 6.1%; their populations were 1.3 billion and 1.1 billion; their population growth rates were 0.87 vs. 1.5; their literacy rates were 90.9% and 59.5%; their Internet users were 79.8 million and 18.5 million; the percentages of their populations below the poverty line were 10% and 25%; foreign direct investment they received in 2001, for example, was US$44.2 billion and US$3.4 billion; and their fixed lines and mobile phones per 1000 people were 247.7 and 43.8 respectively.[18]

China's Permission Society Protects China's Economic Sovereignty

Accepting the effectiveness and legitimacy of China's Permission Society in meeting China's needs will help Americans and American companies collaborate more effectively and profitably with the Chinese government and trading partners.

The Chinese government will be understandably under pressure domestically not to allow foreigners to gain control of the Chinese economy. Although China abandoned the goal of economic self-sufficiency in 1979, it remains a key driver in China's sovereignty which is not negotiable. Even as the government and people seek more foreign capital and expertise, it is ultimately to build, not sell, China. They need to open China up to foreign companies to strengthen it's economy and fuel economic development by importing foreign companies' financial and intellectual capital. It is true that China's leaders have chosen to empower foreign companies, rather than domestic private enterprises in the sale of SOEs and SOE assets. Powerful foreign companies are easier to control than powerful domestic companies.[19]

The dilemma is that China must offer enough long-term benefits to the foreign companies to attract them without losing economic control to them. China's Permission Society and Pre-Rule of Law regulatory system, which Western observers habitually assert is an impediment to China's sustained economic development, has not been empirically proven to be an impediment. China's system, which is so different from Majority-Rule Democracies and Post Rule of Law regulatory systems, provides the tools and flexibility for China to admit foreign companies without submitting to foreign domination. As such, China's system both fosters and protects China's sovereignty and economic progress.

Are there any limits to the ability of the Chinese government to impose zero-sum-game results on foreign companies? Yes, there are. But they are limits set by the Chinese political leadership in dealing with and solving China's economic problems. So far, China's leadership has recognized how to deal with China's problems very successfully. They are adroit at gradual, controlled evolution and have eschewed the "big bang" approach to change that many non-Chinese observers and participants long to see.

Perhaps the systematic, not completely successful suppression of private enterprise in the 1980s and 1990s, as China "opened up" and transformed so many key parts of its economy, was key to China's success then, now, and into the future.

Rule by Law in a Permission Society

As stated, China has the "rule by law" and America has the "rule of law"[20] Law is predominantly an administrative mechanism in China and an administrative and adjudicative mechanism in America. China has a long tradition of rule by moral principles and of the interpretation of those principles by people in authority. It has never adopted the concept that individuals have a right to due process under the law. For example, although the Economic Contract Law was enacted in 1982, there is considerable evidence that the Chinese society at large is unconvinced by the legal principles and processes that this law enshrines. Carolyn Blackman comments:

> People with power override contracts if it suits them because they are used to exercising power without any legal restraints. People bringing contract disputes to court face strong social pressure to settle by mediation rather than to insist on their legal entitlements.... The legal system does not operate as a separate sphere from normal social life. Personal relationships and insider-outsider distinctions affect legal judgments just as much as those in any other areas.
>
> Since the enactment of the first Sino-Foreign Equity Joint Venture Law in 1979, every year has seen a string of new laws and regulations as China attempts to bring its business environment into line with international practice. The lack of a well-understood, respected and integrated commercial legal framework places a burden on negotiations to solve many issues by negotiation rather than by reference to legislation.

One of the commonest complaints from western business people is the Chinese failure to fulfill conditions agreed to and signed on in contracts.… Many western companies have discovered that getting legal redress for failure to comply with a contract is just about impossible. This leaves one way out if a company is to continue in China—negotiation.

In ordinary Chinese life one cannot help but notice the way people get around rules and regulations and do not see them as binding. They have a different view of what constitutes honesty and cheating from the western one.… It is unwise ever to forget that this is a 'haggling society' in which it is legitimate to cheat outsiders.[21]

The law and courts serve critically different purposes in a Permission Society and a Rights Society. Observers inculcated and operating with the assumptions of a Rights Society may not realize or like to tolerate that rulers from a Permission Society have not been inculcated nor operate with a Rights Society's definitions of "law" and "courts." The following explanation captures these distinctions well, and identifies their continuing role in China's historical and social context:

Historical developments can explain many of the contradictions in China's legal system including the central government's commitment to initiate reform and the obdurate problems of implementing this reform. The Chinese economist, Yun, described the Chinese economy as a 'bird in a cage'. The owners must let the bird fly, but only within the confines of the cage, the central plan, lest the bird escape. Both the imperialist legacy and the Maoist overlay failed to differentiate between the functions of law and administration; both placed the judicial system at the same level as the states' bureaucracies in the political hierarchy. Thereby, the emperors and the Communists failed to give authority to the courts over the administration, and limited powers of judicial interpretation. Despite its burgeoning market economy, law in China still serves more as an instrument of control than as a framework to facilitate private transactions or to protect rights.[22]

Each of China and America's systems' economic development critically depends on its different history, traditions, legal regime, and cultural assumptions. Each society's legal traditions, regime, and cultural assumptions work adequately for it. China's Pre-Rule of Law System works well in serving its political, social, and economic customs and practices for its purposes and needs. As we have seen, China's Pre-Rule of Law system protects China's economic sovereignty and development goals and needs. The Chinese government's decision to help drive China's economic and legal reengineering by committing China to the requirements of WTO membership creates a transitional dynamic of a customary law society evolving into a Rule of Law society.

Business people inculcated and operating with a Rights Society's legal regime and assumptions typically view China's Permission Society's Pre-Rule of Law system as defective. But China's system is not defective if one uses the criteria of China's political, social, and economic customs and practices and the protection of China's economic sovereignty and economic development.

The Chinese government is still in the process of developing a comprehensive set of laws and regulations in the course of China's transformation from a centrally-planned economy to a more market-oriented economy. As the legal system in China is still in a state of flux, laws and regulations, or the interpretation of them, are subject to change. Furthermore, any change in the political and economic policy of the Chinese government may also lead to similar changes in the laws and regulations or their interpretation.

China's legal system is based on the People's Republic of China's ("PRC") Constitution and is a codified legal system comprising written laws, regulations, circulars, administrative directives, and internal guidelines. As such, the administration of China's laws and regulations are subject to a notorious degree of discretion by the authorities. As China's economy is undergoing development generally at a faster pace than its legal system, some degree of uncertainty exists in connection with whether and how existing laws and regulations will apply to various events or circumstances. Some of the laws and regulations, and their interpretation, implementation and enforcement are limited. Unlike common-law countries such as America, precedent cases are not binding. Due to such inconsistency and unpredictability, if a business entity, whether Chinese or foreign, is involved in any legal dispute in the PRC, they may, and commonly do, experience difficulties in obtaining legal redress or in enforcing their "rights" in China, or in obtaining enforcement of judgment by a court of another jurisdiction.

Businesses operating in China (outside Special Economic Zones, Hong Kong, etc.) are subject to PRC laws and regulations, including the procurement of licenses and permits from the relevant authorities. Consequent to any breach or non-compliance of these PRC laws and regulations, the relevant authorities may terminate or suspend a company's business activities or impose penalties.

Changes in China's law and regulations, or the implementation of them, at the central, provincial, municipal, and village levels may also require businesses in The PRC to obtain additional approvals and licenses or suspend, change, or not enforce them by or from the PRC authorities at various levels for the conduct of operations in China. Businesses in the PRC incur additional expenses in order to comply with such new or changing requirements.

Businesses operating in China have no assurance that approvals or licenses will be granted promptly or at all. If businesses experience delays in obtaining or are unable to obtain such required approvals or licenses, it impacts their operations and business in China and their financial performance. Businesses can be adversely affected legally in very unpredictable and arbitrary ways.

Since 1978, China's government has undergone various reforms of its economic systems. Many of the reforms are unprecedented or experimental and must be expected to be refined and modified from time to time. Political, economic, and social factors may also lead to readjustment of the reform measures. In particular, China has agreed to undertake a series of measures to liberalize its tariff regime because of its admission as a member to the WTO on December 11, 2001. This refinement and readjustment process will have a material impact on businesses operating in China.

The Fallacy That China Will Quickly Become a Rights Society or Majority-Rule Democracy

These types of uncertainties are and will remain systemic and pervasive in China. But whatever the negative features for foreign and Chinese businesses, as we have noted, China's Permission Society and Pre-Rule of Law system have a very important positive overall impact on China's economic development and sovereignty. If China was a Post Rule of Law society, it would forfeit the degree of flexibility in changing and interpreting its rules, which China requires to protect its economic sovereignty and development.

It is hard to imagine how China could continue to achieve both economic development and sovereignty if it had a Rule of Law system. Why should China adopt the Rule of Law and Rights Society protection of individual rights, which would enable foreigners to more easily gain control of China's economic sovereignty and development? Why should China's government and people give up the stability and economic growth it's Permission Society and Pre-Rule of Law system provides and protects? Such choices are determined by the culture of China as it currently manifests and protects itself. In the process of implementing its

WTO commitments and becoming more active in doing business globally, China will evolve over time, rather than in a "big bang" overnight approach. Lester Thurow has commented:

> In Western societies, states maintain social order and guarantee certain rights through laws that limit other rights and freedoms. In traditional Chinese society, social order is maintained through social pressures—through rites and customs—rather than through laws.... Virtually all nations, and certainly those with extensive trade relations, have developed their own commercial codes. Consequently, codes form primary influences, if not the foundations for national commercial laws. A deeper distinction revolves around rights based systems, as in the industrialized West, or public-law systems, as in China. The U.S. Declaration of Independence in 1776 heralded the first rights-based legal system by proclaiming: "We hold these truths to be self-evident: That all men are created equal; that they are endowed by their Creator with certain unalienable rights...." Public law systems do not endow their citizenry with rights independently of the authorities that grant them. These rights reside with the authorities, not in the "unalienable rights" of the nations' citizens; hence, the authorities can grant or withdraw rights at leisure. With this perspective, China did not develop a legal system, or even written laws, until the 20th century.[23]

Yasheng Huang, in *Selling China,* conjectures that "... China's reform strategy, so far, has been motivated to save, not to dismantle socialism."[24] How quickly will Chinese capitalism erode Chinese socialism? Fan Gang, an economics Professor at Peking University, estimated in 2003 that it might take 20 to 40 years.[25] China's top judge estimates it may take a lot longer for China to design and put in place a legal system that is viewed as binding by China's citizens because there is no tradition in place to support a Rights Society legal system.[26]

Xiao Yang, the Chief Justice of the People's Supreme Court of China stated in 2000:

> In Chinese history, the ideology of rule by man has been dominant for more than two thousand years. Historically there were occasional sparks of rule by law, which always disappeared rapidly in the broad and deep ocean of rule by man.
>
> After the Communist Party took power, the issue of adopting which way to run the country and the society, that is, either adopting a system of rule by man or rule by law became a significant theoretical and practical problem from the beginning. During the earlier period after the founding of new China, this problem was solved relatively smoothly. Regretfully, starting from the later part of the 1950s, due to the influence of all kinds of subjective and objective factors, the answer to this problem had changed. The ideology and phenomenon of rule by man dominated throughout the country and over life and society.
>
> As Deng Xiaoping said, in the past, due to the influence of feudal tradition, the words spoken by leaders were always viewed as "law" in the life of the state and the party. Disagreeing with the words said by the leaders was regarded as "violating the law." As the leaders changed their words, the "law" would also be changed accordingly. This phenomenon mentioned by Deng Xiaoping actually reflects the rule of man. Under a situation of rule by man, man is higher than law, power is superior to law.[27]

The Chinese are pragmatic. Deng Xiaoping made the famous remark in 1962 that "It does not matter whether the cat is black or white. It is a good cat if it catches mice." China certainly caught foreign direct investment in the 1980s, 1990s and so far in the new century. It seems in 2006 in China, that a cat that is half black and half white is better than a cat that is pure gray, or black, or white.

Since China's Socialist Market Economy Capitalism works, it is a good system. A huge majority of Mainland Chinese concur that economic development is more important than multi-party elections and majority-rule democracy that would make China's government and therefore economy less stable and able to enrich China.

China's one-party system and the Chinese government have strengthened China's unsuccessful planned communist economy with Socialist Market Economy Capitalism, but not replaced China's one-party system that successfully managed China's economic transformation. The enduring reality which Americans must accept is that China's one-party system and the Chinese government it produces has been able to produce faster, better, and cheaper economic and social development for China than a Chinese government operating an American-style Majority-Rule Democracy, Rights Society, Rule of Law and capitalist system could.

Laurence Brahm noted in 2001 that:

> The unleashing of a market economy has brought with it a radical shift in people's thinking. Within a span of a mere 20 years, China has gone from a non-materialist society structured around principles of ideology to a now overly-materialistic society driven by the values of conspicuous consumption. While standards of living have improved alongside massive infrastructure development and growing productivity, there has been a rapid breakdown of social morality and an unfortunate loss of ideology and principles in general, leading to corruption and a new proliferation of social vices and rise in crime.
>
> China's leadership, recognizing the dangers inherent in this ideological vacuum, is seeking to piece together a new framework of social values more appropriate for China's modern, and often trend-driven society than the older more rigid moral structure espoused by the Communist Party in the past.... Jiang's introduction of a new theory called the "three representa-tions," which brought into play past values of the Chinese Communist Party such as Mao's "representing the people's inter-ests" and Deng's 'representing modern productive forces' together with Jiang's representing advanced civilization.[28]

The Reality That China's Rule by Law Tradition Cannot Quickly Disappear

China does not currently have sufficient lawyers represented in its legislature to make rules. That can impede China's growth in the medium to long run if not addressed by the Chinese government. The law-making function of the People's Congress could be enhanced. For example, more legally trained representatives and staff for the Standing Committees would assist. Government agencies regulating rule-making functions could be created and enhanced so that social welfare issues such as poisonous foods, unsafe working conditions, etc. are better addressed. Such rules would benefit from being made with consultation with the people who are affected in an open and transparent system. Websites are a modern way of communicating laws and rules to people.

Fan Gang puts the reform process in a realistic perspective, unlike many observers who are hostile to China and impatient with the rate of change. They give too little esteem to the bold and vast changes affecting 22% of humanity that the Chinese government, people, and culture are making with incredible speed and success. Professor Fan wrote in comments published in 2003:

> ... legal reform in China is not just a matter of replacing one set of laws for another, but is also a process of building up the whole concept and whole set of institutions based on the "rule of law" from an initial condition of a rural, even "medieval," society with a long and complex history. Even once the laws have been promulgated, it will take many years, and much testing of them in the courts, for the legal framework to reflect the new realities.
>
> ...while other countries may have one set of problems arising from their being either "developing" or "transitional" economies, China has both. It is undertaking both to transform its rural economy into a modern society and to transform its planned economy into a market system. It is this "dual" nature of its problems that makes the transformation

process in China so difficult, as the two sets of problems complicate and amplify each other.

It will unavoidably take a long time for China to build an orderly, functioning market system. In general, institution building is a long-term process anyway. Seventy years may not be an unrealistic estimate for transforming China from a medieval economy to a modern market economy, given that countries in the West have been undergoing the same process since the 17th century and given that China has no experience with colonialism.

Such an historical, long-term perspective is necessary if we are to understand the current situation. We must expect that there will be problems; the real question is: are the necessary changes being made that will gradually see the present gap between China and the advanced market economies narrowed tomorrow? For instance, although the banking sector is still very poorly organized, it has achieved significant progress in the last five years. The overall political stability that has puzzled many observers is fundamentally based on the fact that most interest groups in Chinese society today are better off, in many senses, than they were 20 years ago, or even five years ago, and have expectations of being even better off in the future, no matter how poor is their current situation.[29]

China's Chief Justice Xiao Yang stated in 2001:

At present, the differences that separate China from the West are fundamental and manifold. These differences encompass culture, social organization, ideology, and political and economic governance, to name but a few. Yet, there are forces both within and outside of China which have been narrowing and transforming the distinctive features of the Chinese landscape.

One of the areas of fundamental difference—namely ideology—needs to be more clearly understood by those in the West. Ideology continues to play an important role in directing the leadership of socialist China. In particular, ideology provides guidance to the Chinese leadership on issues of political and economic governance of the country.

... From an ideological perspective, the primary contradiction facing socialist China at this point in history is that of "economic development." Hence, the primary focus of Party and state activity is geared towards building up the Chinese economy. Such an orientation has characterized Chinese governance since 1978 when Deng Xiaoping launched the "Four Modernizations" in an effort to make China a modern nation-state. This emphasis on economics is also consistent with Marxist-Leninist thought. Perhaps even more interesting is that this preoccupation with things economic has also been the key focus of Western political thinking for the past 200 years. Accordingly, one may say that both China and the West have the same essential political orientation now, although they may differ with respect to the means to achieve similar ends.

Yet, even with respect to the means to be employed to achieve economic development, we have witnessed since at least 1992 convergence between China and the West. In 1992, the Chinese Communist Party launched its "Socialist Market Economy" program in an effort to create Western-styled markets and thereby strengthen horizontal economic relations, while diminishing vertical administrative controls over economic sectors. Such economic reforms have as their goal the creation of an economic system that is compatible with Western and WTO capitalist norms.

Yet the Chinese government may wish to question whether an entirely economic orientation will bring into play China's great strengths and comparative advantages. China's historic future contributions to the emerging global order are likely to be non-economic in nature, and more profound as a result. China may wish to think of itself more in terms of a civilization, rather than as a Western nation-state. Certainly, this would be more consistent with its illustrious past. It would also provide a "new" model for governance—not only for China, but also for the West and for a world of the regions.

China has always been a civilization. A civilization is firstly a moral universe—this has always been appreciated by the Chinese both in the past and present—hence, the continuing importance of ideology in China. One of the greatest of all Chinese inventions may be ascribed to Confucius: the creation of a moral superstructure for Chinese society not connected to any religion. The liberal West of today, having secularized society, operates systems, which are largely amoral, predicated on economic value, rather than moral values. In this sense, the West may be said to fail the test of a civilization as it lacks a moral superstructure. This also points out the fallacy of organizing society primarily for economic purposes.[30]

The Fallacy That America Has the Moral Authority to Demand China Speed Up Its Reform Process

The transition from a Permission Society to a Rights Society was gradual for England and America. A 21st Century Englishman or American doing business in Henry VIII's England would find that most of the "rights" they take for granted did not exist and could not be insisted on. That is the case in China today. Henry the VIII's England was a Permission Society. Legal concepts and rights gradually developed to meet the commercial and international needs of a gradually evolving society in the 17th to 20th Centuries.

Some believe that America embraced being a Rights Society since its birth, but the democracy and rights Americans today take for granted evolved and were extended incrementally. Sean Wilentz in *The Rise Of American Democracy* [31] recounts how:

> ...after the American Revolution and the framing of the Constitution...the very idea of democracy remained contentious. The founders, Jeffersonians and Federalists among them, clashed ferociously over the appropriate role of ordinary citizens in a government of "we, the people."'
>
> The triumph of Andrew Jackson in 1828 redefined this role on the national level while city democrats, anti-Masons, fugitive slaves, and a host of other Americans hewed their own definitions on the local level. In these local definitions Wilentz recovers the beginnings of a fateful division. The free-labor North and the slaveholders' South, although linked by the federal government, were actually two distinct political systems, embodying separate and fundamentally antagonistic

conceptions of democracy. National leaders like Martin Van Buren to Henry Clay succeeded in squelching that antagonism, maintaining a wary balance between the two regions that lasted until the election of Abraham Lincoln sparked bloody resolution.

By combining the political history of the towering figures in early American history with an intimate and surprising look at the influence of innumerable lesser-known figures, The Rise Of American Democracy compels us to understand our democracy not as an historical inevitability or an abstract philosophical system but as a fragile enterprise shot through with human frailties, conflicts, accommodations, and unforeseen events. Those events, from Thomas Jefferson's time to Abraham Lincoln's produced the underpinnings of the democracy we know today.[32]

Americans have little moral authority or right, in light of their historic precedent, to demand that China quickly adopt the American-style Majority-Rule Democracy that evolved slowly in America, with many internal struggles and a civil war, over a century after the American Constitution was in place. More fundamentally, England and America evolved from Permission Societies into Rights Societies over an 800-year period since the Magna Carta. Why and how can China achieve immediately the political reforms that took America over a century to work out? How can Americans ask the Chinese to do quickly what Americans could only do slowly and in stages? Yet, Americans make demands that China become democratic the core driver of America's foreign policy towards China since 1949. China's political evolution is properly a matter for China's citizens to decide, not America's. Americans have always claimed the right of self-determination. How can Americans prudently ignore the right of 1.3 billion Chinese to self-determination?

The American Constitution formulated in 1791 is a new and, in its scope and success, an unprecedented government of laws interpreted by successive generations of men, rather than the intra-generational rule of men by men. In other words, the American

Constitution established a system of the rule of law rather than the rule of men.

In what we will refer to as the "American Experiment," immigrants and a relatively few indigenous people in an unpopulated land have made great progress in mankind's quest for freedom and freedom from want. The American Experiment, to date, is a monumental achievement in building and sustaining a free society:

> The United States is the first nation in the world created by the pen as well as the sword; the ideas expressed in these documents have shaped the lives of all Americans: indeed these ideas, perhaps more than the vast and rich continent and the American people themselves, have given America a unique identity among the nations of history.[33]

The documents referred to include those created by Americans building on many preceding debates and writings. The first is the Fundamental Orders, 1639, created by a group of farmers nineteen years after the Mayflower landed in America, and described as the first written constitution known to history that created a government, and marked the beginning of American democracy. Then came the Declaration of Independence in 1776, the Northwest Ordinance in 1787, the Constitution of the United States of America in 1787, the Bill of Rights in 1791, Jefferson's First Inaugural Address in 1801, the Emancipation Proclamation in 1863, the Gettysburg Address in 1863, Lincoln's Second Inaugural Address in 1865, and John F. Kennedy's Inaugural Address in 1961. These are only a few of the documents in which America was incrementally defined.

Americans are proud of what Majority-Rule Democracy under The Constitution of the United States has achieved. As Thomas Jefferson said, when the American Experiment did not yet have three centuries of proof of the sustainability of that Constitution,

"The example of changing a constitution, by assembling the wise men of the State, instead of by assembling armies, will be worth... much to the world... The Constitution... is unquestionably the wisest ever presented to men."[34] The authors of America's Constitution achieved something revolutionary, as in it, for the first time, the then-radical idea that a government rests on the consent of the people was, by the strokes of pens, made a political and a national fact. The authors of the American Constitution produced a document, a law, that solved a remarkable number of the problems of government and politics that had plagued men and nations throughout history, a document that an early American president called, and history has proven, was "the greatest single effort of national deliberation that the world has ever seen."[35]

Unfortunately, some observers feel that America's avowed mission to spread democracy throughout the world, however fervently felt, is not consistent with America's behavior. The Bush Administration's War on Terror has features that tarnish America's moral authority as a beacon of freedom. But, Mao Zedong referred to the undemocratic treatment of Negro Americans in his *Little Red Book*. Some argue that America is not a "democracy" if that word is reserved for a society where the peoples' will is done,[36] and point out that America has overthrown democratically-elected governments in Iran, Chile, Guatemala and elsewhere. Some argue that America only supports democratic governments if and only if it is consistent with America's strategic and economic interests, which are those of a corporate elite that dominates the country and its policy-making, and not the interests of the American people.

However a reader subjectively thinks and feels about such observations, there can be no objective dispute that the American system of government is not all that exists in the world or in world history. China's governing institutions and processes outdate and have outlasted the American Experiment by 48 centuries. Today,

China's experiment with Socialist Market Economy Capitalism is very successful. The question facing Americans is whether the peaceful rise of China, as a capitalist superpower with five times the population and a different history and culture than America, is possible.

How Can a Pre-Rule of Law Society Comprising 22% of Humanity Produce So Much Economic Growth, Reform and Social Stability?

How can China be doing so well with its undemocratic political system, poorly performing banking and other state-owned sectors, unreliable legal and regulatory system, corruption, serious regional disparities, currency conversion restrictions, etc.? How is China consistently out-performing the developed economies' GDP and other growth rates after 1979 even though in many respects its economy in 2006 is less advanced?

The short, simplistic answer is that in the past 25 years, China's economic growth has been produced by and has maintained social stability. This is not accidental. It is the result of and depends upon exceptional problem-solving and consensus-building skills in the Chinese government, as much as on the innate attitudes, abilities, aspirations, and energy of the Chinese people. China's economic growth and increasing standards of living depend on social stability and collaborative, focused national effort. It is China's Pre-Rule of Law and Consensus Democracy, and not the Rule of Law and Majority-Rule Democracy that have, among other factors, produced China's reemergence as the world's leading high-growth economy.

How Does China's Pre-Rule of Law System Work?

How can a Pre-Rule of Law Society like China economically compete so effectively with a Rule of Law Jurisdiction like America? The Chinese depend on a vast network of social relationships rather than the Rule of Law to get things done. Their system regulates the lives of 22% of the human race and is undeniably demonstrating over the past twenty-five years the ability to outperform majority-rule democracy in producing economic growth and social stability. China's system of dictatorship based on consensus democracy is gaining the "legitimacy" or, at least, the validation provided by a growing global economic power.

How China can be achieving such global power while it is in a pre-legal-system one-party state is one of the great questions and challenges of the 21st century. In European and American history, economic power was thought to be a result in part and to depend to a large degree on a jurisdiction having a well-defined and objective rule of law rather than the amorphous and arbitrary rule of men. How can consensus-dependent dictatorship be more productive than majority-rule democracy?

The question of how China's Pre-Rule of Law system governs the lives and actions of 22% of the human race becomes an even more prominent question when the assumption that China, as it opens up economically, will cease to be a Permission Society is questioned seriously:

> Family ties, especially between fathers and sons, comprise the strongest and most important relationships. Consequently, parental duties include ensuring the families' good behavior. If parents fail to maintain appropriate behavior within their families, then the duty passes to neighborhood and village elders and, finally, to provincial and central governments.[37]

Social norms, rather than individual rights, are inculcated in Mainland China's citizens.

> While Western moral philosophy is sprinkled with truisms such as "Thou shall not kill" or "Thou shall not steal", few truisms exist in Chinese moral philosophy ... Specific and binding moral duties and appropriate behaviors exist for every situation and derive from specific categorizations and grouping of situations and individuals in society.[38]

The Chinese operate by shared inculcated social norms and expected behavior developed during the long history of China's isolation. In the context of such shared social norms and behavior, habits of consensus building, group decision-making and group responsibility for decisions operate in China. After detailed, painstaking consultations, people in authority in China make decisions, but responsibility for the decision is borne by the entire group. It typically takes a long time for the Chinese to arrive at certain types of business decisions, due to their non-majority-rule, consensus-based decision-making traditions.

In America, the rule of law, with its emphasis on the rights and obligations of the individual, has replaced the rule of men and custom and practice as the mechanism of enforcing social conformity. It is common for one person to be given power in America to make the final decision and bear all responsibility. Individual decision-making is often seen as the most efficient method to use. Decisions tend to go from the top down, although Americans believe that those closest to a problem should have input in determining the solution, and individual decision-makers are found at all levels depending on the importance of the decision.

Americans are more inclined to trust strangers than the Chinese, who are raised and operate in a Pre-Rule of Law system, and so have to rely on shared social norms and relationship networks rather than the rule of law and courts to enforce perceived obligations.

Americans, with the benefits and relative predictability of an objective legal system, believe that competition fosters creativity and contributes to high performance. Chinese believe that everything must be in harmony for the world to be in balance and that competition can lead to disharmony.

Americans decide, in the context of the relative predictability of an objective legal system, what to do on the basis of what effect an action will have. They believe most productive thinking is linear, rational, and based on concrete evidence and facts. The Chinese take a long-term view and believe change is disruptive and that non-action is better than action. The Chinese decide what to do on the basis of whether the action fits the existing plan. They do not debate issues on the basis of right and wrong. They base their actions on circumstances, not principles. Americans believe truth is absolute and not dependant on circumstances. The Chinese believe that truth is relative to circumstances and human obligations.

Control, Permissions, Licenses, etc.

Control is more important than efficiency in China's Permission Society. A former head of PricewaterhouseCoopers in China wrote in 2000:

> Control is a dominant feature of Chinese society. Approvals and licenses are required for anything and everything. For the Chinese to secure employment in a different part of the country may be difficult because approval is required. Obtaining a passport to travel abroad, particularly to Hong Kong Special Administrative Region (SAR), takes a long time. To marry or have children requires permission from the work unit. This is a Chinese phenomenon developed over centuries by successive generations of mandarins anxious to ensure that subjects many thousands of miles away obeyed the Emperor's decrees and the wishes of the court in Beijing.[39]

From the perspective of China's economic sovereignty, the plethora of permissions and licenses required from various Chinese government entities and officials is an impediment to foreign economic domination. Foreigners want what China has, want China to submit to their rules, and want to rule China. Human nature being what it is, that is natural, and China naturally resists.

The onerous requirements and number of permissions and licenses required to do business in China are many times greater than encountered elsewhere.[40] It ensures Chinese control of business in China. It is a mechanism in the interaction of consensus building and local autonomy, and in the financing of China's national, provincial, municipal, and village governments. It regulates business and distributes revenues from business in China among the various central, provincial, municipal, and village government entities. Such multi-layered mechanisms of control, autonomy, and consensus are quintessentially Chinese. They also play significant roles in maintaining China's economic sovereignty.

Crony Capitalism

In the aftermath of the politization and blocking of CNOOC's higher bid for Unocal, China may have a better record for permitting direct foreign investment in Chinese companies than America is exhibiting in permitting Chinese companies to invest in publicly traded American companies. All economies have the potential for corruption and cronyism, which are ubiquitous features of human nature. One study under the heading "China's communist crony capitalism" made the following observations:

> In 2002 Forbes magazine listed China's richest multi-millionaires. One-quarter of these declared they were CCP [Chinese Communist Party] members. Most Chinese CEOs of

private companies or transnational corporations also have party connections. Foreign companies seeking to capitalize on opportunities arising by China's development may find that scope for returns has been severely limited by entry of CCP-linked competitors.[41]

Crony capitalism is a problem in China and America. Consider the application of the following comments to China:

> The power elite is composed of men whose positions enable them to transcend the ordinary environments of ordinary men and women; they are in positions to make decisions having major consequences. Whether they do or do not make such decisions is less important than the fact that they do occupy such pivotal positions: their failure to make decisions is itself an act that is often of greater consequence than the decisions they do make. For they are in command of the major hierarchies and organizations of modern society. They rule the big corporations. They run the machinery of the state and claim its prerogatives. They direct the military establishment. They occupy the strategic command posts of the social structure, in which are now centered the effective means of the power and the wealth and the celebrity which they enjoy....[42]
>
> The elite who occupy the command posts may be seen as the possessors of power and wealth and celebrity; they may be seen as members of the upper stratum of a capitalist society. They may also be defined in terms of psychological and moral criteria, as certain kinds of selected individuals. So defined, the elite, quite simply, are people of superior character and energy.[43]

These comments were made about America. Some American observers believe that crony capitalism is a problem in China, but not in America.[44] It can be said to be a problem in America for the following reasons:

1. Most Americans on the *Forbes* list of richest multi-millionaires have "party connections" with the Republican, and to a

lesser extent, the Democratic Party. They are politically well connected.

2. Some American observers argue that the interests of the corporate elite dominate America and its policy making.[45]

3. In America, the gap between the rich and the poor is bigger than in any developed country.[46]

4. Despite a quarter century during which incomes have drifted ever farther apart in America, the distribution of wealth has remained remarkably stable. Some observers assert that the share of aggregate income going to the highest-earning 1% of Americans has doubled from 8% in 1990 to over 16% in 2004, that the share going to the top 0.1% has tripled from 2% in 1980 to 7% in 2006, and that the share going to the top 0.01%, comprising 14,000 taxpayers, has quadrupled from 0.65% in 1980 to 2.87% in 2004.

5. America is second, among all nations, only to Brazil in income inequality.[47]

Political Corruption in China

Financial corruption is wider spread in today's capitalist China than it was during Mao Zedong's leadership. There were less opportunities for corruption in Mao Zedong's communist China. Corruption, a ubiquitous human fault, took other forms. Financial corruption is a very serious problem in China and is recognized as such by China's top leaders. Minxin Pei has described China as a country crippled by leaders who care more about riches than reform.[48]

Hu Angang and Guo Yong take the view that "Corruption is a manifestation of the failure of institutions. In the course of economic transition, as old institutions are undergoing transformation, new mechanisms have not yet taken shape. In this gap, many opportunities and temptations may arise, leading to corruption. It not only absorbs huge economic resources, but also results in serious societal pollution and may cause the legitimacy of the governing regime to be questioned."[49] Hu and Guo assert that administrative monopoly, seen in sector monopoly and regional monopoly, arising from the long-standing overlap of the functions of government and the SOEs, leads to abuses that cause huge economic losses.[50] In a recent ranking of corruption, China, the most successful developing country, was ranked 59th out of 102 countries.[51]

There is a major concern in China's governing party that the Chinese government must ameliorate the conflicts among social groups and corruption among government officials. These are recognized as serious problems and priorities. The Chinese government, in China's Permission Society, can and will seek to impose policy changes that cannot as easily be implemented in America's Rights Society. For example, *The Economist* reported in June 2006:

> The Chinese Communist Party is a highly centralized beast, with a power structure little changed from the days of Mao Zedong. Over the next year or so it will be engaged in what official reports describe as one of the biggest shuffles of leaders at every level, with hundreds of thousands due to change their jobs. Nominally appointments are made by local party committees. In practice top appointments in the provinces have always been made by leaders in Beijing. But that does not mean that Beijing is in complete control....
>
> To be sure, China is not heading towards a break-up, anarchy or the warlordism of the pre-communist era. The armed forces and police remain under the party centre's grip. At the provincial leadership level too, the authority of the center is secure....
>
> The problem today is more a profusion of township, county and prefectural leaderships whose effort to propel growth in their regions produce impressive statistics, but often at a heavy

social, environmental or macroeconomic cost. In the last two years the government has been worrying that the economy might overheat and has been trying to curb investment in industries whose capacity has been growing too quickly. But local officials have often simply ignored these measures....

In March last year, amid growing public complaints about fast-rising house prices, the government issued directives aimed at cooling the market.... But local governments control land supply and have a vested interest in keeping prices high.[52]

The rapid increase in the cost of low-cost housing is being focused on by the Chinese government in the program of the relocation of local officials. It is also cracking down on land-sale corruption,[53] seeking to cut back on lending through state-owned banks, and introducing laws and tax increases to make real estate speculation and quick resales less attractive.[54] In the first quarter of 2006, US$23.6 billion was reportedly invested in residential development in China, but only US$775 million of that was spent on creating low-cost housing. This type of allocation of resources is creating a growing shortage of affordable housing and causing hardship and unrest.[55] *The Financial Times* reported in July 2006 that:

Hu Jintao, China's president, yesterday urged the country's ruling Communist party to maintain its half century-long grip on power by ensuring it remained the most 'progressive' force in the country.

Mr. Hu's speech, made in his role as party secretary—a position that outranks that of president—was delivered in a televised ceremony to mark the 85th anniversary of the founding of the party in 1921 in Shanghai.

"A political party that was advanced in the past does not mean that it can remain advanced today; and a political party that is advanced today does not mean that it will continue to be advanced in the future," he said.

Xinhua, the official news agency, in a commentary about the speech, said the party had succeeded because it had 'associated Marxism with China's realities, throbbed with the pulse of the times, emancipated the mind ... and always represented the fundamental interests of the broadest majority of the people.'

The speech in Beijing was aimed at the party faithful and couched in political language largely meaningless to the populace at large.[56]

In somewhat different language, *The New York Times* reported on the same day that:

President Hu Jintao of China said Friday that his political concept of maintaining the "advanced nature" of the Communist Party was the key to its survival, while warning that corruption threatened to undermine its hold on power.

... He said in his address on Friday that despite a seemingly endless effort to control corruption by demanding internal discipline within the party, abuse remained widespread. "There are continued cases of leading officials abusing power for private gain, engaging in graft and bending the law and falling into corruption and dissolution," he said.

Exposure of several major corruption cases recently has highlighted the problem.[57]

Minxin Pei notes that few top government officials are punished for corruption and that the problem is more widespread than the Chinese government is addressing.[58] *The New York Times* on July 1, 2006, reported that a top Chinese naval officer had been fired for seeking bribes and maintaining a mistress, which violated party rules. A vice governor of Anhui province and several top officials in the city of Tianjin were detained in a bribery investigation, and a vice mayor of Beijing and the top official overseeing China's preparations was fired for corruption and licentiousness.

Corruption is a serious problem in America also. One of many examples was the report also in *The New York Times* on July 1, 2006, of the guilty plea to corruption charges of the previously highly respected Commissioner of The New York Police Department during Mayor Giuliani's administration, who was nominated to head the Homeland Security Department by

President Bush but had to withdraw because of the corruption charges. *The New York Times* on July 1, 2006, also reported the conviction on political corruption charges of the head of Health South, a major American company. America and China's political and legal systems each persistently struggle to combat corruption by publicly punishing government officials and business people in the attempt to discourage others.

China's Innate Barriers to Business

China, under its emperors and after the 1949 Revolution, has always had a culture of locals resisting the central government's power. "The emperor is far away and the hills are very high" is a Chinese proverb. Under the Communist government, the state, and the national, provincial, municipal, and village governments owned the means of production and derived much of their revenue from the businesses they owned, operated, and licensed. A legacy of those arrangements is the need for approval from all levels of government for businesses.

Provincial barriers to competition are traditional in China and block not only the development of foreign companies' domination in the Chinese market, but also non-central government-supported SOEs that are owned by village, municipal, and provincial governments. But provincial and municipal and village barriers to competition do not, in theory if not practice, block the development of SOEs owned and supported by the focused effort of the central government.

These barriers also protect tax revenues and employment benefits critical to village, municipal, and provincial governments. The onerous requirements regarding permission and licenses, and the paying of taxes to village, municipal, provincial, and central governments in China entities is legendary. This reflects the basic organization of both government revenue sources at the central, provincial, municipal, and village levels, and local autonomy, which are at the core of China's dynastic and communist systems of political, social, and economic organization:

> Foreign companies have experienced difficulties seeking access [to] customers beyond the confines of the Special Economic Zone. A recent IMF study cited evidence suggesting that in an effort to protect industries from competition, local governments in China are erecting barriers to entry of goods from other provinces…. Managers of Chinese firms confirmed that they have indeed had trouble in accessing markets in other provinces. The administrative units of the industry and commerce department were reportedly obstructing access to markets through audits or local registration requirements. Unfortunately, it is not possible to directly measure such barriers. As it is illegal to impose trade restrictions, the measures adopted to protect local industries from competition are usually subtler than a direct border tax. IMF research on China's FDI policy points to significant gains in GDP output if internal barriers to trade were removed.[59]

A study by Julius Bar, a Swiss financial services company, offered an analysis that focused on the tension between a centralized political system and a decentralized economy:

> In the coming years China's leadership believes it can maintain a centralized political system while moving to increasingly decentralize its economy. Inevitably, tensions between these two forces will arise. Informal networks exist that control key aspects of commercial life such as the granting of licenses, the allocation of public works contracts, the allocation of bank credit, and pressure on banks not to foreclose on failing businesses because of political connections. As seen elsewhere in Asia, political monopolies tend to spur the development of commercial monopolies. Much is made of anti-corruption drives, which invariably weed out middle ranking bureaucrats taking bribes. But what is arguably more important for foreign investors is "macro-corruption"—the existence of reg-

ulatory barriers that either prevent entry into lucrative markets or measures that bestow significant competitive advantage to local entities, administered by officials who hold pecuniary interests that benefit from the operation of such arrangements.[60]

A 2002 study by the OECD said there remain restrictions on the organizational forms of FDI entry. Industries where Chinese partners must have majority shares include coal-mining, oil and gas delivery, the design and manufacture of civil airplanes, printing and publishing, development and production of grain, medical institutions, and the repairing, designing, and manufacturing of special, high-performance ships, and ships above 35,000 tons.

American Companies' Strategies in a Transitioning Permission Society

China was operated like a single company after the Communist Revolution, with the state as the only shareholder. Over 300,000 SOEs provided employment and tax revenue to the central, provincial, municipal, and village governments, that own the SOEs. The SOE system was not working and in 1998 a bold decision was made to "release the small and seize the large" by the Chinese government. Many SOEs have or are being partly or wholly sold to mostly foreign enterprises and to politically well-connected indigenous Mainland Chinese entrepreneurs and enterprises. This aspect of China's economic development strategy imports the foreign intellectual and financial capital essential to sustaining China's economic progress and ameliorating regional disparities in living standards and other critical social problems. The Chinese government's tradition of not empowering indigenous Mainland Chinese entrepreneurs and enterprises by denying them access to foreign or domestic equity or debt capital to expand their businesses has been assailed as detrimental to them and to China,[61] which it is. But that detriment has a vital benefit. Foreigners are less able than Mainland Chinese entrepreneurs to challenge the leadership of the governing party, which is the only organization that has been capable of ruling China.[62] Today China's Communist Party allows capitalist entrepreneurs to join the Party.

China suffered internal and foreign-initiated destructive conflicts from the Opium War in 1840 until the end of the Cultural Revolution in 1978. With political stability, the innate entrepreneurship drive was released after 1978. Since then, the Chinese people have enjoyed gradually increasing freedom to seek personal well-being. In 1978, 40% of the Chinese did not have enough to eat, but by 2003, only 10% of the Chinese people were living below the poverty level. China experienced the greatest growth of per capita income in Asia between 1980 and 2001 during which China's per capita income grew 425% or an average of 8.2% per year, from US$699 to $3,664. China's urban population doubled in the last 20 years and average Chinese housing increased from 7.4 square meters per capita in 1979 to 22.8 square meters in 2003.[63] China's undemocratic political system, right or wrong, has the strength to provide its people with the political stability China's economic development requires. China may need American-style democracy in the future. But it takes time.

The management of American companies seeking profitable, sustainable "China strategies" must recognize and empathize with the Herculean challenges that China's political leaders confront each day in pursuing economic development and the reduction of poverty in China. Their task is similar to any other manager's, but much larger. "When the president of China wakes up in the morning his biggest concern is how he feeds 1.3 billion people" is the way one foreign executive summarized the management challenge the Chinese government faces.[64]

It is also important for American companies to recognize the influence in China of Chinese feudal and communist ideologies and customs. Foreign observers may not be able to internalize a "sino-centric" view of China. An Amero-centric view leads Americans to assume that China must inevitably, as it opens up, adopt exactly the same economic and political institutions that have been thought to be the driving engines of capitalism and economic development since Adam Smith published *The Wealth Of Nations* in 1776. A sino-centric perspective recognizes it is likely that China will sustain its traditions developed over 5000 years even as it absorbs ideas developed incrementally in European countries and America over the past three centuries.

China's experience with foreigners' "China strategies" drives "China's strategy" of economic development, which is shifting somewhat over time from a zero-sum game strategy to a "win-win" strategic approach. The vulnerability of China's economic sovereignty and growth, and social stability, are key drivers of the Chinese government and people and of the evolving rules of the game in China's "Permission Society." It is useful to compare China's situation in the 19th century and today:

> In 1860, foreign allied forces united with a single purpose: to cripple China politically and force it open to the West on Western terms economically.... Unable to attack the political nerve center of China, the allied forces attacked the cultural. Discovering the vast wealth outside Beijing's city walls, enshrined in the Yuan Ming Yuan and the Summer Palace, they broke into the palaces stealing every item of conceivable value and destroying what they could not take with them.... The statement was clear: precious items of immediate commercial value to China were to be had by foreign interests; precious items of cultural importance and value were to be destroyed completely....The key elements of Western policy towards China at this critical period in history were: to obtain unlimited access to China's market, that is, to sell Western manufactured

and finished goods to the vast Chinese population without restrictions or import duties; to have unlimited access to China's vast natural and crafted products at cheap labor costs; and to control trade. Foreign powers knew that a weak political system would have to tolerate their interests and commercial domination. In addition, Chinese law could not touch the rights of foreigners in China; foreign laws and administration were carried out within foreign enclaves and complete diplomatic immunity was accorded to all foreign interests. These elements of this diplomatic episode have remained part of the collective unconscious underlying both Western diplomatic and commercial initiatives today in opening the China market and the Chinese government's approach to dealing with them.[65]

As the 20th century began, several foreign countries had violated China's sovereignty and dignity and were poised to dismember China. That seemed to be the natural order of things. The strong rule the weak. China's 1949 Communist Revolution and what we term China's "Capitalist Evolution" beginning in 1978, offered the Chinese people more compelling value propositions than the zero-sum-game strategies of successive generations of foreigners seeking to master China's wealth and future. China is relentlessly developing its global economic power to protect its sovereignty, dignity, rising living standards, and its people's happiness. The Chinese government and people remember China's struggles with foreign powers for survival and respect in the 18th, 19th, and 20th centuries. It is against that background that foreign companies come to China seeking their fortunes.

After the Communist Revolution in 1949, China under Mao Zedong focused on self-sufficiency. Only in 1981 did China begin to admit tourists after a 30-year hiatus in which the People's Republic of China was effectively closed to the outside world.

The 18th, 19th, and 20th century foreign approach to China manifested a zero-sum-game mindset and evokes one. "China's strategy" is to use the intellectual and financial capital of foreign companies to facilitate China's economic and social progress and to create Chinese companies that can dominate both China's domestic and the world's markets. Foreign companies attracted by China's huge market, low labor and material costs, and remarkable economic development invested US$650 billion in 350,000 joint ventures in China in 1979–2006.

A zero-sum-game strategy can work in a "Rights Society" with a well-defined legal and regulatory system enforcing rights, i.e., the rules of the game. But such strategy approaches will probably fail in a "Permission Society" if China's government or a foreign company's trading partners can and do change the rules of the game when they like. But win-win value propositions may work in both a Permission Society and a Rights Society. Competitive strategies or flawed collaborative strategies can use zero-sum approaches, but successful collaboration requires a different approach.

Some foreign companies find their China strategy does not perform as they hoped.[66] But that is changing. In 1999, an American Chamber of Commerce in China reported that 58% of their members surveyed had lower profit margins in China than their global average, but 88% of them intended to expand their China operations.[67] Of the 354,000 foreign companies operating in China in 2001, only about 33% reportedly were profitable in 2001.[68] A Deloitte & Touche survey in 2002 reported that 90% of foreign companies in China intended to expand their operations within three years. In 2003, there were reportedly 424,196 small and large foreign companies in China. In 2003, the America Chamber of Commerce in China reported that one third of their members were not profitable, and two thirds were not up to anticipated levels of profit. Although the foundations of foreign companies in China seem to be in "shifting sands," they desperately attempt to placate the Chinese government, rather than abandon the potentially lucrative market.[69]

In 2005, *Business Week* reported that 68% of 450 American companies surveyed by the American Chamber of Commerce in China indicated that their China operations were profitable and 70% of those indicated that their China margins are equal to or greater than their global average.[70] *Business Week* stated:

> Such an answer would have been unthinkable in 2000 before China entered the WTO and began to open its economy wider to foreign companies. The biggest beneficiaries are the pioneering multinationals—such as Proctor & Gamble, Caterpillar, and United Technologies—that arrived in the 1980s, then stuck it out in the worst of times. But now even small and medium-size U.S. companies are realizing they have to play their China hand or lose out altogether.
>
> If a company stays the course, the results can be remarkable. China contributed 9% of Motorola Inc.'s $31 billion in sales last year, and thanks to smart products and marketing the Schaumburg (Ill.) based company is battling Nokia Corp. for leadership in the world's biggest handset market. Low cost exports from China, and the brainwork done at 16 labs, have also helped revive Motorola's fortunes. For many products, "China will become a larger market than the U.S.," says Motorola Asia Pacific Senior Vice President, Simon Leuing. "And it helps our global operation from the perspective of costs, quality and time to market."
>
> The prospects of some companies, in fact, may be brighter in China than at home where they have entrenched competition or are saddled with high cost operations. In China, nobody has home-court advantage, says Jonathan Woetzel, McKinsey & Co's Greater China director. "You can play a new game and get a new lease on life."[71]

Companies, like Motorola and Microsoft, which courageously aligned their "China strategy" with the Chinese government's economic development goals, in spite of intellectual property piracy risks, are benefiting from their commitment to China and the value propositions and relationships their non-zero-sum-game strategies enhance. Some foreign companies may not be able to earn immediate profits in China, because it takes some time for them to understand China's market, companies, customers, laws, and regulations.

But some companies can be quickly and sustainably profitable in China. Immediate profitability was cited in 1998 as the litmus test of the long-term success of a company's "China strategy."[72] Some foreign companies are not passing the Profitability Test and expect not to be profitable in China for some time. That self-defeating and unacceptable expectation indicates that a company's China strategy is weak and perhaps wrong. A China strategy should be presently and sustainably profitable or probably should be changed as quickly as possible. How soon it achieves profitability can depend on how fast and astutely a foreign company can align its China strategy with the Chinese government's economic development strategies and Chinese companies' strategies. Using "win-win" rather than zero-sum-game strategies works better for American companies in China, where the business, legal, and political frameworks are so different from America's. Such strategies aligned with China's needs and goals are the subject of *New China Business Strategies: Chinese and American Companies as Global Partners.*

6

Why China Is Emerging from Hunger

Overview

This chapter examines how the Chinese government and people escaped having one of the most moribund economies and created the most competitive, fastest-growing economy in the world. It examines why and how China's economic growth started, was sustained, and has been so successful. It is unrealistic for Americans to assume that China will collapse or stagnate, or that "easy growth" is over and the hardest part of reform is yet to come. It is unrealistic to think that China's growth will slow or can be contained so that America can win the China Game because China loses it.

How Did China's Economy Grow So Much So Fast for So Long?

How did the Chinese government, people, and culture transform China's failing communist economy into a successful Socialist Market Economy and make China such a formidable capitalist country? They achieved, to date, the largest and fastest economic transformation in history starting in 1978 with an impoverished failed planned economy and a 40% literacy rate. How did China achieve such rapid and sustained success without the Rights Society features of Majority-Rule Democracy and a Rule of Law System? How did the Chinese government achieve a successful balancing of reform policies, sustained economic growth, and political and social stability? How have three generations of China's leaders since 1978 made China work so well?

China's economic progress since 1978 is an unprecedented management feat in human history. Recognizing and accepting how China has been successful in the past 28 years is essential to understanding how the Chinese government is likely to make the China Game work for the next 25 years.

From 1949 to 1979, self-sufficiency was the goal of China's socialist planned economy and China's leadership. Increasingly from 1979 to date, self-sufficiency through economic growth was their goal. They achieved massive sustained economic growth and the social and political stability that China's continuing development depends upon.

In 1962, Deng Xiaoping made his famous comment "Whether a cat is black or white makes no difference. As long as it catches mice, it is a good cat." The integration of that pragmatic focus on "catching mice", i.e., economic development and foreign direct investment ("FDI") in China's strategy, developed gradually into today's Socialist Market Economy Capitalism, winning ground in 1979 only after Mao's death and continuing after 1992 as China really opened up to sharply-increasing annual levels of FDI.

As we have seen, theories considered to be incompatible, namely capitalism and the doctrines of Marx and Mao, have been combined in a very pragmatic Chinese way. Deng Xiaoping, who assumed power in 1978, turned China from a Soviet-style planned economy into a communist market economy. This transition was relatively gentle and, as a result, took much longer than the unsuccessful reforms in the political and economic systems of the former Soviet Union and other nations in Western Europe.

The Chinese government in the 1979 to 2006 stage of economic development and poverty reduction opened China to foreign investment and initiated reforms, which attracted an estimated US$665 billion[1] in FDI needed to drive China's economic growth and sustain social stability and the Communist Party's leadership of China. The graph below shows China's annual growth in per capita GDP from 1986 to 2004 with estimates for 2005 to 2007. In 2005 China's FDI inflow was US$60.33 billion.[2] The huge FDI flow continued although the 2005 appreciation of RMB by 2.1% made investment in China more expensive in US dollars.

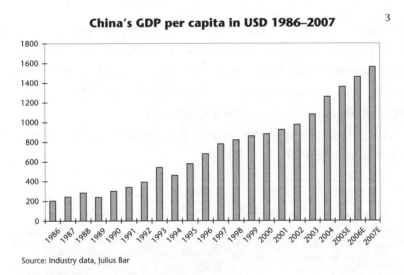

China's GDP per capita in USD 1986–2007 [3]

Source: Industry data, Julius Bar

The graph below shows the percentage of worldwide FDI investments China received from 1980 to 2004, which grew from zero to 12% during that period

China's success in fueling its GDP growth through attracting FDI is due not only to its low-wage labor, but the result of 28 years of the government attracting and managing FDI with policies that include the creation of special economic zones; allowing regional authorities

A Dragon's Share of World FDI   4
China: Foreign Direct Investment Inflows

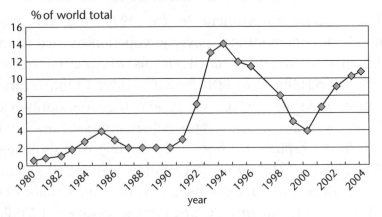

Source: UNCTAD World Investment Report (2004)

to approve FDI investments under US$30 million; aggressive use of tax incentives; duty-free importation of intermediate products and capital goods; providing infrastructure, i.e., land, power, physical security, and transportation; and permitting flexibility within the special economic zones to hire and fire staff.[5]

The graph below shows the FDI flows and stock stated in US dollars between 1980 and 2004:

China Mainland: FDI Flows and Stock (in USD m)   6

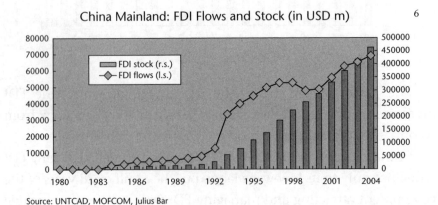

Source: UNTCAD, MOFCOM, Julius Bar

Under the auspices of Deng Xiaoping, China was reintegrated into the global economy. Special economic zones, whose output was destined exclusively for export, were established along China's southern coast. Gradually, foreign investment was allowed in the cities, where for the first time foreign companies were permitted to manufacture for the domestic market. From 1986 onwards, it was possible to establish wholly foreign-owned enterprises, which were also allowed to produce for the Chinese market. In the subsequent years, increased amounts of capital from Europe and the U.S. began to flow into China, converging with the traditional foreign investment sources of Hong Kong and Taiwan.[7]

The Fallacy That Foreign Direct Investment in China Is Fundamentally Good for China

In *Selling China,* Yasheng Huang points out that FDI, as it has been brought into China, has been at the expense of private enterprise, which is efficient, and has supported SOEs that are not efficient or profitable. Yasheng Huang is critical of the government's development of China's economy because it deliberately starved private enterprises of equity and debt capital sources required for private enterprise growth. Capital was systematically directed only towards SOEs.

The Fallacy That Foreign Direct Investment in China Has Been Fundamentally Bad for China

While Yasheng Huang recognizes in the final analysis[8] that the way FDI was allowed by China's leadership in the 1980s, 1990s, and to date has not been optimal or empowered private enterprise and the private sector. It has been a useful method of ensuring the fundamental requirement of China's economic and social development: political stability. The reality is that there is no other organization but the Communist Party that was and is able to deliver political stability and therefore economic progress. As we have seen, the Chinese people have suffered in the past during repeated periods when the absence of a strong governing organization produced political, social and economic chaos.

Yasheng Huang's analysis rests on the assumption, it seems, that for China to be successful, or at least to be optimized, it must have the economic institutions and rules that highly developed Western economies rely on. Why is that so? As we have seen, China presents a new model, which its leadership has named a Socialist Market Economy, in which government regulation is highly flexible, ambiguous, and inconsistent, but permits large parts of GDP to be produced by privatized SOEs and FDI-funded foreign-owned companies rather than what might be called "Direct Domestic Investment" (DDI) in private companies owned by mainland Chinese. FDI is a less formidable threat to the hegemony of the Chinese Communist Party and, therefore, to China's economic sovereignty and progress than DDI. If DDI had been used by China's leadership as the primary engine of economic and social development, that would have created and empowered a new elite. Instead, China's governing party has changed itself from the inside as it has used FDI to change China from the outside.

The Reality That China's Economic Success Is Sustainable

It is often asserted that China's economic success will collapse because China's deficient "undemocratic"[9] systems and state-owned enterprises will be unable to cope.[10] But the reality is that China's political system has successfully created and sustained unprecedented economic development since 1979. Wishful thinking regarding China's political, economic, and social systems' ability to cope with its economic challenges and ability to sustain its economic growth has so far been revealed for what it has been—wrong.

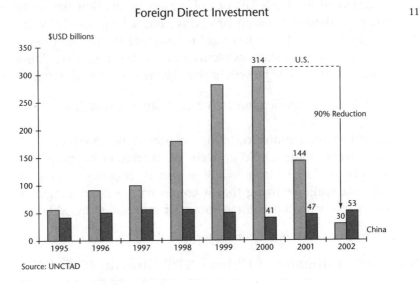

Foreign Direct Investment
Source: UNCTAD

The above graph compares foreign direct investment in America and China from 1995 to 2002.

The sustained reform policies of the Chinese government, the cost and other competitive advantages, and the potential size and importance of China's market led China to pass the United States in 2002 as the leading destination of foreign direct investment.

The Fallacy That Economic Statistics from China Are Fundamentally False

Many observers have asserted that China's economic statistics are false. Lester Thurow, for example, has asserted that published annual growth rates of 9.7% grossly exaggerate Chinese success in the decade of the 1990s.[12] *The China Economic Quarterly,* which is affiliated with *The Financial Times,* is a leading critic of China's economic policies. It reviewed the veracity of China's GDP statistics and commented:

For statisticians that want to have fun, China's gross domestic product numbers have for years provided a marvelous playground. A patchy collection system, a well-entrenched tradition of local officials of puffing up production figures to improve their promotion prospects, and a large incentive for national leaders to lay beautiful numbers at the feet of foreign investors, all gave skeptics plenty of room to argue that China exaggerated its GDP growth in the first two decades of reform.[13]

The China Economic Quarterly's conclusion was that:

... while China almost certainly overstated its growth in 1998, more recent figures hold up well. We therefore encourage our readers to view China's headline growth number as roughly accurate while realizing that it comes with a large margin of error—probably a percentage point or more on either side.[14]

The China Economic Quarterly published the chart below:

How Real? Estimates of China's GDP Growth, 1990–2001. [15]

	Official GDP growth rate (production/income approach)		
	As First Published	As in Statistical Yearbook 2002	Calculated Based on Revised Nominal Growth Rate*	Keidel's Real GDP Growth Rate (expenditure (approach)
1990	3.9	3.8	2.7	6.8
1991	8.0	9.2	12.2	10.1
1992	13.2	14.2	17.2	10.9
1993	13.4	13.5	14.5	10.7
1994	11.8	12.6	15.8	14.6
1995	10.5	10.5	10.6	11.4
1996	9.6	9.6	8.5	9.8
1997	8.8	8.8	8.3	7.3
1998	7.8	7.8	6.4	6.1
1999	7.1	7.1	7.3	5.5
2000	8.0	8.0	8.0	7.1
2001	7.3	7.3	n/a	8.7

*Assuming original implicit GDP was correct.

Sources: China Statistical Yearbooks (1990 through 2002); Albert Keidel.

The Fallacy That China Will Founder Economically Because Japan Did[16]

Many observers have asserted that China will founder economically as Japan did. An example is Garry Shilling's *Forbes* article "Broken China,"[17] which asserted:

> Is the world's largest nation a wonder of growth? Don't believe it. The growth figures are cooked. A lot of problems are kept out of sight. Think Japan 1988...if you are awed by China's current and potential power, think twice. Recall the awe over Japan during its 1980s bubble days. ... I don't believe China's official 8% growth figure. It is a politically mandated number, first conjured up in 1988 by Chinese officials. Independent surveys of industrial capacity, energy use, employment, consumer income and spending and farm output imply much slower growth. Chinese from the top down have long known this: In 1999, Premier Hu Rongji complained that "falsification and exaggeration are rampant." The official 4% urban unemployment rate jumps to 9.3% when laid-off workers, who receive modest stipends, are added to the registered unemployed. And while the official poverty rate in cities is 2%, the Asian Development Bank estimates it's 11%. Note that the Tiananmen Square demonstrations were preceded by urban labor unrest.
>
> So, China needs rapid growth to employ the urban idle and the inflow from farms and to fund adequate roads, housing and farming modernization. Huge education outlays are needed to turn those rural youths into productive urban workers. Pensions and social security, new to China, are gigantic money sinks. The military is another big drain. China also has to rescue the state banks, which are essentially broke because of the bad loans used to support equally bankrupt and overstaffed government-owned businesses.
>
> What's more, China's two recent growth engines are highly vulnerable. First are exports. Official data show that from 1997 to 2001 exports averaged 21% of GDP but accounted for 48% of GDP growth. And most of those exports go directly or indirectly to the U.S. American consumers have

ended their 20-year borrowing-and-spending binge and are embarking on a saving spree, which I forecast in past columns. So, the outlook for Chinese exports is glum. Ditto for foreign direct investment in exporting businesses that employ 6 million.

Government deficit spending is the other growth source, and it's under pressure. Officially, China is running a surplus equal to 2% of GDP. The reality, though, is that if all the off-balance-sheet financing and capital outlays are included, the country is running a deficit of at least 4%. Government debt, 17% of GDP, may seem small, but potential liabilities run that to 150%, gigantic for a primitive financial structure. As for the Chinese middle class, surveys dispute government data and show that both urban and rural consumers are, despite falling consumer prices, big savers, and not lavish spenders.[18]

Comparisons of Japan and China's companies becoming multinational companies, which point out how poorly Japan's acquisitions turned out,[19] overlook the competitive advantages China's 1.3-billion-person economy in the 21st century has over Japan's 120-million-person economy in the 20th century.

Oded Shenkar notes:

> ... China and Japan share a number of traits, starting with partial similarity in philosophy, religion and institutions.... Both countries have been an enigma to Western observers, who oscillated between suspicion and unadulterated admiration for their ancient civilizations and modern achievements. Both nations also have historical baggage: Japan as a member of the Axis during World War II ... and China as a member of the Communist block ... Both Japan and China have had the misfortune of lacking development infrastructure, later reinterpreted as a boon because it enabled them to leapfrog countries with investment sunk in older technologies. Both have benefited from favorable geo-political circumstances: Japan was helped by the cold war ... In the aftermath of September 11, China appears to play a role as a potential ally in the fight against terrorism and in containing North Korea.

Japan ran a coordinated industrial effort that gave priority to 'strategic industries' while maintaining competition within each of those industries—something that China would imitate later. In their foray into foreign markets, both Japan and China used an artificially weak currency to support exports; in fact, both countries continue to do so today. Both countries also have used trade barriers to block foreign—especially U.S. imports. Both benefited from a lingering perception that they were unlikely to become viable competitors with the possible exception of cheap, low technology products. Then and now, this proved to be a serious mistake.

Similarities notwithstanding, China and Japan differ in a number of key areas. One vital difference is size. Although the Japanese economy is larger than that of China's in nominal terms, the allure of a vast and rapidly growing Chinese market with pent-up demand for products and services translates into greater leverage with trade partners than Japan ever had. China's size gives it another advantage: While Japan moved in less than a generation from a low-cost manufacturer to a high-cost producer. ...

China has a vast, untapped hinterland with a huge supply of workers, which will permit it to move up the technology scale without sacrificing its present cost advantage for years to come. China will thus use its dominance in labor-intensive production to advance the knowledge-intensive industries of the future. In addition to having Hong Kong and Taiwan (and to some extent Singapore) as capital providers and knowledge catalyst. China has a vibrant overseas community that plays a major role in its development and globalization. Japan had none. China has the benefit of much larger foreign investment (which Japan rejected at the time for fear of foreign domination and as a threat to Japanese culture). China is also ready to open up its educational system, something Japan never did, and in addition to sending its students abroad, China is the host to many foreign students from Asia and the West. Plus, while Japan's World War defeat limited its future defense expenditure and deployment, China is a member of the Security Council and is becoming more involved in world affairs, participation it will later leverage for economic advantage.

China's potentially stronger impact is also anchored in the timing of its ascent. Its rise and challenge to its trading nations comes at an earlier development than Japan's, driven by stronger internal pressures to provide employment ... and relying on a much lower cost base.... Another difference between China and Japan is that the United States handled its trade conflicts with Japan on a bilateral basis while conflicts with China are handled under the multilateral WTO regime. Given China's trade distribution (a huge surplus with the U.S., a moderate surplus with the European Union, and a deficit with Asia) continuous acrimony between the U.S. and the EU, and a rising conflict between the developing and developed nations over farm subsidies, it would be difficult for the U.S. to garner support for policies limiting China's entry into its markets, especially since much of the world ... views the U.S. as an unfair trader.[20]

In the late 1980s, Japan's buying binge in America quickly became a contentious issue. Chinese companies, knowing this history and recognizing their own current weaknesses in operating internationally and acquiring companies and assets outside China, are using sophisticated Western financial, legal, and other firms.[21] Chinese companies will increasingly be able to use international capital market resources and funding as well as their own, and Chinese banks and government financing.

Best-Case, Slowdown, and Worst Case Meltdown Scenarios of China's Economic Future

In considering the best-case, slowdown, and worst-case meltdown scenarios, Americans must contemplate the ramifications for the American economy of American policy contributing to the occurrence of a slowdown or worst-case scenario.

The "Chinese Market Will Grow Forever" Scenario

This scenario assumes that China will continue its reform and opening up, the global economic environment will remain stable, China's integration into global markets will deepen, there will be a continuous transfer of China's labor force into non-agricultural sectors, and total factor productivity will keep growing at 2.5 to 3 percent.[22]

The "Slowdown Scenario"

This scenario assumes that reforms of China's banks and SOEs will not be effective, the transfer of labor from the agricultural sector will falter, the quality of China's labor force will improve only marginally, the propensity of Chinese to save will gradually decline, and taxes and financial deficits will increase as China's government has to increase welfare and social security programs.[23]

The "Worst-Case Meltdown" Scenario

Another school of thought asserts that China is headed for collapse.[24] This perspective asserts that China's economic growth is not sustainable and questions whether there is much productivity growth in China. China is seen to have failed to complete its transition and is maintaining the illusion of progress in a bubble-like economy built on fraudulent banking practices, which will culminate in China's banks' insolvency as they attempt to support hopelessly inefficient industries. Income disparities will spiral out of control. Continuous rapid degradation of China's environment will lead to a massive humanitarian crisis.[25] Mar & Richter, of the World Economic Forum, are of the view that this scenario is unlikely.[26] One summary of the collapse perspective is set out here at length because it summarizes the Chinese government's leadership challenges:[27]

> Observers such as Gordon Chang, who believe that China is headed for collapse, lead the "worst case" camp. He and others believe that China failed to complete its reformation and is currently maintaining the illusion of progress on a bubble-like economy. Beneath this veneer of success, a corrupt governance system has spawned a host of problems in business, government, and throughout society, which will eventually implode under the weight of its own burdens.

> Indeed, the list of burdens is long, and touches almost every facet of China's being, from the economy and politics to social issues and the environment, and every sector of society, from farmers and blue-collar workers to educated professionals, civil servants, and foreign investors. A roster could never be comprehensive, and presents a damning case for economic collapse. It would start with puncturing a hole in the myth of high growth that is predicted, falsely reported, and then trumpeted by the planners as the makings of a "natural market system under a socialist framework." That China's statistics are doctored is legendary, and could subtract anywhere from 1% to 4% a year from the country's growth.

> Certainly, at the heart of the problem is the state-owned enterprises (SOEs), bloated by workers, rife with incompetence, and maligned by their shoddy products, but somehow kept alive by a financial system that continues to shovel money down the black hole of the SOEs. The scale of debt is astounding, and has been estimated at up to several trillion Renminbi— which will take years to clear and raise government debt much higher than the 13% of GDP at the end of 2002. At one point, it seemed that technology offered a way out, with its promise of increasing productivity of the SOEs while providing an engine for growth through hundreds of small start-ups. Eventually, the majority of the SOEs learned that technology is great for the educated but meaningless for the uneducated and unskilled. As for dot.com dreams, China followed the way of NASDAQ, although perhaps with a bit less waste and debt.

> The problems with China's industry are comparable only to the scale of its agriculture problem. China has among the

lowest percentages of arable land—between 13% and 17%—
for a country of its size and population. Add years of subsidies paid to farmers by bureaucrats, and even with the land
reforms of the 1980s, which put land under the control of
those who know it best, the farmers, China's agriculture
sector is a huge liability. Although it employs over 50% of
the country's workers, it produces only a small fraction of
national GDP. Far from the cities and infrastructure, poorly
educated and ignorant of their basic rights, farmers are beset
with spontaneous taxes, declining commodity prices, and
few options. Farmers' success stories have nothing to do
with farms, and everything to do with making their way to
the city to find a job in a joint venture or private factory.
China's accession to the WTO only increases the bleak lot of
farmers, due to the entry of high-quality, foreign-grown
grains and the scaling back of subsidies.

Farmers have thus seen little of the growth of the past few
years, contributing to an increasing gap between the rich and
the poor, the urbanized and farmers, and the west and the
coast. This disparity is increasingly resulting in social unrest,
with protests by farmers and laid-off SOE workers, which has
the potential to organize and escalate rapidly if picked up by
the media and dissatisfied peasants in other parts of the
country. Their dissatisfaction is in many ways understandable:
the Party has built the country on their backs and with their
support, and now, the managers and local cadres who
represent the Party are able to abscond with their pensions
and severance pay....

China's problems looking outward are almost as grave,
though perhaps not as socially disruptive, as are those on the
inside. China is being called the next great power, but which
supposed power has ethnic unrest (Xinjiang), a desire for
annexation (Taiwan), dreams of expansion (Spratlys), and
makes friends with autocratic regimes (North Korea)? China's
citizens, and especially its Internet-enabled youth, are
increasingly aware of and hungry for the outside world. How
will rulers who still think that the best way to manage
information is to hide it lead them?

All of these threats have been well-known for some time,
but have been neglected, ignored, or suppressed in the belief

that an ever-growing Chinese economy will carry the state through. China has mastered the dance of muddling through.

But what will happen when a stick gets caught up in the spokes of the growth wheel? A whole chain-reaction could be triggered, starting with a financial crisis, leading to mass bankruptcies and lay-offs, a run on the financial system, and finally social unrest. The impetus could be anything, even something seemingly insignificant. As in chaos theory, a butterfly beating its wings may change the course of the planet. China's future may be influenced by a series of small disruptions.

Imagine that one of the four big state banks unearths a corruption case, and as a result faces a run on its deposits, which then forces it to face bankruptcy. This is theoretically a non-event, for sure, as the state still owns the bank and will make every effort to save it. But the pain may be too much. A real Chinese "Enron," combined with a Chapter 14 scenario, might trigger an entire cascade of events that will throw the economy, starting with the financial system, into disarray. The collapse would certainly not come instantaneously, but would be marked by a series of seemingly insignificant events, in the same way that an investigation into account books and a few connected partnerships brought down the houses of Enron and Andersen.

The bankruptcy of one of China's big banks or one of its big resource or trading firms would result in large-scale unemployment, incite instability in other enterprises, and possibly cause social unrest. This would not be new in Chinese history, as the country has experienced repeated incidents of peasant unrest, not unlike the Taiping uprising of the 1850s. Often, peasant rebellions would lead to the overthrow of the ruling dynasty and the formation of a new government allying the peasants with reform-minded elements of the ruling class. Thus is formed a new dynasty. The most significant instance in which this pattern was broken was the Tiananmen incident of 1989, in which the intellectuals led the challenge to authority. The result was a new government that expelled the reformers and empowered the conservatives.

This new rebellion—by peasants, students, or workers— would not necessarily be a cry for democracy, but rather a cry for competent economic leadership that ensures that the masses benefit from the country's prosperity. Although many people in the cities are fed up with corruption, rising unemployment, and lack of social order, the upheaval is likely to start on the margins: in Xinjiang or in the rustbelt of the northeastern provinces.

Social unrest would unsettle foreign investors, for it would remind them that for all its commercial prospects, China is at base a lawless developing country. They will gauge the political and economic risks of doing business in China, comparing it with such unstable countries as Indonesia or Colombia. As many foreign investors have already failed to see profits even after years of investment and marketing, it will only be a question of time before they gauge the risks to outweigh the potential. One need only recall the siege mentality that took over in some American-owned or affiliated factories after the U.S. bombing of the Chinese embassy in Belgrade in 1999 and one can understand that multinational corporations (MNCs) have little patience for political instability. The domino effect caused by a huge MNC evacuating its staff could shake the entire foreign-owned manufacturing base in the country.

Big powers often turn to foreign policy to draw attention away from domestic problems. Although the government has relatively more control over the media than in other countries, there is no doubt that information flows enough in China so that people would become acutely aware of any threats. One could conceive of the government using a geopolitical linked maneuver, such as forcing the return of Taiwan to the motherland, in order to reunite the country under the flag of nationalism. Many Chinese claim that they are prepared to die in order to bring Taiwan back into the fold, and one does not doubt that the government would be prepared to override its military inferiority to attempt this. The toll in terms of lives and resources may be great, but when national pride is at stake, and indeed national disintegration threatens, who is counting? Not the government, and likely not the United States which by that time, or in parallel, could be preoccupied with saving its forces for the Middle East.

An exchange of hostilities across the Taiwan Strait could be disastrous for regional integration and stability in East Asia.

Global supply chains would be disrupted; Taiwanese would flee, or attempt to flee, en masse from the mainland; Hong Kong would be submerged in protest and worry; and the rest of Southeast Asia would shrink from the "China as ogre" image. It is unlikely that any country in Southeast Asia—least of all ASEAN—would dare to protest, in spite of the investments that would be jeopardized, for fear that they would be denied a future slice of the China pie. Indeed, ASEAN investors, who may have more tolerance for political instability (or simply a greater thirst for a slice of the commercial pie), may end up replacing some of those Western investors who would feel compelled to withdraw, either because of the unrest or because of a need to uphold certain "principles." Either way, China's economic powerhouse would be stopped in its tracks.

The most important point is that the fallacy that an unstable, unsuccessful China would be good for America rests on the erroneous assumption that America and 300 million Americans would benefit from China and 1.3 billion Chinese being unstable and unsuccessful. If American policy contributed to China's instability and failure, what is the likely result? If America has a neutral policy if such a thing is possible or a constructive approach to China, and China becomes unstable and unsuccessful due to internal problems, that might benefit America, some might argue. But, as discussed in Chapter 7, what sort of leaders in China would an unstable and unsuccessful China produce? What sort of leaders in America would it evoke?

Would an unstable and unsuccessful China be capable of harming America in a war? As discussed in Chapters 7 and 12, in the Age of Species Lethal Weapons, the friendship or hostility of 22 percent of the human race, with the abilities and accomplishments of the Chinese in less than 30 years of relations and trade with America, must be material to America's national security and homeland defense. But some Americans believe that an unstable or unsuccessful China is necessary for American national security.

To be believable, those championing this fallacy must convince us that war in the 21st century between America and China would be good for America. Were the Korean and Vietnam wars good for America? The Korean and Vietnam wars were the armed-conflict testing points between China and America in the late 1950s, 1960s, and early 1970s. China in the 21st century would be a much more formidable enemy for America than North Korea and North Vietnam were.

In ending the Vietnam War, President Nixon obtained China's tacit consent to arrange a way out of the conflict and to put pressure on the expanding Soviet Union in Asia. Nixon made the best possible decision for America at that time. Was the decision to accept the need for peace that led him to offer diplomatic and trade relations with China wrong? What would have been the impact on American political, economic, and social stability of a never-ending Vietnam War or other military conflict with China?

In the traumatic experience of the Vietnam War, President Nixon opened diplomatic and trade relations with China. Were the instincts and need for peace that led him to offer diplomatic and trade relations to China wrong? If it was a mistake, it is too late to reverse 28 years of political, economic, and social development in China?

America already has many implacable adversaries among the 1.2 billion Muslims in the world. The fundamentalists, who seek to destabilize and reshape the Muslim world in their mold, are not prepared to accept America or American influence. That is likely to be a lasting ideological confrontation. It is hard to believe that American national security will be served by fostering hostility and zero-sum military and economic competition with 1.3 billion Chinese seeking success as capitalists in the new century.

The Genius of the Chinese Government, People, and Culture from 1979 to 2006

In 1987 Deng Xiaoping admitted, "In the rural reform our greatest success—and it is one we had by no means anticipated—has been the emergence of a large number of enterprises run by villages and townships. They were like a new force that just came into being spontaneously.... The Central Committee [of the Chinese Communist Party] takes no credit for this."[28]

Yasheng Huang has highlighted that:

> This is a powerful insight into both the success and the limitations of China's economic reform. The biggest success of the reform is to have allowed a substantial degree of flexibility in an otherwise rigid and statist economic system. This flexibility gave an opportunity to innovative and hard-working entrepreneurs to create and expand businesses, which over time would eclipse China's inefficient and wasteful state sector. Some of the specific economic policies and reform measures have also been important. These would include price liberalization, opening up the country to foreign direct investment in overseas export markets, creation of central banking and tax institutions essential to a functioning market economy, and a gradual emergence of a rule leading, though not rule-based, government interventions in the economy and business government relationships. These policy measures have led to macro stability, illumination of shortages, and abatement of anticompetitive barriers, all very impressive achievements during a short period of time.[29]

Although Yasheng Huang criticizes the reform path the Chinese government's economic reform has taken in many respects, he affirms the overall impressive achievements of the Chinese government since 1978.[30] He acknowledges that:

> The huge success of China's reforms is indisputable.... Poverty has fallen dramatically and the Chinese economy

has been transformed from a shortage economy in the 1970s to one that today faces a chronic oversupply of many goods and services.... The Chinese people are enjoying economic and social freedoms unprecedented in the history of the People's Republic. Yes, an inefficient political pecking order of firms has persisted through the reform era and has led to a high dependency on FDI [Foreign Direct Investment]. But, in the grand scheme of things, this is not the worst possible outcome and many countries have done considerably worse. One should also recognize the enormous challenges confronting Chinese policy makers over the last twenty years. The leadership has been managing two parallel developments, each fraught with a high degree of complexity and uncertainty. One is the transition from a planned to a market economy and the other is the transformation from a rural to an industrial economy. In the presence of massive uncertain contingencies about policy outcomes, as a number of economists stress, gradualism is a superior strategy ... our overall assessment of China's gradual reforms is strongly positive.[31]

The reality is that the Chinese government recognized and used the unexpected emergence of a large number of enterprises run by villages and townships, and combined that with policy shifts that attracted sustained foreign direct investment that produced extraordinary economic growth providing the social stability that economic reform required.

The Chinese government still has much to do in its determined and adroit march to improve the lives of China's people. China's reserve of unused and not fully used human capital is one of it's greatest competitive advantages. The success of the first 28 years of the Chinese government's "China strategy" of economic development suggests that China will develop and deploy its full human capital. The stability of China and the economic development it causes and requires have been and are likely to remain compelling motivators for the government in the next 25 years of China's strategy. The Chinese government is committed to sustained economic and social development. It has many challenges and problems, but has the abilities, energy, resourcefulness, and irrepressible genius for capitalism of the Chinese people.

The Economist has commented that:

> Domestically, the government [of China] is well aware that its political acceptance derives solely from rapid economic growth and will do whatever is necessary to meet its internal benchmark, an annual rise of 7%. China's leaders call themselves communists, but they have become capitalists, in practice.[32]

The ruling party's leaders, as well as being self-interested, love their country and their people. Ideology and patriotism, as well as the desire for enhanced living standards and social stability, drive China's emerging global economic dominance. After the "century of humiliation" in which it sought to ignore the rest of the world and live in external and internal peace but suffered foreign imperialism, China's current top leadership is made up of seven pragmatic patriots. They are leading their people because they are capable managers and share their people's cultural and national values.

The map across shows the high rate of per capita growth in China of above 2.5% annually between 1980 and 2000. The second map shows the incidence of poverty in China relative to other countries: In 1978, 64% of the Chinese people lived in extreme poverty on less than $1 per day but, by 2001, this had been reduced to 17%.

Average Annual GDP per Capita Growth, 1980–2000   33

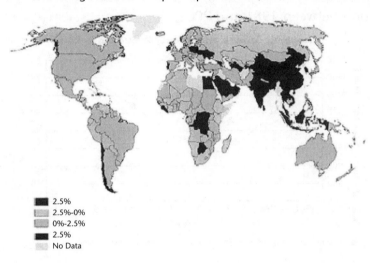

- ■ 2.5%
- □ 2.5%-0%
- □ 0%-2.5%
- ■ 2.5%
- □ No Data

Source: Calculated Using Data From World Bank 2004

Moderated and Extreme Poverty   34

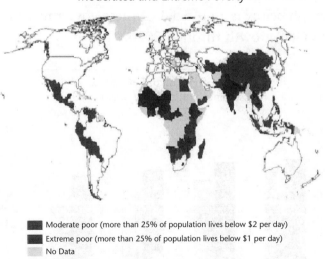

- ■ Moderate poor (more than 25% of population lives below $2 per day)
- ■ Extreme poor (more than 25% of population lives below $1 per day)
- □ No Data

Source: Data From World Bank (2004)

The graph below shows China's economic growth and poverty reduction between 1981 and 2001:

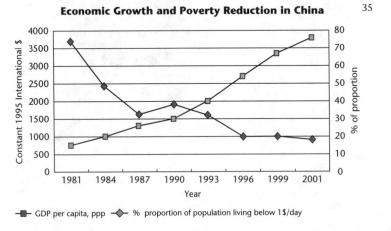

Economic Growth and Poverty Reduction in China 35

The Chinese government's ability to continue to provide social stability and economic growth is essential to pulling more and more of China's vast population out of extreme poverty into sustainable prosperity. That is a noble and demanding challenge that the government must meet successfully if China and the world are to be at peace.

The graph below is an official Chinese government projection of China's GDP growth through 2020.

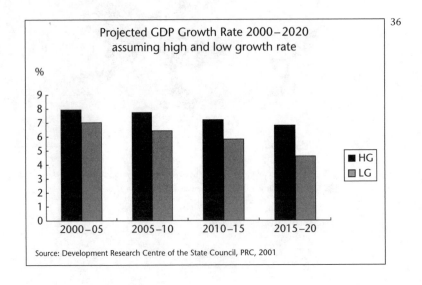

The graph below shows China's GDP per capita from 1800 projected to 2050:

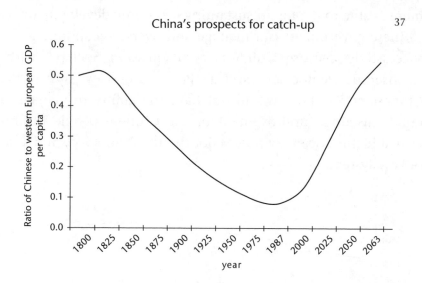

When Mao Zedong took power in 1949, the population of China was 550 million. By 2020, China's population is projected to be at least 1.5 billion. China's One Child Policy stemmed the danger of making national poverty inescapable simply due to economically unsupportable population growth. China is unique among developing countries in stabilizing population growth while its national wealth is skyrocketing. Less dynamic and well-managed developing countries are being impoverished by population growth, among other factors.[39]

Since the mid-1970s, the Chinese government's promulgation of measures to reduce China's annual birthrates reduced them from 39.6 live births per 1000 persons to 17.6 live births per 1000. Population growth is expected to drop from an annual average of 1.2% in 1980–1981 to 0.6% between 2001 and 2015.[38]

The controlling of China's population growth is the quintessential demonstration of the power the Chinese government is able to deploy in sustaining economic development. The Chinese government can manage and oversee economic growth successfully because China is a "Permission Society" with a "Consensus Democracy" and a "Pre-Rule of Law" system. The Chinese government would not have the ability to manage the rapid, sustained improvement of the Chinese people if China were a Rights Society with a Majority-Rule Democracy and a Rule of Law system.

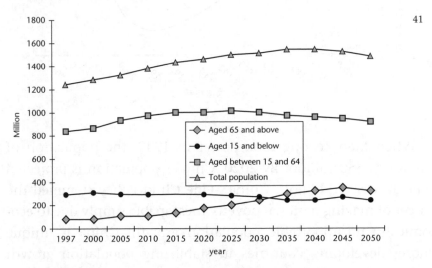

41

At current growth rates, the chart above shows that China's current 1.3 billion population will theoretically pass 3 billion by 2100.[40]

By controlling population growth with astonishing effectiveness, China's one-party political system of government has safeguarded the conditions for the economy doubling in size every six years since the government began economic reforms in the 1980s. As we have seen, China has been the highest recipient of foreign direct investment of all countries, except America, since the 1980s.[42]

Non-Chinese Analysis of China's Future Economic Competitiveness

We have highlighted that many Western observers insist that China can only progress if it quickly adopts non-Chinese style institutions of a Rights Society and Rule of Law system. For example, the Director of the World Economic Forum and its Associate Director, China, commented in 2003:

> A Chinese proverb says, "Wealth only lasts three generations. The first generation builds it up, the second consolidates it, and the third squanders it".
>
> In retrospect, this can be a metaphor for almost all epochs of Chinese history, in terms of the rise and fall of the dynasties. We see repeatedly that dynasties came to power led by a visionary leader or reformer, but whose less charismatic successors squandered the people's goodwill in the dynasty's steady decline. China's major dynasties—the Qin, Han, Tang, Song, Yuan, Ming and Qing—have gone through the same cycle of ruthless but hope-filled establishment, a height of glory and cultural renaissance, followed by decline due to incompetence and corruption. Dynastic endings were bloody, marked by social unrest, peasants' revolts, and a leader's catastrophic end.
>
> After a period of chaos and power shifts, a new aspiring leader would summon his forces and move into power.
>
> The cycle seems predictable, save for the somewhat astonishing feat that throughout the country has always been able to put its house in order and rise to catharsis and renaissance once again. In this way, China seems to be a striking exception to Paul Kennedy's proposition that great powers rise and fall. Indeed—the Roman and Spanish empires fell, and the British Empire disintegrated—only China, although certainly experiencing its ups and downs, had the wherewithal to survive. Only the rulers changed.
>
> At the end of 2002, the People's Republic witnessed the hand-over of power from the third generation to the fourth generation of leaders, and aside from much ado in the media, not much happened to mark what is supposed to be a seminal change of power. Business seemed to be as usual.

Appearances may be deceptive. The real meaning of the proverb above lies not in the numbers, exact generations or years. Instead, it refers to the fact that Chinese history is a cycle of ups and downs, successes and failures, rises and falls. Indeed, even during the past 50 years the country has seen constant shifts, with periods both of booming growth and national austerity, of cultural freedom and tighter control. There are people who claim that China has finally broken this cycle. The past 10 years, since the post-Tiananmen years of austerity, have been one of the longest periods of sustained strong growth. Of course, in history, 10 years is nothing, but there are those who say that with WTO accession, and the winning of the 2008 Olympics for Beijing, and in late 2002, World Expo 2010 for Shanghai, there is no turning back. China's story of globalization and economic growth is now a one way trend.[43]

A 2005 Swiss study made the following comment:

China's economic development undoubtedly has been impressive, particularly in the last 10 to 15 years. Cities whose appearance changed almost completely in a matter of a decade, fleets of cars that drove the traditional bicycles out of the city centers, booming economic regions along the coast, they all are among the most obvious testimonies of China's progress. The nation's economic growth is increasingly being felt on a global scale. China's enormous hunger for commodities is having major effects on the prices of oil and many other raw materials such as metals. In addition to these effects, which are tangible to a greater or lesser degree abroad...China has become an integral part of the strategic plans of...industrial companies. Regardless of whether the subject is the purchase of intermediate products, production or the sale of goods in China: for large and even medium-sized enterprises, it is impossible or very difficult to avoid the tremendous potential the Chinese market has to offer. Yet there is no doubt that a commitment in China does not only offer enormous potential but also entails a number of risks. The interpretation of local rules and relevant federal laws can sometimes be bewildering for those affected. The unwanted transfer of know-how to Chinese partners may also spawn uncomfortable local competitors. And the protection of intellectual property, though improved since China entered the WTO in 2001, remains a far cry from what is desirable from a western point of view.[44]

The Evolution of Capitalism With Chinese Characteristics in the First 28 Years

In 1978, the Chinese government decided that to develop China's economy, it was necessary to reopen the country's borders after 30 years of isolating China's economy from the global economy. In fact, China's borders had been closed for 5000 years. Foreign trade and investment brought much-needed modern technology and capital from outside China. This "opening up" slowly but steadily progressed through the 1980s, actually increased after the Tiananmen Square incident, and accelerated after Deng Xiaoping's historic visit in 1992 to Guangdong Province near Hong Kong. Chinese from Hong Kong, Taiwan, and Singapore were the first to appreciate the significance of Deng Xiaoping's 1992 initiative. By the mid 1990s, the world's major corporations began to recognize the potential offered by China's huge market and large pool of low-cost labor. A gold rush mentality seized many global corporations.[45] From 1990 to 1994, the Chinese government approved an estimated 256,000 joint ventures. In 1992 China's GDP increased to 14% and consumer price inflation at 24% in 1994.[46] From 1995, China's one-party government began to reduce the rate of inflation by slowing growth. The standard of living increased each year as the Chinese people enjoyed the newfound prosperity after the Chinese Revolution. An economic revolution was created by the interaction of China's current government and people. The new "Socialist Market Economy" and economic liberalization brought economic benefits previous generations had neither experienced nor imagined.[47]

The Suppression of the Domestic Ownership of China's Private Sector

As we have seen, the Chinese government has been criticized for not making reforms empowering Mainland Chinese to participate in private sector growth and to own successful private businesses, and maintaining policies that suppress their development.[48] The Chinese government no doubt did that deliberately to protect the rule of China's Communist Party. However, the reality is that the Party is the only entity that can currently provide stability and economic progress in China.

The chart below shows the gradual evolution of the official formula of reform objectives between 1978 and 2001. It can also be characterized as showing the gradual creation of Socialist Market Economy Capitalism. For a detailed step-by-step analysis from 1985 to 2004 of the reform process see the Appendix reproduced in this book.

The Rationale for Only Stimulating the Growth of China's Foreign-Owned Private Sector

The Chinese government saw several advantages to favoring foreign businesses and suppressing private Mainland Chinese entrepreneurs. Foreigners are more controllable. Economic development and reform required political and social stability, which only the ruling party was able to provide. Policy questions were debated within the ruling party, rather than in a proliferation of parties competing for power and policy control, which would have destabilized China and made economic development and reform unachievable. Foreigners also brought the capital, management skills, and technology that China needed. The Chinese govern-

The Gradual Evolution of the Official "Formula" of Reform Objectives Since 1978 [49]

Time	Formulation of Reform Objectives
1978–1984.10	Planned economy supplemented by some market elements
1984.10–1987.10	Planned commodity economy
1987.10–1989.6	"State regulates the market and market regulates enterprises"
1989.6–1991	"Organic integration of planned economy and market regulations"
1992	Shareholding system and security market (started) can be used by socialism
1992.10	Socialist market economy
1994	"Corporatization of SOEs and reform of property rights"
1997	Developing the state sector together with all other kinds of ownership; "holding on to large SOEs while letting small ones go to the market"
1998	Constitution amendment: private ownership should be equally promoted and protected
1999.10	SOEs withdraw from competitive industries; diversification of ownership of corporate and "mixed ownership"; executive stock options for SOEs
2001.7	"Three representative functions of the Party"; allows owners of private and individual enterprises to be Party members; further develop various ownership forms

Source: Various official documents of the Central Committee of the Chinese Communist Party (CCCCP).

ment could not have looked to Mainland Chinese to provide, in the time frame available, what China needed.

By 2000, 400 Fortune 500 companies had already invested in China.[50] The amount of FDI rose steadily from US$12.5 billion in 1979–1982 to US$59 billion in 2000. In 2002, the private sector accounted for over 60% of service industry capacity, 50% of exports, 24% of GDP,[51] and China surpassed America as the leading destination for investment capital.[52] By 2010, it has been estimated that the private sector will comprise as much as 40% of China's GDP.[53]

After 1995, the initial enthusiasm of foreign corporations yielded to the realization that China was not an easy country in which to do business, because its regulatory environment was difficult and its laws and regulations kept changing and were interpreted in different ways in different parts of China. Foreign companies were also directed by China's central or local governments to joint ventures with SOEs, which often turned out to be less-than-satisfactory partners. The Chinese government's and SOE's objectives differed from the foreign corporations, and the SOEs had shortcomings that were not recognized at the time many of the joint-ventures agreements were negotiated.

In spite of the difficulties, by 2002 China and America were already among each other's leading trading-partners. According to the Ministry of Commerce of China, the leading trade partners for China are currently the European Union, America, and Japan. The trade between America and China started from less than $2.5 billion in 1978 and experienced tremendous growth, but has been hurt by American anti-dumping activities in recent years.[54] International trade has expanded even faster than China's economy, with merchandise exports and imports together growing by 22% in 2002 and by 37% in 2003 to reach US$360 billion.[55] In 2003, 31% of consumer goods bought in America were from China.[56]

China accounted for about 5% of global GDP growth in 2003. However, the conversion of China's[57] currency accounted for 0.008% of the 2003 global US$471 trillion foreign exchange turnover.[58] Chinese companies are required to surrender their foreign earnings to China's government, but this requirement is changing.[59] China had foreign currency reserves of US$659.1 billion in 2004, second only to the United States,[60] and had invested US$243 billion of that as of June 2005 in US Treasury Bonds making Japan, China, and England the largest holders of America's national debt.[61]

A Combination of the Structure of China's Economy, the Spontaneous Entrepreneurial Capitalism of China's People, and the Chinese Government's Policy Choices Enabled China to Transform Itself

There is a debate over why and how China has succeeded (unlike the former Soviet Union, which collapsed) in transforming itself into the world's emerging economic superpower while not transforming itself politically. Understanding that debate is important to understanding China's history and future.

Some observers attribute the Chinese government's successful management of the economic development and reform process to the structure of China's economy, rather than the policies chosen by the government. Jeffrey Sachs in *The End Of Poverty*[62] provides the following analysis of China's reform process:

> China was booming in the course of its market reforms, whereas Eastern Europe and the former Soviet Union were experiencing a huge and very painful contraction of heavy industry. Had China chosen a superior reform path? What could it teach Eastern Europe? And what did China need to understand about the events in Europe and the former Soviet Union? ...
>
> The standard take on these questions is one that I gradually discovered to be wrong both on the facts and in economic interpretation. The standard view is that China proceeded gradually, whereas Eastern Europe proceeded radically, indeed, by shock therapy (that awful term that continued to follow me about). China's gradualism was humane; Eastern Europe's radicalism was dislocating. China, said many, had been wise to forestall democracy altogether, waiting until the economy was better placed to handle political freedom, whereas Eastern Europe had rushed headlong into democracy.
>
> From the start, this line of thinking did not sit with me for several reasons. First, I knew that Gorbachev had tried

gradualism in the Soviet Union during the era of pere-
stroika and, indeed, had modeled many of the Soviet
reforms on the obvious successes in China. Yet, that course
had not worked.

Our diagnosis began by noting a fundamental difference
between the economies of Eastern Europe and the Soviet
Union and the economy of China. As of 1978, when it began
its market reforms, China was still a largely rural and agricultural economy. Roughly, 80 percent of the population lived in
rural areas, and 70 percent lived as peasant farmers. During
the 1960s and 1970s, these peasants were organized in
communes, with communal land tenure and communal pay.
Individual families were not rewarded for their own efforts
or investments in the land. Yields in the communes were
extremely low, reflecting the absence of incentives at the
household level. Only 20 percent of the population worked in
cities, and about the same proportion of the labor force
worked in state-owned enterprises of all sorts. These, too, were
very inefficient. Workers were guaranteed their wages and
benefits (including, for example, healthcare), and could
not be laid off. They had, as the common expression put it,
an "iron rice bowl" that could not be broken by an
economic downturn.

Eastern Europe and the former Soviet Union were utterly
different in structure. Unlike China, roughly 60 percent of the
region's population lived in urban areas in 1978, whereas
about 40 percent lived in rural areas. The industrial labor force
was about 40 percent of the labor force; the service sector was
another 40 percent; and the agricultural sector was only
around 20 percent.... Even the farms were organized not as
Chinese communes, but as state-owned enterprises with
workers on salary. It could be said that 100 percent of the
labor force in the Soviet system enjoyed the wheat-based
equivalent of the iron rice bowl.

The difference in starting points made all of the
difference. In both contexts, the state enterprise sector posed
an enormous challenge. With workers guaranteed their wages,
jobs and benefits, the state-owned enterprises were both
inefficient and big drains on the budget. Only force, or the
threat of force, kept down the workers' demands for wage

increases, since the workers knew that they could press for higher wages without fear of layoffs or unemployment. Only subsidies from the budget and the state-owned banks allowed the state enterprises to keep operating and to cover implicit or explicit losses.

On the other hand, China's peasant commune sector was taxed by the state, rather than subsidized. The government bought all of the food from the farmers at low prices in order to subsidize the urban workers via low food prices. Moreover, the peasant farmers had no guarantees of incomes or benefits—in short, no iron rice bowl. As was true of China's peasants from time immemorial, they just wanted to be left alone by the state, rather than taxed by it. The communes were also very inefficient, with grain yields that were very low because of the lack of appropriate work incentives. The farmers' incomes did not depend on their own efforts or production, but rather on the overall commune output. The return to a "household responsibility" system in which individual farm households farmed individual plots, with the benefits accruing mainly to those households, dramatically improved the work incentives.

China was able, therefore, to begin its reforms with a major burst of agricultural production and a radical market reform of the food sector. Between 1977 and 1979, the commune system was spontaneously dismantled, not so much by top-down command, but by bottom-up action of villages across the country in the wake of the power vacuum after Mao's death. After decommunization spread like wildfire, the Communist Party of China validated it in 1979, but the real action was spontaneous.

There was nothing gradual about this change. This was shock therapy par excellence. Around seven hundred million individuals in farm households were suddenly farming on plots assigned to the household rather than to the commune. This new household responsibility system gave massive incentives to individual farmers to work harder, apply inputs with more care, and to obtain higher yields. Food yields boomed, and food supplies to the urban areas increased rather than decreased with decommunization. In short, the early stage of China's reforms was a burst of output that was "win-win" for both the rural and urban sectors. The next steps of China's reforms, in the 1980s and early 1990s, were also rather swift and had highly positive results. First, the rural peasants were given the freedom to leave the farm and begin work in rural industry, known as township and village enterprises (TVEs). Suddenly, millions of industrial jobs opened up in hundreds of thousands of these enterprises. Second, international trade and investment was liberalized, initially in specially designated free-trade zones, known as special economic zones (SEZs). Foreign investors saw moneymakers at hand. They could bring in foreign technology and capital to employ low-wage Chinese labor for the production of labor-intensive exports for world markets. Chinese workers flocked into the free-trade zones from the countryside. In effect, the liberalization of the farm sector freed up labor for the manufacturing export sector. Within a few years of the establishment of the free-trade zones, China began an export boom based on labor-intensive exports in garments, textiles, footwear, plastic, toys, and electronics assembly. Within just two decades, manufactured exports soared, from a few billion dollars in 1980 to more than $200 billion dollars by 2000.

The designation of a few favored free-trade zones had historic precedent in China's long history with world markets, particularly in the nineteenth century. It turned out that the special economic zones were, with a remarkable degree of overlap, the same sites of the initial opening of the Chinese economy in the mid-nineteenth century after the Opium Wars. The major difference between the early and the more recent period was that in the mid-1800s, China was under quasi-colonial rule, whereas the current episode was a matter of sovereign choice. This made the legitimacy of today's free-trade zones vastly greater and the reforms much deeper. The idea of using key centers of industrialization as a strategy of development, picking areas where the industrial investments would be encouraged, also has had a proven track record elsewhere in Asia, from Japan's successful economic development to the post-World War II successes of Korea, Taiwan, Hong Kong, Singapore, Penang Island (Malaysia) and many other parts of Asia.

The rest, as they say, is history. These zones took off. They combined very low-cost labor, availability of international technology, and an increasing and eventual torrent of investment funds, both from domestic savings, but increasingly in the 1990s, foreign direct investment.

That foreign direct investment had three components. Part of it was long-distance international capital flows from the financial and industrial centers of Europe and the United States. Another very important part was money from the offshore Chinese communities of Asia, the leaders of which were able to identify excellent business opportunities, frequently family centered. And a third part was what was called round-tripping money, money that was taken out of China, usually from state enterprise accounts, passed through Hong Kong financial intermediaries, and then reinvested in mainland enterprises. However it was done, the combination of low-cost laborers numbering hundreds of millions, modern technology, ample capital, and a safe and sound business environment produced one of the great moneymaking machines of modern history.

One area of China's reforms was indeed gradual: the state enterprise sector. China partly liberalized, but did not privatize, the state enterprises in the 1980s and 1990s. The government did not attempt to break the iron rice bowl, and the results were not good, as might have been predicted. Wages increased, profits decreased, and the burdens on the budget and banking sector multiplied. Still, the government kept the state enterprises in operation with few layoffs or ownership changes until state enterprise reforms began in earnest at the end of the 1990s. Only then did urban unemployment begin to rise with the layoffs of hundreds of thousands, and then millions, of state enterprise workers.

Gradualism, then, Chinese style, meant radicalism in rural reforms, a quick opening of the economy to trade, and only gradual reform of the state enterprises. In that sense, China saved the hardest for last in the sequence of reforms. This was a prerogative made possible by the structure of China's economy as of 1978."[63]

Probably no country in the world, not even Russia has experienced the extent of tumult and swings from misery to triumph, economically and socially, that China has since its revolution of 1949. The Maoist period, looking back, had a few huge successes, mainly a dramatic improvement in basic healthcare in the country, and many huge failures, especially socialist industrial development, which failed in ways similar to those of the Soviet economy. The public health successes are striking, and deserve careful note, because they surely formed part of the foundation of China's economic boom after 1978.

At the time of independence, life expectancy was forty-one years and infant mortality (death before the first birthday for each 1,000 births) stood at an astounding 195. Women gave birth to an average of six children. By 1978, when market reforms began, life expectancy had risen to sixty-five years, infant mortality had declined to 52, and the total fertility rate stood at around three. These successes reflected several major policy initiatives during the Maoist era. First, major public health campaigns reduced or eliminated the transmission of several infectious diseases, including malaria, hookworm, schistosomiasis, cholera, smallpox, and plague. Second, there was the innovation of the barefoot doctor, a community health worker for rural areas with basic training in essential health services, including the prevention and treatment of infectious diseases. Third, important improvements in basic infrastructure (roads, power, drinking water, and latrines) raised the safety of the physical environment. Fourth, major increases in crop productivity were achieved, in part through the introduction of high-yield crops during China's green revolution. Cereal yields, for example, went from 1.2 tons per hectare in 1961 to 2.8 tons per hectare in 1978, according to the official data.

China also had its share of tragic disasters caused by the madness of one-person rule. The two greatest of these disasters were the Great Leap Forward between 1958 and 1961 and the Cultural Revolution between 1966 and 1976. The Great Leap Forward was a mad scheme of Mao's to accelerate industrialization through the introduction of so-called backyard steel mills. Millions of peasants throughout the country were told to stop planting and to start producing steel in tiny and ineffective, and totally misconceived, backyard mills. The policy ended up causing mass starvation, the news of which did not reach those in charge because of false reports and the fantasy world of the top leadership at the time, particularly of Mao. Tens of millions of deaths resulted. The Cultural Revolution, which began in 1966, was Mao's decade-long attempt to create permanent revolution through upheaval in normal planning and bureaucratic processes. It turned Chinese society upside down, destroyed livelihoods, led to suicide and displacement, and disrupted for a decade or more the education of a whole generation of China's young people. Many of China's current scholars and leaders spent that decade in the countryside. It was Mao's death in 1976, the arrest of the Gang of Four in 1976, and Teng Hsiao-ping's ascension to power in 1978 that began the great opening of China.

Since 1978, China has been the world's most successful economy, growing at an average per capita rate of almost 8 percent per year. At that rate, the average income per person has doubled every nine years, and thus had increased almost eight-fold by 2003 compared with 1978. The reduction of extreme poverty in the country has been dramatic, as shown in Figure 2. In 1981, 64 percent of the population lived on an income below a dollar a day. By 2001, the number was reduced to 17 percent. The engines of growth are still running strong, with per capita growth currently only slightly slower than a few years ago. It is typical for a fast-growing country like China to experience a gradual moderation of its growth over time, just as Japan did in the second half of the twentieth century. The basic reason is that much of the growth is catching up, specifically adopting the technologies of the leading innovative countries. As those technologies come into use, and the income gap is thereby narrowed with the leading countries, the opportunity for "easy" growth through the importation of technologies is narrowed.[64]

Jeffrey Sachs's analysis needs to be considered with five additional comments regarding the Chinese government's goals. First, the Chinese government is focused on reducing regional and income disparities in China in the next 25 years of China's economic development strategy. It will take longer than Sachs predicts for China's "catching up" growth to abate because seventy percent of China's people are still to be deployed. Secondly, China's economic growth will continue to accelerate rather than experience a gradual moderation of growth over time as Japan did. Japan has a much smaller population and therefore less human capital than China. Thirdly, instead of only adopting technology developed by the leading innovative countries, China also will become a leading country in developing and deploying innovative technologies in the next 25 years of the Chinese government's strategy of economic development.

Fourthly, Jeffrey Sachs's emphasis of the structure of China's economy in the 1978 to 2004 stage needs to be augmented by recognition of the key role that the policy choices and management abilities of the government in developing the competitive advantages and tools of China's "Permission Society," "Consensus Democracy" and "Pre-Rule of Law" system. The astute use of those Chinese cultural characteristics, institutions, and decision-making processes must be recognized and respected in predicting China's future. As we have seen, the government is unlikely to give up those competitive advantages and tools essential to China's sustained economic growth and adopt a Rights Society, Majority-Rule Democracy, and Rule Of Law approach that many commentators assert are necessary for continued economic growth.

Finally, Sachs's analysis also can be usefully considered with and augmented by John McMillan's analysis in *Reinventing The Bazaar: A Natural History Of Markets*,[65] which provides the following analysis of the Chinese government's economic development and reform process:

> The experiences of China and Russia could hardly have been more different. In China, reform was followed by world-record growth for twenty years. In Russia, incomes plummeted. Differences in their initial conditions—China was poor and agricultural, Russia was middle-income and

industrial—account for some of the differences in responses to reform. But much of it is accounted for by their policies.

The most conspicuous difference between China and Russia is in the form of government. Throughout its reform period, China remained under communist control, whereas Russia became democratic. Does this political difference rule out the possibility of general economic lessons from China? Did China need its authoritarian government in order to follow its economic path, or could it have reformed as successfully under a democratic government? This is impos-sible to determine. There are reasons to believe, however, that China's economics is inseparable from its politics, and that it could not have followed a similar economic path if it had been democratic.

China's reforms were those of a relatively weak state. Formidable political barriers stood in the way of economic reform. The reformers had to craft a political coalition that favored reform: they had to engage in ordinary politicking to get their policies enacted. Having discarded Marxism and Maoism, the Communist Party had little legitimacy beyond its ability to deliver economic growth. The political commitment to reform came not from any inherent strength of the state but from the early and cumulative reform successes.

Russian shock therapy differed from Chinese gradualism, at root, in the degree of government activism. Paradoxically, newly democratic Russia chose a reform path that demanded a strong state, while authoritarian China chose one that did not. "The crucial requirement for success" of shock therapy, said economist Robert Skidelsky, one of its advocate is also the most difficult: "a strong and legitimate state." Russia's privatization program was implemented by presidential decree (apart from initial legislation, passed by the parliament). Because of the need to move quickly, shock therapy meant bypassing the democratic processes of debate and deliberation.

Whereas in Russia the government controlled the transition, or tried to, in China the government was largely passive. Its main role was to repeal prohibitions: it removed the ban on farmers working individual plots, the ban on entrepreneurs forming new firms, and the ban on state firms trading on markets. It left in place the existing mechanisms by which the economy was running, and let people build the new economy around the old. Bottom-up changes drove China's reforms. The new economy arose more from the initiatives of the Chinese people, who built new firms and created new ways of doing business, than from changes imposed by the government.

Some top-down changes were needed also; in fact, more than what occurred. The government was unduly laggard in acting to correct China's hopelessly inadequate financial and legal systems; undoubtedly some of the growth was based on misallocated investment. Privatization was delayed too long. But what China's success shows is that a transition economy does not have to set everything right all at once. It can get by with temporary solutions, devices like the township and village enterprises that may not exist in Western practice or in economic textbooks.

In any of the planned economies, the starting point for transition was misaligned prices, unproductive firms, and unfilled market niches. Such inefficiency offered large scope for improvement. Introducing a few incentives and some competition into a highly distorted economy could have dramatic effects, just as the situation in China illustrates. It was hard to predict, however, just which incentives would work in the peculiar circumstances of the transition economy. It follows that it is prudent to take an experimental approach, and be willing to live for a while with unconventional institutions, if they work. These band-aid solutions may well not be discovered in a finance ministry, let alone in the World Bank or a Western University. They are more likely to be discovered by people whose livelihoods are on the line.

The amount of reliance on foreigners' advice highlights the difference between shock therapy and gradualism. Russia leaned on lawyers, economists, and bankers from the West for advice on how to privatize state firms, develop capital markets, and reform the legal system. The U.S. government spent $2.3 billion in grants for technical assistance and exchanges to support reform in Russia. China by contrast called little on foreign consultants. This was not a matter of Chinese xenophobia versus Russian open-mindedness. It went to the very nature of the reforms. In China, many of the important decisions were made in the local regions. Beijing had less use for experts than Moscow because it was deciding less. "Reflecting on the first eight years of China's reforms, paramount leader Deng Xiaoping said, "All sorts of small enterprises boomed in the countryside, as if a strange army appeared suddenly from nowhere. The rapid growth of the new township and village enterprises was not something I had thought about. Nor had the other comrades. This surprised us."

These new firms were arguably the single most important factor in China's reform success. They were a prime contributor to China's reform momentum and economic growth. They strengthened the nascent market economy by creating jobs, supplying needed consumer goods, mobilizing savings, and ending the state firms' monopoly on industry. As Deng said, however, their growth was "not the achievement of our central government". The reformers failed to foresee, by Deng's admission, the pivotal feature of their own reforms.

The township and village enterprises were, on the face of it, a strange way of organizing firms. The planned economy had failed because of public ownership, yet China's path away from the planned economy, it turned out, involved creating additional publicly owned firms. With hindsight, we can explain the new firms' success. Each was subject to intense product-market competition from the many similar firms. Since local governments owned them, they could raise funds without a financial market yet could not expect to be bailed out by the government if they failed. They effectively co-opted the local Communist Party officials, who otherwise might have sabotaged the reforms, by giving them a stake in the emerging economy. The fear of failure induced the managers to run the firms efficiently. But these explanations came after the fact; these firms' success was not foreseen."[66]

It is necessary to add the recognition of the genius of the leadership of the Chinese government in the first 28 years of rapid economic development to analyses that assert that China's growth is significantly accidental and mismanaged in fundamental ways[67] and that the structure of China's economy[68] and bottom-up generated spontaneous economic growth, and that muddling through by China's leadership, account for China's economic growth and competitiveness. The unique combination of the genius of the Chinese government, people, and culture, and the advantages and tools available to the government in designing, accepting certain bottom-up changes, and managing China's "Socialist Market Economy Capitalism" must be recognized if "The China Game" is to be successfully dealt with by America's political and business leaders in the next 25 years.

The Chinese Communist Party's Capitalist Mindset Shift

The Chinese Communist Party ("CCP") is committed to capitalism in the reform of China. Kishore Mahbubani believes that "CCP" more accurately means the Chinese "Capitalist Party."[69] He asserts:

> The Chinese Communist Party, despite its name, bears no relation to its Soviet counterpart, which used to be run by aging bureaucrats. Today, the Chinese Communist Party is almost as ruthless as Harvard in its search for young talent to fill key positions. The average age of the Chinese leadership is now among the youngest in the world, a remarkable achievement in a society that venerates age and has hitherto equated age with wisdom.[70]

There has been no retreat from economic capitalism within the CCP. The internal debates among members occur within the CCP and then are announced as CCP and Chinese government policy. As mentioned, *The Economist* has asserted that:

> Domestically, the government [of China] is well aware that its political acceptance derives solely from rapid economic growth and will do whatever is necessary to meet its internal benchmark, an annual rise of 7%. China's leaders call themselves communists, but they have become capitalists, in practice.[71]

The Reality That Very Able Political Leaders Are Selected Within China's One-Party Government System Since 1978

Information not previously available to American observers became available in late 2001 about the leadership selection process then occurring within the CCP and the type of people who emerged as current leaders of the CCP and China. It is important to note that elections held within China's current one-party political system did play a role in the selection of China's current seven top leaders. American observers Andrew Nathan and Bruce Gilley, in *China's New Leaders: The Secret Files*[72] have described the method used in choosing China's current top leadership team:

> The Chinese Communist Party is a secretive, selective organization of about sixty-five million members who have positions of influence in all sectors of Chinese society, whether managers, newspaper editors, or bureaucrats in charge of everything from public health to police intelligence. The Party's national congress consists of about two thousand persons divided into provincial delegations, elected by Party members throughout the country. It meets once every five years to elect a Central Committee, currently of about 370 persons.
>
> The election of the Central Committee is important because being a member or alternative member of it is a necessary qualification for the most senior positions in the Party, the government, and the military. In the past, Party congress delegates ratified a list of names prepared in advance by the Party's Organizational Department—which handles appointments and promotions—under the guidance of the senior leaders. Since 1987, the congress has been allowed to vote on a list of candidates slightly larger than the number of Central Committee seats. This means that a small number of candidates fail to be elected, an advance for inner-Party "democracy" in the eyes of the reformers. The leaders usually accept the verdict of the congress, but sometimes they

improvise—in one case ... by decreeing the existence of an extra seat so a favored candidate could be elected.

Once elected, the Central Committee approves a Politburo of twenty-plus persons, the makeup of which has been agreed upon in close door bargaining among Party elites. Five to nine of those members are designated as the Politburo Standing Committee, which meets weekly and really runs the country. The highest ranking member of that group is the general-secretary.

On paper just a Party organ, the PBSC makes all the important decisions on national policy concerning the economy, foreign affairs, defense, science and technology, welfare, and culture—policy in every sphere of life. It can deal with any issue it wants to. No other organ of the Party or the government has the power to contradict its decisions. The only exception to this general rule was a group of highly esteemed former PBSC members, sometimes called the "Party Elders," headed by Deng Xiaoping, who from 1987 to 1997 exercised behind-the-scenes veto power over major decisions. But since Deng's death, retired senior leaders have not exercised such power.

Each member of the PBSC takes on other important responsibilities. Some supervise crucial activities in which the Party exercises authority. Among these are internal security, including the police; high-level-appointments to jobs in the Party and government; propaganda; and other work carried on by the powerful Party Secretariat and high-level Party committees or commissions. Others hold top positions in the state apparatus—as state president, premier, vice premier, or chairman of the national parliament. But those roles are secondary to their position as PBSC members. Members of the Politburo may hold similar posts or may serve as Party secretaries of major provinces or provincial-level municipalities.[73]

To the degree that China's selection process produces competent leaders, it also has the characteristics of a *meritocracy* of sorts. The CCP selection process has produced groups of leaders under Deng Xiaoping, Jiang Zemin, and Hu Jintao, who have managed China's economic miracle. A huge majority or "consensus" of Mainland Chinese support that economic miracle and its further development throughout China.

The CCP's Organizational Department assembles information on government and party officials who are candidates for membership in the CCP's Politburo Standing Committee, China's highest governing body. Andrew Nathan and Bruce Gilley provide an assessment of China's current top seven leaders in *China's New Leaders: The Secret Files:*[74]

> For many, our portrait will be reassuring, since it shows the new leaders to be determined modernizers, intent on integrating China's economy with the rest of the world and on maintaining good relations with the United States. They are competent managers with wide experience in China's complex party-state bureaucracy, and pragmatic technocrats who are capable of keeping order and promoting development in the world's most populous country. Some of them are willing to subject the ruling Chinese Communist Party to more political competition and to trust the state-controlled Chinese media, including the press, radio, and television, with more freedom to criticize the performance of lower level officials.
>
> For others, however, the portrait will be frightening. This is a group of men who believe in authoritarian rule as a precondition for pushing their country through the turbulent passage to modernization. They believe in stopping dissent against Communist rule before it gets started and in deterring crime by widespread use of the death penalty. They believe that their government has been more than generous to the grievances of the residents of Taiwan, Tibet, and Xinjiang, and have little sympathy for the grievances of the people in these areas. Although they share many Western economic values, they share fewer Western moral values. They expect strategic competition with the West, and intend to resist American dominance, yet they believe that the West will eventually have to cooperate with China because of common economic interests. For the

> West, the new leaders present a dilemma: it will be economically and strategically necessary to deal with them, but many Western policymakers may also feel a moral obligation to oppose their methods of rule.[75]

The leadership selection process now operating in China as described by Andrew Nathan and Bruce Gilley above, has important democratic features. In 2001, there were 65 million CCP members throughout China from whom 2000 persons, divided into provincial delegations, were elected as participants in the CCP's National Party Congress. The CCP's National Congress meets once every 5 years to elect a Central Committee, and in 2002 had about 370 members from whom China's current 7 top leaders were selected.[76] To the degree that 65 million participate in selecting the 370 CCP National Party Congress members, who then participate in selecting and have an opportunity to be among China's top leadership, it can be said that within a one-party state system, China has a "democracy," which we have termed a "Consensus Democracy." It is just a different type of democracy than America's Majority Rule Democracy.

"Democracy" has many definitions.[77] Robert Dahl has written about American democracy,[78] and questioned whether the American Constitution is democratic[79] and was democratically adopted.[80] Dahl has shown the incremental expansion of the right to vote in America over many generations after the Constitution was adopted, from a restricted property based ownership right to vote to universal adult suffrage. The expansion of the right to vote was achieved gradually over hundreds of years.[81] Some observers, such as Noam Chomsky, believe universal adult suffrage remains unachieved even in America.[82]

America does not have the moral authority today to demand that China do immediately what America took many generations to do, and in many observers' views, has not yet achieved itself. Few objective observers would argue that neither America nor China are perfect. There is the opportunity for improvement in both nations.

As a percentage of total population, more Americans are able to participate in the selection process of America's future leaders than Chinese are able to participate in their selection process. Only 5% or 6% of China's population, who are CCP members, are able to participate in the selection process of China's political leaders.

Although there are more people notionally involved in selecting America's *future* leaders than in selecting China's future leaders, America's Majority-Rule Democracy and two-party system results in large percentages of American voters being out-voted by small majorities or even large minorities of the popular vote. In American elections, the candidates that emerged as president are often selected by an incredibly tiny majority, or even a minority, of the popular vote. Democracy *imposes widely unwanted political leaders* on America. Just how unwanted each American president is can be seen in the popular vote totals. However, when *representative* leaders are selected, "democracy" in both America and China is a process, not a result. American democracy also reflects widely-held but shifting major divisions of popular opinion. Tolerance of the opinions of others is an essential requirement of democracy's survival and success since America was established.

China's "Consensus Democracy" is a larger "democracy" than America's Majority-Rule Democracy *when measured by numbers of participants allowed to be involved* and compete in the leadership selection process. With 65 million CCP members participating in the selection process of China's *future* leaders, there are more Chinese *"actively"* involved in the selection of their future leaders, than Americans *"actively"* involved in their selection process.

The Fallacy That Western Policymakers Are Entitled to Interfere with China's Sovereignty and Right of Self-determination

If the above assessment of China's current top seven leaders by Andrew Nathan and Bruce Gilley is correct, and we concur with it, then we submit that a key problem in the relationship of China and America's political leaders is that some Western policymakers feel they have a "moral obligation" to oppose the leaders of China's methods of rule. Such moral obligations must be reconciled with the basic concepts of China's rights to self-determination, sovereignty, and economic progress. Americans, in reconciling these principles, should remember how intolerant they would be of foreign policymakers who felt a "moral obligation" to oppose the methods of rule of America's political leaders.

What special rights or abilities to govern China have Western policymakers who feel a moral obligation to oppose China's government methods of rule? American policy makers who feel a moral obligation to oppose China's leaders' methods of rule nonetheless opposed China exercising the feelings of "moral obligation" that China's policymakers felt during the Cold War about America's "methods of rule."

Hopefully, the feelings of moral obligation that American policymakers have will find their proper focus in improving America and leaving it to China to produce the leaders who, in the case of China's seven current top leaders, are said to be "…competent managers with wide experience in China's complex state-party bureaucracy and pragmatic technocrats who are capable of keeping order and promoting development of the world's most populous country" and who "believe in authoritarian rule as a precondition of pushing their country through the turbulent passage of modernization."

China in Transition: A Scenario for the Road Ahead

Expect the unexpected from 21st century China. But study China's 5000-year past. China has a long history of political, economic, and social evolution driven by pragmatism and incremental experimentation. The ability to remain in government has always demanded providing leadership capable of preventing social unrest or military failure. Within the context of a 5000-year history of dynastic rule, China's one-party political system could be compared to a modern dynasty-like rule, based not exclusively on family links but membership in a single governing party whose members constitute a small elite drawn from throughout China that internalizes policy struggles so they do not destabilize a state comprising 22% of humanity.

Incremental economic change has worked well for China since 1978. As we have seen, at this period in history, China needs stability, which its current one-party political system is able to provide. China's economic performance is growing at a higher rate than "democratic" countries from 1979 to 2006. India's growth rate has averaged 6.1% cumulatively since 1993. America, Japan, Germany, France, Britain, Italy, and Canada's rates were 3.3%, 0.9%, 1.4%, 2%, 2.8%, 1.7%, and 3.3% respectively. The Chinese government has used its style of economic reform and development combined with some political reform successfully since 1978. It is likely this will continue if America is not aggressively promoting political change in China in ways that seek to increase social instability in China.

Observers of future events in China may be astounded by the solution the government may use to protect China from the real and present danger of armed conflict over Taiwan triggering armed conflict with America. The governments of China and Taiwan are now both operating capitalist economies. The Chinese government is introducing democratic elections of government officials within the CCP from the bottom up as a means of rooting out corruption. As that process continues, China and Taiwan will increasingly share democratic election procedures for officials. The Taiwan government has much experience in operating a capitalist economy. The economy of Taiwan is now dependent upon and interwoven with the economy of the rest of China. The problems of regional disparity and the reconciliation of different groups' interests in a harmonious society face whoever rules China's 1.3 billion people.

The solution that the Chinese government is developing for the danger of armed conflict with America over Taiwan, and for the reintegration of Taiwan back into Mainland China, could include Taiwan's leadership in the government of Mainland China. In other words, since Mainland China and Taiwan are now both capitalist, the danger of a counter-revolution is disappearing.

China should not become a two-party political system unless the Chinese government is satisfied that a constitutional mechanism had been devised and will work reliably. A stable two-party state and elections is difficult to achieve currently in China.

A solution to the danger of an unwanted war with America over Taiwan must also meet the vital requirement of preventing political contests or chaos from weakening or wrecking China's economic success and social reform.

Ironically, Li Tenjhisie's political experiment in Taiwan is an interesting case study for the Mainland Chinese government. Although the Taiwan democracy is not a very successful one, in the sense that it produces extreme nationalistic leaders and the extreme polarization and potential to cause conflict with the Mainland Chinese government, it came about in a largely peaceful transition from absolute party rule. China must find institutions that avoid the extreme politicians that the Taiwan model has generated. As we have seen, the government of 22% of humanity must seek consensus rather than majority rule in which 50.01% of voters can impose their will on 49.99%.

In the Chinese government's pragmatic way of doing things, *within the political, social, and economic stability of a one-party system,* free elections of party officials are being introduced gradually from the lower levels upwards to fight corruption and as experiments with majority-rule voting within the CCP. The governing party may even introduce a novel form of pluralism into China's political life. China might remain a one-party system but absorb senior members of Taiwanese parties into roles of some kind in the central government of the People's Republic of China.

For both America and China to win, what else could China's political leaders do domestically to help American political leaders cope with China's rapidly growing economic and geopolitical power? That is a key question. Any successful scenario will require close and constant collaboration between America and China's political leaders. Here is one scenario of what China's political leaders might choose to do. It would be encouraged by the creation of a committed, genuine partnership between America and China. But with or without America's cooperation, China's political leaders can implement the following.

China will gradually become more open to the rest of the world and communicate its intentions and purposes better. It will reduce its dependence on exports by increasing internal demand and investing in infrastructure, education, and research and development. As a poor and developing country, China might gradually decide not to accumulate large foreign exchange reserves and a large current account surplus just to lend its hard-earned savings to others. There is a defensive character in China doing so, which helps protect its economic growth and sovereignty. But there is another road China can follow. China may invest more in itself. Professor Laura D'Andrea Tyson, Dean of the London Business School, has put forward an argument for such an approach.[83] This has to be balanced with the international payment obligations and the security of China's domestic financial systems.

The kind of rapid and large one-time appreciation of the yuan demanded by the American Congress is very dangerous for the world financial systems and would destabilize the American economy as well as China's. But China will gradually and systematically allow its currency to appreciate without rapid moves that could shock the global markets and destabilize international trade. New technology such as the Forexster foreign currency trading system[84] will make that possible. Its use will eventually achieve a higher value for the yuan while allowing enough time for China's producers, exporter, customers, and borrowers to adjust. The use of the Forexster technology can also help prevent speculative funds rushing in and out of China to benefit from short-term appreciation prospects. This may also reduce the interest-rate risks for the American and world economies.

China will make successful efforts to allow the currently under-utilized rural population's innate productivity to become increasingly part of the national economy. One important way to achieve this integration and participation is to invest heavily in the rural economy. Infrastructure pathways for rural products and services to reach the cities are helpful. Monetary and fiscal policies of providing loans to farmers based on their needs and business plans is also very important. The demand thus generated, for agricultural machinery, and consumer and industrial products, would produce a major boost to the overall domestic demand. The net long-term effect of such a boost to demand would more than justify an eventual forgiveness of repayment of the entire financing package to farmers. But to avoid wasteful and short-term-focused behavior, such financing has to be initially tied to payback obligations as well as mortgages on the farmers' properties. Local officials could be generous in enforcing such security interests, using such enforcement only when it is necessary to ensure responsible behavior by borrowers, and not for improper purposes.

"Friends of China"

Americans who are genuinely what the Chinese refer to as "friends of China" have the advantage of having the right spirit in communicating and working with the Chinese. Those who are hostile to China will never have such advantages. The more Americans' understanding grows of the worldview, hardships, relentless drive, and capabilities of the Chinese people and the goals of the Chinese government, the more the mutual respect essential for success in the China Game is engendered.

Friends of China who recognize the incredible achievements of China's leadership and people since 1978 will be better able to see that what seemed impossible can be achieved incrementally by modern China. Who would have believed the story of China's economic miracle and reforms if it had been written in 1976 instead of 2006? Observers who recognize the genius that the Chinese leaders and people have deployed so successfully are less likely to underestimate the boldness and pragmatism that the Chinese government may use to align China's needs for political, social, economic, and military stability and development with America's needs. The Chinese government may solve the problems of simultaneously maintaining stability and growth, reconciling with Taiwan, and eliminating the conditions facilitating corruption with the creativity, daring, and determination that is making China so successful.

That is what is required, because chaos, less than 8% GDP growth per year, armed conflict with America over Taiwan, and the social disease of corruption are problems that must be solved.

They can be solved with the creativity, daring, and determination that the Chinese government has demonstrated since 1978.

Americans who realistically accept that a paradigm shift is occurring and that a mindset change is essential can be "friends of China." Unless the logic and empirical basis of this book are incorrect, that is the smart choice for America. America's containment policy is the key factor in how The China Game can be played out. As we discuss next in Chapter 7, President Hu is offering to collaborate with American political leaders in seeking win-win responses to the inevitable problems in the relationship.

PART 2

China's Capitalism
and American Capitalism

7

Can America Peacefully Accept China's Peaceful Rise?

Overview

This chapter examines why America should collaborate with China's growing economic power, and whether American political and business leaders and the American people will be able to peacefully accept that China's economy is going to become much larger than America's. It also examines China's willingness to persistently and unilaterally use win-win strategies consistent with the development of a committed partnership with America, even when America is operating in a zero-sum-game mindset.

What Are the Needs of American "National Security" in Response to China's "Manifest Destiny"?

American economic, political, and military policies of containment against what has been called China's "Manifest Destiny"[1] in the 21st century is currently perceived by many Americans as a zero-sum-game. A "Nash Equilibrium"[2] of sustained reciprocal benefit for America and China must be possible in this century. Is it beyond the abilities of America and China to coexist peacefully and prosper?

Accepting the Reality That China's Economy Will become Larger Than America's

America has 300 million people and China has more than 1.3 billion people.[3] The ramifications of this simple fact is difficult for many Americans to accept. China's emergence from solitude and poverty is redefining the global economy, just as the emergence of England's economy did in the 19th century, and the growth of America's economy from poverty did in the 20th century.[4] China was the world's leading economy before the 18th century, England was in the 19th century, and America was in the 20th century.

Americans fear and resent that the competitive advantages and wealth of nations are being rapidly affected by new competitive advantages emerging in the 21st century's global economy. China's competitive advantages will be overwhelming in the Knowledge Revolution, as computers and communication make education increasingly available, and the productivity of China's 1.3 billion people catches up to and surpasses America's 300 million people.

The "Knowledge Revolution" refers to what Carl Dahlman of the World Bank Institute defines as the ability to create, access and use knowledge as becoming a fundamental determinant of global competitiveness. There are at least five key elements of the "Knowledge Revolution":

1. Increased codification of knowledge and development of new technologies.

2. Closer links with science-based increased rates of innovation and shorter product life cycles.

3. Increased importance of education and up-skilling of labor forces and life-long learning.

4. Investment in intangibles, i.e., R&D, education, software, are greater than investments in fixed Capital in OECD nations.

5. Innovation and productivity increases are more important in competitiveness than GDP growth and increased globalization.

Many Americans assumed that "globalization" meant that American and European multinationals would dominate the global economy. Suddenly, "globalization" increasingly entails that the American and European economies and companies cannot compete effectively with China's developing economy or companies, or dominate the global economy in the new century. The awareness of this is creating "future shock".[5] China is poised to become the world's largest economy and American companies without profitable "China strategies" will find it difficult to remain profitable, whatever their competitive advantages were in the 20th century.[6]

The Fallacy that China and America Will Be Equal Economic Powers in the 21st Century

The first difficult step in establishing America and China's successful partnership in the 21st century is accepting that China will emerge as a "mega-economic superpower." In 2003, Frank-Jurgen Richter, the Director of the World Economic Forum for Asian Affairs, and Pamela Mar, Associate Director, wrote:

> China could even assume the mantle of a real global growth driver. Indeed, no country could possibly dream of replacing the United States in this role. While many things could derail the Chinese economic miracle... it is worthwhile just to envisage what China as a 'first among equals' economic power would mean.[7]

In 2004 The World Economic Forum China Summit focused on a model where America and China would share hegemony in the 21st century. That may not be a realistic model because of the rapidly growing economic and intellectual competitive advantages China's 1.3 billion people have. The unprecedented success of the

Chinese government's economic development strategy and the resourcefulness of the Chinese people have demonstrated China's economic drive to emerge from hunger and poverty. As we will show, China's economy is becoming much larger and more innovative in science and technology than America's economy. China's transition from a Communist planned economy to Socialist market economy capitalism is freeing up so much pent up talent and energy that America's post-Cold-War role as the only global superpower is also transitioning.

The Reality That China has the Capability to Displace America Globally in the Long Term as the Dominant Power [8]

Joseph Nye Jr., the Dean of Harvard's Kennedy School of Government, has asserted in *The Paradox Of American Power* that some believe:

> "… China is the likeliest of suspects for future peer competitor status" [with America and] "… Polls show that half the American public think China will pose the biggest challenge to U.S. world power status in the next hundred years."[9]

Nye asserts that if:

> …China aims in the near term to replace the United States as the dominant power in East Asia and in the long term to challenge America's position as the dominant power in the world. Even if this is an accurate assessment of China's intentions (and that is debated by experts), it is doubtful that China will have the capability….[10]

Nye also asserts:

> The fact that China is not likely to become a 'peer competitor' to the United States on a global basis does not mean that it could not challenge the United States in East Asia or that war over Taiwan is not possible. Weaker countries sometimes

attack when they feel backed into a corner, such as Japan at Pearl Harbor or China did when it entered the Korean War in 1950. Under certain conditions, Beijing will likely be fully undeterrable. If, for example, Taiwan were to declare independence, it is hard to imagine that China would forgo the use of force against Taiwan, regardless of the perceived economic or military costs, the likely duration or intensity of American intervention, or the balance of forces in the region. But it would be unlikely to win such a war. The U.S.-Japan Alliance, which the Clinton-Hashimoto declaration of 1996 reaffirmed as the basis for stability in post-Cold War East Asia, is an important impediment to Chinese ambition. This meant that in the triangular politics of the region, China cannot play Japan against the United States or try to expel the Americans from the area. From that position of strength, the United States and Japan can work to engage China as its power grows, and provide incentives for it to play a responsible role. How China will behave as its power increases is an open question, but as long as the United States remains present in the region, maintains its relationship with Japan, does not support independence for Taiwan, and exercises its power in a reasonable way, it is unlikely that any country or coalition will successfully challenge its role in the region, much less at the global level. If the United States and China stumble into war or a cold war in East Asia, it will more likely be caused by inept policy related to Taiwan's independence rather than China's success as a global challenger.[11]

Nye notes that some observers believe:

"sooner or later, if present trends continue, war is probable in Asia... China today is actively seeking to scare the United States away from East Asia rather as Germany sought to frighten Britain before World War I... Chinese leaders chafe at the constraints on them and worry that they must change the rules of the international system before the international system changes them. *Each side, believing it will end up at war with the other, makes reasonable military preparations, which then*

*are read by the other side as confirmation of its worst fears."[12]
(Emphasis added)*

Fortunately, some American business and political leaders recognize that collaboration with China is essential to America's prosperity and national security. The nationalistic military and working people in the two nations may not ever be able to adopt a new collaborative mindset. Forty-four percent of Americans reportedly believe that America has not been tough enough in dealings with China.[13] Many of America's political and military leaders fear a scenario where China attacks America in the 21st century, as Japan did in the 20th century. That fear must not be permitted to create such a reality.

The Fallacy That Trade War, Cold War or Armed Conflict with China Would be Good for America

America's then Federal Reserve Chairman, Alan Greenspan, warned Congress in 2005 that a big increase in tariffs on Chinese imports would "materially lower" U.S. living standards. He urged American lawmakers to let financial markets resolve trade imbalances with China.[14]

The Economist noted in 2005 that if the Chinese government liquidated even one tenth of its American Treasury Bond investments, the impact on America's economy would be "devastating".[15] Those investments were reportedly US$280 billion in April 2005[16] and US$242.1 billion in September 2005. China is the second largest holder of US Treasury Bills.[17] Chinese government controlled passive investments in American corporate equities are of a similar magnitude and importance.[18]

The Cold War in the 20th century cost trillions of dollars and diverted a high proportion of the world's intellectual and financial resources away from important needs. China, historically, including when it was the world's most innovative and largest economy prior to 1800, has shown little interest in international military aggressiveness. China has nuclear weapons and a limited ballistic missile delivery capability threatening America.[19] It is estimated that America has 3000 ballistic missiles with nuclear warheads targeting China. But wars in the future may be "unrestricted wars" in which nuclear and other high technology weapons capability may not protect America from terrorist, economic, computer virus and other attacks that are impossible to successfully defend against.[20]

Colin Powell in a June 2005 speech asserted that China's increased spending on its military does not make it a threat to America. Powell's view is that "China wishes to live in peace with its neighbors and the U.S." He pointed out that China's military expenditure is far less than America's[21] and stated that America and China have a "strategic partnership" and a "complementary relation." In his experience, "the most important thing to do is to sit down and jointly probe solutions." He indicated that the Chinese are great people who must work hard to earn a living for 1.3 billion people. Commenting on Chinese-American trade disputes, Powell indicated, "China needs to do a better job to explain to the U.S. public how U.S. consumers will benefit from quality goods coming in at low costs". In his view, China-U.S. trade and economic cooperation benefits Americans and helps create jobs.[22]

Richard N. Haass, the President of the Council on Foreign Relations, has written that:

> It is not clear the United States could prevent China's rise even if it wanted to. But should the United States want to? The answer is "no." For one thing, attempting to block China's rise would guarantee its animosity and all but ensure its working against U.S. interests around the world. More

important, the United States shouldn't want to discourage the rise of a strong China. America needs other countries to be strong if it is to have the partners it needs to meet many challenges posed by globalization, the spread of nuclear weapons, terrorism, infectious disease, drugs, and global climate change. The issue for American foreign policy shouldn't be whether China becomes strong but how China uses its growing strength.[23]

The Fallacy That China Will Inevitably Confront America

China's natural and historic enemies are its neighbors the former Soviet Union, Japan, and Taiwan. China's relationship with the former Soviet Union was the continuation of relations rather than an alliance.[24] Mao Zedong wished to see China align with America and establish relations with America.[25] But America's trade embargo against China from 1949 to 1979 and China's long period of economic and political isolation was, in part, the result of America's policy of containment. Deng Xiaoping wished to see China emulate America's economic success. Jiang Zemin wished America and China to be "strategic partners" in a "new relationship."[26] Good relations with the United States are good for China's economic development and national security. Trade wars and military wars are not. Jiang Zemin stated in 2000:

> We are now in a new century and China-U.S. relations should strive to advance to construct a strategic partnership. Whoever is the next president, regardless, from the perspective of world strategy, should try to straighten out the China-U.S. relationship... Sometimes China-U.S. relations are good and sometimes in a storm. There are certain people in America who do not want to see China and the U.S. having good relations. They always make some problems.[27]

China's current President, Hu Jintao, seeks to strengthen dialogue with America's political leaders, and to increase mutual trust and cooperation for common development.[28] "While each country should be able to pursue its own strategy," President Hu said in July 2005, "we hope that business issues will prevail and the issues will not become politicized."[29] China's Ambassador to America, Zhou Wenzhong has stated that China and America's relations are very important and the two countries have more in common than differences: "What is important is to handle the differences through consultations and dialog. ..."[30]

The Reality That the Chinese Admire and Want to be Friends of America

The Chinese government has the temperament among its leaders to act unilaterally for peace using strategies that are consistent with and designed to facilitate the strategic partnership that each Chinese leader since 1949 has proposed to America. President Hu Jintao's speech at Yale University on April 21, 2006 contained a message of friendship and respect:

> The Chinese and Americans have always had an intense interest in and cared deeply about each other. The Chinese admire the pioneering and enterprising spirit of the Americans and their proud achievements in national development. As China develops rapidly and steady headway is made in China-US cooperation, more and more Americans are following with great interest China's progress and development. Understanding leads to trust.[31]

The Chinese people also have a similar desire. For example, a Chinese newspaper reporter, upon learning of the thesis of this book, in a very unusual gesture in the Chinese culture, jumped up and hugged one of the authors. The reporter said:

You will be loved throughout China when the book is published in Chinese. There is nothing more that the Chinese people want than to be friends with America. We admire America's awesome achievements. We know that it was Americans alone among the nations who invaded China, who gave China schools, universities, and hospitals.

The Fallacy That America Should Seek to or Can Contain China

Henry Kissinger, in a June 2005 editorial in *The Washington Post* entitled "China: Containment Won't Work," set out his views that collaborating with China, rather than confronting it, is the only sound American strategy.[32]

China's emerging role is often compared to that of imperial Germany at the beginning of the 20th century, the implication being that a strategic confrontation is inevitable and that the United States had best prepare for it. That assumption is as dangerous as it is wrong.... Only the reckless could make such calculations in a globalized world of nuclear weapons. War between major powers would be a catastrophe for all participants; there would be no winners; the task of reconstruction would dwarf the causes of the conflict. ... Military imperialism is not the Chinese style. ... China seeks its objectives by careful study, patience and the accumulation of nuances— only rarely does China risk a winner-take-all showdown.... There is no doubt that China is increasing its military forces, which were neglected during the first phase of its economic reform. But even at its highest estimate, China's military budget is less than 20% of America's. ... The challenge China poses for the medium-term future will, in all likelihood, be political and economic, not military. ... The test of China's intentions will be whether its growing capacity will be used to seek to exclude America from Asia or whether it will be part of a cooperative effort.... China, in its own interest, is seeking cooperation with the United

States for many reasons, including the need to close the gap between its own developed and developing regions, the imperative of adjusting its political institutions to the accelerating economic and technological revolutions; and the potentially catastrophic impact of a Cold War with the United States on the continued raising of the standard of living, on which the legitimacy of the government depends.

But it does not follow from this that any damage to China caused by a Cold War would benefit America. We would have few followers anywhere in Asia. Asian countries would continue trading with China. Whatever happens, China will not disappear. The American interest in cooperative relations with China is for the pursuit of a stable international system. Preemption is not a feasible policy toward a country of China's magnitude. It cannot be in our interest to have new generations in China grow up with a perception of a permanently and inherently hostile United States. It cannot be in China's interests to be perceived in America as being exclusively focused on its own narrow domestic or Asian interests. ... As a new century begins, the relations between China and the United States may well determine whether our children will live in turmoil even worse than the 20th century's or will witness a new world order compatible with universal aspirations for peace and progress.[33]

Fallacies in America's Republican and Democratic Parties' China Mindsets

Henry Kissinger stated in 1998:

> Republicans see China as a threat; Democrats view it as a laboratory for the spread of American values. Both view China through the prism of their party's experiences over the past thirty years. Unfortunately, too many Republicans have substituted China for the collapsed Soviet Union and seek to deal with it by the methods that accelerated the collapse of the Soviet empire: diplomatic confrontation, economic ostracism, and ideological warfare. Too many Democrats act

as if the sole goal of American policy should be to replicate our institutions and principles in China, even at the cost of many of our other interests at stake in Asia and without regard to the complexities of Chinese history.[34]

Fallacies Arising from Americans seeing China as a Threat and Laboratory for the Spread of American Values

There are many dangerous fallacies that result from what Kissinger described in his statement above:

1. Aggressive American foreign policies that seek to affect the stability of China's political, economic, or social systems are unrealistic and counterproductive in attempting to make China more like America.

2. American foreign and domestic policies based on China being perceived or treated as a threat or laboratory for the spread of American values are not in America's national security or economic interests.

3. Americans' ideological belief in majority-rule democracy is one that America itself does not practice or at least is perceived internationally to not practice.[36]

4. America has exhibited understandable intolerance of other governments seeking to interfere with America's political system. But, America has repeatedly interfered with democratically, elected governments that it did not favor.[37]

5. Without a genuine global partnership of America and China, the growth of China's economy could undermine Americans' belief in their system of government, and America's economic interests and national security.

6. American ideological assertiveness ignores other societies' right of self-determination. In China's case, 300 million

Americans should not ignore the right of 1.3 billion Chinese to determine for themselves what type of government, economy, society, and culture they want.

7. At the core of American democracy is a requirement of the tolerance of the rights and opinions of others.

8. Notwithstanding Americans idealogy, there is a limit to the human, political, and financial costs Americans will willingly bear, which in the 1950s, 1960s, and 1970s was tested and measured in America's involvement in the civil wars in Korea and Vietnam on China's border.

To facilitate a genuine and sustainable partnership between America and China, each must accept the other's need for self-determination. Ironically, such tolerance of the other nation's differences may in itself facilitate the two societies having fewer and fewer differences over time.

The Reality That America Is using a Self-Defeating Zero- Sum-Game Approach

During his 2000 election campaign, President George W. Bush described China as a "strategic competitor" whose ambitions for global influence must be contained. Like Presidents Reagan and Clinton, President Bush came to office convinced that if he set tougher rules about engaging China, the Chinese would change their behavior. Presidents Reagan and Clinton came to abandon that view, and President George W. Bush seems to be being moved along in a similar reappraisal.[38] He promised in his second inaugural address to confront "every ruler in every nation" that resists the tide of freedom.[39] But the relationship with China is increasingly important to America. In 2006, President Bush characterized America's relationship with China as "complicated" and said "China and the United States share extensive common strategic interests."[40] Those common strategic interests and China's economic power require a collaborative breakthrough, which has not yet occurred, but must occur.

America and China's leaders must directly collaborate in real time to deal effectively with increasingly complex geopolitical dangers. Diplomacy carried out by press conference is not a prudent way for the world's current and emerging superpowers to communicate effectively. The speed and seriousness of "real time" daily events throughout the world require a committed and formalized partnership between America and China and therefore between their Presidents.

America's political leaders need to see more than their traditional zero-sum view of America's relationship with China. The American government increasingly needs the Chinese government's help. For example, America needs China's help in dealing with North Korea, where China has the most influence and controls its oil supply; with Iran, where China is a major oil customer; and with America's trade deficit with China and many other complex issues. President Bush appears unlikely to get the fullest support of China with his administration's mindset. Nonetheless, each day, in many foreign and domestic matters, China is helping America.[41]

But a committed formal partnership would enormously assist America. For example, after North Korea's launch of seven missiles on July 4, 2006, the public positions of America and Japan's leaders, who called for a strong, united condemnation and major economic sanctions, contrasted with China and Russia's leaders, who did not favor the response that America and Japan wanted. China and Russia, North Korea's neighbors, fear that the North Korean government will collapse. America and Japan, which do not have borders with North Korea, are less concerned about such a regime change.

Chinese Ambassador to the UN, Wang Guangya, being interviewed after a Security Council meeting regarding China's role in the North Korean nuclear issue.

If a committed global partnership was in place, America and China might have more ability to manage world affairs. The July 2006 North Korean missile launch was an outrage to the leaders of America, Japan, Russia, and China. Each had applied pressure that proved to be ineffective in preventing North Korea from moving further along a dangerous course.[42] As committed global partners, America and China would make the world that much more governable. Lacking a committed partnership with America, China is entering a more dangerous alliance with Russia, which will take a different approach to world problems than America does. China could take greater risks for America if America were collaborating with it in all geopolitical issues than China can in the current America and China relationship.

It is hard to imagine either America or China dealing successfully with future challenges without a committed and genuine geopolitical, economic, and business partnership. A new mindset and framework is required for working out solutions. What is preventing a win-win partnership is America's political leaders' rejection of it.

In a meeting in 2005, President Hu departed from the prepared remarks in his briefing books and candidly told President Bush that fighting China's political corruption, rural unrest, widening differences in wealth, and severe pollution consumes nearly all his time. President Hu said that such domestic problems left China with neither the will nor the means to challenge America's dominance in world affairs.[43] President Bush reportedly responded well to President Hu's uncharacteristic candor. The overture is part of the Chinese government's effort to reduce American anxiety about China's growing economic, political, and military power.[44]

On April 19, 2006, at a lunch and meeting in Seattle Washington, President Hu said that China and America "enjoy extensive common interests" and could avoid major problems in their relationships if they "avoided politicizing" the issues that divide them. "China and the United States are fully capable of settling problems that have occurred in the course of business growth, and keeping their business relations on a sound track," President Hu said.[45]

President Hu met with President Bush five times in 2005 and 2006. The meeting on April 20, 2006, was the first White House meeting granted by the American Administration to President Hu since he became China's top leader in 2002. The Chinese government called it a "state visit." But, the Bush Administration described it as a "working visit" or "visit." It was not recognized by the American Administration as the "full state visit" that President Hu wanted.[46] In spite of the importance of their meeting, given **America's need for China's help**, President Bush was the first American President since the founding of the People's Republic of China in 1949 not to accord the visiting head of state of China a "state dinner."

The reception for President Hu at the White House was also jarred by a White House announcer confusing the official name of the Peoples' Republic of China with that of Taiwan, the seat of power of Kuomintang Party, which lost the Chinese Revolution in 1949.

Chinese officials made it clear they felt slighted by President Bush's decision not to offer the customary honor of a "state dinner." President Bush did not extend this customary honor, although such a dinner is of great importance in the Chinese culture. This persistent refusal of the respect due the head of state of a major world power is hard to understand.

Instead, in a lower-profile lunch and a ninety-minute meeting, President Bush presented demands regarding how China should operate its economy and political system, urged China to speed up its reform process, raised issues of controversy between the two nations, coached China on the role it should play in the world as "a responsible stakeholder", and sought China's help with major domestic and foreign policy problems America faces, without the opportunity being granted for Presidents Hu and Bush to have a press conference together or make common statements.[47]

President Hu's speech at the White House was interrupted by heckling by a member of a dissident group in China, the Falun Gong spiritual sect, who was accredited by the White House as a reporter.[48] The Secret Service did not immediately react to the security breach and took a minute or two to arrest and remove the heckler. A member of the Bush Administration's National Security Council told reporters that President Bush expressed his regrets. The advisor said "I would be extremely surprised if the Chinese blame us for this".[49] Other security analysts said the security breach might heighten the distrust between the two nations.[50] The heckler faced a misdemeanor charge of intimidating, coercing, threatening, and harassing a foreign official, but later "reached a deal with prosecutors under which all charges against her will be dropped."[51]

As the White House welcoming event ended, photographs showed President Bush first steering President Hu off the podium and then, realizing that he had done so prematurely, grabbing the Chinese leader by the arm and pulling him back into the proper position.[52]

The visit produced little of substance for the main items on either the American or Chinese leaders' agenda, except the photo opportunity President Hu wanted at the White House with President Bush. The tension and frustration of both sides was unmistakable. President Bush's frustration was evident in his voice.[53] The years of persisting in the insulting refusal to show the respect normally due to President Hu as a head of state in a state dinner, the White House announcer's reference to Taiwan, rather than the People's Republic of China, the breach of security by the heckler, the dropping of charges against her, and the photos of President Bush manhandling President Hu are not helpful to America obtaining China's full help in solving America's geopolitical and economic problems.

President Bush, Vice President Cheney, and many cabinet members have visited China and were not subjected to insulting or embarrassing episodes of this kind. The Chinese are not likely to believe that the world's most powerful nation could botch a formal White House ceremony of this importance through ineptness. Some of the insults, such as the refusal of the state dinner were deliberate. Whether the others were deliberate or resulted from ineptness, America is not presenting a collaborative approach to China, while seeking a collaborative approach from China. Fortunately, China is persisting with its wish to have a collaborative approach with America and continues to quietly help America.

54

Presidents Bush and Hu at the White House on April 20, 2006 offering contrasting win-win and zero-sum-game approaches for the peace and prosperity of the 21st century's leading capitalist nations.

At the same time, there are reports that the Bush Administration "behind the scenes is busy preparing for a possible military conflict with China" and "to better gird itself is reaching out to a willing partner: Japan."[55] China's ambassador to America, Mr. Zhou Wenzhong, has indicated that China does not want to see the America-Japan alliance expanded "beyond what is needed for Japan's defense."[56] However, the trend is clearly, in the Chinese Ambassador's view, "to enlarge the scope of the joint defense. The question… is whether they think that Taiwan falls within that responsibility."[57] China and Japan have a long history of bitterness and mutual suspicion. The depth of hatred in China towards Japan is very dangerous because of the Japanese invasion of China and atrocities in World War II.

Behind the concern of the American military about China is the realization that in time, because of American budgetary constraints, China's naval presence may outweigh that of America's in the seas around China.

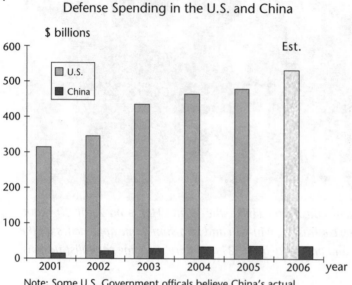

Defense Spending in the U.S. and China   58

Note: Some U.S. Government officals believe China's actual
defense spending is higher than its offical figure.

Source: Office of management and budget; globalsecurity.org

In the War on Terror, America has moved to aggressive "preemptive strike" and "regime change" policies, rather than a defensive military philosophy of deterrence. Some observers believe the doctrine of preemptive strikes risks accelerating the crises that it is meant to avert.[59] The CIA, Pentagon, and other American observers recently raised alarms about China's military expenditure, which has been growing by 10% per year in recent years. But, China's military spending is less than 1% of the world's military expenditure while America's is 51%.[60] America's military spending dwarf's China's and is accelerating many times more quickly than China's military spending. The graph above compares America and China's military spending since 2000.

America may unnecessarily goad China into an accelerated military buildup. Bernard Cole of the America's National War College notes, "It's not really that the Chinese are doing something evil, bad or unnecessary, but that their path is on the upswing, and ours is on the downswing." "There is a self-fulfilling prophecy element here." In Mr. Cole's view: "U.S. military planners must have something to plan against, while China is a new rising power that needs to modernize its military."[61]

There are some signs of the beginning of a new American mindset reflecting current realities and the limitations of even American military power. Thomas P. M. Barnet regularly advises the Office of the Secretary of Defense, Special Operations Command and the Joint Forces Command. Barnett has asserted in two influential recent books, *The Pentagon's New Map: War and Peace in the Twenty-first Century*[62] and *Blueprint For Action: A Future Worth Creating*[63] that the training, skills, and resources in fighting wars are not what it requires for post combat peacekeeping, a mission is required to protect America's national security and make a dangerous world safer.

The Reality That a Partnership Between America and China Can Be Achieved

After the collapse of the former Soviet Union, President George H. W. Bush declared that a new world order was being born with the end of the Cold War:

> We have a vision of a new partnership of nations that transcends the Cold War. A partnership based on consultation, cooperation, and collective action, especially through international and regional organizations. A partnership united by principle and the rule of law and supported by an equitable sharing of both cost and commitment. A partnership whose goals are to increase

democracy, increase prosperity, increase the peace, and reduce arms.[64]

The expansion of democracy, in many Americans' view, is a goal for all nations and is a driver of the American vision of the world. President Clinton stated:

> In a new era of peril and opportunity, our overriding purpose must be to expand and sustain the world's community of market-based democracies. During the Cold War, we sought to contain a threat to the survival of free institutions. Now we seek to enlarge the circle of nations that live under those free institutions for our dream is of a day when the opinions and energies of every person in the world will be given full expression in a world of thriving democracies that cooperate with each other and live in peace.[65]

Former American Defense Secretary Donald Rumsfeld, who has long been hawkish regarding China, voiced America's alarm in 2005 at the rise in Chinese defense spending. However, in 2006, Mr. Rumsfeld's tone began to shift after a worsening of America's diplomatic and military situation in Iran, Iraq, and Afghanistan, and political challenges in Venezuela and elsewhere in South America. Even Mr. Rumsfeld began signaling an American desire for a more cooperative security relationship with China.[66] The military and geopolitical logic of not confronting China may be gaining currency within the American government. Secretary of State Condleezza Rice, who favors a conciliatory approach, met with China's leadership to discuss America's fear of China's growing military power and the creation of a new alliance of China and Russia. The Chinese leadership indicated that China would not follow the path of aggression that Japan followed in attacking America in World War II.

The Reality of China's Win-Win Approach

Having personally suffered the economic hardships during the leadership of Mao Zedong, China's subsequent leaders have focused on economic development. The Chinese government shifted to capitalist and "peaceful rise" mindsets in the 1980s, 1990s, and in this decade. Before becoming China's top leader in 2002 as head of the Chinese government, the ruling party, and the Chinese military, Hu Jintao had no military experience and little international experience.[67] He spent much of his career running remote inland territories in China and had made few trips abroad. At a luncheon in Seattle on April 19, 2006 with American corporate leaders, Hu Jintao hugged Henry Kissinger, who is revered in China for his role in re-establishing political and trade relations between America and China. That is a very unusual gesture, given President Hu's normally aloof style and in Chinese culture in general. It reflects the Chinese leader's spontaneous reaction to a known friend in the unfamiliar world outside China. Few if any have lived outside China.

Looking beyond the slights and heightening of tensions by the American administration, President Hu emphasized economic cooperation in his April 20, 2006, discussion with President Bush, saying that it provided an important foundation for China-U.S. relations. President Hu told President Bush:

> We are ready to work with the U.S. in the spirit of seeing mutual benefit and *win-win outcomes* to properly address each other's concerns and facilitate sound and steady economic co-operation and trade.[68] (*Emphasis added*)

After his meeting with President Bush at the White House, President Hu met with several members of the United States Congress. They liked the Chinese leader and commented that he shares their views on the threats and opportunities facing the world. Republican Congressman Mark Kirk of Illinois said the Chinese leader responded very favorably when he broached the idea of setting up a hot line linking the Pentagon with China's military command.[69] The collision of a Chinese jet fighter and American spy plane in 2001 and the bombing of the Chinese Embassy in the Bosnia War created dangerous spikes in tensions that enflamed Chinese public opinion and reflected the belief that such events were not accidental.

President Hu chose Yale University to deliver a speech on April 21, 2006, to convey his views of China's past and future so Americans would understand what China's goals are:

> China firmly pursues a strategy of opening-up for mutual benefit and *win-win outcomes*. It genuinely wishes to enter into extensive cooperation with other countries. It is inclusive and is eager to draw on the strength of other civilizations to pursue peace and development through cooperation, and play its part in building a harmonious world of enduring peace and common prosperity.[70] *(Emphasis added)*

Unfortunately, America's political leadership may not yet be as interested in establishing a "win-win" relationship.[71] President Hu Jintao also said:

> China and the United States are both countries of vast territory where many ethnic groups co-exist and different cultures intermingle. Both our two peoples are hard working and talented. Due to different historical backgrounds and national conditions, there are differences between China and the United States. But this enables us to learn from each other and draw on each other's strength. Closer China-U.S. cooperation serves the fundamental interests of our two countries and peoples and is of far-reaching significance for peace and development of the world.

Vast as it is, the Pacific Ocean has not stood in the way of exchanges and cooperation between our two peoples over the past two hundred years, and many moving episodes of mutual learning and mutual help between our two peoples who represent different civilizations have been recorded. In the twenty-seven years since the establishment of diplomatic relations in 1979, China-U.S. relations have maintained steady momentum of growth despite twists and turns on the way, bringing tremendous benefits to both countries and peoples.[72]

The Reality That China is Acting Unilaterally Using Win-Win Strategies

The Chinese government is patiently seeking a win-win rather than a zero-sum-game relationship with America. It is acting unilaterally to ameliorate entrenched problems that could impede such a relationship. For example, the first Cross-strait Economic and Trade Forum in Beijing on April 14 and 15, 2006, achieved seven-point joint proposals and fifteen new policies for the Chinese Mainland to promote economic and trade relations across the Taiwan Strait.

73

Kuomintang Honorary Chairman Lein Chan and President Hu Jintao at the April 15–16, 2006, meeting between the leaders of winning and losing parties in China's 1949 Revolution. The meeting reduced tensions and strengthened trade and economic ties across the Taiwan Strait.

Top Chinese government officials attended the forum from the Chinese Communist Party (CCP) and Taiwan's opposition party, the Kuomintang (KMT), the CCP's adversary in the 1949 Chinese Revolution, and the People First Party and New Party, and economic and business people. KMT Honorary Chairman Lien Chan, who headed the KMT delegation, said at the press conference at the end of the forum, "These policies, along with the consensus reached at the forum, are more than we expected."[74]

KMT Vice Chairman, Wu Po-hsiung, said at the forum's closing ceremony that with these policies, the Taiwanese people will feel the sincerity of the Mainland.[75] The policy package covered issues related to Taiwan's agricultural and aquatic products, cross-strait agricultural cooperation, recognition of university diplomas issued in Taiwan, visits between mainlanders and Taiwanese, and Taiwanese becoming customs agents and being engaged in medical services on the mainland.

The new Chinese government policies may erode President Chen Shuiban's base of supporters in the southern part of Taiwan.[76] Chen Shuiban won the Presidency of Taiwan in 2000, ending 50 years of KMT's monopoly on power. He is known for opposing closer ties to the mainland, which considers Taiwan a breakaway province.

The CCP and KMT jointly issued a press communiqué on April 29, 2006, that states that the two parties have reached a five-point consensus for "promoting peace and development across the Taiwan Strait." According to the communiqué, "the two parties have agreed to work together to promote an earlier restoration of cross-strait talks, the formal end of hostilities across the Taiwan Strait, all-around economic and trade relations and "three direct links" across the Taiwan Strait, discussions of Taiwan's participations in international activities and the establishment of a regular platform for party-to party exchange between the CCP and KMT parties."[77]

Chinese press reports indicated that these new policies toward Taiwan were a gift, on the eve of President Hu Jintao's state visit to America, trying to convey to America that the Chinese government has the sincerity to promote cross-strait economic and trade relations, communication, and an end to hostility between Mainland China and Taiwan.[78]

On June 13, 2006, the Taiwan government unexpectedly announced it had reached a deal with Beijing to allow many charter flights to and from Mainland China.[79] People traveling between the two could not previously do so directly. The Chinese government is making Taiwan an official tourist destination for Mainland Chinese and pushing for further regularization of travel.[80] On August 1, 2006, the Taiwanese government announced new policies to liberalize cross-Taiwan-Strait economic ties with China, lifting key restrictions on semiconductor technology investment and on business travel to Taiwan by Mainland Chinese. Further reforms are expected. Taiwan law limits mainland investments by Taiwanese companies to 20 to 40 percent of a company's net worth. But, more than 70 percent of Taiwan's outward foreign direct investment in 2005 went to Mainland China.[81]

The Reality That China Is Improving Economic Human Rights

Hank Greenberg, Chairman and CEO of American International Group, commented in 2000:

> You have to look at the facts. China is a big country. It covers a huge part of the globe. It has 1.3 billion people. China is making dramatic progress, with change in almost every facet of human life. If you just go back to 1975, when

I first went to China, and look at the progress made since then, China today is like another planet. Not only is the physical infrastructure of China changing, but also the lifestyle of the people has probably never been better at any time in their 5000-year history. Having said that, China still has a long way to go. But the speed at which they are making progress in every facet of life is remarkable. Even for those who criticize China's human rights policies, if they go back, look at China in 1975, and then look again at China today, the progress including in the field of human rights, has been enormous. When you feed and clothe and shelter 1,300 million people, that is human rights, compared to what it was before. What China cannot tolerate is chaos. Chaos would destroy China. To create political instability in a country with that mass of population, until there is further progress and maturity in a political and social sense, would be quite wrong. Change will come in China's time, not on or of a timetable of external forces.[82]

President Hu Jintao reviewed for Americans the progress China has made in its reforms and goals during his speech at Yale:

... I would like to speak to you about China's development strategy and future against the backdrop of the evolution of Chinese civilization and China's current development. I hope this will help you gain an understanding of China.

...Between 1978 and 2005, China's GDP grew from US$147.3 to US$2.22257 trillion. Its import and export volume went up from US$20.5 billion to US$1.4221 trillion, and its foreign exchange reserve soared from US$167 million to US$818.9 billion.... On the other hand, I need to point out that despite the success in its development, China remains the world's largest developing country with a per capita GDP ranking behind the 100th place. The Chinese people are yet to live a well-off life, and China still faces daunting challenges in its development endeavor.... We aim to raise China's GDP to US$4 trillion by 2020.... By then, China's economy will be better developed; and its democracy will be further enhanced.

> We are pursuing today a people-oriented approach toward development because we believe that development must be for the people and by the people, and its benefit should be shared among the people. We care about people's value, rights and interests, freedom, the quality of their life, and their development potential and happiness index because our goal is to realize the all-round development of the people."[83]

The defining and protection of human rights is evolving gradually in China. It also evolved gradually in America and its evolution there continues even today in ebbs and flows.

The Reality That America Does Not Have the Moral Authority to Demand That China Adopt America's Protection of Human Rights

The development of human rights defined and protected by law is a defining characteristic of American civilization, which has an inspiring but blemished record, marred by the American Civil War and 200 years of human rights violations and struggles that continue today. The United Nations human rights committee rebuked America in July 2006 for violation of human rights and international law in America and abroad.[84] Some American observers assert that America's record of human rights violations is the worst in the world.[85] One of the earliest examples of the incremental development of concepts of human rights in America is the Bill of Rights. It was left out of the U.S. Constitution initially in order to achieve agreement to create the United States. The Bill of Rights was adopted in a separate step.

The Fallacy That American-Style Majority Rule Democracy in China Is in America's National Security Interest

As we have seen, America's political leaders and the American people's vision of the world sees the promotion of the spread of democratic institutions as a key goal of American foreign policy. This seems self-evidently laudatory to Americans. Americans may, as a result, overlook the rights of other nations, such as China, to self-determination in evolving their political institutions and fostering their economic and social development as their priority rather than the creation of American-style democracy. Democracy has worked well in America, so it is assumed by many Americans that it will work well everywhere at any time. However, China has a different history than America and is at an earlier stage in building a modern economy and nation. The irony is that China is more stable and friendlier towards America, Japan, and Taiwan under the leadership of the Chinese Communist Party today than China would be if it adopted American style democracy.

The Fallacy That an Unstable, Unsuccessful China Is Good for America

China is one of the most important engines of world economic growth. The International Monetary Fund estimated that the global economy would increase by 5% in 2004 and 4.3% in 2005. Since the beginning of 2005, the world economy continues to recover despite the lower growth rate of GDP in 2004. China's economy maintained a fast growth with a GDP of 9.5% in 2004 and 2005, and above 11% in the first half of 2006. China's GDP increased from US$1.1 trillion in 2000 to US$1.6 trillion in 2005.[86]

In 2004, China became the third largest country in world trade. Its international trade volume was US$1154.8 billion, an increase of 35.7% per year. In 2005, it grew 23.2% to US$1.422 trillion.[87] China is the largest recipient in the world of foreign direct investment, receiving US$60.6 billion in 2004. China had the second largest foreign exchange reserves in the world, which were

US$659.1 billion at the end of March 2005, exceeded US$1 trillion in 2006, and reached US$1.3 trillion in March 2007.[88] Much of China's foreign-currency reserves are helping to finance the United States fiscal deficit. This has a profound impact on the global economy and a direct impact on the US economy. The stability and growth of China is vital to the American economy and the global economy's stability.

8

Leadership Failure and American Resentment and Fear of China

Overview

It is obviously true and compelling that if America and China's political and business leaders are unable to collaborate successfully, both countries will easily move into military competition, confrontation and armed conflict in a lose-lose outcome.

The Reality of Leadership Failure if America Cannot Accommodate China's Economic Development

In China, hard-line, centrists, and reform factions struggle for input in Chinese-American relations, while in America, the President, Congress, Senate, media and electorate all impact the delicate formulation of America-Chinese relations.

In July 2005, Major General Zhu Chenghu, a dean at China's National Defense University, made a statement, which China's foreign ministry quickly recanted, that China would be prepared to sacrifice all the cities west of Xian in a nuclear exchange with America.[1]

In 2006, two Americans, Jeb Babbin and Edward Timperlake, published the book *Showdown: Why China Wants War With*

The United States,[2] which was described on its cover as "A thrilling and chilling look at what war with China might look like." The book presents various scenarios of how a war between America and China might arise. In that respect, it is a useful guide to how such a war can be "won" by being prevented by America and China's leadership. America can do without the "thrill" of armed conflict with China. Such books reflect a 20th century Cold War mindset that is wrong and dangerous in dealing with 21st century capitalist China. China is a peace-loving nation, which built a wall—still in place a thousand years later—seeking, often unsuccessfully, to protect itself from foreign aggression.

The Cold War between communism and capitalism in the 20th century cost trillions of dollars, redirected a high proportion of scarce global intellectual capital into weapons system research, and created a climate of fear[3] that some are now trying to use to poison the relationship between American and Chinese capitalism. Military analysts worry that armed conflict in the future will be unrestricted and fought on many fronts in multi-dimensional ways that combine military and non-military forms, including terrorism, drug trafficking, environmental degradation, and computer-virus and other attacks that ignore boundaries and restrictions.[4]

There is unnecessary risk of failure in the current ad hoc operation of America and China's relationship. For example, Chinese Premier Zhu Rongji visited President Clinton in 1997 seeking to finalize China's admission to the World Trade Organization. During the visit unnecessary difficulty in reaching effective decisions occured. Premier Zhu commented with frustration during a joint White House press conference with President Clinton:

> In my view, the gap between the two sides is really already not very significant. If you wish to hear some honest words, the problem does not lie with some big gap, but with the political atmosphere."[5]

President Clinton had tried to temper America's media's attitude before Premier Zhu Rongji arrived, saying:

> We cannot allow a healthy argument to lead us toward a campaign-driven cold war with China. No one could possibly gain from that except for the most rigid, backward-looking elements in China itself.[6]

The Chinese respect and admire the character or "right spirit" of America when it manifests itself. In Chapters 12 and 15 we will examine the interest groups in America seeking a campaign-driven cold war with China. China's political leaders do not want trade war, cold war, or armed conflict with America.[7] They want to use China's economic success and resources to continue to eliminate poverty in China.

What types of leaders would come to power in China if American policies hostile to China's emergence from poverty were successful? If China's economic development falters, the resulting social instability is likely to produce a dangerous dynamic in China's government, foreign policy, and Sino-American relations globally. China's economy must grow at 8% per year to avoid faltering. China has a recent history under Mao Zedong of ideological and militaristic leadership. As a result, China has focused on economic development and returned to its innate entrepreneurial and capitalist mindset.

There is nothing worth having in America seeking to undermine China's economic development. There is a consensus currently among the Chinese government and people for peaceful economic development. China's political and business leaders recognize that peace with America is essential to China's prosperity and success. The Chinese are a shy people that do not wear their hearts on their sleeves or easily communicate their feelings to foreigners.

The Fallacy of "Amero-centric" Analysis of China

Joseph Nye, Jr. recognizes in *The Paradox Of American Power*[8] that:

> ...the "rise of China is a misnomer." "Reemergence" would
> be more accurate, since by size and history the Middle
> Kingdom[9] has long been a major power in East Asia.
> Technically and economically, China was the world's leader
> (though without global reach) from the year 500 to 1500.
> Only in the last half millennium was it overtaken by Europe
> and America. The Asian Development Bank has calculated
> that in 1820, at the beginning of the industrial age, Asia
> made up an estimated three-fifths of world product. By 1940,
> this had fallen to one-fifth, even though the region was
> home to three-fifths of the world's population. Rapid
> economic growth has brought that back to two-fifths today,
> and the bank speculates that Asia could return to its histori-
> cal levels by 2025. Asia, of course, includes Japan, India,
> Korea, and others, but China will eventually play the largest
> role. Its high annual growth rate of 8 to 9 percent led to
> a remarkable tripling of its GNP in the last two decades of the
> twentieth century. This dramatic economic performance,
> along with its Confucian culture, enhanced China's soft
> power in the region.[10]

Joseph Nye Jr. offers what may be characterized as a traditional
"Amero-centric" analysis, which some observers may see as myopic
and internally contradictory:

> Almost every commentator has for some years been regard-
> ing China as the likeliest suspect for future "peer competi-
> tor" status. Polls show that half of the American public
> thinks China will pose the biggest challenge to U.S. world
> power status in the next hundred years. ...Nonetheless,
> China has a long way to go and faces many obstacles to its
> development. At the beginning of the twenty-first century,
> the American economy is about twice the size of China's. If
> the American economy grows at a 2% rate and China's

grows at 6%, the two economies would be equal in size sometime around 2020. Even so, the two economies would be equivalent in size but not equal in composition. China would still have a vast underdeveloped countryside—indeed, assuming 6% growth and only 2% American growth, China would not be equal to the United States in per capita income until somewhere between 2056 and 2095 (depending on the measures of comparison). In terms of political power, per capita income provides a more accurate measure of the sophistication of an economy. The Asian Development Bank projects Chinese per capita income will reach 38% of that of the United States by 2025, about the same level relative to the United States that South Korea reached in 1990. That is impressive growth, but is a long way from equality...[11]

The assumption that America's economy will grow at 2% and that China's will grow at 6%, rather than at over 8% for decades, may not be seen to be correct in retrospect. Additionally, the comparison of China in 2025 to South Korea in 1990 seems to overlook many differences between the economic development characteristics of each. The "Knowledge Revolution" and "Globalization 3.0" had not really begun in earnest in 1990, but will be big economic growth factors from 2005 to 2025 and beyond. Comparing previous eras' economic development assumptions and results in the "Knowledge Revolution" and "Globalization 3.0" period is comparing very different eras. It is open to question, also, as to whether China was "overtaken," or whether, after inventing most of the key inventions that underpinned the Industrial Revolution in Europe and America, China deliberately chose to chart its evolution according to its own values, along a different and entirely insular, and perhaps in retrospect, unfortunate path in the 19th and 20th centuries.

Accepting the Right of the Chinese to Escape Poverty with Capitalism

"Genius" is seen in things that are obviously true, compelling, and that no one thought of. The genius of the Chinese government, the resourcefulness and energy of the Chinese people, their way of doing things, and capitalism with Chinese characteristics, changed China from one of the poorest and least economically competitive countries in 1978 with a GDP of US$64.7 billion to the world's most competitive country in 2005 with a GDP of US$1.6 trillion. What China achieved should be the basis of mutual respect between China and America, particularly if looked at as the astounding management and entrepreneurial feat that it is.

Although China's success frightens Americans, it does not take genius to see that the 21st century must not be defined by trade war and armed conflict between America and China. It takes good-will between 300 million and 1.3 billion people. The American and Chinese peoples must produce leaders able to prevent conflict.

In order for America and China to become genuine partners in the 21st century, it is essential that Americans recognize and accept the genius of the Chinese. Chapters 3, 4, 5, 6, 11, and 13 examine China's achievements in order to assist Americans in doing so.

After securing China's sovereignty with the Communist Revolution in 1949, China's leadership again sealed off China from much of the world for 30 years, partially by choice but also due to isolation imposed by Western powers. American governments, although not all Americans, were hostile to China. For many years, an American embargo against China was so absolute that a single bag of grain would violate the embargo rules. Some observers chose to forget about the trade embargo against China and blame China for its isolation.

From 1949 to 1979, under Mao Zedong, China's government focused on solidifying an authoritative national governing mechanism, namely China's Communist Party, for uniting and making China self-sufficient. The rapid integration of America and China's economies from 1978 to 2005 and the globalization of Chinese companies that is emerging today, so that Chinese companies can remain competitive, is driving the relationship of America and China to a point where the choice between the roads to economic and military conflict or collaboration must occur.

Today, American consumers increasingly like Chinese products. Oded Shenkar notes:

> Chinese products would not be on so many retail shelves if potential customers were not willing to buy them. Leo J. Shapiro and Associates, a Chicago based survey research firm, studied the attitudes of Americans towards China and Chinese products in May 2002. A nationally projected sample of 450 U.S. households were surveyed about their interest in buying Chinese products.... The interest was moderate, with more than half of respondents showing a high-to-mid level interest but more than 40 percent not showing an interest. These proportions will probably change as Chinese products become more known and uncertainty regarding quality diminishes, though other factors (such as animosity) may dampen a growing enthusiasm.
>
> That interest is high in electronics and computers and not only in arts and clothing...suggests that China is beginning to acquire a reputation for providing reasonable quality in technology products. Indeed, when people are asked why they are interested in Chinese products, cheap price still comes first but is immediately followed by positive perceptions regarding product quality and technological experience as well as by positive experience with Chinese products. ... This perception of Chinese products as providing good quality at a reasonable price is noteworthy because it is not far from the value proposition that many global customers attach to U.S. made products. This suggests that, down the road, "made-in-China" goods will

be in direct competition with American products in world markets.

[The graph below] lists the reasons why people would *not* buy Chinese products. [It] suggests that poor quality remains a major concern, which is consistent with the Chinese Ministry of Commerce's observation that foreign quality standards in developed-country markets pose the biggest obstacle to increase Chinese exports. This is immediately followed however, by non-product-related issues such as the perceived treatment of Chinese employees or concern for U.S. jobs—both of which also play an important role in the purchasing decision. This suggests that the decision to buy made-in-China products may become entangled in social and political considerations. Marketers know that animosity can play an important role in purchasing decisions. It is quite possible that such animosity may develop toward China based on perceptions regarding anything from working conditions to geopolitical development (say aggression toward Taiwan). A Zogby International poll of likely voters released on September 30, 2003, shows China at the top of a list of non-allied countries, ahead of Saudi Arabia and France. An earlier poll (released June 13, 2003) found that more than 80 percent saw China as a serious threat to U.S. national security.[12]

What is it about products from China that makes you think they would not be so good to buy?   13

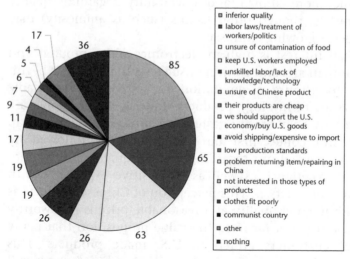

source: Leo J. Shapiro & Associates

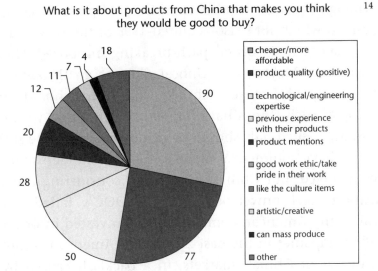

What is it about products from China that makes you think   14
they would be good to buy?

- ▣ cheaper/more affordable
- ■ product quality (positive)
- ▢ technological/engineering expertise
- ▢ previous experience with their products
- ■ product mentions
- ▣ good work ethic/take pride in their work
- ▣ like the culture items
- ▢ artistic/creative
- ■ can mass produce
- ▣ other

The Reality of America's Declining Economic Competitiveness and CNOOC Jingoism

Agonizing reappraisals of deeply entrenched feelings and beliefs are a typical prelude to mindset changes. In August 2005, *Fortune* summed up the sudden awareness of the change China is causing in America:

> It's a crisis of confidence unlike anything America has felt in a generation. Residents of tiny Newton, Iowa, wake up to the distressing news that a Chinese firm—what's it called? Haier? That's Chinese?—wants to buy their biggest employer, the famed, but foundering Maytag appliance company. Two days later, out of nowhere, a massive, government-owned Chinese oil company muscles into the bidding for America's Unocal. The very next day a ship in Xinsha, China, loads the first Chinese-made cars bound for the West, where they'll compete with the products of Detroit's struggling giants.
>
> All in one week. And only two months earlier a Chinese company most Americans had never heard of took over the personal computer business formerly owned—and mismanaged into billions of dollars of losses—by the great IBM.[15]

Although Legend's acquisition of the IBM personal computer business (in which IBM also acquired 19% of the new company Lenovo) succeeded, other path-breaking proposed Chinese acquisitions of Maytag and Unocal did not go through. That Chinese companies make such acquisition bids should not be surprising as such things have happened in the past with other nations. More such bids should be made and should be successful if they have commercial merit to the shareholders and companies involved. But Chinese companies considering American acquisitions feel unwelcome after CNOOC's failed bid for Unocal. Many American companies have invested in or bought Chinese companies in the past 20 years. If American companies are shut out of China's markets, in a backlash caused by the blocked CNOOC bid, their ability to compete globally will be weakened.

The politicization of Chinese acquisitions by jingoistic American companies, interest groups, and politicians should trouble American political and business leaders. But it does not trouble a sufficient number of them yet. Chevron successfully used nationalism and national security jingoism to create fatal political opposition to CNOOC's aquisition. Then Chevron asked Unocal's shareholders to accept a lower bid instead of raising Chevron's bid. In doing so, Chevron successfully asked Unocal's shareholders to ignore capitalist market norms. The normal goals of America's capitalist game, which it plays globally, include making money and creating shareholder value. America's capitalism's fairness and charisma is damaged by such hypocrisy.

Some observers will say that American capitalism is not, nor does it purport to be, fair. Its charisma comes from its sustained success and power, not its fairness. That view must deal with the fact that suddenly, early in the 21st century, the power of American capitalism is in jeopardy. If America can no longer depend on the raw power of its globally dominant companies and capitalist economy, Americans should not further undermine America's and American capitalism's charisma by highlighting its unfairness. What we term "CNOOC jingoism" harms America's reputation and the economic competitiveness of American companies.

The Reality That American Companies' Global Competitiveness Is Enhanced by an Enhanced America and China Relationship

The international competitiveness of American companies requires the relationship of America and China to be stable. Randy Yeh, Chairman of Lucent Technologies China Co. Ltd has noted:

> For any American company, whether it is low tech, medium tech, or high tech, a sound, stable, and good relationship between the U.S. and PRC (Peoples' Republic of China) is key to business success in China. Since I took over as head of operations here, I have tried to show that Lucent is not just a strong global high tech company, but also a friend of China. At Lucent, we try to help foster a more constructive relationship between the United States, the great superpower, and PRC, the great emerging superpower....It doesn't hurt anyone to increase communications...when we increase communications, we have a better understanding of each other's position. While we may continue to have differences, and they may sometimes be substantial, we might still find them acceptable. We try to demonstrate that we take a long-term approach to China and that we have China's interest at heart, as well. In 1997, we established two Bell Laboratories in China, one in Beijing, and the other in Shanghai. Bell Labs, which in our view has the finest communications technology in the world, has received eight Nobel prizes to date.
> President Jiang Zemin has visited Bell Laboratories on two occasions. On the most recent visit, in 1997, he penned his own message in Chinese calligraphy: "To launch a new sphere of cooperation in high technology." The Chinese leader has

always shown that he is willing to welcome senior Lucent executives during their visits to PRC and to discuss technology and recent innovations.[16]

The Reality That America's Response to China's Emergence from Poverty Endangers the Survival of America's Democratic System of Government

There are other fundamental issues revealed in the "CNOOC jingoism" in addition to whether America's current policy of containment of Chinese capitalism is hypocritical, unfair, and economically unwise. One is: If American capitalism and companies are unable to compete and dominate the global economy in the 21st century, will American democracy survive?

America's character and charisma globally are based not only on American economic and military power, but also on America's idealistic and ennobling Constitution, which created a government of laws with checks and balances and rights (a Rights Society), rather than a government of men not ruled by law (a Permission Society). The inspiring power of the ideas and ideals so boldly committed to in America's Constitution and championed in America's historical struggles since then define America's character at home and it's charisma globally. How strong is American democracy today and how strong will it be tomorrow? That is an issue of fundamental concern.

A question of moral principle now confronts America (and China): Are there two sets of rules in American capitalism—one for American companies and another for Chinese companies? Out of that question arises an issue of profound importance for American power: Is America becoming a "Permission Society" like China, even as Americans are exhorting China to become a "Rights Society"?

Many Americans believe that America should do all it can to block China's economic development and expansion in international business. If that "containment" strategy remains America's policy, it will increasingly harm America and threaten China. How America's leaders and 300 million people respond to China's leaders' and 1.3 billion people's pursuit of China's "Manifest Destiny" in reemerging as the world's largest economy is one of many key issues that will determine mankind's viability as a species.

Americans believe with religious zeal that it is America's democratic institutions and processes that created America's historically overwhelming productivity and competitive advantages. However, as we have seen, China's economy is poised to surpass the productivity of America's economy. This is possible, in part, because of China's lack of American-style democratic institutions and processes. The Chinese view America's productivity and competitiveness with admiration. But, it is important for Americans to recognize that China would have been hindered rather than empowered from 1979 to 2006 if it had American style democratic institutions and processes. In the long run, China will likely have to adopt parallel but very Chinese-style institutions and processes to deal with its increasingly more advanced and sophisticated economy and society. Some observers assert that China's gradual rule-making or system-design process is slowing down it's economic growth. But China's sustained economic growth is already astounding. Even at a still-early stage in it's transition from poverty to economic superpower, China's success is already having a fundamental economic, social, and political impact on America.

The Reality That America and China May be Trading Places in the 21st Century

It has been suggested that America and China may be trading places. In August 2005, a *Fortune* article titled "America Isn't Ready" pinpointed that paradigm shift assumption as a serious possibility.[17] The rise and collapse of nations are influenced by their decision-making abilities and energy of their people, and by their resources and their people's hunger for, or satiation with, better lives. The hungry, frugal, energetic capitalism of China's five-times-larger population, combined with it's Socialist Market Economy, are likely to get larger and larger. In the process, America's economy could be, but does not have to be, the loser.[18]

Kishore Mahbubani notes:

> America was probably the first major society to demonstrate that a totally non-feudal order could be built: Almost from the very beginning (apart from the slaves), American society had no class barriers. Instead, with each passing generation there were more and more success stories among the very poor. To make it against great odds was part of the American dream.
>
> This American dream is essentially the magical stardust that America has sprinkled into the eyes of many of the poor around the world. America did not intend to do this. Most Americans believe that this American dream has been confined to American shores. But as the world shrank and American TV became ubiquitous...the American way of life became known to billions. The poor were astute enough to see America's greatest strength: that it had created a social order where even the very poor had an opportunity to advance. ...
>
> Given the remarkable historical contribution that America as a society has made to other societies, it is hard to imagine how world history would have turned out if America had not been born. It is conceivable that in the late twentieth and early twenty-first century, our world could have continued with the zero sum games that

nations played with each other. Whenever one nation became powerful, it felt almost an obligation to expand, dominate, or conquer its neighbors. This strain of behavior had been almost genetically imprinted into every nation of the world.

Perhaps America's greatest contribution may have been to smash the natural continuation of this age-old tendency. In 1945, at the peak of its power, America decided to create a rules-based order that allowed any nation to flourish. ...

This generous attitude of the American government towards the rest of the world also reflected the generous attitude of individual Americans toward the world. Indeed, the best face of America emerges when individual Americans meet individual foreigners. Hence, when the density of face-to-face contacts increases with Americans, the inevitable result seems to be an accumulation of goodwill towards America.[19]

This explains a particularly counterintuitive fact. America dropped over 7 million tons of bombs in Vietnam (as opposed to only 2 million in World War II); it also killed hundreds of thousands of Vietnamese in brutal battles. The natural result of all this when the United States pulled out in 1973 and the war ended in 1975 should have been to leave behind a huge reservoir of hate in Vietnam. The Vietnamese people do not hate the Americans. Indeed, at a time when Americans are increasingly feeling unloved and threatened, one of the safest places in the world for an American to visit is Vietnam. America has left behind in Vietnam a huge reservoir of good will.

How could this happen? Only a Vietnamese can explain this unnatural phenomenon fully. But let me venture a simple theory. Most individual Americans tend to be generous souls. They seem to have a natural instinct to help the underdog. Through the Vietnam War, millions of Vietnamese and millions of Americans dealt closely with each other face-to-face. At the nation-to-nation level, the North Vietnamese government successfully demonized the American government. But at the face-to-face level, the Vietnamese encountered many generous and kind Americans who certainly did not show them contempt. Many Vietnamese may have been puzzled by the naiveté of the

Americans they met, but they could see clearly that most came with good intentions, to help not to destroy Vietnam.

At the end of the Cold War, America made an awesome strategic error: It decided to behave like an ordinary country. There is nothing inherently wrong with behaving like an ordinary country. The only problem is that over the course of two hundred years, America had succeeded in convincing mankind that it was an extraordinary country. It had demonstrated this both in word and deed.[20]

... America does not want to be perceived as a cynical ordinary country. America believes that it represents a more principled state, not a petty, scheming Machiavellian operation.

Herein lies the nub of the problem. Like any other state, America wants to have the freedom to engage in cynical deeds for short-term gains. However, unlike any other state, it does not want to be perceived as a cynical actor motivated by realpolitk. It wants to be viewed and respected as a country that stands by certain values and that it is constantly trying to develop a political order based on certain principles. That is what America proclaimed that it stood for during and after the Cold War.

After the Cold War ended, the visions expressed by President George H. W. Bush and President Bill Clinton were similar. When President George H. W. Bush declared that a New World Order was being born with the end of the Cold War and the success of the Gulf War, he reached into the best Wilsonian traditions of American foreign policy to describe the new world:

"We have a vision of a new partnership of nations that transcends the Cold War. A partnership based on consultation, cooperation, and collective action, especially through international and regional organization. A partnership united by principle and the rule of law and supported by an equitable sharing of both the cost and commitment; a partnership whose goals are to increase democracy, increase prosperity, increase the peace and reduce arms."[21]

Fortune stated in 2005:

> "Can America compete?" is the nation's new No. 1 anxiety, the topic of emotional debate in bars and boardrooms, the title of seminars and speeches...and countless schools and Rotary Clubs. The question is almost right, but not quite. We're wringing our hands over the wrong thing. The problem isn't Chinese companies threatening U.S. firms. It's U.S. workers unable to compete with those in China—or India, or South Korea. The real question is, "Can Americans compete?
>
> ...More worrisome is the chance that if the world's most powerful nation finds itself getting poorer rather than richer, some kind of domestic or even global political crisis could follow.[22]

This statement is not hyperbole. The combination of the American hubris Kishore Mahbubani cites,[23] and the declining competitiveness of America that *Fortune* cites is so appalling that cognitive dissonance, denial, resentment, and fear are an understandable reaction for Americans, but not a solution. The employment prospects for Americans that Oded Shenkar cites below is an added ingredient that makes America's hubris, competitive weakness, and job loss combination ominous:

> In 2004–2005 Occupation Outlook, forecasting job growth between 2002 and 2012, the U.S. Department of labor lists thirty occupations as offering the brightest prospects. Of those, five are in healthcare (such as nurses, home health aides) and four are in education (such as teacher assistants). Next, however, are three food service categories (such as waiters). Jobs as security guards, janitors and repairmen, and sales clerks and truck drivers...follow—not exactly the twenty-first century jobs that you may have had in mind. Only three of the jobs are managerial (including managerial analysts) and only two are technogically intense (including computer service engineers).

Indeed, perhaps the most dramatic employment challenge of the Chinese century is that education is no longer the insurance policy against trade displacement and other forms of job migration it once was. As the IEEE's Ron Hira noted in his testimony before the House Small Business Committee, in the thirty years in which the Department of Labor has collected such statistics, the unemployment rate for electrical and electronic engineers has never exceeded that of the general employment rate. That is until now. Much of the U.S. technological edge rests on an influx of talent from abroad that in the future may seek other venues and, despite great efforts, the U.S. educational system is not exactly a model of readiness for the new technology frontiers. According to the National Center for Educational Statistics, the math test scores of 13-year-olds in the U.S. rank 31 out of 35 participating nations and provinces—ahead only of the French population of Ontario, Jordan, two Brazilian provinces, and Mozambique. China ranks first, Taiwan third. Truly, the U.S. has some great universities, but it would be a dangerous mistake to take the current innovation lead for granted. The arrogant comment of MIT's career director that "the jobs that are being outsourced aren't the jobs that its students are seeking" may come back to haunt us all.

Take, for example, electronic chips. Interviewed in Fortune magazine Lin Stiles of the executive search firm Linford Stiles and Associates, declared that for high tech firms, "...product design and marketing really have to stay in the U.S. [and]...aren't getting outsourced." She should not be so sure. Israeli's scientists already do groundbreaking chip development for Intel and may do so for others in the future. China, in the meantime, is offering significant tax rebates for companies to locate chip design on its soil. Hewlett-Packard already designs computer servers in Singapore and in Taiwan, and there is no reason to believe it will not eventually do so on the mainland. And, as far as marketing is concerned, why is it preordained to stay in the U.S. when many markets abroad (such as China) are growing faster? In an age of global supply chains, the organizational 'brain' will be staffed with people who understand other cultures and environments. American diversity helps greatly in this respect, but business education that is increasingly devoid of any country's specific information does not.

The increasing complexity of the global labor environment suggests that we do not take old assumptions for granted. In the words of Wachovia Securities' chief economist, John Silva, "…because of the globalization of the labor market, the relationship between economic growth and employment is different this time than it has been in the past … in other words, the models are permanently broken." China will play a central role in how the new models turn out, and we better be prepared.[24]

How Did America, with 25% of Annual Global GDP and 51% of Global Military Spending, Become So Vulnerable?

How does a great civilization reach hubris, declining competitiveness, and unsustainable economics?[25] Such a dangerous combination is more consistent with failure than success. Many of the signs in America's situation reveal a proud, great power in a process of negative change. The situation in China reveals a proud, great power in a process of positive change. The collision of two such extraordinary nations is a deadly serious test of their leadership and national characters.

Without the care and attention of an overt, committed partnership between America and China, their political and business leaders will only have ad hoc, zero-sum-game options. Prosperity and peace are not destinations on the road to trade war and jingoism. China and America's political and business leaders must help each other solve the problems each has in the relationship. They must help the other to win. To do so, Americans and Chinese must understand and empathize with each other.

The New Definition of 21st Century "Realism" Regarding America and China's National Security

Many American and other observers are looking at the present and future of America and China's relationship through the assumptions and realities of the past.[26] As we have seen, China's way of doing things is usually studied by Americans from the perspective of comparing it to America's. That comparison assumes that China *can and has* to become like America. If that fallacious assumption is dropped, the analysis can change to "How can China's way of doing things work so well for China when it is so different from America's?" Consider the relationship of America and China in the 21st century from that new perspective.

One part of the mindset shift required is that Americans must accept the Chinese government and people's right and drive to eliminate hunger and achieve their full potential again. Another part is that China must accept Americans' drive to preserve their standard of living and achieve their full potential again. Mutual respect is an essential part of the changes needed to enjoy prosperity and, therefore, peace together in the 21st Century.

During the geopolitical and economic paradigm shift underway, can mindsets change without armed conflict? America's acceptance of China's right of self-determination, a genuine partnership between America and China, and successful genuine global joint ventures between American and Chinese companies are parts of a formula for success. To achieve that success, America and China's political and business leaders must combine the wisdom of the zero-sum and win-win mindsets and strategies without the errors of each.

9

Conflict or Collaboration Among the Elite Capitalist Superpowers

Overview

The Chinese government's wholly- and partially-owned companies and non-government-owned Chinese companies are now moving into investing directly in and acquiring American companies. The Chinese government's huge foreign currency reserves and the criteria used for their deployment in China's Socialist market economy capitalism are changing the financing dynamics of American Capitalism. As seen in the 2005 acquisition bid of CNOOC for Unocal, wholly or partly Chinese-government-owned or favored companies have capital costs and borrowing terms that neither American companies nor American capitalism can match.

Chinese Companies' Multifaceted International Financings, Investment, and Merger and Acquisition Initiatives

In 2002, we entered a new era of capitalism in which the Chinese state and privately owned companies are becoming global competitors, with the growing intellectual and financial resources of the Chinese government managing 22% of humanity. Those advantages herald a new type of capitalism: "state capitalism." We refer to this new era as being defined by the emergence of China's Socialist Market Economy Capitalism.

From 1990 to 2004, Chinese foreign acquisitions never exceeded US$2 billion annually. In 2004, Chinese companies spent US$2.3 billion, most of it in the Legend acquisition of IBM's personal computer business (which was also coupled with IBM's acquisition of 19% of Legend), creating the new company, Lenovo. It was estimated that Chinese companies' foreign acquisitions would increase to US$20 billion in 2005.[1]

The Chinese government's international merger and acquisition (M&A) initiatives, through wholly or partly state-owned enterprises and those of privately owned Chinese companies, are the most obvious examples of the government's investment criteria of seeking to secure resources essential to China's economic growth and fostering international experience and growth of Chinese companies competing inside and now outside China with foreign companies.

China's political and business leaders are upgrading and positioning companies to be both domestically and globally competitive.[2] They realize that Chinese companies cannot be domestically dominant unless they are globally competitive. However, many globally successful American companies are unable to accept that Chinese companies that are weak today may soon have overwhelming competitive advantages. Chinese companies will displace many current Fortune 1000 companies by surviving the ruthless domestic competition in China and bringing a new corporate mentality, cost control, and aggressiveness to both China's domestic economy and the global economy.

Wholly and partially Chinese-government-owned companies and privately owned Chinese companies are increasingly using acquisitions,[3] debt, and equity financings in and outside China. Growing "Mega-Multinational Companies" are or will be listed on stock exchanges outside of China. These companies, if well managed and advised, will be well positioned for IPOs and subsequent equity and debt financings in the global capital markets that can provide huge funding for major acquisitions. For example, Warren Buffett invested $1.2 billion through Berkshire Hathaway for a 1.2% stake in PetroChina. That investment more than doubled in value since Buffett disclosed it. PetroChina is the biggest of China's giant energy companies, with 17,400 gas stations, a 29% share of retail gas sales in China, and 2,500 miles of natural gas pipeline across China.[4]

The Reality That China Must Have Oil and Is Building Multinational Oil Companies

Before examining CNOOC's bid for Unocal it is important to examine the geopolitical and economic context in which the American government made such an imprudent move in the China Game. America's response to China's emergence from poverty must not be built on the ultimate zero-sum-game strategy of offering China "heads I win, tails you lose" scenarios. For example, Dan Blumenthal and Phillip Swagel have written:

> While American leaders view high gasoline prices as a political liability, the Chinese Communist Party sees energy instability as a threat to its rule. Beijing is in a panic over the growing financial burden arising from soaring energy use, and panic does not make for good policy.
>
> Inexperienced in global commodity markets and suspicious of the United States, China's policy makers are vainly seeking to insulate themselves from the global energy market by locking up energy supplies. To do this Beijing has supported regimes that promote geopolitical instability, overpaid for energy assets, and invested in expensive infrastructure projects as alternatives to transporting oil by sea. China is also developing the capability to project its military power into the sea-lanes used by oil tankers. It has every right to waste resources in this way, but its

clumsy approach harms others by raising international tensions and oil prices...

The irony in China's attempts to build its own energy infrastructure is that Beijing benefits immensely from U.S. protection of the current global energy system. The ability of countries in the Middle East to produce and export crude oil depends heavily on America's commitment to keep the region secure. The oil that fuels the Porsche Cayenne SUVs roaming Shanghai's streets is conveyed along sea lanes from the Persian Gulf through the Straits of Malacca, which is patrolled by the U.S. navy.

Yet Beijing seems unhappy with this arrangement, and is developing alternate oil delivery routes meant to circumvent the U.S. military shield.[5]

Blumenthal and Swagel's analysis is not realistic, persuasive, or sound. Their analysis might make more sense from the perspective of the Chinese government in the context of a well-functioning, committed partnership between America and China. But suggesting that China rely on America to protect China's oil supplies is not good for China and therefore not realistic for America in the current zero-sum-game, ad hoc containment, confrontation context. Unfortunately, Blumenthal and Swagel's analysis may seem persuasive and sound to the American government.

Blumenthal and Swagel's analysis also reflects the nascent struggle of American capitalism to come to grips with "capitalism with Chinese characteristics":

China's oil policy is driven by the mistaken belief that locking up energy sources will insulate Beijing from the vicissitudes of global energy markets. That belief has prompted Chinese companies to vastly over pay for oil, as the largest state owned oil company, China National Petroleum Corporation (Sinopec), did last August when it paid $4.18 billion for PetroKazakhstan's oilfields in Central Asia—a 21% premium over that company's share price at the time. The Wall Street Journal reported ... that another Chinese state owned conglomerate is negotiating to buy Nations Energy, a Canadian company whose main asset is an oil field in Kazakhstan.

Such purchases betray a profound lack of understanding that the $70 a barrel price of oil represents not just the amount that a buyer must pay, but also the tradeoff between consuming one's own oil and using the $70 for another purpose. Even if China owned all its own energy, the global price of oil would still indicate how much Beijing gives up by not selling its oil to others. China should purchase oils assets if the terms are financially attractive. But over-paying for oil wastes China's financial resources without providing security against price spikes.

If Beijing does not respond to price and simply puts some energy sources off limits to others, energy price volatility will increase...

The United States and other nations have much to gain if China participates constructively in the global energy market. So too does China, which—once it learns how better to respect intellectual-property rights-could cooperate with other nations on developing new energy sources such as hydrogen and nuclear fusion. However, such cooperative efforts will be fruitless if China, motivated by the troubling mixture of fear and great-power ambition, continues to try to create an alternative structure for energy security by locking up its own energy sources, propping up troublesome regimes, and developing a global military reach that threatens others.

While investing in new oil sources can have positive effects for the world as a whole, that is outweighed by the risk of increased geopolitical instability as a result of China's blundering quest for energy.[6]

Dan Blumenthal is a former senior country director for China and Taiwan in the Office of the U.S. Secretary of Defense, and Phillip Swagel is a former Chief of Staff of the President's Council of Economic Advisors. Blumenthal and Swagel's analysis reflects a desire to preserve the status quo when, realistically, the status quo cannot be preserved. It reflects the ultimate zero-sum-game strategy of offering

China a "heads America wins, tails China loses" scenario. It reflects an inability to respect China's needs and to persuade China to act as they propose. It is vital that American foreign and domestic policy respect China's needs in order to successfully persuade China to collaborate rather than compete with American oil needs. Why should China respect America's needs, if America does not respect China's needs? Blumenthal and Swagel's lecture to China is alarming, whether they expect China to adopt the course of action they propose or if it is a call to arms for Americans. They make demands of China, perhaps in order to justify conflict. America's reactions to China's oil needs have not been in America or China's best interests.

A *New York Times* editorial took a different view of America and China's relationship regarding oil than the approach illustrated by Blumenthal and Swagel. It stated:

> How is this for nerve? The leader of a country that consumes more than 20 million barrels of oil a day is warning the leader of a country that consumes some 6.5 million barrels not to try to lock up world oil resources. When President Bush welcomes the Chinese president, Hu Jintao, to the White House today, the American complaint will be that China's appetite for oil affects its stance on Iran, Sudan, and other trouble spots.
>
> In other words, China is acting just like every one else: subjugating its foreign policy to its energy concerns. The United States does it, too—witness its long-running alliance with Saudi Arabia.
>
> Still, the size of China's population—1.3 billion people—puts things into an alarming context. China recently over-took Japan as the world's second biggest consumer of oil. Its real gross domestic product is growing at 8 to 10 percent a year, and its need for energy is projected to increase about 150 percent by 2020. China's move from bicycles to cars has accelerated its oil consumption; by 2010, China is expected to have 90 times the number of cars it had in 1990, and it will probably have more cars than America by 2030.
>
> That leaves the world with two options. The first is to manage energy resources better. The other is to look for

another planet. Simply continuing the current trends isn't viable, especially with the growing needs of India, with its one billion people and a growing economy of its own.

The United States doesn't have the right to tell a third of humanity to go back to their bicycles because the party's over. Clearly, Mr. Bush and Mr. Hu must tackle energy in a real and meaningful way. That can be done only if the United States both helps China find alternative energy sources and shows that America is doing the same thing itself.

The best possible course would be for China to leapfrog an oil-based economy and head toward sustainable alternative fuels, just as other companies are jumping past the construction of land lines for telephone service and going straight to wireless systems. ...

China like America has a lot of coal. But the world can't afford for it to go ahead with a proposal to build hundreds of coal-fired power plants; that would be an environmental disaster. The United States can help stave that off by sharing clean coal technology.

None of this cooperation will work unless the United States provides leadership by making sacrifices of its own. Asking other countries to lay off the world's oil supply so America can continue to support its gas-guzzling Hummers doesn't really cut it.[7]

Michael T. Klare published *Resource Wars: The New Landscape Of Global Conflict*[8] in 2001, suggesting that armed conflict in the 21st century will be fought not over ideology, but over dwindling supplies of natural commodities. In 2004, after the attacks on America on September 11, 2001, Klare published *Blood and Oil: The Dangerous Consequences of America's Dependency On Imported Petroleum*[9] noting that, by 2020, America will need to import twice as much fuel per year as it did in 1990. Most of this oil will come from chronically unstable, strongly anti-American regions—the Gulf, the Caspian Sea, and Africa. In Klare's view, American recurrent involvement in armed conflict "is sure to follow."

The world had 1.2 trillion barrels of proven oil reserves at the end of 2005. If overall production continues at the rate in 2005, known oil will last 41 years. However, it will run out more quickly in some countries.[10] The graph below shows the barrels of oil left at the end of 2005 for the oil-producing countries and the years remaining before the oil in each country is used up. It indicates that in twelve years the domestic sources of oil in America and China will have been used. Consider the impact on the American or Chinese economies of war or other events affecting the ability of the top five countries to produce oil. Both nations have a common interest in preventing such interruptions affecting either of them. But without a committed, genuine partnership, their need for oil is a zero-sum-game neither can win even if they secure their oil needs.

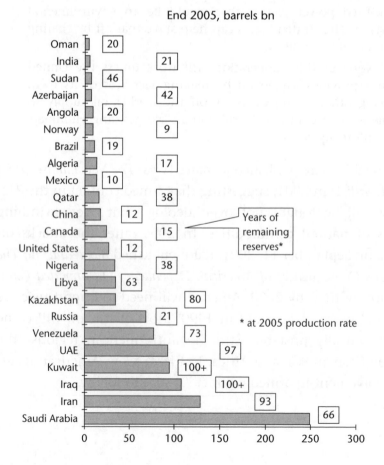

End 2005, barrels bn   11

Oman — 20
India — 21
Sudan — 46
Azerbaijan — 42
Angola — 20
Norway — 9
Brazil — 19
Algeria — 17
Mexico — 10
Qatar — 38
China — 12
Canada — 15   Years of remaining reserves*
United States — 12
Nigeria — 38
Libya — 63
Kazakhstan — 80
Russia — 21
Venezuela — 73   * at 2005 production rate
UAE — 97
Kuwait — 100+
Iraq — 100+
Iran — 93
Saudi Arabia — 66

0   50   100   150   200   250   300

As China's economy has grown, it has been unable to meet its demand for oil domestically. China's production capacity is not expected to increase as demand is projected to grow. The graph below shows China's oil consumption since 1980 and projected demand through 2030, and China's sources of total crude oil imported in 2005.

The table on page 266 shows the changes in China's sources of crude oil imports in 2003–4. The graphs below and on the following pages show the sources of proven foreign oil reserves and projected growth of American and Chinese oil consumption exceeding domestic production.

A Growing Thirst for Oil   12

As China's economy has grown, the nation has been unable to meet it: demand for oil domestically. The country's production capacity is not expected to increase, but the demand is projected to grow significantly

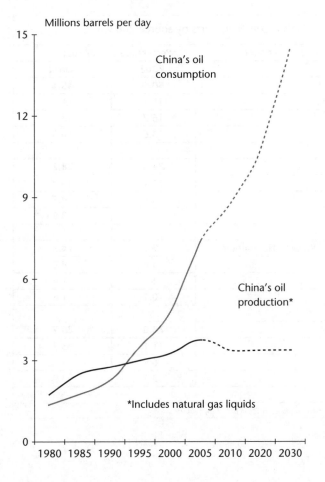

Millions barrels per day

China's Sources of total crude oil imported in 2005   13

Middle East	Africa	Asia Pacific	Europe
47%	30%	15%	8%

	Saudi Arabia	17.5%
	Angola	13.7%
	Iran	11.2%
Largest	Russia	10.1%
Suppliers	Oman	8.5%
2005	Yemen	5.5%
	Sudan	5.2%
	Congo	4.4%
	Indonesia	3.2%
	Equatorial Guinea	3.0%

14

China's crude oil imports by source 2003–4		
Region and top three suppliers	Percentage of total supply	
	2003	**2004**
Middle East	**50.9**	**45.4**
Saudi Arabia	16.7	14
Oman	16.2	13.3
Iran	13.6	10.8
Africa	**24.3**	**28.7**
Angola	11.1	13.2
Sudan	6.9	4.7
Congo	3.7	3.9
Europe and Western Hemisphere	**9.6**	**14.3**
Russia	5.8	8.8
Norway	1	1.6
Brazil	0.1	1.3
Asia-Pacific	**24.3**	**28.7**
Vietnam	11.1	13.2
Indonesia	6.9	4.7
Malaysia	3.7	3.9
Source: Calculated from data in China 6DP, FEB, 1, 2005		

PROVEN RESERVES OF THE MAJOR OIL-PRODUCING
COUNTRIES, AS OF END 2002

15

Major producer (in rank order)	Proven reserves (billion barrels)	Percentage of world total
1. Saudi Arabia	261.8	25.0
2. Iraq	112.5	10.7
3. United Arab Emirates	97.8	9.3
4. Kuwait	96.5	9.2
5. Iran	89.7	8.6
6. Venezuela	77.8	7.4
7. Russian Federation and Caspian Sea states	77.1	7.4
8. United States	30.4	2.9
9. Libya	29.5	2.8
10. Nigeria	24.0	2.3
11. China	18.3	1.7
12. North Sea (Norway, U.K., Denmark)	16.3	1.6
13. Qatar	15.2	1.5
14. Mexico	12.6	1.2
All others	90.2	8.6
World total	1047.7	100.0

Source: BP, *BP Statistical Review of World Energy* (London: BP, June 2003), p. 4.

America and China need oil that they do not produce. Chinese foreign policy is increasingly driven by China's unprecedented need for resources. In exchange for access to oil and other raw materials to fuel its booming economy, the Chinese government is focusing on its bilateral relations with resource-rich states, sometimes striking deals with governments American political leaders view as "rogue states" or entering the competition for resources in relationships

The Dependency Dilemma U.S. Oil Production and Consumption
History 1950–2000; Projections 2010–2020   16

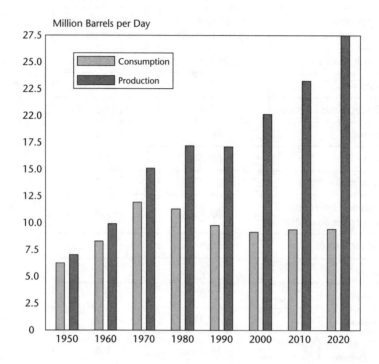

Million Barrels per Day

that American political leaders view as belonging to America. China and America should collaborate rather than compete for oil. They could also jointly develop alternate energy sources and energy conservation innovations.

A Partnership Between America and China on Oil Needs

America and China's need for oil cannot prudently be left to zero-sum commercial or military competition. A collaborative, "win-win" committed economic partnership is vital to both nations' future peace and prosperity. China's economic development and social stability require increasing amounts of oil, like America's. China is, in the well-oiled traditions of capitalism, using its emerging mega-multinational companies to obtain the oil it requires. Unfortunately, American political leaders are seeking to block the use of capitalism to resolve China's legitimate and compelling commercial needs. This is another vital reason why a formal, overt, committed partnership between America and China is needed to enable both countries to obtain the oil they each require for their economic and social stability.

David Zweig and Bi Jianbai note:

> In the past, most of China's disputes, with both its neighbors and other states, centered on trade issues. But its rising need for resources affects its foreign relations in new ways. Like other resource analysts, Mikkal Herberg ... said ... that he could not foresee any scenario that would not lead to confrontations between the United States and China over energy.
>
> By no means are such conflicts a certainty, however. In assessing the dangers of China's growing energy needs, certain important mitigating factors tend to be overlooked. For example, Beijing has set out to replace some of the oil it consumes with alternate forms of energy, such as coal, of which it holds the world's third largest-reserves. China is projected to become the world's largest producer of nuclear energy by 2050. It is also promoting conservation and the efficient use of petroleum. Following President Hu's December 2004 exhortation to balance "consumption and resource exploitation" with "actively developing oil substitutes," last spring Beijing established a new powerful energy agency, the State Energy Office, which reports directly to the prime minister. The SEO's job is to lower China's energy dependence—the ration of the energy China imports to the total it consumes—to 5 percent, as Prime Minister Wen has advocated. This is an ambitious goal, but China is far ahead of the world's other top consumers; according to the political scientist, Robert Ross, it imports only 12 percent of the energy it consumes, compared with 40 percent for the United States and 80 percent for Japan.
>
> Nor should the dangers posed by China's rising energy needs be overstated. For one thing, China's hunt for resources is helping some developing states. The rising cost of resources may be hurting poorer countries that import

oil, but it is helping those that supply it. Other states will also benefit. According to Homi Kharas, a chief economist at the World Bank, 45 percent of China's total annual imports come from developing countries, and these sales help developing states offset the increased cost of crude oil and gas.

China's hunt for resources may have less dire consequences for developed nations, such as the United States, than is often assumed by a strict zero-sum vision of the world's natural resource markets. China typically picks up secondary deals or moves into markets from which the United States is absent; thus in many places the two countries are not really in direct competition.

A much bigger issue is how the magnitude of China's energy needs affect the international oil market: China's demand is so great—and likely to get much greater—that it could affect global supplies and prices. Yet it is precisely because China and the United States are both great oil guzzlers that there are grounds for cooperation. Some energy experts, such as Amy Myers Jaffe at Rice University, argue that big consumers can best protect their interest in keeping oil supplies steady and prices predictable by joining forces to counterweight the influence of producers rather than by trying to forge privileged relations with them. One strategy is to create joint reserves of oil. Members of the International Energy Agency, an organization of 26 industrialized states, including the United States, created to manage energy emergencies, have already contributed to such a common pool. Some analysts, such as Herberg, have urged Congress to invite China to participate.

Similarly, Washington and Beijing share a common interest in securing open sea-lanes to ensure the unhindered passage of cargo ships. That both governments want stability in the Malacca and Taiwan straits does not pit them against each other—just the opposite. Moreover, developing an oceangoing navy to defend far-off sea-lanes is an arduous and expensive project, which will take Beijing decades to complete. In the meantime, China must cooperate with the United States to maintain its sea-passage security, in particular the security of its energy shipping lanes. This should not be a problem, so long as China and the United States avoid war over Taiwan.

It is true that difficult times may be ahead. U.S. officials, particularly the Department of Defense, the Pentagon, and Congress, see China's resource hunger as a new strategic challenge. Consider for example, Congress' response to the China National Offshore Oil Corporation's recent bid to buy the American energy company Unocal. Few impartial analysts see any serious threat to U.S. national security in the deal, yet in a statement approved by 398 votes to 15, members of the House of Representatives said the sale would "threaten to impair the national security of the United States." Under its resource-based foreign policy, China has become quite assertive in seeking the raw materials it needs to keep its economic juggernaut rolling. Just how benign China's rise remains is partly in the hands of China's leaders. Supporting pariah states that scoff at global norms, all in the name of economic growth, will not endear China to the world, especially not to the United States. Washington and Beijing must reach some accommodation on how to view China's ties to such rogue states.

Yet, China has a right to pursue energy sources through market strategies, and unlike the Soviet Union, it is not orchestrating regime changes to advance its interests. Washington must recognize that it would be irresponsible for China's leaders not to increase the country's energy supply. Washington must learn to cooperate with this rising China and continue to work to integrate it into the global economy. Beijing for its part must develop ties that do not flout international standards of good governance and human dignity or threaten U.S. security interests. The world needs farsighted leaders on both sides of the Pacific to adapt to rapid changes in the global distribution of economic and political power, not leaders who let such shifts push them into an increasingly acrimonious confrontation.[17]

Case Study: CNOOC's Acquisition Bid for Unocal

The Cold War "realism" of the 20th century is unnecessary and dangerous in the 21st century. The shift of China from a communist to a capitalist economy needs to be recognized by American political and business leaders. A Cold War "realism" is an unrealistic, unnecessary, and imprudent perspective for American political leaders to pursue. Such a perspective can create conflict that is not sought by China or beneficial to either nation. The most noted example of the new stage of Chinese companies that "go global" is in the pursuit of the rapidly growing amounts of oil that the Chinese government requires to produce at the minimum 8% annual GDP growth that China's social stability requires.

Chinese companies have competitive financing advantages in acquisitions that non-Chinese companies, which are constrained by "rational economics," cannot match. For example, NYSE listed, partly Chinese-government-owned, partly privatized CNOOC was able to make its all-cash US$18.5 billion bid, plus the assumption of debt and a break-up fee totaling US$2 billion, for the American oil company Unocal without crushing CNOOC's share price or financial ratios. This was possible because CNOOC's financing for the bid was made up of $7 billion from the parent company owned by the Chinese government, which owns 71% of CNOOC, and US$6 billion from four Chinese state-owned banks. On the US$7 billion portion of the financing package, CNOOC would pay no interest on US$2.5 billion and 3.5% on US$4.5 billion on a loan with a 30-year term.

At a time when a 30-year American Treasury bond yields 4.2%, CNOOC is able to borrow more cheaply than the American government. Chinese state-owned firms, including most big Chinese companies, have access to financing that does not have to make commercial returns and may not even have to repay loans from state-owned parent companies or state-owned banks. That makes Chinese companies' cost of capital much lower and the rates of return on capital much lower than their foreign competitors. Chinese firms' competitive financing advantages include no interest loans, long-term loans with low interest, or loans that will be forgiven. Post acquisition, Chinese companies can also cut costs in some acquisitions by relocating manufacturing to China, which can reduce labor costs from 70% to 17% in some instances. Such Chinese companies also have the competitive advantage of being able to know the Chinese government's plans, affecting the levels of demand for products in China. They also have competitive advantages in tapping China's already vast and growing domestic market.[18]

CNOOC CEO, Fu Chengyu, was raised in northeastern China near Siberia. He was a student during the Cultural Revolution, and received a Master's degree from UCLA in 1986. Fu Chengyu hired leading American law and public relations firms, lobbyists, and investment banks. CNOOC would have moved earlier than Chevron but for the caution of a Non-Chinese member of its board. Because of the three-month delay, CNOOC's bid was preempted by Chevron's and was raised because Chevron bid first.[19]

CNOOC, China's third-largest energy company, found itself competing against Chevron, which bid US$16.4 billion for Unocal. Ironically, Chevron has joint ventures with CNOOC in China. Many American companies have major investments and joint ventures in China. Shell Oil's investments in China are a case study in our business strategy book. The Chinese, quite understandably, given that China has accepted so much American investment in China, will view jingoistic attacks by companies such as Chevron, which are supported by the American government, in order to thwart the success of bids by Chinese companies for American companies as unfair. The Chairman of Exxon, the world's largest publicly listed oil firm, was quoted as declaring, before American politicians blocked CNOOC's higher bid for Unocal, that it would be a big mistake for America to block the CNOOC bid.

But over 40 Congressmen signed a letter expressing concern about the CNOOC bid; some indicating the bid raised "national security concerns" and the White House rejected a request from CNOOC for an expedited review of the deal.[20] Such delays in regulatory approval can in themselves be used to block Chinese acquisitions in which there are multiple bids, which require timely shareholder consideration and approval. Shareholders have to factor in the regulatory threats to bids. The American regulatory hurdles, and the delay they caused, blocked CNOOC's higher bid for Unocal. We refer to this phenomenon as "CNOOC jingoism."

Former President Clinton, indicating his support for Chinese companies acquiring American companies, stated while visiting China: "We cannot expect to be welcomed in China and not welcome you in the United States."[21]

The Wall Street Journal commented:

> A zero-sum neurosis has taken hold on Capital Hill that the Chinese with their double-digit rates of economic growth are creating too much wealth and that all this wealth is coming at America's economic expense. The real lesson of China's economic miracle of the past decade is that capitalism works.[22]

The Economist noted before the CNOOC acquisition of Unocal was blocked, "How America reacts will have huge ramifications on future energy policy and military strategy. The signs are not good."[23]

The competition between the American company, Chevron, and China's partially state-owned, partly privately owned CNOOC was played out as a zero-sum-game in which CNOOC obviously lost. Chevron may feel the consequences of "winning" in its China Strategy. But, far more significantly, China lost. China's government needs to secure sufficient oil resources to meet economic development and consumer needs. As CNOOC withdrew its bid for Unocal, there were gasoline shortages in China.[24] This "lose-lose" result, obviously for CNOOC and less obviously for Chevron, if it encounters subsequent reciprocal problems in China, occurred even though Chevron and CNOOC were joint venture partners in China.

CNOOC's bid for Unocal failed for a variety of reasons. The most obvious reason is that Chevron and American politicians politicized a commercial transaction. The less obvious reason reflects CNOOC's executive team's transactional inexperience in such an acquisition of an American publicly traded company. CNOOC and its acquisition team made several critical mistakes in this charged commercial transaction, giving Chevron an advantage it did not initially have. CNOOC top executives kept its board members, particularly its independent board members, in the dark. That management mistake contributed to one of CNOOC's outside director's cautious reaction on learning of the deal at the last minute, when it was presented by CNOOC's CEO as a fait accompli, and delayed the acquisition. The resulting decision inadvertently allowed Chevron to make its bid before CNOOC's higher bid.

The mentality of secrecy in CNOOC's executives in not pre-briefing and dealing with their own board in such a huge transaction reflects inexperience in dealing with the power of independent directors to approve or disapprove a transaction. CNOOC's Chinese-government-owned parent company no doubt had been informed of and approved the acquisition and the financing for the bid. The initial failure to approve the transaction by independent directors made it impossible for CNOOC to pursue the transaction in a timely manner. This resulted when CNOOC's top executives failed to communicate with and prepare CNOOC's board for the transaction, although financing had been arranged with CNOOC's parent company. The delay prevented CNOOC from being the first and highest bidder. Had

CNOOC's executives initially prepared necessary briefing material and research and prepared its board for such a transaction, Chevron would not have had the opportunity to come in as a first and lower bidder and win as the capital markets would not have allowed it.

As a second bidder, CNOOC's later bid had to be compared to Chevron's lower but earlier bid in all respects, including the political risks of not getting CNOOC's acquisition approved by American government entities in charge of evaluating national security interests.

The failure of CNOOC's management to form alliances with American companies and investors also hindered CNOOC in gaining the support of American investors and shareholders. This occurred in spite of CNOOC's executive team hiring leading American investment banking and law firms.

How Might Chevron and CNOOC Benefit from a Win-Win Strategy for Unocal?

How might the Chevron—CNOOC bid for Unocal play out in a win-win strategy in The China Game? As we recommend throughout our books, Chevron and CNOOC's shared interests in acquiring Unocal might have better outcomes for all concerned if Chevron viewed its joint venture with CNOOC not merely as a joint venture in China. We call such an approach a "Genuine Global Joint Venture" in which Chevron and CNOOC collaborate in building a much larger and firmer-based joint venture outside as well as inside China. Such a Chevron—CNOOC joint venture in the acquisition of Unocal would not have aroused as formidable political reactions in America or its ultimate failure resulted in ill will in China. It would have forestalled Chevron and American politicians politicizing the acquisition. It would have prevented a contested acquisition. It also would have given CNOOC's executive team the benefits of Chevron's experience in operating and making acquisitions outside of China. Chevron and CNOOC could have divided or shared the Unocal assets, as their respective needs required. Chevron and CNOOC would have strengthened and extended their existing joint venture. Both companies could collaborate on further acquisitions to meet their respective needs. Both companies could have used less of their financial, business, and political resources by making the Unocal acquisition in collaboration.

Such a collaboration could be either public or in a less obvious multiple-stage process in which Chevron would acquire the American company and, in a later transaction or transactions, deal with its assets by agreement with CNOOC. Such win-win collaborations may have compelling, but perhaps unthought of advantages for an American company's "China Strategy," the Chinese company's strategy for becoming a global company, and the Chinese government's need to secure resources that are vital for China's economic development. Perhaps CNOOC and Chevron can still implement such a Genuine Global Joint Venture.

James LeJeune, President, Middle East and North America, of Chevron, United Kingdom, stated at the World Economic Forum on May 15, 2005 in Jordan:[25]

> Access to reserves, while important, will not induce the oil majors to significantly boost investment in production unless oil-producing countries recognize the increasing difficulty of getting new sources to market. He cited four recent exploration projects that succeeded in raising Chevron's output—but at a cost equal to US$17 billion for 1 million bbd. "There aren't too many companies or countries that can come up with that kind of money, especially when they don't know what the market is going to do". The longer lead times between discovery and production have also left the industry less capable of responding to sudden spikes in demand—such as the surge in Chinese consumption. His company is open to participating in down-

stream joint ventures as a condition for access to upstream reserves, but only if both projects make commercial sense.[26]

Chinese SOEs are not restricted to whether "projects make commercial sense". They are securing China's supply lines. The goals and national resources of the Chinese and American governments in securing oil sources will either be deployed in zero-sum-game contests with companies like Chevron/CNOOC or in win-win collaborations. Such collaborations, in advanced structures such as the Genuine Global Joint Venture Model, could provide Chevron with access to the Chinese government's financial resources and knowledge of "what the market is going to do". Such a venture would assist the Chinese government and oil companies in reducing political opposition generated by companies like Chevron and American politicians, and probably reduce the amounts of foreign currency reserves the Chinese government would have to spend in bidding contests to acquire non-Chinese sources of oil. Paying more than necessary for foreign assets and companies reduces confidence in the capital markets[27] in the management of Chinese companies, and wastes money that can be better used in other projects.

It is hard to imagine how such interrelated advantages can be achieved unless Genuine Global Joint Ventures become an ubiquitous and enduring template. Achieving the successful design and operation of such ventures requires mindset shifts from zero-sum-game attitudes and strategies to win-win attitudes and strategies. If such a template is widely implemented, it can also yield the priceless dividends which the partnership of America and China in the 21st century uniquely offers both.

Case Study: America Blocks CNOOC Acquisition: America Loses and India and China Win

America loses with a zero-sum-game strategy of containment. Within a month of blocking CNOOC's acquisition of an American company, China and India announced an energy alliance:

> India said its national oil companies would team up with China's to bid jointly for selected energy assets abroad, cutting the cost of feeding their oil guzzling economies while making Asia's two fastest growing economies even stronger competitors in global energy markets.
>
> India and China have been engaged in cutthroat competition in recent years for access to some of the world's richest oil and gas deposits. Consumption of crude oil is rising sharply in both countries, which are heavily dependent on imported oil. ... New Delhi's collaboration with Beijing would forge a "formidable" presence in world energy markets. Major Western oil companies see Indian and Chinese national oil companies as a growing threat, analysts said, as they are viewed as willing to take a lower rate of return to secure assets.[28]

Both countries have been following different but complementary growth strategies. China relies on export-driven manufacturing, infused with high rates of direct foreign investment. India's growth has focused on expanding the service sector more rapidly than manufacturing. In the information sector, China can develop hardware while India focuses on software. India and China's reliance on low labor costs is now being joined by improved knowledge industry productivity.[30] Indian and Chinese companies may submit a joint offer for oil assets.[29]

India and China have shifted their zero-sum competition to win-win collaboration in many instances. This is an example of how zero-sum-game strategies of competitors do not work to their mutual advantage (i.e., to America or China's advantage) and of how win-win strategies work (i.e., China and India's advantage, but not America's advantage). America's political and business leaders must find ways to ensure that American companies are China's companies' partners in such arrangements. The signal sent by the Chinese government immediately after the CNOOC bid was blocked is unmistakable. The Chinese government simply moved on and China reversed its zero-sum-game with India's state-owned oil companies and entered into a far more formidable alliance with India. American oil companies that were already alarmed by the changing competitive dynamics in their dealings with China have even more to fear because of the China-India alliance. American political and business leaders who blocked the CNOOC acquisition of Unocal, but few, if any, recognized the losing result from their zero-sum-game strategy immediately after blocking CNOOC's bid for Unocal.

The Reality That Trade War Is a Zero-Sum-Game America Will Lose

Zero-sum-game strategies by America beget similar strategic reactions from China. That reciprocity of motive and behavior suggests that exploration of win-win strategies to ameliorate CNOOC jingoism is very much in America's economic and national security interests. America and China should treat each other as they would like to be treated. Demanding "fairness" of others while acting unfairly lacks moral authority and persuasiveness, and is counterproductive. In June 2006, the United States Congress considered the National Security First Act, which, among other things, automatically subjects any foreign state-owned company that is acquiring an asset in America to a full 75-day investigation of the deal by the Treasury-chaired executive branch committee. The Senate is considering similar legislation, which is thought to have even more chilling effects on foreign investment interest in America.[31] At the same time, Senator Charles Schumer of New York dropped resistance to the confirmation of Susan Schwab as chief U.S. trade negotiator after receiving assurances that the American Administration intended to pressure China to remove trade barriers affecting American Banks expanding their operations in China.[32] China is preparing antitrust legislation and other restrictive measures as America prepares legislation for vetting foreign acquisitions of American companies and putting high tariffs on Chinese imports.

In June 2006, the Chinese government signaled that it had reached consensus on proposed anti-trust legislation that can have broad ramifications for Chinese and foreign businesses. The new "anti-monopoly law" could come into effect, giving the Chinese government new powers over the expanding private sector of China's economy. It has been under discussion for over a decade. The new law would require any companies engaging in mergers anywhere to notify the Chinese government if the size of the deal or the extent of the companies' operations in China surpassed certain thresholds. The Chinese government would review such transactions if it felt the deal might reduce market competition. America and European countries have similar legislation to that which China is creating.

China has been adept at attracting and managing foreign investment in fueling its economic success. This leads us to believe that it will remain adept at attracting foreign investment, even if America prevents Chinese investments in American businesses although it needs Chinese investment in America's national debt. America is becoming less attractive to foreign investment and has trade deficits with China. China is attractive to foreign investment and its trade surplus with America is increasing.

The effect of America's new National Security First Act and China's new anti-monopoly laws may be to prevent American companies from expanding their operations in China and to prevent Chinese companies from expanding their operations in America. One of the questions this book raises is whether America can afford to restrict the investments and operations of Chinese companies when the rest of the world is accepting Chinese companies' investments and business.

There are negative economic and national security consequences for America using zero-sum-game strategies with China. The first is that it is America, rather than China, that loses in the short run. The second is that if either or both nations use zero-sum-game strategies as the basis for their relationship, in the longer run neither can win in the Age of Species Lethal Weapons.

Case Study: America Blocks CNOOC Acquisition: America Loses and Canada and China Win

As American politicians and business interests expressed anti-Chinese sentiment and blocked CNOOC's investment in Unocal, Canada was more hospitable. In 2005, CNOOC paid C$150 million for a 17% stake in an energy firm with an oil sands project. In a second deal, China Petroleum & Chemicals, known as Sinopec, agreed to pay C$150 million for a minority stake in another oil sands project. A Canadian pipeline company also announced in 2005 that it planned to partner with PetroChina Co. Ltd to build a new pipeline from Alberta's oil sands regions to Canada's west coast. Oil would then be shipped to Asia rather than Canada's usual buyers in America. Canadian federal, provincial, and municipal government officials have been back and forth to China, and China has opened a consulate office in Alberta. Canada and China also have a petroleum center in Beijing that helps bring Canadian oil technology to China's oil fields.[33] Canada is collaborating profitably with the Chinese government's "China strategy" of economic development and thereby ameliorating Canada's trade imbalance with China. Canada is "a friend to China." American government officials are growing concerned about China's interest in Canadian oil.[34] Alberta's former Energy Minister, who heads Alberta's trade office in Washington, commented, "We're open for business. Open markets and free trade build a strong and prosperous Alberta and will continue to do so."[35]

After a bidding contest in August 2005, and negotiations in September, a Chinese state-owned oil company, China National Petroleum Corp. (CNPC), signed an agreement in October 2005 to acquire 33% of PetroKazakhstan Inc, an oil company based in Canada with all its assets in the Central Asian state of Kazakhstan, for US$4.18 billion. The deal includes a joint venture to split ownership of a refinery with the Kazakhstan state-owned oil company and to process crude oil at the facility. CNPC offered a far higher price than many people expected. Other bidders stated they intended to top CNPC's offer. None did.[36]

In January 2006 CNOOC made a US$2 billion offer for Canada-based energy company, Nations Energy Co.[37] In June 2006 Canada's Husky Energy and CNOOC announced a major deep-water natural gas discovery in the South China Sea.[38]

Case Study: America Blocks CNOOC Acquisition: China and Russia Win and America Loses

China's second immediate move in the aftermath of America's blocking of the CNOOC acquisition of Unocal was exactly what *The Economist* predicted. China announced that it is going to hold its first-ever joint military exercises with Russia.[39] The long-term ramifications of decisions involving China may be much larger than American political and business leaders envisage.

Prior to America's CNOOC jingoism, Russia and China also had little practical cooperation in energy. But in 2006, China and Russia agreed to build pipelines and expand oil shipments.[40]

CNOOC jingoism helped China and Russia strengthen ties of a "multipolar" world, which is a euphemism for countering American interests.[41] Pragmatism, not love, is drawing Russia and China closer.[42] America's CNOOC jingoism is detrimental to America's national interests and national security.

In February 2006, the Bush Administration said that Chinese companies' efforts to buy international energy assets were not economically damaging to America, dismissing growing concerns among Members of Congress and the Senate that China is hoarding global energy supplies.[43] One difficulty CNOOC jingoism exacerbates is that a Chinese company has not been permitted to invest in an American oil company, and yet the American government does not want China to do business with despotic regimes. This is America offering a lose-lose proposition that China cannot accept, and which America would not accept. There are increasing examples of the effects of CNOOC jingoism, which is not a viable or wise domestic or foreign policy initiative for America.

In March 2006, President Putin of Russia committed to supplying gas to China. President Hu Jintao and President Putin met for the fifth time in less than a year and pledged to pursue closer political and economic ties between the former Cold War enemies that previously prevented any major oil pipelines and rail access across their shared border. For years China has pressured Russia to build more links and expand shipments.[44] China wants access to Russian oil and gas. In the aftermath of the CNOOC jingoism exhibited in the battle for Unocal, both nations have made new progress in building a political alliance to counterbalance American dominance in world affairs. President Hu Jintao pledged to promote links between energy, telecoms, transportation, and other industries. President Putin commented, "Our relations serve not only as factors for geopolitical stability. They demonstrate an example of open international partnership, which is not directed at any third country and serves to develop a more perfect system of peace." President Putin endorsed China's claim to Taiwan, the self-ruled territory that the People's Republic of China says is part of its territory.[45]

In June 2006, Chinese state-owned oil companies and Indian companies were likely strategic investors in the IPO, intended to raise US$10 billion, of the Russian oil giant Rosneft. Financial investors were more responsive to concerns about the questionable acquisition of Rosneft's main asset and short-term volatility of the equity markets.[46]

Case Study: America Blocks CNOOC Acquisition: China Wins, Africa Wins

In the year following the unsuccessful CNOOC bid for Unocal, trade between China and Africa increased 35%, reaching US$39.7 billion, and will continue to rise dramatically. In January 2006, an unprecedented flurry of diplomatic activity began with an African tour by China's foreign minister, Li Zhaoxing. That was followed in April by President Hu's trip to Morocco, Nigeria, and Kenya. In June 2006, China's Premier, Wen Jiabao, made a seven-country tour of Africa. Between them, the three Chinese leaders have visited 15 African countries in six months (shown on the map below) as part of China's securing of oil and raw materials required to maintain its greater-than-8% annual GDP growth, which is running above 10% in 2005 and 2006.[47]

Some Western observers predict that China's ventures are on rocky roads in investments and trade with Africa.[48] In early reports, other observers indicate that Mainland Chinese business people carrying out such investments in Africa have an unusual ability and success on an interpersonal basis in doing so. The latest visit by China's Premier reportedly assured countries such as South

Africa that their relationship with China will produce balanced benefits.[50] South Africa's President Thabe Mbeki commented:

> ...the Chinese will invest on the African continent in all sorts of ways—in the first instance in raw materials, energy and other things...They are making capital and expertise available for general infrastructure development. This co-operation results in our development. But there might be other elements that might have other results.[51]

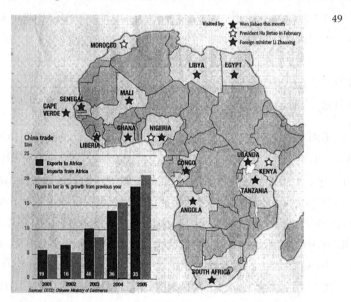

49

Mr. Mbeki expressed confidence that the two sides would talk to each other about any possible concerns over Chinese acquisitions in sectors such as mining or manufacturing, stating:

> I suspect that in the event that the South African government would say we do not believe this kind of action is in our interest and it can only spoil relations, the Chinese would positively respond.[52]

Africans admire China's achievements as a model of rapid economic development. Many Americans may view China's achievements in rapid economic development as a threat. This difference in zero-sum-game and win-win mindsets presents a competitive disadvantage to America in responding to China's peaceful rise and an advantage to developing African nations.

African nations seem not to be being required by China to sacrifice their own economic sovereignty to their nation-building needs. President Mbeki's confidence may reflect an understanding already reached with China's top leaders. China understands what it is to be a developing country, the value of mutually beneficial long-term relationships rather than zero-sum-game strategies that work in developed countries, and has a culture that emphasizes consensus in decision-making. All these attributes make China suited to a balanced, sustainable, win-win strategic relationship with African countries.

The Financial Times commented:

> China offers Africa many of the same advantages as western donors do: aid, debt relief, medicines, training, technical support and tariff exemptions. State-run Chinese companies have committed billions of dollars to oil exploration and production from the Red Sea to the Gulf of Guinea. China has placed a strategic bet on Angola's growth as an oil exporter, providing a hefty mortgage against future supplies. This is a kind of long-term package that no western country—not, at least, since the privatization of France's oil industry—can offer. And it comes with no strings attached.[53]

For example, in January 2006, CNOOC purchased a 45% stake in a Nigerian offshore oil and gas field for US$2.27 billion. This was CNOOC's biggest acquisition to date and a sign that China's largest offshore oil company has moved beyond its bitter defeat in the 2005 battle for Unocal. CNOOC will invest an additional US$2.25 billion toward a US$5 billion capital expenditure required to develop the Akpo field, which is to begin production in 2008. CNOOC's CEO indicated, "This is a world-class asset and this also feeds into our strategy and is very highly attractive in value".[54] The deal was financed with CNOOC's own cash.

An American oil company with a genuine global joint venture with CNOOC might find its global and China strategies enhanced in ways that give it major competitive advantages over other oil companies.

Win-win strategies take advantage of synergies that can be unrecognized or ignored when zero-sum-game strategies are used. For example, in June 2006, China and South Africa signed an agreement to cooperate on peaceful nuclear technology. South Africa is a leading producer of uranium. China is pursuing an ambitious nuclear power plant-building program. Both China and South Africa have similar French-built nuclear power plants and will be exchanging operating experience and personnel. China is developing a high-temperature nuclear reactor similar to a pebble bed modular reactor under development in South Africa, and they may cooperate on developing the system. China and South Africa are each expanding their use of nuclear energy in response to power shortages resulting from faster than expected economic growth. Both countries are experiencing undesired power blackouts. Both countries are seeking to reduce reliance on low-grade coal, which currently generates much of their electricity.[55]

President Mbeki is a vocal advocate of cooperation in politics and trade. President Bush and many American political leaders, so far, are not. What might be characterized for purposes of comparison as the "win-win China and South Africa strategy" contrasts with the current "zero-sum-game America and China relationship" that, as discussed in Chapter 7, China would like to improve.

Case Study: America Blocks CNOOC Acquisition: Iran Lobbies China and Russia to Help Curb America

The results of CNOOC jingoism can rapidly affect America's relationships with many countries. In June 2006, Iran's President urged China, Russia, and other central Asian nations including Kazakhstan, Kyrgyzstan, Tajikistan, and Uzbekistan to boost cooperation and blunt the interference of "domineering powers" in global affairs, and used Iran's energy supplies as inducements to such collaboration. His call was made at the Shanghai Cooperation Organization's (SCO) annual meeting focused on energy and security issues.[56] America is increasingly concerned about energy security and reactions to American foreign and domestic policy, such as the SCO, that point out the fast-paced, losing consequences of American zero-sum-game strategies to contain China.

CNOOC jingoism's loser is America. The SCO has been referred to recently by American critics as "Oriental NATO" and "OPEC with nuclear weapons." It is an emerging focus of global power that is competing with America. One American observer stated that the SCO's agenda, especially after Iran's President's participation as an observer in June 2006, is to dictate to the U.S. how things are done, and at what pace. The reality is that zero-sum-game strategies produce zero-sum-game results that may not please or benefit even powerful zero-sum-game players.

The SCO has its roots in a group called the Shanghai Five, set up in 1996 to analyze territorial disputes in central Asia following the collapse of the Soviet Union, and which evolved into the SCO in 2001 with a focus on security and economic cooperation.[57] The development of SCO is occurring while America is rejecting direct talks with Iran but is seeking to use European countries, China, and Russia to communicate with Iran about Iran's nuclear weapons program,[58] which many Europeans fear may lead to pre-emptive and destabilizing American military action.[59] Many Europeans see America as a greater threat to peace than Iran, a view that President Bush angrily dismissed as "absurd."[60]

Case Study: America Blocks CNOOC Acquisition: Chinese Company Seeks Acquisition of Major Canadian Mineral Company

The Chinese government and companies will avoid CNOOC jingoism and move to secure its energy and commodities needs with commercial deals. China's state-owned Minmetals bid C$6 billion in 2005 to acquire Canada's Noranda, one of the largest zinc, nickel, and copper producers in the world. The deal broke down[61] amid the surging prices for mining companies. However, Minmetals may just be testing its bargaining skills.

Noranda executives are studying Mandarin and attending mining conferences in China.[62] The Canadian government's approach, in spite of Canadian laws designed to prevent foreign ownership in acquisitions over C$250 million if deemed not to be in Canada's interest, and some Canadian politicians' negative comments, shows a political and economic choice to work with and benefit from China's economic developments.[63] "We don't feel you can have it both ways," said a spokesman for the Mining Association of Canada.[64] Canada's trade with China nearly doubled since 2000, which made China Canada's second-largest trading partner after America. Although China's exports to Canada are much greater than China's imports from Canada, Canada's natural resources ranging from forest products to nickel and other ores helped Canada's exports to China increase 40% from 2003 to date. Canada is eager to boost exports to China.[65]

The Reality That America Loses with Zero-Sum-Game Strategies Seeking Containment of China

Other countries competing with America will take win-win collaborative strategies with the Chinese government and companies at America's and American companies' expense. American companies will have more opportunities to remain competitive and profitable inside and outside China if America makes the collaborative policy choice. A key issue in "The China Game" is whether America's political and business leaders recognize that American companies will be less able to compete successfully with foreign and Chinese companies if America pursues a zero-sum-game containment policy.

Ameliorating America's CNOOC Jingoism

The Chinese government and Chinese companies going global should do what American companies like IBM do in China in proposing the IBM + Legend = Lenovo genuine global joint venture, namely seek the advice and approval of American political leaders at the national, state, and municipal levels in formulating Chinese investment strategies in America.

Abrupt hostile takeovers of American companies was not the strategy pursued successfully by IBM and Legend. Just as American companies seeking successful China strategies in China must align their goals and means with the Chinese government's economic development strategies, Chinese companies seeking successful "American strategies" in America must align their goals and means with American economic strategy.

American companies seek the advice of Chinese officials in formulating their China strategies. An additional way to help ameliorate CNOOC jingoism would be to take into account, in selecting which states and cities Chinese companies establish manufacturing or other operations in, to collaborate with American leaders of states most negatively and most positively affected by exporting goods and jobs to China. Such consultation, collaboration, and support-building must be as transparent and public as possible, so that the message is clearly sent that Chinese direct investment in American operations seeks, with the "right spirit," to ameliorate the local impact of China's economic development in areas in America that are most negatively affected. If the Chinese government and companies are "friends of America" they will likely, all other things being equal, ameliorate CNOOC jingoism.

Accepting the Chinese Companies Establishing Operations in America

Congressmen Tom Lantos from California, Tom Conyers from Michigan, and Congresswoman Carolyn Maloney of New York expressed agreement with the game-theory-based thesis of this book.[66]

The maps below show the relative impact of the benefits of American exports to China and of the projected loss of American jobs to China. American national, state, and municipal political and business leaders in locations negatively impacted by China's economic progress need new investments that create jobs and tax revenues. Chinese companies should seek the advice and support of American leaders in locations negatively affected by exports to China.

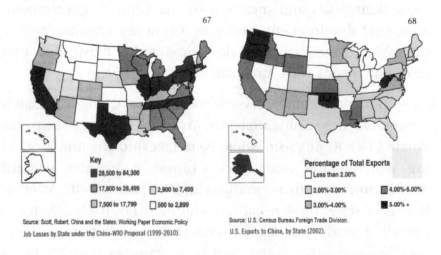

Key
■ 28,500 to 84,300
■ 17,800 to 28,499   □ 2,900 to 7,499
□ 7,500 to 17,799   □ 500 to 2,899

Source: Scott, Robert. China and the States. Working Paper Economic Policy
Job Losses by State under the China-WTO Proposal (1999-2010).

Percentage of Total Exports
□ Less than 2.00%
□ 2.00%-3.00%   ■ 4.00%-5.00%
□ 3.00%-4.00%   ■ 5.00% +

Source: U.S. Census Bureau.Foreign Trade Division.
U.S. Exports to China, by State (2002).

The chart on the following page shows the projected jobs gained and lost in various industry sectors in America.

Job Losses by Industry in the China-World Trade Organization Proposal 1999– 2010   69

	Jobs Gained From Growth of Total Exports	Jobs Lost From Growth of Total Imports	Net Jobs Lost Due to Change in Trade Balances
Agriculture Foresty, Fisheries	23,631	−28,726	−5,095
Mining	3,917	−6,675	−2,758
Consutruction	2,692	−7,564	−4,872
Manufacturing	189,941	−932,041	−742,100
Transportation	11,486	−31,709	−20,223
Uitilities	1,800	−5,748	−3,948
Communication	2,737	−7,208	−4,471
Trade	3,952	−14,768	−10,816
Finance, Insurance, Real Estate	6,754	−19,604	−12,850
Services	26,725	−85,116	−58,391
Government	2,667	−9,153	−6,486
Total	276,221	−1,148,313	−872,092
Manufacturing Share total	**68.70%**	**81.20%**	**85.10%**

Source: Economic Policy Institute 2003

The three members of the U.S. Congress's advice was also sought regarding a proposal of a Chinese company wishing to establish a plant in America to assemble parts made in China that is designed to be "win-win" for America and China because locations for the new Chinese investments and operations in America are chosen with great sensitivity to the views and needs of American political and business leaders and American workers. Their support is sought in the matching of the new operations of Chinese companies in states and cities being affected by China's emergence from poverty. Congressmen Lantos, Conyers and Congresswoman Maloney indicated that this new model is useful and welcomed it for their states.

This type of data must also be factored into the useful rather than threatening direct Chinese investment in America. This somewhat complex combination of economic and political factors can be focused and collaborated on by American and Chinese political and business leaders in enabling American businesses and workers to benefit from China's continuing economic development. Examples of China being a friend of America can be seen in China purchasing eighty 737 airplanes from Boeing for US$5.3billion. China spent an estimated US$15billion on

American items, from soybeans to software, just before President Hu's April 2006 visit to America, and spread the purchases among 13 American states and 14 cities.[70]

Case Study: The KHD Model

China Jiangxi Greatsource Display Tech Co., Ltd. (abbreviated as "KHD") is a leading emerging technology company in the field of Liquid Crystal Display (LCD). KHD, using the American-designed state-of-the-art LCOS (Liquid Crystal on Silicon) in conjunction with its own expertise on liquid crystal packing as well as key optical engine production and other industrial technology in manufacturing, is forming a complete LCOS HDTV production chain.

John Milligan-Whyte and Dai Min, Chairman and President of America-China Partnership Foundation met Representative Tom Lantos, Chairman of the U.S. House Foreign Affairs Committee who represents Silicon Valley in April 2006 to discuss the win-win US-China relations and American and Chinese companies as global partners, i.e. utilizing the expertise of both the American and Chinese companies to create a "win-win" Sino-American commercial partnership: using American design and parts produced in China but assembled in the United States for the vast American market. Gui Song, Chairman of KHD was invited to the meeting.

Congressman Tom Lantos agreed with the game theory based thesis of the books that neither America nor China could succeed in the 21st century if neither did not ensure that both it and the other were successful.

John Milligan-Whyte, Dai Min and Gui Son also met with John Conyers, member of Congress from Michigan and Carolyn Maloney, Congresswoman from New York. All agreed with the "game theory"

John Milligan-Whyte (left) and Dai Min (right) met with Congressman Tom Lantos (second left), Chair of House Foreign Affairs Committee to discuss the emerging partnership between China and US in their new books using the game theory to explain the "win-win mind-set" for both country's leadership in government and commercial sectors.

*Representative Carolyn Maloney, Chair of the House Financial Institutions reading the introduction of John Milligan-Whyte and Dai Min's books: **"China & America's Emerging Partnership"** and **"New China business Strategies"** and support the game theory used in the book to promote the "win-win" US China cooperation. .*

John Milligan-Whyte (second from left) and Dai Min(one from right) met with John Conyers Jr., member of Congress and Chairman of the House Judiciary Committee to discuss the cooperation between Chinese and American companies in automobile sector.

and cooperation between American and Chinese companies. A wise American company should carefully selecte American strategic and financial investors/partners and target customers are being put in place to implement this new model. To utilize American leverage the KHD Model combines American and Chinese capital and technologies that match their perspective advantages, yet adopt America as the final assembly site—thereby ensuring that most of the jobs remain in the United States. Together with innovative product design

Case Study: COSCO's Help and Success in Boston

After the terrorist attacks on America on September 11, 2001, the port of Boston, Massport, felt the economic impact. Some liner companies decided to withdraw from using Boston's port facilities. Massachusetts faced a severe impact in the economic downturn and a job loss crisis. The Governor of Massachusetts, Jane Swift, wrote a letter to COSCO Group President, Captain Wei Jiafu,

Captain Wei Jiafu of COSCO answered Massachusetts Governor Jane Swift's request for COSCO's help supporting Massport in Boston.

requesting COSCO's support at that critical time. COSCO is one of China's largest partly state-owned shipping companies.

Considering the international significance of the educational and economic influence of Boston and the New England area, Captain Wei recognized the great potential of doing business in the area. Despite the challenges and economic risk for COSCO to ship through the port of Boston, Captain Wei had a vision of the long-term positive impact on the trade relations between China and the New England area.

COSCO America, the COSCO Group's American subsidiary, conducted a careful study of the business and trade in the New England area and provided COSCO Group with a series of in-depth reports. With the support of the government of Massachusetts, Massport, customers in New England, COSCO America and the COSCO Group responded to Governor Swift's request for help. Massport helped COSCO coordinate relations among local shippers to minimize the economic risk for COSCO in adopting Boston as a new port of call.

On March 21, 2003, COSCO's container ship Zhen He made her maiden voyage to the Port of Boston. COSCO's using the Port of Boston resulted in leaders of Massport frequently complimenting them for its cooperation, which they said "reinstated Boston's economic leading position in the New England area." *The Boston Globe* reported on the cooperation as New England's "Renaissance of China Trade." COSCO's responsiveness to Boston's economic needs saved about 9000 shipping, logistics, and related jobs, created many new job opportunities, and was highly appreciated in the region.

On December 19, 2003, China's Premier, Wen Jiabao, visited the Port of Boston and shook hands with local longshoremen, visited where the COSCO vessel Da He docked, and greeted the COSCO crewmembers. President Wen highly commended COSCO's success in exploring business opportunities and cited the "COSCO Model" for many Chinese companies to follow. In November 2004, the Massachusetts Alliance of Economic Development awarded COSCO the special "Economic Stimulation Award." It was the first time this award went to a foreign company.[71]

10

America and China Are
Currently Economic Partners

Overview

This chapter examines how America and China's economies
currently operate in a fragile partnership in which collaboration
rather than conflict is essential for the American economy to be
stable and thrive. This chapter also addresses the debate on how
America should respond to China's growing competitive advantages and participation in the global economy by examining key
"fallacies" and "realities" important in the American political and
economic choices that lie ahead.

The Reality That America and China Are Currently
Economic Partners

The success or failure of the world's leading developed and
developing nations' economies, in the short and medium terms,
are interdependent. This reality must be widely accepted in the
formulation of successful rather than inadequate American and
Chinese domestic and foreign policies. Inadequate policies will be

recognizable by their result, which is that America and China slip into a trade war, and its consequences.

Since 1979, America, whether it fully realizes it or not, has grown into a relationship with China in which they ultimately share the economic profits or losses that each enjoys or endures. The reality of the interdependence of America's big economy and China's rapidly emerging much bigger economy has not been sufficiently focused on in the growing political and economic policy debate within America regarding how to respond to China's economic power. Instead, the major focus in America is on America's growing loss of jobs and trade deficit with China, and Chinese companies' desire to invest in America as they go global.

The current interdependence of America and China economically is well understood by the Chinese government. But without the committed partnership between America and China argued for in this book, how can the Chinese government not increasingly shift away from reliance on America? As China does so, the American economy will suffer, accelerating the two superpowers into lose-lose confrontations.

The Fallacy That China Is taking Jobs from America

As we have seen, it is new economic realities, rather than China, that are taking jobs from America. Fundamentally, China is a much poorer nation than America and wages in the two countries reflect that. The graphs across indicate that labor costs in China are much lower than the other countries listed, and that in Dongguan, China, for example, where the demand for labor is high, it is encouraging wages to increase.

The division of labor as envisaged by Adam Smith in the 17th century still applies in the 21st century. But in the 21st century's global economy, which American companies led in creating in the 20th century, manufacturing and other functions

a. U.S	$21.33	1
Europe	20.18	
Japan	18.83	
Korea	9.16	
Singapore	7.27	
Taiwan	5.41	
Brazil	2.57	
Mexico	2.35	
China	.69	

a. Employer cost including bonuses and mandated insurance.
b. Average for Austria, Begium, Denmark, Finland,
   France, Germany, Greece, Ireland, Italy, Luxembourg,
   Netherlands, Norway, Portugal, Spain, Sweden,
   Switzerland, and the UK.

Source: Bureau of Labour Staristics;
China Statisicial Yearbook.

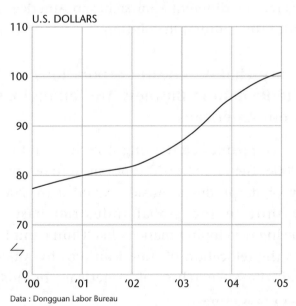

AVERAGE MONTHLY WAGES
FOR WORKERS IN DONGGUAN

2

Data : Dongguan Labor Bureau

go to the most efficient producers for the benefit of global consumers. Americans lead the world in the consumption of manufactured goods. The cost disadvantage that America's prosperity has created currently causes, Ted Fishman estimates, the loss of approximately 400,000 primarily manufacturing jobs a year in America and the loss of 2.9 million jobs since 2000.[3] Jobs that were once done in America are going to poorer nations such as China, India, Mexico, Malaysia, Brazil, and other countries. The loss of American jobs to poorer countries, including China, is going to increase. But America gains high-tech and service-sector jobs, often at the expense of poorer nations. As America lost 5% of its manufacturing jobs in the past decade to more competitive labor markets, China lost 15% of it's manufacturing jobs due to inefficiencies in its SOE-based economy, a problem which the Chinese government is address-ing. America similarly must address difficulties in its economy rather than ignoring them or blaming foreigners. Economic solutions require different approaches in America, as they did in China after the Cultural Revolution.

The Reality That American Corporations Trying to Remain in Business Are Taking Jobs Away from Americans

American companies are costing Americans jobs. For example, in July 2006, General Electric announced that it would make the majority of its products outside America by 2009, marking a historic shift in the global industrial base to low-cost, fast-growing developing markets like China and India.[4] *Fortune* describes the relocation of American jobs by American compa-nies and the ownership of American brands by foreign companies as follows:

> Many iconic U.S. firms—Coca-Cola, Proctor & Gamble, Texas Instruments—already do most of their business and employ most of their workers outside the U.S. Conversely, some of

the most American brands you can think of—Hellmann's Mayonnaise, Jeeps, BV California Wines—are owned by non-U.S. companies (Unilever, Daimler Chrysler, and Diageo, respectively). To complicate matters further, many products of U.S. companies are made outside the U.S.— Maytag refrigerators are no longer made in Galesburg, Illinois, but in Mexico—while many non-U.S. companies make products here—your new Toyota may have come from Kentucky. Now add a few more twists: Your Dell laptop may have been assembled in Malaysia from parts made by American companies in Thailand.

The truth is that large companies transcended nationality long ago, and globalization gives them as many opportunities as problems. It increasingly lets them hire, source, and sell wherever they like, and that is good news no matter where the incorporation papers are filed.

For American workers, globalization is a radically dicier proposition—far more so than most of them realize. The fast-changing economy is exposing vast numbers of them to global labor competition, and it's a contest millions of them can't win right now.

Three main factors are changing the game. First, the world economy is based increasingly on information, bits and bytes that have to be analyzed, processed, and moved around, examples: software, financial services, media. Second, the cost of handling those bits and bytes—that is, of computing and telecommunications—is in free fall. Wide swaths of economic activity can be performed almost anywhere, at least in theory.[5]

The Reality That American Companies Need to Remain Competitive in the Global Markets

Richter & Mar of the World Economic Forum commented in 2003:

> The seeming flight of manufacturing to China is merely one step in a longer chain of productivity enhancement and comparative advantage. But it is not a zero-sum game, and replacements are not absolute. The demand for core competitiveness and a niche advantage has always been

the prevailing law of business survival. The only way companies and countries have prospered over time is by honing their competitiveness and efficiency in identifiable markets.... One cannot deny that there is dislocation and pain in communities that are experiencing the so-called flight of manufacturing to China. The task for these countries is to view these as freed resources that should be put to alternative uses. At the same time, companies that gain in productivity will invest back into economies, thus completing the cycle. This may be an idealistic view, but it is one that carries the credence of the history of trade and investment flows. It is also being mimicked domestically within China.[6]

But such a view is not a solution to the problems that unemployed workers in America and the politicians that represent them face. Unfortunately, currently, the loss of so many manufacturing jobs in America to China, among other developing nations, has a zero-sum-game result. America is losing jobs and has not found the solution to this major economic trend and growing political problem. A key political dynamic in the America and China relationship is the social and political impact of the Americans who have lost or who might lose their jobs as China moves from not only being the "factory floor of the world" but also the "innovative economy of the world."

Many American corporations seek to remain competitive by ceasing to manufacture in America. But the compelling necessity of their economic rationalization strategies do not solve the backlash problem in America that the Chinese government must manage. The Chinese government must ameliorate the damage in America caused by the loss of jobs to China. Doing so is in China's interest. The loss of jobs and America's trade deficits with China pose a real and present danger to America. At the same time, American consumption of Chinese exports plays a key role in China's wealth creation. The Chinese government is shifting away from that dependency on exports to America. Thus, the problems America has are not decreasing, but China's reliance on America is decreasing.

As we have seen, the Chinese government could and would assist American political leaders in dealing with the angry public view regarding the loss of jobs to China. For example, Chinese companies could establish operations in cities where jobs have been lost, using the trained labor pool that is available in such locations. One motivation for doing so is their need to increase Chinese companies' American marketing knowledge and their products' brand recognition in America. The demonstration of "the right spirit" of being concerned for others by the Chinese government and Chinese companies will be very impressive. Such a move might also help reduce American political pressure to block acquisitions like CNOOC's bid for Unocal. Japanese companies have established plants in America. American and Chinese political and business leaders must develop collaborative solutions.

Such a Chinese policy of collaboration could be directed by the Chinese government, just as President Hu Jianto directed the "go global" policy shift in 2002 for Chinese companies to acquire Western skills, market knowledge, experience, etc. The Chinese government's "Socialist Market Economy Capitalism" can look beyond a simplistic cost comparison between operating a plant in China or America. Larger goals are involved than the narrow cost rationalization perspective American companies follow when moving jobs to China. Such pragmatic policy initiatives by the Chinese government could be best carried out through an overtly declared partnership of America and China in the 21st century.

It is also possible for the Chinese government to unilaterally and repeatedly declare that it wants partnership with America and begin implementing pragmatic initiatives to seed and grow the partnership. The cultivation of the partnership of America and China must begin in soil that requires careful nurturing to bear rich fruit.

The Fallacy That the Financial Benefits of Chinese - American Trade to China Are More Significant Than the Disadvantages to America

Americans currently see China's increasing economic power as a threat. But the reality is that it simultaneously both threatens and benefits America's economy. America and China's political leaders must collaborate on this complex, interwoven problem that neither can solve without the help of the other.

China increases American standards of living in many ways: for example, by providing cheaper goods for American consumers, enabling American companies to compete effectively globally, and by investing in U.S. Treasury bonds and in American companies. American companies are heavily invested in China. Their success there can enrich their American shareholders. But the political ramifications of China's economic successes on American domestic and foreign policy can be devastating to both America and China.[7] American companies would experience great problems in manufacturing and operating in China if a trade war develops. That would reduce the ability of American companies to compete with other foreign companies globally.

Ted Fishman has focused on how America and China's economies have become interwoven and asserts that the financial benefits of America's trade with China are less than the costs to America:

> China saves American consumers enormous amounts of money. It takes at least a 20 percent savings for American companies to move their factories offshore. The nearly US $150 billion of manufactured goods coming annually from

China to America, by and large, came from outside America anyway. It has been asserted that America imports a trillion dollar's worth of goods whose prices are pushed down by Chinese competition. If the savings to Americans on nearly a trillion dollars of non-Chinese trade are just 3 to 5 percent, instead of the 20 percent the Chinese can deliver, the average American household enjoys savings that start at about $500 per year. For an American family of four earning $75,000 a year, the savings from China could easily have equaled at least half of the $1,100 in savings that the tax cuts delivered in America's Jobs and Growth Tax Relief Reconciliation Act of 2003 which President Bush said was designed "to deliver substantial tax relief to 136 million American taxpayers ... adding fuel to America's economic recovery."[8] The downward pressure from Chinese manufacturers occurs even when prices of raw materials rise due to Chinese demand increased i.e. the cost of steel, copper, aluminum, nickel, plastics, and nearly every other important industrial commodities in 2003 and 2004, but the price of cars in major markets dropped. In America, from 1998 to 2004, prices fell in nearly every product category in which China was the top exporter. Personal computer prices dropped by 28 percent, televisions nearly 12 percent, cameras, and toys by about 8 percent and other electronics, clothing, shoes and tableware also dropped in price. As the U.S. cost of living rose 16 percent in the same period, the price drops resulting by goods shipped from China provide welcome relief. In 1981, America imported $319 billion (using constant Year 2000 dollars) worth of goods and services equal to just 6 percent of its GDP. By 2001, Americans bought $1.44 trillion imports, equal to more than 14 percent of its GDP. By 2001, countries with lower incomes, primarily China, are estimated to be 24 percent of every thing America imports.[9]

Fishman describes the situation as follows:

This, of course, creates many businesses lobbying for American government protection, but American consumers benefit. The businesses and their employees who lose their jobs face the problem that they cannot compete. Countries that face competition from China and other lower cost manufacturing countries than America must weigh the competing interests of business and consumers. Economists argue that by embracing the forces of the free market, nations give themselves the best chance of being prosperous. China's competitive challenge also pits Americans against themselves as investors as well as consumers and workers. Nearly all Americans have conflicting interests. Union workers who lose their jobs often have a stake in American companies whose success is increasingly determined by their ability to make it in China because those workers have pension and retirement accounts held by such companies. Those pension and retirement accounts frequently invest in China, which is "a once in a life time growth opportunity." America's largest pension funds invest in Wal-Mart, Motorola, GE, Philips, and thousand of other companies investing in China. American institutional investors, universities, and hospitals also invest in the same investments. Investors trying to avoid an economic stake in China will find it no easier than avoiding contact with the American economy, Japan's, or OPEC's because it cannot be done because China's currency is pegged to the US dollar.[10]

Fishman describes the dilemma America faces as follows:

Walk into nearly any retail store, examine price tags and labels, and it is clear that China saves consumers enormous amounts of money.... When one considers that the nearly $150 billion worth of manufactured goods coming from China to America are, by and large, goods that once came from somewhere else, the magnitude of the savings begins to come into view. But the savings that come directly from China's factories are just the beginning. China's prices have a downward pricing effect on the rest of the world's manufacturers that dwarfs this savings offered by Chinese goods alone...that adds up...to nearly a trillion dollars worth of additional goods whose prices are pushed down by Chinese competition.... In fact, in the United States between 1998 and 2004, prices fell in nearly every product category in which China was the top exporter.... The declines are impressive in themselves, but considering that the U.S. cost of living rose 16 percent over the same period, the price drops forced by goods shipped out of China provided especially welcome relief ...

Over the last quarter of a century, there has been a surge of imports into the United States from the fifty-eight countries where people earn one-twentieth or less, of what Americans earn.... By 2011, low-income countries, primarily China should account for 24 percent of everything Americans buy from outside the country's borders.... China's competitive advantage not only puts Americans against themselves as shoppers and workers but as investors too.... As a commentator, Lou Dobbs, the influential CNN financial commentator whose vociferous stand against companies that outsource jobs overseas ... serves as an example of this entanglement. As a commentator, Dobbs finds deep fault with companies that abandon American workers, but as an investment adviser, he recommends the shares of companies that have eliminated American jobs while taking big stakes in China and India. ... This dilemma is played out throughout the economy, where nearly everyone has varied interests that incline against one another. Even union workers who lose their jobs often have a stake in companies' success that are increasingly determined by their ability to make it in China. China bets are made through investments held by pensions and retirement accounts. Many state governments in the United States have considered laws that would ban sending state contracts to overseas companies, and yet the states' employees, as beneficiaries of giant pension plans, are stakeholders in the largest investment pools in the world. ... and they would be foolhardy not to invest in China. America's largest pension funds invest in Wal-Mart, Motorola, GE, Philips, and the thousands of other companies investing billions in China.[11]

American corporations are shifting jobs to where the work can be done most inexpensively. A trade war seeking to protect American workers in uncompetitive economic sectors would be, ironically, like China's policies of seeking to protect China's failing SOEs and China's economy from being overwhelmed by American and other foreign companies. China chose in the 1990s out of necessity to reform the SOEs, which were failing, by embracing the financial and intellectual capital of foreign companies and has been very successful in re-engineering its economy. America must re-engineer its economy. China's political leaders can assist America's political and business leaders in doing so.

The Fallacy That Harming China's Economic Development Will Benefit America

If America, instead of re-engineering its economy and opting for an economic partnership with China, attacks China's economy by imposing such controls as the 27.5% tariff proposed in the Schumer-Graham Bill in Congress, America will not benefit. It would take tariffs of that magnitude to eliminate the low cost of goods made in China, which underlie American's current trade deficits annually with China. But such aggressive and shortsighted moves would severely damage America's economy. The benefits to America, outlined by Fishman above, would be greatly affected. Presumably, America would buy what it could afford from other countries. More importantly, China would sell what it could to other countries. Almost all countries want to do business with China.

As Chinese businesses began buying foreign companies, America faces a similar dilemma. Policies of containment blocking such acquisitions, as occurred in CNOOC's bid for Unocal in 2005, could backfire, making the American economy weaker. But the Chinese economy will adjust, which it immediately did after the political blocking of CNOOC's bid, and invest in and form businesses with non-American companies, and continue its growth. In such a scenario, America's economy would get weaker, although China's economy might continue to grow at the 8% per year rate that the government needs to retain political stability.

If the Chinese government was not able to achieve 8% annual GDP growth and instability developed in China because American policies of containment materially damaged China, the prospects of trade war leading to armed conflict between America and China is likely to grow.

Solving America's Emerging Competitive Weaknesses

Fortune's proposed solution in August 2005 to America's diminishing economic competitiveness was:

> We are not building human capital the way we used to. Our primary and secondary schools are falling behind the rest of the world's. Our universities are still excellent, but the foreign students who come to them are increasingly taking their education back home. As other nations multiply their science and engineering graduates—building the foundation for economic progress—ours are declining, in part because those fields are seen as nerdish and simply uncool. And our culture prizes cool.
>
> No one is saying that Americans can't adapt and win once more. But look at our preparedness today for the emerging global economy, and the conclusion seems unavoidable: We are not ready.[12]
>
> Ever since the collapse of the Soviet Union, Americans could reasonably dream of a world dominated by a single superpower: the U.S. No longer. The rapid transformation of China into an economic powerhouse, and the likelihood that India will follow in its footsteps, means the U.S. must prepare for a far different future, one where it must learn to share economic power as never before. Such a change won't be welcome or easy. But as America's economic dominance is challenged—China could surpass the U.S. by mid-century, with

China and India combined accounting for roughly half of all
global output—Washington must craft fresh strategies that will
still allow the U.S. to thrive in this new tripartite world order.[13]

Business Week's proposed solution in August 2005 to America's
competitive weaknesses was:

> … a renewed commitment to innovation, and education."[14]
> "But, that is only a response, not a solution. *Business Week*
> notes, "The sheer brain power in both countries [China and
> India] gives them an edge."[15]

If America persists in a policy of containment towards China it is
investing its youth's future in armed conflict at the cost of educational pursuits. The lessons of the Korean and Vietnam Wars must
not fade with the passage of time. The only solution for America
in dealing with China's emergence from poverty is America and
China's partnership, because 1.3 billion Chinese make better prosperous partners than angry competitors.

The Fallacy That Appreciation of China's Currency Will Be Good for the America Economy

Many American political and business leaders attribute
America's growing trade deficits with China to China's currency
being pegged at 8.3 yuan to the US dollar. Such a view is
based on the assumption that China is "artificially" holding
the value of its currency down is what creates such huge
demand for Chinese goods among Americans. But the
compelling competitive advantages China has in the cost of
producing goods is that China is so much poorer than America.
America's average per capita income in 2004 was US$40,000.
China's per capita income averages US$3500 per year among
the 400 million Chinese in the regions enjoying rapid

economic development and US$345 among the 800 million in the rest of China.

Nonetheless, American political leaders have been applying pressure and issuing trade embargo ultimatums to China, which the Chinese government is seeking to ameliorate. The Chinese government announced its decision on July 21, 2005, to unpeg its currency, the yuan or RMB, from the U.S. dollar and let its currency appreciate, but pegged to a basket of currencies. The Chinese government will manage this new basket of currencies, functionally pegging RMB within a strict trading range of about 2%, gradually but steadily increasing RMB against the value of the U.S. dollar. Under the new currency system, China has not surrendered control of its currency, just moved from a fixed rate pegged to the U.S. dollar. The change did not affect China's strict control over money flows into and out of China. The change also gave the Chinese government much more flexibility to adjust their domestic economy, to attack inflation or inject new capital to re-engineer banks without throwing the exchange rate out of kilter.[17] RMB has appreciated 12 percent since 2005.

Some observers estimate that the RMB would have to appreciate 15% to 30% against the U.S. dollar to materially reduce Chinese goods' price advantages, and point out that American consumers will simply pay more for them, feeding inflation, or big retailers will force Chinese suppliers to absorb the increased costs by lowering the cost of goods.[18]

American political pressure and trade embargo threats which preceded China's unpegging its currency from the U.S. dollar were based on the assumption that increasing the value of RMB relative to the U.S. dollar will make Chinese goods more expensive outside China, therefore slowing the sales of goods produced in China in world markets, saving U.S. jobs, and helping reduce America's

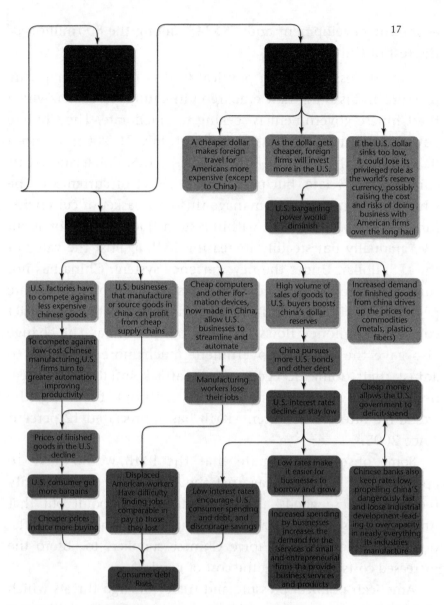

17

- A cheaper dollar makes foreign travel for Americans more expensive (except to China)
- As the dollar gets cheaper, foreign firms will invest more in the U.S.
- If the U.S. dollar sinks too low, it could lose its privileged role as the world's reserve currency, possibly raising the cost and risks of doing business with American firms over the long haul
- U.S. bargaining power would diminish

- U.S. factories have to compete against less expensive chinese goods
- U.S. businesses that manufacture or source goods in china can profit from cheap supply chains
- Cheap computers and other ifor-mation devices, now made in China, allow U.S. businesses to streamline and automate
- High volume of sales of goods to U.S. buyers boosts china's dollar reserves
- Increased demand for finished goods from china drives up the prices for commodities (metals, plastics fibers)

- To compete against low-cost Chinese manufacturing,U.S. firms turn to greater automation, improving productivity
- Manufacturing workers lose their jobs
- China pursues more U.S. bonds and other dept
- U.S. interest rates decline or stay low
- Cheap money allows the U.S. government to deficit-spend

- Prices of finished goods in the U.S. decline
- U.S. consumer get more bargains
- Displaced American workers Have difficulty finding jobs comparable in pay to those they lost
- Low interest rates encourage U.S. consumer spending and debt, and discourage savings
- Low rates make it easier for businesses to borrow and grow
- Chinese banks also keep rates low, propelling china's dangerously fast and loose industrial development-lead-ing to overcapacity in nearly everything its industries manufacture
- Cheaper prices induce more buying
- Consumer debt Rises
- Increased spending by businesses increases the demand for the services of small and entrepreneurial firms tha provide business services and products

Ted Fishman produced this flow chart illustrating the interaction of the benefits and results of America's economic relationship with China arising from China's yuan being discounted against the American dollar, which he called "The Cycle Of Co-dependency."

2005 US$205 billion trade deficit with China. What if those assumptions are false? It is poverty that enables China to produce low-cost goods. Imports from China constitute about 13% to 14% of American imports.[19] Americans will buy cheap goods from other countries if the U.S. imposes a 27.5% tariff on all goods entering America from China.

Some observers saw the timing of the change in pegging the value of 8.3 RMB to 1 U.S. dollar as a goodwill gesture by China's President just before a visit of America's president to China. The change is an example of the Chinese government's willingness to collaborate with America, even as America pursues the disadvantageous policy of containment.

If the change means China will buy less U.S. Treasury bonds, it will push American interest rates higher.[20] The unpegging of China's currency from the U.S. dollar and repegging it to a basket of currencies, including but not limited to the U.S. dollar, begins to uncouple the relationship China seeks to build with America.

China responded to American pressure to let China's currency float, but that did not materially increase the cost and reduce the competitiveness of Chinese goods in America. The demand from America, which is a containment, could be viewed as a bad zero-sum-game strategy for America engendering a "win-win" or a "win-lose" reactive move in "The China Game" by China. Either way, it can be asserted that America is choosing moves that are not in either America or China's best interests. China's response, in shifting from pegging RMB to the US dollar to a basket of currencies indicates that China may currently be the wiser player.

China's former Premier Zhu Rongji has pointed out:

> Since 1997, China has maintained the value of its currency at about 8.3 yuan to the dollar. As the value of the U.S. dollar rises or falls, the yuan moves with it. China is the only large trading nation that pegs its currency to the dollar. It does it by requiring that whenever the yuan is converted to foreign currency, the

transaction must be made at the pegged rate through a Chinese state owned bank.[21] China has invested about US$500 billion in U.S. Government Treasury bonds. When China was asked in 2004 by the G 8 countries to revalue the yuan by not pegging it to the U.S. dollar, the Deputy Governor of China's central bank responded: If you force China to change, it will hurt the U.S. You destroy a goose that will give you a golden egg.[22]

As we have seen, China's foreign currency reserves exceeded $1 trillion in 2006 and reached $ 1.5 trillion in 2007, giving China the world's largest foreign currency reserves.[23]

Ted Fishman has offered the following analysis:

> China's imports more or less equal the value of its exports. ... As a matter of demand, then, China's currency would seem to face little upward pressure, except that private citizens have been bringing foreign money into China to acquire local assets, a trend reflected in China's enormous reserves of American dollars.
>
> If China simply spent its dollars, it could flood the world market with American currency and quickly drive the dollar down. But China, no fool, is not interested in pushing the dollar down. So, instead of spending its dollars, it *lends them* to the United States by purchasing U.S. Bonds.
>
> The logic here is complex; because China buys so much on the U.S. bond market, China actually pushes up the price not only of U.S. currency, but also of American debt overall. And because any change in the yield on a debt instrument usually moves in the opposite direction of any change to its value, China's heavy buying of U.S. Treasury bills and other forms of public and private debt serves to push down the U.S. interest rates.
>
> For example, China almost certainly has a large stake in the market for bonds issued by Fannie Mae and Freddie Mac, the companies that buy home mortgages from banks and thrift institutions and resell as bundled securities. This means that billions of dollars worth of investments belonging to the Chinese are plowed, indirectly, into the American real estate market, and that an ever increasing share of Americans' mortgage payments pour into the coffers of the government of China.

China keeps tight wraps on the value, composition, and trading of its portfolio, but Wall Street commonly assumes that the country also owns a large amount of high-grade U.S. corporate bonds, intertwining its national fortunes all the more with America's blue chips—many of them the same corporations reaping fortunes in China itself. Thus does China indirectly profit from American corporations profiting from China.

...as long as China is an aggressive lender, Americans—whether borrowing for their own private purchases or acting in the roles of taxpayers—can borrow money at low rates. Much of the recent boom in real estate prices in America, especially in the East and West coast markets, is attributable to those low interest rates. And low American interest rates help keep interest rates low worldwide, a boon for borrowers everywhere. That includes China.

Low interest rates in the United States inform how Chinese banks lend, and their resulting low domestic rates that have propelled China's dangerously fast and loose industrial development—leading to overcapacity in nearly everything its industries manufacture and to a highly speculative real estate market.[24]

Many observers assert that the size of the American government debt is not prudent for America. Fishman estimates that for the future obligations which the American government already has committed to pay, each American household's share of the government's debt is $473,456.[25] It is predicted that America's national deficit in 2006 will be $423 billion or 3.2% of GDP.[26]

What Does Realism Require?

The Chinese would like America to accept that "America and China are friends and not competitors."[27] This assertion must be supported by deeds aligned with it.

China' s Household Saving as % of Disposable Income   28

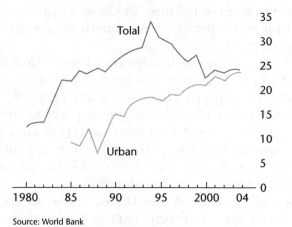

Source: World Bank

Getting richer without trying   29
United States, as % of Disposable Income

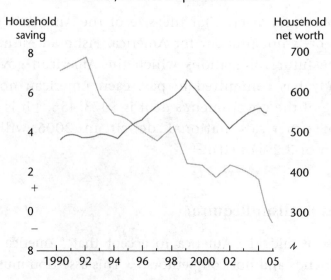

Source : Federal Reserve US Department of Commerce

From an American viewpoint, economic and geopolitical "realism" requires that the reality that China is emerging from hunger and joining the global economy is changing both China and America. American political and business leaders must avoid seeking solutions in fallacies and inadequate domestic and foreign policies, which may be politically attractive at the moment. The graphs across show that the Chinese household saving habits in 2004 had increased to 35% of their disposable income and that American household net worth is declining.

Ultimately, who is likely to prevail in the circumstances of our new century:

> 1.3 billion Chinese, who earn 12% per capita of what Americans earn and save a national average of 35% or higher of their earnings in Chinese government owned banks, who are seeking to emerge from poverty; or

> 300 million Americans who have a declining household net worth and save 1% to 2% as a national average of what they earn, who are trying to not decline into poverty.

Realism requires the acceptance that America's zero-sum-game strategy against China cannot be successful for America. America must resist the temptation to present China with loss-producing value propositions. China must resist the temptation of presenting America with loss-producing value propositions. Only a win-win strategic approach can work.

11

The Partnership Solution to America's Trade Deficit with China

Overview

This chapter examines China's import and export trends and makes the point that in the framework of a committed, genuine partnership, China could balance its trade with America by ensuring that it purchased enough goods and services to do so. Without such a partnership, America's trade deficit with China is likely to lead to a trade war in which China collaborates with the many other nations that want to do business with it. That would not benefit America, the competitiveness of American companies globally, or the employment or standard of living of Americans.

China's Growing Role in Global Imports and Exports

China's foreign trade has been growing at 15% per year since 1978.[1] Since 2000, it's imports have been growing faster than its exports.[2] China accounted for around 6% of world merchandising trade flows and was the world's third largest importer and exporter of goods in 2004. In 2004 and 2005, China had trade surpluses of US$31.98 billion and US$101.88 billion.[3] In 2004 and 2005, China's trade grew 37.5% and 23.3%, increasing from US$1.155 trillion to US$1.422 trillion.[4]

A Growing Share of Global Export Markets   [5]
Share of Selected Export Markets

Source: WTO International Trade Statistics 2004

China's share of world merchandising exports rose from less than 1% in 1980 to 6.5% in 2004, and its share of merchandise imports rose from 1% to 6%. From 1995 to 2000, its merchandising exports grew at twice the rate of world export growth. Since 1990, China has been the most important country contributing to the growth in world trade.[6] The value of China's industrial-export shipments in the first nine months of 2005 grew 28.6% from a year earlier to US$418.8 billion, and China's retail sales grew 13% in the same period.[7]

China's share of world imports grew from 1.5% in 1990 to 3.6% in 2000, and to 5.7% in 2003. In 2003, China consumed 7.4% of all the oil produced in the world, 30% of coal, 27% of iron ore, and 40% of cement. China has displaced America as the world's largest importer of copper, iron ore, aluminum, and

A Rising Force In World Merchandise Trade 8
China's Share of World Merchandise Trade

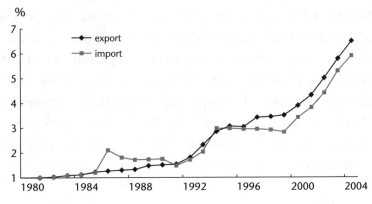

Source: WTO International Trade Statistics Database

platinum. Its share of worldwide demand for metals was about 19% in 2004. In 2004, China was the world's second largest consumer of oil at 8% while America remained the largest at 25%.[9] In 2004, China's steel imports were more than 10% of world steel imports and it imported more than 33% of the world's soybean imports and 25% of the world's cotton imports. In 2005, China's estimated share of global consumption was 47% of cement, 37% of cotton, 32% of rice, 30% of coal, 26% of crude steel, 21% of aluminum, 20% of copper, and 16% of wheat.[10]

China's Exports

China's participation in world exports has grown rapidly from 1.9% in 1990 to 6% in 2003. Between 1980 and 2003 China's exports of manufactured goods rose from 1% to over 7% of global totals. In 2003 and 2004, it accounted for about 12% and 11% respectively of growth in world exports by value, while America contributed about 3% and 6%.[11] Manufactured products constitute about 35% of China's GDP and about 90%

of China's exports. Reportedly, 70% of China's exports consist of labor-intensive products such as garments, toys, shoes, and furniture[12]. Chinese companies are increasingly producing capital-intensive products such as computers, cars, and semiconductors, but were not exporting them as of 2004.[13] China already produces over 50% of the world's shoes,[14] 21% of the world's personal computers, over 50% of cameras, and over 25% of color televisions.[15] In 2004, China produced 16% of textiles, 23% of the world's clothing exports, and 13% of office machines and telecommunications equipment.[16]

China's Imports

In 2003, China's total imports exceeded its total exports. China's trade surplus in 2004 was US$32 billion and was expected to be US$100 billion in 2005.[17]

The value of China's imports were more than the value of its exports in 2004.[18] China's global trade position shifted from a deficit of US$6.8 billion in the last half of 2004 to a surplus of US$39 billion in the first half of 2005. It was estimated that the value of China's exports would exceed the value of its imports by US$100 billion in 2005.[18] It was estimated that in 2005, China's global trade surplus would reach US$140 billion, according to reports prepared by a manufacturers association in America.[19] China's imports have grown at a rate of 26% in the past 4 years. There has reportedly been a slowdown in the growth of China's imports.[20] China's major trading partners are America, Japan, South Korea, Taiwan, and Germany. China has trade deficits with Germany, Asian countries, and other countries that supply commodities.

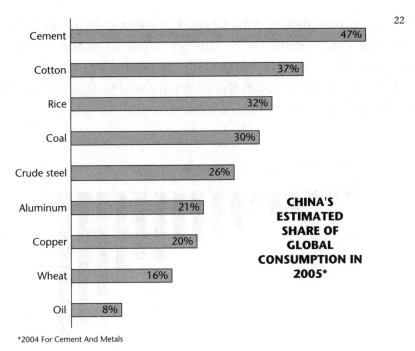

22

CHINA'S ESTIMATED SHARE OF GLOBAL CONSUMPTION IN 2005*

*2004 For Cement And Metals

Data: U.S. Geological Survey Energy Dept, Agriculture Dept.

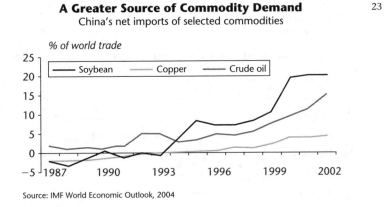

A Greater Source of Commodity Demand   23
China's net imports of selected commodities

Source: IMF World Economic Outlook, 2004

The Reality That China's Exports to America Currently Exceed China's Imports from America

China's exports to American have grown by 1,600% from 1990 to 2005, while America exports to China grew 415%.[24] Since 2000,

America's trade deficit with China has been growing at 25% per year. The graph below shows the development of the imbalance. In 2003 and 2004, China sold America US$152 billion and US$162 billion more goods than America sold to China.[25] In 2005, America's trade deficit with China was over $200 billion.[26]

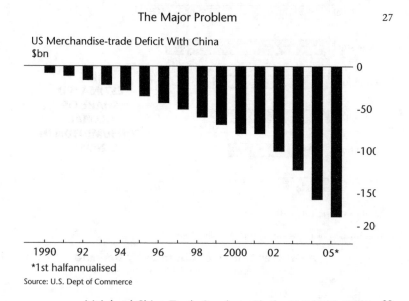

The Major Problem   27

US Merchandise-trade Deficit With China
$bn

*1st halfannualised

Source: U.S. Dept of Commerce

Mainland China Trade Surplus with the U.S.1996–2003   28

Source: Census Bureau's Foreign Trade (FT-900), US International Trade In Goods And Services Annual Issue. Updated 5/15/2003

As mentioned, America hopes that China's move to begin to revalue its currency may help. They have done so.[29] But as we have seen, in reality, the problem reflects a combination of the fundamental cost advantages that China has over America and Americans' consumption habits, which reflect the standard of living that America enjoys. China's poverty makes it more economically competitive than America. This is not a complete answer, but it is a key factor.

Fallacies About China's Exports

Many Americans hold China responsible for America's huge and growing current account and trade deficits. That is the first important fallacy. America is largely responsible for causing and fixing its deficits. The reality is that China accounts for only 25% of America's trade deficit. The graphs below and following show the sources of America's trade deficit and where America's current account deficits stand relative to China and other economies and as a percentage of global GDP.[30]

The second fallacy is that America's economic problems resulting from trade and current account deficits can be cured by protectionist threats or policies. The reality is that America has dangerous economic self-management problems and might respond to them by imposing tariffs or engaging in other demands that make

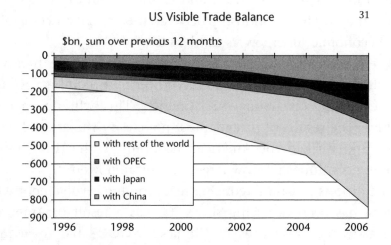

US Visible Trade Balance   31

$bn, sum over previous 12 months

legend:
□ with rest of the world
■ with OPEC
■ with Japan
□ with China

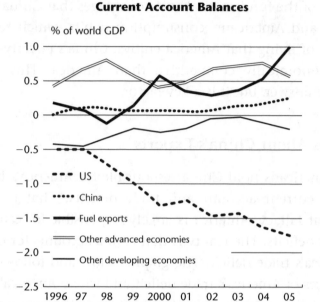

Current Account Balances   32

% of world GDP

Sources: IMF; Department of Commerce; JP Morgan

economic matters ones of power and prestige in which to "win" is to impose power and to "lose" is to sacrifice prestige. At present, America is more powerful than China. If America imposes its will by threatening or imposing tariffs, it will inflict harm or humiliation on China. A series of economic and trade confrontations between American and Chinese political leaders will destroy the working relationship between the current and emerging global economic superpowers for decades.[33]

The reality is that China must continue to react to threats or impositions of American economic power by becoming less and less dependent on trade with America. This will not benefit America. The results of protectionist policies or threats will be to isolate and weaken the American economy, while the Chinese economy continues to grow larger and more powerful.

The process of China reducing its economic involvement with America has been occurring since 2005 as a result of American political leaders' responses to China's CNOOC's bid to acquire

Unocal, pressure by America on China to revalue its currency, and the American administration's request to the Chinese government that it fuel continued Chinese economic development with higher consumer spending in China's domestic economy. The Chinese government stepped up its investments and alliances with nations other than America, shifted China's foreign currency reserves from U.S. dollars into a basket of currencies, and is developing greater self-sufficiency in fueling China's 8%-or-greater annual GDP growth with Chinese consumer spending and Chinese companies "going global."

Demands for protectionist policies are less virulent while the American economy is expanding. However, a downturn is likely since it is only exceptionally low savings and high borrowing by American consumers that have sustained domestic demand at levels able to offset America's huge trade deficits.

The third fallacy is that Chinese companies are causing America's trade deficits with China. As we have seen, a lot of China's exports to America are actually those of American companies manufacturing products they sell in America. About 50% of China's exports are funded by foreign enterprises.[34] Manufacturers in China "suck in imports and dictate the prices in everything from steel to microchips."[35] However, as shown on the graph over, 50% of China's exports come from foreign-invested factories in China,[36] many of them owned by American companies.

China's import figures into America include products manufactured by American companies in China because American companies are seeking to remain globally competitive with other nations' companies operating in China and exporting into America, and global markets American companies need to remain competitive in.

The fourth fallacy (or assumption), which underlies the other fallacies, is that America will permanently dominate the global

China's Exports and the Share of Foreign Affiliates 37

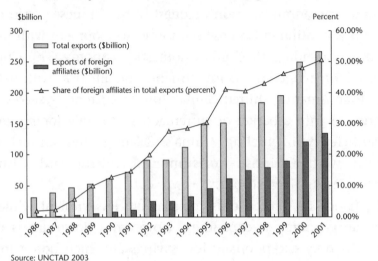

Source: UNCTAD 2003

Comparisons: trade in goods and services 38

(2004)	China	US	India
Merchandise exports	US$593b	US$819b	US$73b
% of world total (rank)	6.5% (#3)	9.0% (#2)	0.8%
Merchandise imports	US$561b	US$1,526b	US$95b
% of world total (rank)	5.9% (#3)	16.1% (#1)	1.0%
Comm. Service exports	US$60b	US$319b	US$32b
% of world total (rank)	2.8% (#9)	15.2% (#1)	1.5%
Comm. Services imports	US$70b	US$259b	US$38b
% of world total (rank)	3.3% (#8)	12.4% (#1)	1.8% (#5)

Source: WTO World Trade Report 2005. Rank reported for top 20 economies only

economy. China's population size, roughly 4.5 times America's, and per capita income that was 12% of America's in 2004, suggests that China's economic growth, exports, and imports could continue to rise commensurately for decades to come.

The graph above compares China, America, and India's trade in goods and services in 2004.

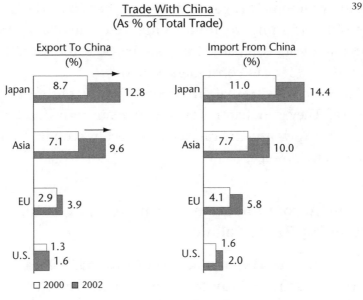

Trade With China   39
(As % of Total Trade)

Source: International Trade Statistics 2003 (WTO).

Imports From China   40
(2002)

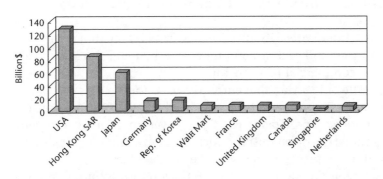

Source: UNCOMTRADE, Business Week (October 6, 2003)

America needs China more than China needs America. The graph above compares China's imports and exports with its major trading partners and indicates that in 2002, China's trade with America was 1.6% of China's total exports, and China's imports from America were 2% of China's total imports. The second graph indicates that America's imports from China in 2002 were much larger than from other countries and notes that Wal-Mart's imports from China were remarkable. Wal-Mart is an American company that has become the world's largest because of American consumers' support.

The basic fallacy is that protectionist policies or threats "protect" America. They can harm America in many ways and they can obscure the ways America can act to protect its economic prosperity, prestige, and power.

An Elite Accommodation of America and China's Partnership Trade Balance

There is a need for a better relationship between America and China. The problems the two economic superpowers have make that true, but not enough Americans have realized it to make it a reality. It is surprising how nascent and underdeveloped the communication channels are in the relationship. John Frisbie, president of the U.S.-China Business Council stated on April 20, 2006:

> ...as China enters its fifth year as a WTO member, the two countries still lack a comprehensive bilateral framework for their commercial relationship.
>
> The only forum that currently exists for the U.S. and China to address commercial disputes is the Joint Commission on Commerce and Trade (JCCT), a government-to-government consultative mechanism, which met on April 11 [2006] and resulted in progress on several key trade issues.
>
> The JCCT was created in 1983 as a means to promote commercial opportunities. In recent years, it has focused solely on resolving trade problems. Its roughly annual frequency and one-day schedule limit its ability to address the breadth of issues in the U.S.-China commercial relationship. U.S. government and industry need more consistent engagement with China.
>
> A more comprehensive framework would lay out the common goals and objectives for what will soon be the two largest economies in the world and establish a better bilateral

mechanism through which to resolve their increasingly complex and wide-ranging commercial differences. George W. Bush, U.S. President, and Hu Jintao, Chinese president, have an opportunity to set in motion such a comprehensive framework when they meet in Washington today, thus cementing a more stable foundation for the U.S.-China relationship for years to come.

America is China's largest trading partner and China is America's third largest trading partner. It is hard to believe that a comprehensive framework is not in place to guide these two economies. Its absence threatens to undermine the achievements made not just in the commercial relationship but in the political one as well. The economic relationship between the U.S. and China clearly is a bellwether for political and strategic relations.

My 20 years of doing business with China include 10 years living and working in Beijing and dealing directly and frequently with all levels of government. This experience has shown that establishing mutually beneficial goals and outcomes is the best way to achieve progress on the very real issues that adversely affect American companies and the American economy. Chinese companies and the Chinese economy, too, benefit in the long run from such outcomes, which generally aim to foster a rules-based economy and introduce greater competition.

A broad framework would identify the commercial priorities for both sides and lay out carrots, not just sticks, along the way to achieving each side's goals. For the U.S., the framework would, among other things, address better protection and enforcement of intellectual property rights in China, the top problem cited by U.S.-China Business Council members. It would also address the array of market-access issues, as well as greater regulatory transparency, that confront U.S. companies there.

A comprehensive framework would have to address China's concerns as well, for example, one of China's priorities is gaining U.S. recognition of China as a market economy. U.S. law clearly spells out the criteria for market economy status, one of which is the extent to which a country's currency is convertible. An over-arching framework would include a clear road map of how China could meet those criteria and address the crucial financial reforms and market openings needed to get there. It might also outline steps China would need to take to become a member of what then becomes the Group of Nine industrial nations.

U.S. and Chinese businesses, directly and through their representatives at private organizations, such as the council [U.S.-China Business Council], have long played a valuable advisory role for government officials involved in drawing up the JCCT agenda. Under a more comprehensive commercial framework, businesses would surely continue to assist both sides to define priorities for discussion—and devise potential solutions.

Presidents Bush and Hu have a long list of pressing strategic issues to discuss. By taking time to propose a framework to address the commercial relationship, they have the potential to use the solid commercial ties that China and the U.S. have forged since 2001 as a foundation on which to build a broader co-operative relationship in the 21st century.[41]

As we have seen, the White House meeting of Presidents Bush and Hu on April 20, 2006, did not produce a proposal for such an urgently required comprehensive commercial framework. President Hu would have welcomed the breakthrough John Frisbie and others see is required. We believe that such a commercial and political breakthrough could be of profound and far-reaching mutual benefit to America and China. However, it cannot occur as merely a comprehensive commercial framework as Treasury Secretary Paulson envisages. Treasury Secretary Paulson's approach is discussed here in Chapter 15 and in Chapter 7 of our business strategy book.

We assert here that three things are required to achieve the comprehensive commercial framework America and China need. The first is a mindset change among American political leaders and the American people that accepts that China is an emerging capitalist mega-superpower. That mindset change includes the realization that America and American companies must align their prosperity with China's prosperity. The second requirement is the establishment of declared, committed global partnerships between America and China and therefore American and Chinese companies, so that win-win collaboration replaces the ad hoc zero-sum-game geopolitical and commercial contests. The third requirement is "the right spirit" among the Americans and Chinese implementing the successful global partnerships of the two nations and their companies. Good partnerships require good partners.

In 2008, in the annual update of how America and China are doing in dealing with each other, we will publish *America and China's New Economic Partnership* and *America and China's Partnership in Creating a Future for Mankind.* They will continue with the examination of how America and China are doing in achieving the shared mindset changes, a committed global partnership and "the right spirit" required to sustain their prosperity and peace.

The Reality of the Partnership Solution to Trade Deficits

China's lower standard of living and huge population give it cost advantages that America cannot currently compete with. At the same time, American companies need to take advantage of China's cost advantages and huge emerging market. These are major social and political realities for America, and therefore for China. China's emergence from poverty must not impoverish America.

America and China's political and business leaders have not yet found solutions to these problems. It may be possible that with sincere and sustained collaboration, a resolution of trade imbalances can be managed. At least, small steps are being taken away from the myopia of containment towards a better vision of collaboration.

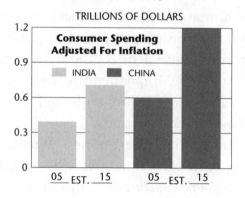

As they get richer, they'll increase consumption...

42

TRILLIONS OF DOLLARS

Consumer Spending Adjusted For Inflation

INDIA   CHINA

...Contributing to growth in overall U.S. exports

TRILLIONS OF DOLLARS

U.S. Exports of Goods And Services

Collaboration may work. Containment has much less chance of producing results that both nations would benefit from. America and China need Nash Equilibrium in their already existing economic partnership. What characteristics does sincere and sustained collaboration require? Hostility and brinkmanship are counter-productive. Hubris and hypocrisy are counter-productive. The "right spirit" is required. Candor and concern for other nations' needs and goals are required. American exports to China are increasing and can continue to increase; China is one of America's largest trading partners. In a burst of checkbook diplomacy, China purchased US$16.2 billion of American-made aircraft just prior to President Hu Jintao's April 2006 visit with President Bush.[43] As the graphs above show, China's wealth creation is contributing to the development of a huge and growing Chinese consumer economy, which is and can continue to contribute to American exports of goods and services.

President Hu indicated to President Bush in their September 2005 meeting that trade friction with America is "inevitable."[44] However, President Hu said that China "does not pursue a huge trade surplus" with America and was willing to take steps to increase American imports to China, mainly by strengthening intellectual property piracy rules and increased purchases of big ticket items.[45] Shortly before the two presidents' meeting, Chinese airlines ordered 42 jets from Boeing in a $5.04 billion deal.[46]

The Chinese government, with its control of China's economic development and its partial ownership of many of China's major companies and control of the others, could in the context of the new economic partnership between America and China help ensure that the trade between America and China is not in a deficit position for America. As China increasingly imports more as its economy reaches and surpasses the size of America's, America could find solutions to many of its economic challenges caused by the growth of China's economy. American farmers are already enjoying the profits from China's imports.

The Chinese government can ameliorate China's trade surplus with America. But American political leaders will also have to address America's economic consumption and production imbalances. America is a net importer. Trade imbalances with China are only part of America's trade deficit problem, albeit a critical part.

The Chinese saving habit is often viewed as a general trait, but the younger generation does not save as much as older Chinese do. A survey done by a Chinese company, the Horizon Group, indicated that 93.5% of young Chinese female consumers (age 18 to 35) have a tendency to buy things that are not needed. This type of consumption accounted for 20% of their total consumption budget, and 55.7% of the young women said they buy things only to make themselves happy.[47]

The Reality of the Development of China's Domestic Consumer Demand

In October 2005, America's Treasury Secretary Snow presented a new strategy for lessening America's trade frictions with China: Get Chinese consumers to save less and spend more. The Chinese government has pursued the same goal with limited success. America is proposing that China revamp its tax code, make consumer credit easier to get, and rebuild the social safety net, lost with the reform of state owned enterprises and the "iron rice bowl," so the Chinese people can dip into their savings and spend more.

The *Wall Street Journal* stated:

> Mr. Snow extolled the virtues of the average Chinese buying "more stuff", be it Chinese-made sofas or new ovens. "We see the growth of consumerism…as going directly to what is most on our mind, which is the global imbalance in trade," he said.
>
> Mr. Snow's new consumerist line has another attraction. It gives him a softer alternative to twisting China's arm over its still-rigid currency system, now the main sore spot in the two countries' trade relationship. China is set this year to rack up a trade surplus with the U.S. of more than $200 billion, up from $162 billion last year.…
>
> The U.S. wants China to spend more and save a little less not simply to get the Chinese to buy more American imports—though that would be applauded. The idea is to get China's domestic market moving faster so its big companies grow by selling to people at home, not only by shipping more goods to the U.S., which adds to America's trade deficit and

generates political pressure for protectionist measures that the Bush administration doesn't want.

Mr. Snow's new tack has won supporters in Beijing, but may earn him little breathing room at home. Measures to liberate China's consumers could take years to put in place, while critics in Congress and within U.S. industry want immediate action. Hence their focus on China's currency, the yuan, which they argue is kept at an unfairly cheap price to spur exports.

Treasury secretaries going back to the Reagan era have pursued a similar save-less-spend-more line with Japan. But in the China case, Mr. Snow jumped on the consumer wagon just in the past few months, largely at the urging of his new undersecretary for international affairs, Timothy Adams.

China...has the highest savings rate—at around 50%—of any major economy. The reasons for that are many. China has no real pension system, or government-funded health care, and housing costs are soaring. "There is enormous precautionary savings" Mr. Adams says.[48]

President Hu indicated during his April 20, 2006, visit to President Bush at the White House, "China is pursuing a policy of boosting domestic demand, which means that we'll mainly rely on domestic demand to further promote economic growth."[49] China is reacting to America's unwillingness to accept a strategic partnership, which China has offered. Thus, America is prompting China to be less reliant on trade with America. As we have seen, China is also, as a result of America's rejection of its offers of a strategic partnership, simultaneously deepening and accelerating its relationships with other countries. This is a "lose" scenario for America and a "win" scenario for China. America's global trade deficit climbed to a monthly record of US$68 billion in January 2006.[50]

The thrust of American policy toward China appears to have changed in September and October 2005, causing the far-reaching accelerating shifts in China's domestic and foreign policy. But the tendency of American political and business leaders to see China as some sort of would-be copy of America persists.

The Wall Street Journal reported that:

> ... U.S. Federal Reserve Chairman Alan Greenspan warned China's economic leaders in private that they shouldn't be complacent in reforming their financial markets. China has been lucky, he told Chinese Finance Minister Jin Renqing and central bank Governor Zhou Xiaochuan. The country has had several years of "benign economic conditions" that did little to test the resilience of its financial system, he said.
>
> According to Treasury officials present at the meeting, Mr. Greenspan gave the Chinese officials a 10-minute tutorial of sorts on how changes in the U.S. financial system had helped the U.S. motor through 20 years of international economic ups and downs with only two mild recessions.
>
> The discussions took place during a summit of the Group of 20 developed and developing countries. ...
>
> China's top officials were unavailable to comment on their talks with the U.S. They have repeatedly maintained that China needs to strengthen its broader financial system before allowing the yuan to appreciate significantly.
>
> U.S. Treasury officials today also plan to recommend an array of additional reforms for China's finance sector, beyond what China is obligated to achieve under its World Trade Organization commitments. For example, the U.S. wants China to speed up the removal of "caps" on the percentage of a Chinese bank that a U.S. Bank can own. And the U.S. is urging China to establish a national credit-rating system and a bank supervisory structure.
>
> Timothy Adams, the Treasury's undersecretary for international affairs, said the recommendations show "the enormity of the reform effort that needs to be undertaken" and represent "a quantum leap in sophistication and scope'"in Treasury's approach to Beijing.[51]

It would be encouraging to see a "quantum leap in the sophistication and scope" in the American Treasury Department's approach to China. However, it is ironic that America, which has not done as well economically as China in the past 20 years, presumes to lecture China on reforms China must make, and assumes that to solve America's economic problems, China must make itself like America. America, the world's most developed economy, is in trouble. America's political leaders are not addressing the real problems in the American economy. America's Treasury Secretary Hank Paulson may be more demanding. But the world's largest and fastest growing developing economy is thriving. The real problems in China's economy have been and are being addressed by China's political leaders. The real problems of America's economy have not been addressed by America's political leaders.

12

Will America Choose 1.3 Billion Chinese Friends or Enemies?

Overview

This chapter examines the political choice that Americans must make of how their domestic and foreign policy will respond to China's emergence from centuries of poverty and humiliation. Attempting to contain China's economic growth is America's usual choice, but collaboration is the better choice. Hypocrisy by America or China, or American cognitive dissonance, containment, and hostility to China's development do not facilitate peace or prosperity. Moral authority is an essential reciprocal ingredient of a successful, committed partnership of America and China.

China and America Remain Strangers to Each Other

China is the world's oldest surviving civilization. But for all but the most recent 28 years in the 50 centuries of the Chinese civilization, China remained a world to itself. Only a relatively tiny number of the 300 million Americans and 1.3 billion Chinese have ever met or worked together. There are approximately 150 million persons of Chinese origin living outside of China who have experienced other cultures. But the vast majority of 1.3 to 1.5 billion Mainland Chinese have not.

Most Americans are unaware that China was the largest, most innovative leading economy in the world until 1800. Many observers underestimate the creativity and genius for capitalism of the Mainland Chinese, whose pent-up abilities and aspirations have been released after a century of humiliation and hunger.

The Chinese have viewed outsiders as barbarians who lack morality, as their civilization defines "morality." Foreigners repeatedly showed themselves to be aggressive, tricky, would-be invaders, who quickly resorted to force when they did not get their way.

Will the 1.3 Billion Chinese Emerging from Poverty Become America's Friends or Enemies?

The genius and conflicts of human beings in the 20th century created nuclear and biological weapons. Those scientific and military innovations require a stabilizing leap of genius in human problem solving and moral abilities. The partnership of America and China will enrich both intellectually, and create wealth by improving both peoples' problem-solving skills. Similarly, the comparative study and more widespread understanding of Chinese and American moral philosophies, economics, and political science can yield very pragmatic rewards. A successful, sustained partnership of America and China will be more interesting and safer than choosing the road of containment and conflict.

The xenophobia and jingoism exhibited in American political leaders and an American oil company in blocking a partly state-owned company's acquisition of an American oil company in 2005 suggests that America is currently instinctively choosing not to be a friend to China. A second important point in this chapter is that in the Age of Species Lethal Science And Weapons, xenophobic instincts are a blind guide leading to economic confrontation and perhaps accidental armed conflict. The road to trade war, Cold War and armed conflict is avoidable only by not taking the incremental steps along that road. The leaders and people of America and China must choose another road not yet taken. Finding that other road is a test of the character and intelligence of human beings.

The Reality That America's National Security Requires That It Be Both Loved and Feared

American national security in the 21st century requires that America ensure that it is loved as well as feared. Both forms of respect are essential. To protect American national security interests, America must prudently use all its resources. We believe America's best choice is to ensure that it is both feared and loved and that a collaborative partnership with China is one of the necessary and realistic ways America can protect its economy, national interests, and security.

America's annual GDP is 28% of the world's total and China's is 4%. American military spending is 51% of the world's and China's is 1%. Those facts lead America to be feared and therefore respected by other nations. After the collapse of the Soviet Union, America currently is the only global superpower. Nonetheless, America could over-extend itself economically and militarily by taking on commitments beyond its resources. Some observers assert that in acting unilaterally in recent foreign policy initiatives in Afghanistan, Iran, and Iraq, America is overextending itself.[1] Some observers believe that America is overextending itself with its growing national debt, which on either "soft" or "hard" landing scenarios can wreck America and the global economy.[2]

America had, in the 20th century, a powerful resource of moral authority, which in addition to wealth and military resources are important to its national security. Socrates pointed out the reality that sometimes the strong fail to correctly understand and act in their self-interest.[3] Their character as well as their strength measures the power of nations. America's character has been defined by its idealism and past restraint as a conquering superpower and protector of many nations. These national assets are a vital source of America's power throughout the world, in addition to America's economic and military power.[4]

Choosing the Road to Containment or Collaboration

Two books published in 2005 by Kishore Mahbubani and Constantine Menges present the very different domestic and foreign policy win-win and zero-sum-game roads America's political leaders and people must choose between. In an attempt to facilitate mindset change, we present these authors' views in their own words. Mahbubani argues that American national security requires that it have both military might and moral authority, and use both very carefully. In his view, America is misusing both currently. Menges argues that China is a growing threat to American national security that must be contained and confronted. He argues that America is currently not doing either effectively. Which view should shape American domestic and foreign policy?

A Win-Win Mindset

Kishore Mabhubai's *Beyond The Age Of Innocence: Rebuilding Trust Between America And The World* champions a collaborative approach. Mahbubani's mindset was shaped by his experience as a Sunhi growing up in Singapore, his career as a diplomat and Singapore's Ambassador to the United Nations, and as the Dean of the Lee Kuan Yew School of Public Policy in Singapore. Mahbubani's view is that America had vast reserves of goodwill and respect, but with the end of the Cold War it has abandoned allies, destroying the trust of other nations inadvertently, and created formidable foes.

Mahbubani writes:

> America's relations with the 1.2 billion Muslims in the world are clearly in trouble. If America is not careful, its relations with 1.3 billion Chinese could be heading the same way. In strategic terms, it would be unwise for the 290 million Americans to have a difficult relationship simultaneously with two groups of people who, combined, have a population almost ten times that of America. Their minds enveloped in the current mood of hubris, it is difficult for some key American thinkers to accept the suggestion that a little bit of prudence should be injected into American politics.
>
> America has been imprudent in its policies towards China. It has used China when it suited American geopolitical interests and ditched it when it no longer served American interests. Since the end of the Cold War, as part of the post-Cold War hubris, America has presumed that a young nation just over two centuries old could remake a five-thousand-year-old civilization in its image.
>
> In the 1990s, China was beginning to enter into one of its most peaceful and prosperous periods after more than a century of civil wars, foreign humiliations, internal convulsions, and wars at its doorstep. It was precisely at the moment when the Chinese felt that they were standing up with dignity that America noisily discovered that China's human rights record was blemished. Hence, America decided to portray China as an unfortunate relic of the Soviet Communist era, one that would be washed away by the new tide of freedom and democracy spilling all over the world ... thoughtful Americans saw the Chinese government on the verge of extinction. The

Chinese saw themselves as finally having surfed the tide of history that would restore China to its rightful place in the first league of nations. How could America have so misunderstood China?"[5]

Mahbubani states:

One of the goals of this book is to encourage Americans to revisit the ideological assumptions they use to understand the rest of the world. The twenty-first century will be immensely different from the nineteenth and twentieth centuries. Americans are only disadvantaging themselves if they believe that the ideological perspectives for the past two centuries, even those that have served them well, are sufficient to help them understand the different world of the twenty-first century.

One ideological premise that should be discarded is the belief that the removal of any undemocratic regime can only lead to good, not harm. In the real world, many countries are held together by politically weak regimes, which have to forge untidy and difficult compromises to sustain the unity of the country. Their removal need not lead to the people being better off. In this regard, the decapitation of the Saddam Hussein regime may provide the world with a live laboratory experiment on the management of regime change....

A sudden end to Communist Party rule in China at this point would prove disastrous and painful for the people of China, the people of the region, and indeed the world as a whole. There are strong populist and nationalist forces within the Chinese political fabric. They are carefully controlled and managed by the skilled political leadership of the CPC. If these populist forces were ever unleashed, the nationalism that might emerge and confront the world in the twenty-first century may well be angrier and more difficult to manage. Hence, the CPC may well be doing the world an enormous favor by managing the gradual but positive transformation of Chinese society and steering it in the direction of integrating with the new globalized society as a responsible citizen. The whole world has a vested interest in the success of this great

Chinese experiment. America must become a constructive, not an antagonistic, stakeholder in it.

America also needs to understand the enormous impact of its actions on other countries. Even societies as large as China's can be affected by American moves. Americans believe that no harm can be done if they support political dissidents. They believe that they are only helping individuals in distress, not trying to damage or shake a political system. By contrast the Chinese leadership is acutely aware that in this period of political transition as they try to move from Communist Party rule to a more open and representative political system, they will be moving through treacherous political territory. The political ground they are walking on is very unsteady ... they hear the verbal assurances by American leaders that America is not trying to politically destabilize China. Yet, they can also see the deeds: support of dissidents, encouragement of nationalist forces in Taiwan, the lionization of the Dalai Lama. All these actions can impact China's political stability.[6]

A Zero-Sum-Game Mindset

In contrast, Constantine C. Menges' *China: The Gathering Threat,* champions a containment approach, which manifests a zero-sum-game mindset and strategic response to China. Menges was shaped by his experience in the White House as special advisor to the president on National Security Affairs, at the CIA as a national intelligence officer and a senior fellow at the Hudson Institute, and as a professor of International Relations at George Washington University. His government responsibilities included the development of several major successful foreign policy strategies including the liberation of Grenada as well as efforts to counter Soviet indirect aggression while encouraging transitions to democracy throughout the world.

Menges presents a confrontational and zero-sum-game view of the relationship between America and China:

> China and Russia are two globally active major powers that have recently signed treaties of political-military alliance. China remains a Communist dictatorship while post-Soviet Russia is in the process of a fragile, reversible transition to political pluralism and democracy...
>
> A gathering danger hidden in plain view may seem hypothetical until we know that Communist China has, since 1990, again defined the United States as its 'main enemy'; has used espionage to steal nearly all the U.S. nuclear warheads and many other military secrets; has focused its military modernization, doctrine, and increasingly lethal advanced weapons on U.S. forces in the Pacific; and has explicitly threatened to destroy entire American cities if the U.S. were to help the democratic country of Taiwan defend itself against Chinese military assault.
>
> ...The main gathering threat derives from China's stealthy strategy of geopolitical and economic dominance. This is a strategy rooted in four thousand years of imperial history and the more recent brutal lessons of Marxist-Leninist power politics.
>
> An increasingly assertive and wealthy Communist regime in China intends to dominate the nine-tenths of Asia. Beijing has historically claimed it as its sphere of influence, and then used that as a springboard to global dominance. This goal puts China on a direct collision course with the United States and its security, political and economic interests.
>
> China's stealthy pursuit of strategic and economic dominance without open war includes global strategic and economic positioning and its little-noticed but important new alliance with Russia. Additionally, China uses its more than one trillion dollars in cumulative trade surplus gains and an additional $400 billion in Western investment and aid since 1990 to build up its economy and its advanced nuclear, missile, and other weapons systems aimed primarily at the U.S. Chinese officially contends that all U.S. security alliances in Asia constitute an infringement on 'Chinese sovereignty'

and should be ended. At the same time, China has territorial claims on fourteen of twenty-five nearby countries and asserts that it has full sovereignty over the 450,000 square miles of international waters in the South China Sea, through which half of all world trade passes, including energy supplies vital for Japan and South Korea.

China sells more than 40 percent of its exports to the United States, providing much of the money for its economic growth and military build up. At the same time, China uses unfair trade practices to take millions of American jobs as it seeks to become the world's factory for high-technology products, software, and services. Therefore, the Chinese Communist regime poses a large but little-recognized threat not only to American security but to the jobs of American workers as well.

The new strategic challenge also includes a politically unsettled and evolving Russian state poised at a political crossroad while still heavily armed with thousands of nuclear weapons on long range missiles. One road leads to increased democracy and peaceful, cooperative, economically productive relations with the West. The other road leads to further political and ideological retrenchment and to the strengthening and broadening of the new Chinese-Russian 'strategic partnership.' China is seeking to use this alliance to move Russia away from cooperation with the U.S. It also hopes to move Russia away from its fragile, emerging, and reversible democracy so the Chinese people will not have the example of a large, former Communist regime, making a successful transition from dictatorship.

China and Russia signed two treaties of alliance in 2001 and have been pursuing a two-level strategy with the United States: normal relations in pursuit of political and economic benefits, while at the same time using discreet means to counter and contain the United States. In the ongoing major foreign policy challenges the U.S. and the civilized world now face in the war on terrorism—North Korea, Iran, the proliferation of weapons of mass destruction, the stabilization of Iraq and Afghanistan, and the Middle East peace process—China and Russia are partly, secretly on the other side. For example, even after the massive 9/11 terrorist attacks inside the U.S., China and Russia remain the leading suppliers of weapons of mass destruction and ballistic missile components and expertise to the anti-U.S. state sponsors of terrorism with which they have remained political-military allies, including North Korea, Iran, Syria, Libya, and Cuba.

The Chinese communist regime poses a large but little-recognized threat both to American security as well as to the jobs of American workers. Yet, much as was true of the gathering threat of global Islamic terrorism prior to September 11, 2001, few American political and opinion leaders or citizens are familiar with the facts presented in this book that reveal the emerging threats.[7]

Menges reports that:

The November 1994 congressional elections resulted in... Republican control of the Congress for the first time in forty-four years. The dramatic events and revelations in the U.S relations with China in 1995 and 1996, especially the Chinese firing of ballistic missiles near Taiwan in March 1996, led the Republican leadership in the House of Representatives to become increasingly concerned with the single minded commercial focus of the Clinton administration's China policy.[8]

The House passed a resolution by a vote of 417 to 7 in June 1996 supporting legislative initiatives towards China, resulting in eleven bills in the House combined into one bill in the Senate defining a "policy of freedom" toward China. Menges states:

The purpose of these legislative initiatives...was that: America's China policy should aim to bring freedom, human rights, and the rule of law, religious and political freedom, free trade and free markets. For our longstanding relationship with China can only reach its full potential when its people enjoy the freedoms we cherish—freedoms, which increasingly flourish along China's own borders. And America's China policy should aim to

promote peace and security for China and all of its neighbors—
the essential precondition for further economic, political, and
social progress in the entire region...The Chinese people have
repeatedly shown their strong support for these common goals.
It is time for the United States to enshrine them in law.[9]

The House Republican Committee suggested, among many
other things, "preventing Chinese communist military-controlled
corporations from operating in the United States."[10]

In 1997 the Rumsfeld Commission, headed by Donald
Rumsfeld, the Secretary of Defense in both the Nixon and George
W. Bush administrations, was set up to report to Congress, and
concluded that China was modernizing its long-range missiles and
nuclear weapons in "ways that will make it a more threatening
power in the event of a crisis". The Commission also concluded
that China "poses a threat to the U.S. as a significant proliferator of
ballistic missiles, weapons of mass destruction, and enabling technologies."[11] The CIA reportedly estimated in 1998 that thirteen
Chinese long-range ICBM missiles were targeted at America cities.[12]
America reportedly has about 3,000 missiles targeting China.

Menges states:

Despite these efforts by the Republican majority in the U.S.
Congress to introduce an emphasis on freedom and realism
into U.S. policy toward China, President Clinton and his
administration essentially ignored these aspects and con-
tinually worked to grant China more economic benefits.[13]

Will America Choose Zero-Sum-Game or Win-Win Realism?

Menges's rhetoric talks of America helping China, but such containment and confrontational policies are a hostile zero-sum-
game approach. Looking at Menges' public policy recommenda-

tions from the perspective of the Chinese government, it is hard to find win-win features in them.

The focus of the American political leaders was changed by the terrorist attacks on September 11, 2001. But America still faces the choice between containment or collaboration in defining its relationship with China. Within America, the policy choice may be characterized as a contest of will between zero-sum-game "realists" and win-win idealists. But it is not possible to definitively conclude that either approach is the "right" solution. On one hand, the real world combines many zero-sum-game and win-win features. Perhaps both approaches are right and realistic.

But in considering that possibility, it is useful to note Mahbubani's observation that:

> Hard-headed American thinkers, especially those who belong to the culturally dominant "realist" school of strategic thinkers, will scoff at the suggestion that cultural recognition [of China] as number one can satisfactorily replace military dominance [by China]. These thinkers are culturally programmed to believe that China will behave like a normal European power and engage in a military, not a cultural or political, race with America. And since many of these thinkers have dominated American policymaking in recent decades, they have planted in many key American institutions an ingrained tendency to see China as the real big "threat": namely that when China succeeds, it will engage in a major military contest with America. Hence, in some of these circles there is an understandable desire to plot and plan ways and means of tripping China up before it becomes a rival military power to the United States (including plans to push for greater democracy in Hong Kong and Taiwan) to embarrass or spread political ferment in the Chinese mainland.[14]

The Reality That Human Beings Combine Zero-Sum-Game and Win-Win Strategies

If American political and business leaders do chose the collaboration road, one challenge will be to somehow manage the features in each human being that react to life simultaneously both as a zero-sum and a win-win game. The formal partnership of America and China, overtly committed to by both, is more likely to make the yin and yang of mankind's selfish and altruistic nature work successfully. One of the biggest challenges is that for people with a predominantly zero-sum-game mindset, competing may be more important than winning. The challenge, conflict, competition, and chance to defeat an opponent are an intrinsic reward for such persons. Hawks are hawks. Doves are doves. How can the zero-sum instincts of the hawks and win-win instincts of the doves be combined successfully? It is not realistic to expect either instinct to disappear in the next 25 years.

The policy formation and implementation habits of a Cold War worldview will be hard or impossible to change. But the contest now is not between capitalism and communism. It is between American capitalism and Chinese capitalism. The ideological obsessions of the capitalism vs. communism mindsets must give way to the pragmatic contests between the leading developed capitalist nation and the fastest growing under-developed capitalist nation. Armed conflict between a capitalist and a communist nation is inherently a zero-sum-game. But business between two capitalist nations is not inherently a zero-sum-game if two nations in order to prosper must continuously do business with each other.

The Reality That Neither America nor China Can Win Using Zero-Sum-Game Strategies

As we have seen, if America takes the road to containment leading to trade war, China will suffer the results and focus on other global markets and alliances. American companies would be hindered or excluded from participating in China's economic growth and market, increasingly the most important and largest in the world. This would exacerbate friction between America and China.

If America takes the road to collaboration and formalizes that approach in a partnership with China, American companies will have competitive advantages they do not have today in participating in China's economic development and growing market.

It is hard to see how the containment road ultimately benefits either America or China. However, zero-sum-game strategies used by either America or China exacerbate economic friction and make economic and geopolitical conflict more likely. Let us hope America and China's political and business leaders explore whether it is the zero-sum-game mindset and strategies that themselves are the problem.

Let's explore whether, when the many permutations of possible economic collaboration between America and China contain win-win possibilities sufficiently attractive to offer an alternative to zero-sum-game mindset and strategies. Since America and China's economic interdependence is so advanced in merely 28 years of trade relations, it is likely that win-win strategies are viable and economically compelling. If they are empirically, that is a first step towards win-win strategies replacing the current dynamic in America and China's relationship.

Accepting the Lessons from the America-China Cold War

As we have seen, the Cold War between America and China between 1949 and 1978 included zero-sum-game armed conflict in the 1950s and 1960s in Korea and Vietnam. After measuring China's capabilities, America backed away from attempting to use military power as a way of imposing its will on China. President Nixon's win-win overtures in 1978 coincided with a new leadership coming to power upon Mao Zedong's death, and China promptly established diplomatic and trade relations with America.

New generations of Americans have grown up without personal experience of how unpopular, divisive, and unsustainable the costs of conventional war were in Korea and Vietnam. But conflicts in Afganistan and Iraq have revealed the limits of American military power. America's leadership could have but did not use nuclear weapons in the Korean and Vietnam Wars. China did not have America's capabilities to make nuclear war. But conventional warfare was too costly for Americans to sustain and nuclear war offered no sane hope of victory or post-nuclear war stability for America. In the 21st century, conventional war or nuclear war with China is not a strategy with an acceptable outcome as it will bring untold destruction and suffering to mankind.

America's zero-sum strategies failed, but President Nixon's win-win strategies worked with China. Under Deng Xiaoping, Jiang Zemin, and Hu Jintao from 1979 to 2004, China's government implemented the first 25-year phase of China's strategies for economic development, preserving social stability and sovereignty by opening it up to foreign investment and technology. This occurred initially in Special Economic Zones, but later extended to other parts of China.

The Reality That Win-Win and Zero-Sum-Game Strategies Can Be Combined in America and China's Foreign Policies

Features of the win-win and zero-sum approaches seem to operate empirically in American foreign policy. Mahbubani's description of the relationship of America and China illustrates that a win-win strategy can be integrated with zero-sum tactics in China's response to America:

> After several decades of close encounters with Americans, the Chinese leaders have developed a reasonably sophisticated feel of how to work with America. They now know that argument alone will not be enough to persuade America to be more careful and restrained in carrying out actions that impact on China. China has learned that America, like any other country, responds when its own national interest is directly affected. It serves Chinese interest to see the emergence of situations when America needs Chinese assistance. This happens whenever America gets into political trouble... it develops an interest in seeking China's cooperation. It then serves China's interests to calibrate its cooperation to reflect Americas' behavior towards China at that moment. It would be foolish to underestimate China's ability to play delicate geopolitical games, requiring deft footwork.
>
> Two recent issues that have preoccupied American leaders, Iraq and North Korea, have demonstrated Chinese diplomatic dexterity. When America announced its decision to launch a military invasion of Iraq, China, as a matter of principle, had to oppose it. Unlike France, which tried hard to prevent America's invasion of Iraq, China did so quietly. Perhaps China did not want to aggravate the American leadership. But could it also have been because of a sophisticated Chinese calculation that an American invasion of Iraq would lead to America being stuck in a protracted and difficult overseas commitment? An America caught in an Iraqi quagmire would have less energy and ability to add to China's challenges.

Such an America would also need China's assistance in gatherings such as the U.N. Security Council. When America came back to the Security Council several months after the war began in an effort to secure legitimacy for its occupation and rule of Iraq, the Security Council agreed unanimously in Resolution No. 1511. A remarkable number of diplomatic twists and turns preceded the passage of this resolution; through these twist and turns, China played a quietly helpful role, which was much appreciated in Washington.

Similarly, when America decided to ratchet up the pressure on North Korea by declaring that North Korea was part of "the axis of evil," the Chinese probably anticipated that given the difficult and unpredictable nature of the North Korean regime, America would eventually seek China's assistance to persuade the North Korean leader to be more cooperative. This is exactly what happened. After releasing a lot of verbal bluster on North Korea, America discovered that it had few real levers to exert pressure. Bilateral economic sanctions would not work: North Korea had already isolated itself. Nor was military invasion feasible. The price that South Korea, and possibly Japan, would have paid from a military conflict would have been too high. The North Korean economy has been badly crippled, but despite this, the North Korean military machine remains formidable. Hence, when America needed to assert influence over North Korea, only one country had "persuasive" powers: China. America asked for help and China responded positively. Indeed, at one stage, in a powerful message of its serious intentions, China, virtually the sole supplier of oil to North Korea, cut off its oil supplies to North Korea for a few days.[15]

A stable world requires that both America and China be stable and collaborate. That does not mean that they will collaborate or that the world or their relationship will be stable. But there is some reasons to be hopeful. Human beings adapt to new environments and evolve, sometimes more quickly than expected.

Collaboration-Growth-Rate Breakthroughs

It was only 11,000 years ago that mankind began to live in villages and cultivate plants and animals. However, for the past 500,000 years, human beings have been anatomically equipped to perform intellectually at the levels we do today.[16] But they did not, as far as we know. Collaboration is a strong catalyst in human learning. The more we collaborate, the better we become at collaborating, and the more we prosper.

If a documentary were made, which would take a year to watch, of the evolutionary adventure that produced contemporary mankind, human beings that are anatomically similar to us would appear in the last 11 minutes. The habits of competition and conflict and human decision-making, which evolved over billions of years, have not changed in The Age of Species Lethal Weapons, in which our problem-solving and moral capabilities may be inadequate for mankind's survival.

Through billions of years of evolution, strangers were either strong enemies or weak victims. Strangers were unknown people to whom one had no obligations of kindness and care. Through most of mankind's history, our ancestors' perceived obligations of kindness and care were to their family, tribe, and village. That concept of obligation in a customary or Pre-Rule of Law society, such as China, remains today. America's legislating and enforcing laws, binding on friends and strangers alike, define a Rule of Law society. One of the many interesting things about the relationship of China and America is that they are a Pre-Rule of Law society and a Rule of Law society with interdependent economies.

What we will term a "collaboration growth rate breakthrough" that began 11,000 years ago has accelerated perhaps exponentially in the last hundred years. In only five generations since the discovery of how mankind can fly, men have gone to the moon and back and are exploring the galaxy. Since the discovery of how to communicate by phone, radio, television, and other electronic means, the planet has become "a global village." Since 1993 the Internet has been a further catalyst to the Knowledge Revolution and Globalization 3.0. The collaboration growth rate breakthrough's exponential development is unprecedented in known human history. Today we find mankind in a global village. We also find mankind, in what H.G. Wells, anticipating the communications and Internet revolution, termed "The World Brain." The discoveries mankind will make in the 21st century can only be imagined. But mankind must survive in order to make those discoveries. President Kennedy made the statement in 1963 that man can accomplish anything. Perhaps in doing so, he was assessing the potential future of mankind, rather than the last 11 minutes of a documentary of mankind's history to date.

The Collaboration-Rate Breakthroughs of America and China

It is likely that the collaboration growth rate will accelerate further, if our billions of years of being suspicious of strangers and xenophobic habits do not destroy mankind. Let us focus our collaboration-rate breakthrough on solving the problems our decision-making habits and xenophobic instincts present each day. The Vietnam War (conventional war) and the Cuban Missile Crisis (potential nuclear war) are enlightening guides to what armed conflict between America and China can be if America travels down the path of containment. Let America and China instead follow the path of collaboration. Let their leaders and people look at the relationship of America and China and stabilizing their economic relationship as a challenge where they can make collaboration growth-rate breakthroughs and create reciprocal prosperity and its reward of peace.

The politicization of the acquisition of American companies by Chinese companies should trouble American political and business leaders. But it does not trouble a sufficient number of them yet. Chevron successfully used nationalism and national security jingoism to create political opposition to CNOOC's bid. Then Chevron asked Unocal's shareholders to accept a lower bid instead of raising Chevron's bid. In doing so, Chevron successfully asked Unocal's shareholders to ignore capitalist market norms. The normal goals of America's capitalist game, which it plays globally, include making money and creating shareholder value. American capitalism's fairness and charisma is damaged by such hypocrisy.

The Reality That Perceiving and Playing The China Game as a Zero-Sum-Game Makes It Impossible to Win

Viewing the relationship of America and China as a zero-sum-game will *inevitably* facilitate trade war and armed conflict and harm either America or China. The use of zero-sum-game strategies by either America or China leads to neither superpower being able to win. Therefore, the relationship of America and China must not be perceived or played as a game of containment or domination in which America and China can only win if the other loses. On a theoretic basis, the relationship between America and China must be perceived and played as a win-win game in which both superpowers ensure that the other superpower wins also. If that is correct theoretically, then the next problem is: how can America and China ensure that both of them win in The China Game?

Is a Win-Win Strategy in America and China's Co-existence Possible in the Real World?

Some readers will smile or laugh at the "naiveté" of the notion that such win-win behavior is sound theoretically or can exist in the real world. They may be correct in the case of the relationship of America and China. But, if they are, four questions for such "realists" are:

1. Is it possible for either America or China to "win" if the other loses in their competition?

2. If it is possible for one nation to win while the other loses, how exactly can one of the nations succeed when the other fails, given the interdependence of America and China's economies in the 21st century?

3. If it is not possible for either to win if the other fails, what will we do as the relationship of America and China deteriorates?

4. Is armed conflict between America and China desirable? If so, how can it be contained and prevented from escalating catastrophically?

If it is true that neither nation can deal with the other except on a zero-sum basis, and that produces only negative possible outcomes in the real world that are too horrible to be acceptable, perhaps America and China's political and business leaders should consider even the "naïve" and unrealistic suggestion that America and China can and must have a win-win relationship. If it is impossible from a zero-sum person's perspective for America and China to have a win-win relationship, how can the genius of the American and Chinese political and business leaders and people make it possible?

An Asian, like Kishore Mahbubani, sees that America's moral authority is its greatest power. An American, like Constantine Menges, sees America's economic and military power as it greatest power. This difference in the Asian and American mindset is significant. In the real world, both views are correct. America must be respected for its economic and military power and most of all for its moral authority. That is what America's national security in the 21st century requires. The American hawks and doves are both correct, and America's political leaders must combine their wisdom without succumbing to either the folly of the hawk or of the dove.

The hawks must recognize and accept that the zero-sum-game of containment and Cold War with China rather than "realism" in the interaction of American and Chinese capitalism in the 21st century is "unrealism" that undermines American national security. They must also recognize that American domestic and foreign policy, like the Rumsfeld Commission Report and the 1997 Resolutions of Congress issuing ultimatums regarding Chinese public policy, are premised on an interference with China's right of self-determination.

Perhaps equally important to "realism," Americans must accept that just as they would not tolerate regime-change policies aimed at America's political system, China can also not tolerate it either. Americans must realize that regime-change policies attacking China's government and therefore China's stability and economic development are counter-productive. They force the Chinese government to be hostile to America, American companies, and American geopolitical power. The Chinese government proposed a "strategic partnership" in 2000 and a "cooperative relationship" in 2005. Americans must recognize that China is a capitalist country (with Chinese characteristics) and that the Chinese government is experimenting incrementally with political reforms that American regime change policies obstruct rather than promote. Outdated 20th century Cold War realists, like Constantine Menges, are realistic in seeking to try to balance Chinese power with America's power, but the methods they would use are counterproductive.

America must accept the Chinese government and people's drives to eliminate hunger and achieve their full potential again.

The Chinese government must accept America's drive to preserve its standard of living and achieve their full potential again. Mutual respect is an essential part of the mindset that America and China enjoy prosperity and therefore peace together. How can America and China facilitate reciprocal respect?

The Reality of Human Fallibility and the Power of "Moral Authority"

All human beings, including political, military, and business geniuses, have finite and therefore fallible minds. We all grapple with varying degrees of success and failure with an infinite number of facts and cause-and-effect relationships that are beyond our ability to completely perceive or understand. When we strip away our pride and arrogance, all of us (geniuses, often, most of all), are guessing about most things that determine our fates. Realizing that can help Americans and Chinese to be more tolerant and better understand and deal with new things. Their ability to do so is at the cutting or melding edge of human intellectual evolution. Learning and conflict resolution are enhanced by comparison and tolerance of different ideas and ways of doing things. The partnership of America and China, in order to provide reciprocally sustainable prosperity and peace, must involve comparison and tolerance of the two nations' mindsets. This in time will lead to an integration of the two that is likely to be quite different, in each nation, than the mindsets at the beginning of the process.

Realizing that can also help us understand that in the 21st century it is not safe or sufficient for Americans to rely merely on economic and military power. America must also protect itself with the power of its national character and charisma.

America's "China strategy" must not overlook the power of the Chinese admiring America. To the degree America shows candor and concern for other nations, it has "Moral Authority," which is a critical strategic power in The China Game. The Chinese, for their part, will have to accept Americans as partners who have to be treated fairly.

The Chinese admire and revere America, but the Chinese expect to be treated fairly. Americans expect to be treated fairly. What is "fairly" in a "Rights Society" and "Permission Society" dichotomy? The common feature in both societies is that "you should not do unto others what you do not want done unto you."

The Beginning of a Mindset Shift Toward a New Model of the 21st Century World

A mindset shift to a win-win driven dialogue with China might be beginning to occur. But if so, it is in its earliest stage. The first step in the shift is the consideration of the notion that America and China can be equals. This is the stage in which they develop mutual respect, which previously was not a major feature of the relationship. America and China are working through a process, driven by compelling economic interdependence and necessity, and moving on a path on which there is a fork where strangers choose to be friends and partners or become barbarians.

As we have seen, the World Economic Forum's 2004 China Summit focused on a model in which America and China, the world's two giant economies, would share hegemony in the 21st century. That model may not be realistic given the overwhelming economic and intellectual competitive advantages China's 1.3 billion people have to outperform America's 300 million in the Knowledge Revolution. Even if it is realistic to think of America and China as economic equals in the future, China's economy will not become much larger than America's.

But Chinese culture views the stronger party as having duties of benevolence to the weaker, with whom there is a lasting, reciprocally beneficial relationship. The partnership between America and China is necessary to formalize such a Nash Equilibrium for America and China.

At the World Economic Forum 2004 Annual Meeting, the General Manager of the Bank Of China suggested that America "needs to reposition itself." He said:

> Manufacturing is gone; services are going. [The United States] needs to move up the development chain.[17] America has already lost 2.9 million jobs since 2000.[18] As China and other countries take U.S manufacturing jobs away, America also loses the industrial expertise and infrastructure needed to create the high end products [that] moving up the development chain requires.[19]

In 2005, a cover story in *Fortune* entitled "America Isn't Ready" stated:

> Respectable analysts believe it is possible—not certain, but possible—that the U.S standard of living after decades of steady ascent, could stall or even begin to decline. As for the big question at the center of it all—can we compete?—the answer is not obvious. The don't-worry-be-happy crowd points out that our last national fit of wailing and garment rending, when Japan was going to smite us in the 1980s proved unfounded. We adapted and prospered, as we always had (and Japan didn't). But today's situation is so starkly different that it's tough to find comfort in our experience then. We are not building human capital the way we used to. Our primary and secondary schools are falling behind the rest of the world. Our universities are still excellent, but the foreign students who come to them are increasingly taking their educations back home. As other nations multiply their science

and engineering graduates, building the foundation for economic progress, ours are declining.[20]

The New York Times reported that at the World Economic Forum's 2005 Annual Meeting:

> In almost every panel discussion at the annual meeting of the World Economic Forum there comes a moment when somebody mentions China. A hush typically ensues as panelists struggle to put the bewildering vastness of the topic into a few words. "China is going to be the change agent for the next 20 years" said Bill Gates, the chairman of Microsoft, when asked about the country's future while on a panel.
>
> China's staggering potential, coupled with the steep language barrier and cultural discomfort of many Chinese who came to this conference, has made it Davos' annual enigma. After three days of outsiders dissecting its motives and prospects, China finally took the stage on Saturday, with a speech by its executive vice prime minister, Huang Ju. "China's development will by no means pose a threat to other countries," Huang declared.
>
> He said little on the two issues of overriding importance to the investors and business people here: whether China would allow its currency to rise against the dollar, and whether the Chinese would crack down on the theft of intellectual property. "We have to maintain the exchange rate at a reasonable level" said Huang, who directs China's finance policy. Huang also did little to ease investors' concerns about China's regard for intellectual property rights, saying only that through new laws, and tougher enforcement, China was trying to achieve in a dozen years what it had taken the Western world a century to do.[21]

The Chinese government must develop a plan in collaboration with America's political and business leaders regarding what opportunities China can offer America to prosper from China's emergence from poverty. China must convince American leaders

and the American people that its growing economic competitiveness is not a threat. Is that possible? Is China's emergence
from poverty innately a threat or merely a problem that can be solved?
Is the China Game inherently a zero-sum-game? In our view, it is
not, and must not be perceived as, nor played as a zero-sum-game.

The Moral Authority of Candor and Consideration for the Needs and Goals of Other Nations

Tom Friedman's *The World Is Flat: A Brief History Of The 21st
Century*[22] quotes a Chinese central banker reportedly saying in a
private conversation with a Mexican central banker "First, we
were afraid of the wolf, then we wanted to dance with the wolf,
now we want to be the wolf."[23] The Chinese government's claim
that China's economic development "will by no means pose a
threat to other countries" pinpoints a key danger in The China
Game: hypocrisy. If China's claim that its development will not
harm other countries, particularly America, is not believed and
increasingly turns out to be wrong, China's development will be
attacked by America, either economically, militarily or both.
China's development is already felt by Americans as a threat to them.

Zero-sum-game strategies do not win friends and influence
people as well as win-win strategies. Therefore, all other things
being equal, zero-sum strategies are not as sustainable as "win-
win" strategies are. In the global village, there is no press or media
control, and no enduring secrets. A nation's policy and practice
must be aligned to be admired and respected. Candor and
concern for other nations also has profound "moral authority,"
which will safeguard and honor China in its relationships with
other nations. Zero-sum approaches may succeed in the short run,
but will ultimately fail because of their inherent limitations, as they
generate resistance and impede collaboration.[24]

Another example, from among an avalanche of alarming messages in the American and international press and media coverage of the economic threat China poses to other nations, is *Newsweek,* in a May 9, 2005, cover article, which commented:

> ...Americans like size, preferably super size. That is why China hits the American imagination...It is a country whose scale dwarfs the United States—1.3 billion people; four times America's population ... China is very big, but very poor. All that is changing. But now the so very alluring is beginning to look ominous and Americans are wondering whether the 'China threat' is nightmarishly real.[25]

The Chinese government realizes that it must use win-win strategies to ameliorate the increasingly perceived threat to America of China's relentlessly growing economic power.

Zero-Sum vs. Win-Win Strategies Debate: Will America and China Choose to Succeed?

Even if the Chinese government strives to use win-win strategies, what might such strategies be, and would America respond with zero-sum strategies to the use of win-win strategies by China? Optimists would say "The Chinese government must find and use such win-win strategies and America will respond with win-win strategies." Pessimists will say "America and China can't and won't use anything but zero-sum strategies in competing with each other. In any event, if China's government were to use win-win strategies unilaterally, nonetheless, America will respond with zero-sum strategies." We believe that the optimists are currently correct and must be correct. That is why we present, for debate and acceptance, the case for America and China becoming overt, committed partners using win-win strategies to solve each other's problems.

13

China's Past and Future Scientific and Technology Contributions to America

Overview

This chapter examines China's world leadership in exploration, science, and technology prior to the 18th century, and again in the 21st century, in order to change the mindset that assumes China lacks scientific and technological creativity. The reality is that China, having become "the factory floor of the world," now will become the "innovative economy of the world." It is very likely to succeed in doing so. The best strategy for America and American companies is to collaborate with China in exploring space, science, and technology.

The Beginning of America and China's Relationship

As we have seen, China was the leading economy in the global economy up until 1800 when its 400 million people produced 25% of the world's gross domestic product. China's status as the world's most advanced and largest economy was reflected in its leadership in discoveries of many of the technologies that helped create the Industrial Revolution and enabled the creation of America's wealth. It is useful to recognize this in laying the foundations for enhanced American respect and understanding of China's potential and character.

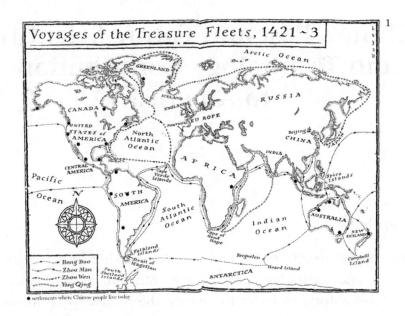

Christopher Columbus discovered America in 1492, but he was trying to reach India and China. China's involvement with America is believed to have begun in 1421. The map above shows the exploration of the world that made China a world leader in 1421–1423. Evidence was published in 2002 by Gavin Mendies in "1421":

The Year China Discovered America:

> On March 8, 1421, the largest fleet the world had ever seen set sail from China. Its mission was 'to proceed all the way to the ends of the earth to collect tribute from the barbarians beyond the seas, and unite the whole world in Confucian harmony."

When it returned in October 1423, the emperor had fallen, leaving China in political and economic chaos. The great ships were left to rot at their moorings and the records of their journeys were destroyed. Lost in China's long, self-imposed isolation that followed was the knowledge that Chinese ships had reached America seventy years before Columbus and had circumnavigated the globe a century before Magellan. Also concealed was how the Chinese colonized America before the Europeans and transplanted in America and other countries the principal economic crops that have fed and clothed the world.[2]

The Fallacy That China Is Less Technologically and Scientifically Capable Than America

China's status as the world's most advanced and largest economy was reflected in its leadership in discoveries of many of the technologies that helped create the Industrial Revolution, which enabled the creation of America's wealth. It is useful to recognize this in laying the foundations for enhanced American respect and understanding of China's potential and character.

Robert Temple's *The Genius Of China, 3,000 Years Of Science, Discovery, And Invention*[3] reviews one hundred critical inventions that assisted Europe and America's development since the Industrial Revolution:

> One of the greatest untold secrets of history is that the 'modern world' in which we live is a unique synthesis of Chinese and Western ingredients. Possibly more than half of the basic inventions and discoveries upon which the "modern world" rests come from China. And yet few people know this. Why?
>
> The Chinese themselves are as ignorant of this fact as Westerners. From the seventeenth century onwards, the Chinese became increasingly dazzled by European technological expertise, having experienced a period of amnesia regarding

their own achievements. When the Chinese were shown a mechanical clock by Jesuit missionaries, they were awestruck. They had forgotten that it was they who had invented mechanical clocks in the first place!

These myths and many others are shattered by our discovery of the true Chinese origins of many of the things, all around us, which we take for granted. Some of our greatest achievements turn out to have been not achievements at all, but simple borrowings. Yet there is no reason for us to feel inferior or downcast at the realization that much of the genius of mankind's advance was Chinese rather than European. For it is exciting to realize that the East and the West are not as far apart in spirit or in fact as most of us have been led, by appearances, to believe, and that the East and the West are already combined in a synthesis so powerful and so profound that it is all-pervading. Within this synthesis we live our daily lives, and from it there is no escape. The modern world is a combination of Eastern and Western ingredients, which are inextricably fused. The fact that we are largely unaware of it is perhaps one of the greatest cases of historical blindness in the existence of the human race.

Why are we ignorant of this gigantic, obvious truth? The main reason is surely that the Chinese themselves lost sight of it. If the very originators of the inventions and discoveries no longer claim them, and if even their memory of them has faded, why should their inheritors trouble to resurrect their lost claims? Until our own time, it is questionable whether many Westerners even wanted to know the truth. It is always more satisfying to the ego to think that we have reached our present position alone and unaided, that we are the proud masters of all abilities and all crafts.

...people belonging to the Euro-American civilization, are subconsciously inclined to congratulate themselves, feeling with some self-satisfaction that, after all, it was Europe and its extension into the Americas which developed modern science and technology. In the same way I think that all my Asian friends are subconsciously inclined to a certain anxiety about this matter, because their civilization did not, in fact, develop modern science and technology.

It would be better if the nations and the peoples of the world had a clearer understanding of each other, allowing the mental chasm between East and West to be bridged. After all, they are, and have been for several centuries, intimate partners in the business of building a world civilization. The technological world of today is a product of both East and West to an extent, which until recently no one had ever imagined. It is now time for the Chinese contribution to be recognized and acknowledged by East and West alike. And, above all, let this be recognized by today's schoolchildren, who will be the generation to absorb it into their most fundamental conceptions about the world. When that happens, Chinese and Westerners will be able to look each other in the eye, knowing themselves to be true and full partners.[4]

China's critical contributions to America and mankind's scientific and technological development include:

In warfare—chemical warfare, poison gas, smoke bombs, and tear gas, the crossbow, gunpowder, the flame thrower, flares, fireworks, bombs, grenades, land mines, sea mines, the rocket, and multi-staged rockets, guns, cannons, mortars, and repeating guns.

In transportation and exploration—the kite, manned flight with kites, the first relief maps, the first contour transport canal, the parachute, miniature hot-air balloons, the rudder, masts and sailing, watertight compartments in ships, the helicopter rotor and the propeller, the paddle-wheel boat, land sailing, the canal pound-lock;

In astronomy and cartography—recognition of sunspots as solar phenomena, quantitative cartography, discovery of the solar wind, Mercator map-projection, equatorial astronomical instruments;

In mathematics—the decimal system, a place for zero, negative numbers, extraction of higher roots and solutions of higher numerical equations, decimal fractions, using algebra in geometry, a refined value of Pi, 'Pascal's' triangle;

In magnetism—the first compasses, dial and pointer devices, magnetic declination of the Earth's magnetic field, and magnetic induction;

In the physical sciences—geo-botanical prospecting, the First Law of Motion, the hexagonal structure of snowflakes, the seismograph, spontaneous combustion, 'modern' geology, phosphorescent paint;

In engineering—spouting bowls and standing waves, cast iron, the double-acting piston bellows, the crank handle, the 'Cardan suspension', or gimbals, manufacture of steel from cast iron, deep drilling for natural gas, the drive belt (or driving belt), water power, the chain pump, the suspension bridge, the first cybernetic machine, essentials of the steam engine, 'magic mirrors', the 'Siemens' steel process, the segmental arch bridge, the chain-drive, underwater salvage operations;

In domestic and industrial technology—lacquer: the first plastic, strong beer (sake), petroleum and natural gas as fuel, paper, the wheelbarrow, sliding calipers, the magic lantern, the fishing reel, the stirrup, porcelain, biological pest control, the umbrella, matches, chess, brandy and whisky, the mechanical clock, printing, playing cards, paper money, permanent lamps, the spinning wheel;

In agriculture—row cultivation and intensive hoeing, the iron plow, efficient horse harnesses, the rotary winnowing fan, the multi-tube seed drill;

In medicine and health—circulation of the blood, circadian rhythms in the human body, the science of endocrinology, deficiency diseases, diabetes, use of thyroid hormone, immunology; and

In sound and music—the large tuned bell, tuned drums, hermetically sealed research laboratories, the first understanding of musical timbre, and equal temperament in music.[5]

China's previous economic, technological, and scientific world leadership is the first basis for realizing that China will reemerge in the 21st century as the world's economic, technological, and scientific leader, with all the potential for "peer leadership" that it entails. China had and has the ability to be the

"innovative economy of the world." China's strategy is the past 25 and next 25 years is the other basis.

The Reality of the Chinese Government's 21st Century Science and Technology Strategies

Deng Xiaoping, who re-opened China to the world, recognized that China must lead the world in science and technology in order to preserve its sovereignty in the modern world. In 1984, while visiting a science fair in Shanghai, Deng Xiaoping placed his hand on the head of the boy sitting at the computer in the picture above and proclaimed that such brilliant youths are the future of China and that computer education should begin with children. The scene was captured in a poster that was distributed throughout China. In a massive campaign to boost science and technology education, tens of millions of Chinese saw the poster, which became known as "Deng touched my head."

Microsoft is using many of the beneficiaries of Deng Xiaoping's science and technology education initiative.[8] Kai-Fu Lee, shown in the photo above right, headed a global research and development lab in Beijing that Microsoft created in 1998.[9] Google hired Kai-Fu Lee away from Microsoft.[10] The battle for Chinese talent will intensify. Many Chinese companies going global will increasingly attract such talent, many with experience leading foreign companies, as China becomes the "innovative economy of the world."

China's President, Jiang Zemin, stated in 2000:

> China will focus on developing high technology and push forward the informalization of the domestic economy and society...China is a developing country and the tasks of industrialization are yet incomplete. Now we are facing a hard task to realize informalization...Our strategy is that during the process of completing industrialization we will bring in information technology to enhance the level of industrialization and during the process of pushing forward informaltionazation, use information technology to reform traditional industries and use information to leap industrialization. We must endeavor to achieve a big technology leap.[11]
>
> China's current program of developing the information industry involves the promotion of an industrial strategy to activate information industry product manufacturing, software production and telecommunications facilities and network technology applications. There is no question that China is now [2001] an aggressive program to promote the information industry...[12]

China's Minister of Information Technology said in 2001:

> The new technology revolution of our contemporary world, represented by information and network technology, is vigorously pushing forward the development of social productive forces and changing the appearance of human society. First, the rapid development of microelectronics and software technology is causing the ratio between the operation capacity of chips, computers, performance and price to continue to increase in accordance with the rule of geometric progression, thus creating conditions for large scale and highly efficient collection, storage and processing of digitized information.
>
> Second, under the impetus of three technologies—microelectronics, software, and laser—telecommunication network technology has realized the transfer from simulation

to digital, from low speed to high speed and from single media to multimedia. In particular, the broad application of Internet and IP technology brought another leap of telecom network technology, promoting the emergence of a new generation of public network systems.

Third, the technologies of computer, telecom, and media technology are undergoing reciprocal penetration and merging into each other. They are pushing the development of information and network technology into a brand new epoch.[13]

Rapid development of information and network technology is speeding up the process of information online, leading to the rise of a network economy. While raw material suppliers, producers, and consumers are commonly connected through the network, the means of connection in the productive activities of mankind will be greatly improved. Due to unimpeded information between the supply and demand chain and the reduced role of the middle man and resultant savings in operating costs, the economic operating efficiency of our entire society will be greatly enhanced. For this very reason, at present, enterprises throughout the world will spend hundreds of billions of U.S. dollars on computers, software, and networks aimed at coping with the ever-growing challenges of the network economy now on the rise.

The network economy is the direct embodiment of electronic commercialization, reflecting the progressive organizational and structural adjustment of enterprise productivity. It is the reflection of the contemporary progress of technology in economic life. Meanwhile, online social services, which include government, education, medical treatment, and media-entertainment, are becoming a reality.

The Network Economy has now gone beyond just theory. Its realization has come upon us.[14]

While speeding the development of information technology and information network infrastructure facilities, we will emphasize the spread and application of information and network technology in all trades and professions. At present, we will focus on the online projects in connection with government, enterprise, and family; spread information knowledge; and promote the development and utilization of information resources.

We will vigorously support all kind of public departments and government institutions including finance, accounting, and taxation; customs; scientific research; education; culture; and hygiene. We will actively utilize the information technology and telecom networks to establish and perfect highly efficient and reliable social service information systems that must face specialized application. In addition, we will also encourage enterprises, in particular the large and medium sized enterprises, to utilize the spread and application of information and network technology as a tool to push forward the upgrade of traditional industries, improve enterprise management, and enhance the quality of products and the efficiency of enterprises.

We will put into play the enterprise activities encouraging enterprises to develop online electronic services. The government shall closely operate with enterprises and jointly promote the development of a network economy in order to create a proper environment of law and regulation, information security environment, and commercial environment for developing online commerce.

We will continue to adhere to the policy of reform and openness. Under the principle of mutual benefit and interest, we will continue to intensify economic and technical cooperation with countries all over the world. We will jointly develop information and network technology and industry and push forward national inforationalization and the cause of modernization.[15]

It is now a known fact that the information industry is the leading industry of our national economy. It is a catalyst and multiplier of economic growth. Over the past ten years, the average growth rate of the information industry has been more than three times the growth rate of the national GDP. Its contribution to national economic growth and the leading role it plays in affecting other industries increases daily. Over the next ten years, it is expected that China's information industry will continue to maintain a growth speed three times over that of GDP growth. In comparison with 1999, the proportion of China's information industry out of total national GDP has increased to 7.6% from 3.3% and the information industry's direct contribution to GDP growth is expected to rise to around 40% from the current 10.5%.[16]

In 2001, Mainland China's Internet users constituted 17 million of China's people.[17] In 2005, there were reportedly 100 million users in China.[18] In 2006 there were reportedly 316 million Chinese Internet users. *Business Week* noted:

> A contrived comparison maybe, but one that vividly illustrates how fast the Chinese Internet is evolving and how vast its long-term potential is. Just as impressive, using the same rate of growth [100% per year] Internet penetration in China, now at only 1.3%, will match the present United States level of just over 50% within the next ten years. By then this vast nation will be a full member of the World Trade Organization. No doubt, it will have cycled through several more rounds of economic reform programs and its infrastructure—technical and otherwise—will be on par with that of its competitors and trade partners in the West.[19]

On those assumptions, even if 100% of Americans were Internet users in 2011, they would in relative terms number approximately 300 million. If China reached 100% Internet penetration that would involve 1.3 billion people.

The Reality That China Is Becoming Both the "Factory Floor of the World" and "Innovative Economy of the World"[20]

In 2006, President Hu Jintao and Premier Wen Jiabao and other top Chinese government officials committed China to the

National Medium Term and Long Term Programme for Scientific and Technology Development (2006–2020). One goal of the programme is to reduce China's dependence on imported technology to 30% or less by 2020. Research and development spending will be increased from 1.23% to 2.5% of China's GDP by 2020. China's banks and government departments will support the program with their credit, taxation, and currency exchange polices.[21] China's educational system will also seek to do so.

Successful economies go through three stages in acquiring technology: mobilizing human and capital resources to fully exploit existing technology, copying technology from more advanced countries, and then building new industries based upon the advances in knowledge developed from their own research and development.[22] In 2006, foreign firms in China received 60% of the profits from China's high-tech exports.

China will move from copying 20th century technology to creating 21st century technology sooner and more significantly than many observers expect. As we have seen, China has led the world in creating many of the inventions that foreign economies used in their development in the past.[23] Many observers underestimate China's ability to suddenly leap forward in scientific genius:

> "China is still a decade—possibly much more—from serious scientific competition with the U.S., Europe and Japan. ... In short, the idea that China will soon leapfrog the U.S. in any major area of science is at war with the facts, with the notable exception of research on new energy sources."[24]

Is that realistic? China's leadership is focusing on making China a leader in technology to reduce its own manufacturers' reliance on foreigners for key components, and to narrow the gap with Taiwan, Japan, Europe, and America.[25] China's leader-

Learning Curve   29

Foreign doctoral candidates, who once flocked to
U.S. universities, increasingly stay home

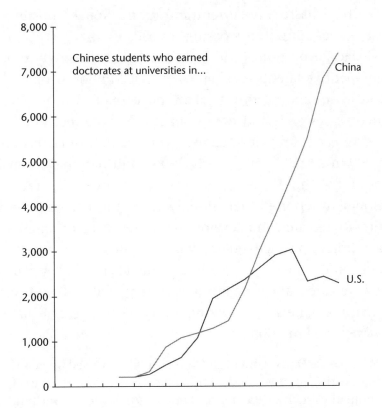

ship is focused on finding and developing breakthrough technologies that Chinese companies can use in becoming domestically and globally competitive and has deployed some of China's best minds and resources.

America graduates 50,000 engineers a year in a mature economy and China graduates 250,000 a year in an early-stage, developing economy.[26] In 2005, *Fortune* estimated that China would produce over 600,000 engineering graduates and America 70,000.[27] *Fortune* highlighted the crisis in a recent cover article that included the previous graph.

Already, Chinese nationals or Chinese Americans have founded twenty-five percent of America's Silicon Valley companies.[28] China has many current and future Nobel laureates who have been learning and working abroad. In the 21st Century's Knowledge Revolution, China will harvest increasingly more of the competitive talents and genius of its 1.3 billion people.

Low costs and plentiful talent have made China a global magnet for research and development. The number of foreign-funded research and development centers in China has grown from 200 in 2002 to 750 in early 2006. Multinational companies surveyed by the United Nations Conference on Trade and Development reported that China was the most frequently cited location for research and development, well ahead of America and India. China's attractiveness will increase as its intellectual property enforcement laws evolve.[30] China is now a key source of original research and intellectual property, with 60,000 science and math engineers graduating every year.[31] *The Wall Street Journal* reported in 2006:

> Whereas R&D investment in China initially focused on adapting existing products and technologies to the Chinese market, companies such as Procter & Gamble Co., Motorola Inc. and International Business Machines Corp. among many others, have been investing to expand their Chinese R&D operations to develop products for the global markets.... giving impetus to the R&D expansion in sectors such as biotechnology to pharmaceuticals to semiconductors in China's government. Having enlisted foreign investment to transform China into a manufacturing powerhouse over the past few decades, Beijing now is mounting a campaign to strengthen domestic innovation that could help push the country into more advanced niches of the global economy.
>
> In his annual report at the National People's Congress in Beijing ... Chinese Premier Wen Jiabao said the central government will

increase spending on science and technology by nearly 20% this year. "China has entered a stage in its history where it must increase its reliance on scientific and technological advances and innovation to drive social and economic development," he said.

China's State Council, or cabinet, recently said the country would seek to boost R&D investment to 2% of gross domestic product in 2010 and 2.5% by 2020...senior officials outlined tax breaks and other tools they plan to use to meet that target. Last year, total R&D spending in China—not including foreign investment—reached $29.4 billion, rising steadily from $11.13 billion in 2000, according to the government.

China still faces numerous obstacles to joining the ranks of the world's innovation leaders—beyond its weak intellectual-property protections. Research spending is still small compared with that of developed countries; the U.S., for example, spends about 2.7% of GDP on R&D, compared with 1.3% of GDP in China last year. And much of what is spent in China still comes from foreign companies: Less than a quarter of Chinese midsize and large enterprises had their own science and technology institutions in 2004. Of China's high-tech exports, valued at $218.3 billion last year, nearly 90% was produced by foreign-invested companies, according to the Ministry of Commerce.

Still, the R&D trend is bolstering China's position relative to other developing countries, particularly India, which is also seeking to build its innovation abilities. India's total domestic spending on R&D rose an estimated 9.7% to $4.9 billion, or 0.77% of GDP, in the fiscal year ended March 2005, according to India's Ministry of Science and Technology....

There has been a paradigm shift among foreign companies in China," says Chen Zhu, a Chinese Academy of Sciences vice president. "Now, more foreign companies realize China is not just a market but a country with huge amounts of talent."

Motorola, which began investing in low-level R&D in China in 1993, now has 16 R&D offices in five Chinese cities, with an accumulated investment of about $500 million. The U.S. company has more than 1,800 Chinese engineers, and the number is expected to surpass 2,000 this year. They have recently begun developing new phones and other products for sale not only in China, but also overseas, executives say. ...

Microsoft Corp.'s basic-research lab in Beijing was only its second outside the U.S. when it opened in 1998. That China lab now employs about 200 full-time scientists, and the software giant expects its total R&D headcount in China to double in this year to about 800 researchers.

At IBM's research lab in Beijing, Chinese scientists have led the development of several technologies now being used abroad. Among them: 'voice morphing' software that can convert typescript of a recorded voice into another voice. 'Our R&D now has a global mission,' says Thomas S. Li, director of IBM China Research lab.

At the state-run Institute of Computing Technology, engineers are taking on technology's tougher challenges: designing a computer microprocessor. Though still many years behind industry leaders like Intel Corp., the institute last year unveiled its second-generation microprocessor, with about the same computing power as mainstream chips in the late 1990s. This year, it plans to finish work on a third-generation chip that could narrow the gap.

China is also emerging as an R&D force in such sectors as nanotechnology, biotech and genetically modified crops. It was the first country to establish a full rice genome database, which has helped Chinese scientists develop hardier and higher-yielding strains of the staple cereal.

Swiss pharmaceuticals companies Novartis AG and Debiopharm SA have teamed up with the Shanghai Institute of Materia Medica under the Chinese Academy of Science to conduct research into traditional Chinese medicines to look for treatments for malaria and Alzheimer's disease. "This last decade, the progress we have seen in China's scientific research sector is phenomenal," says Ju Li-ya, director of Debiopharm's China department.[32]

Chinese companies increased yearly research and development spending from US$8 billion five years ago to US$18 billion in 2005. China's low wages for engineers allow companies to have shifts of them working twenty-four hours a day. China's best in each industry is first class. China's announcement that it is going to send men to the moon when America can no longer afford to do so was a declaration of intended future superiority. It seems that, together with India, China's intellectual and scientific capital will match and then surpass that of America in the 21st century.

Chinese companies are also focused on finding new technology breakthroughs to leap ahead of non-Chinese companies globally. Chinese companies are increasingly able to compete in China and globally in the high tech sector. Chinese-owned Huawei overtook an Alcatel joint venture to become the dominant supplier of digital switches and routers in China. Nonetheless, global market leaders Cisco, Nortel, and Alcatel did not feel threatened because they believed their high-end products were superior. Huawei entered the low end of the international market with routers that were 40% cheaper and took 3% of the world market by 2002. One Wall Street analyst was quoted in 2003 as saying that Huawei is "… the biggest reason I know to short Cisco's stock."[33]

In some areas, such as stem cell research, Chinese science already leads the world.[34] Even without foreign joint ventures' financial capital, Chinese companies' lower costs, intellectual and financial resources, and drive can take global market share faster than foreign competitors anticipate. For example, in the 1980s tourists from China brought lighters back from Japan and learned how to produce replicas. By 2002 they had 70% of the world market and the Japanese and South Korean lighter companies had gone out of business.[35]

The growth of Japan's economic power after 1945 started with a focus on cheap goods, but led to the global domination of many sophisticated industries including America's automobile, electronic, computer, etc. The growth curve of China's economic power after 1979 is similar, but its "thickness" and steepness reflects China's much larger and rapidly expanding domestic market and human, natural, intellectual, financial, and other resources.

America and China's Science and Technology Trends

Fortune commented in August 2005:

> No one is saying that Americans can't adapt and win once more. But look at our preparedness today for the emerging global economy, and the conclusion seems unavoidable: We are not ready.
>
> The key to fighting back is maintaining technological superiority—continually creating high-value new jobs that workers in the rest of the world can't do yet. What are the chances? A worrisome sign is that the brightest students from many Asian countries are staying home to get their Ph.D.s, rather than coming to America as they did in rising numbers until the mid-1990s. Those foreign Ph.D.s have been the driving force in scores of America's most successful and innovative tech firms, but now we are getting fewer of them, and other countries are getting more.
>
> Perhaps worse, those who still come to America for their Ph.D.s.—arguably the best of the best—are returning home in increasing numbers. In economies like China's or India's, growing two or three times faster than America's, elite students see huge opportunities. Even foreign nationals well established in the U.S. are heading home. "Many of my friends are going back", says Professor Godwin Wong of Berkeley's Haas School of Business. They're leaving big corporate jobs here because they can make more money in China.
>
> For the U.S. the loss of technology leadership could be historic. Without that advantage, there would be little to prevent living standards in the world's interconnected economies from equilibrating. The rest of the world's living standards would rise and—at least in the near term—America's would decline.[36]

What is important is that the current temporary weakness in Chinese business management skills and the inexperience of many Chinese executives and companies in doing business outside of China presents a window of opportunity for a non-Chinese company with "win-win" rather than "zero-sum-game" value propositions and strategies to position itself and profit immediately by partnering with Chinese companies to increase their SME management skills and learn how to operate the global companies they are now designing and deploying.

While American politicians, trade protectionists, and union leaders strive to preserve labor intensive, out-of-date industrial sectors, trying to delay competition and innovations, China has boldly tackled the out-of-date and inefficient SOEs and "iron rice bowl" at the price of great and painful unemployment, and focused on education and preparing its people to lead and be prepared for "Globalization 4.0." American political and union leaders must similarly focus on preparing America for the inevitable changes. The choice between resisting change or preparing for and adjusting to new realities determines the future of societies.

For-Profit Management Skills

America is a successful, rich, developed learning society. China is a knowledge-hungry, developing, learning society. China is rapidly absorbing non-Chinese-generated knowledge. The competitive advantages that China's hunger for knowledge gives presents the scenario of two highly intelligent "students of the future," one of whom is rich and the other poor. All other things being equal, the poor boy works with greater passion, desperation, and dedication than the rich boy.

In 1978, few Mainland Chinese were studying abroad, but now 600,000 have and 200,000 have returned home.[37] China's for-profit management skill will dwarf America's as more of the Chinese studying abroad are attracted home by the enormous opportunities to pursue personal wealth and contribute to their homeland at the same time.

Some observers may underestimate China's ability to suddenly leap forward in business management skills. For example:

> Weak management is the major constraint on the competitiveness of Chinese companies. Despite two decades of joint ventures and enormous investments in training, Chinese managers continue to fail the critical tasks of systems integration and optimization. The problem is fundamental, embedded in the economic system itself. The dominance of state-owned enterprises in major manufacturing and service sectors, together with extensive state intervention through the economy, has sustained the premium on good political skills over modern management capabilities.[38]

Generations of Chinese business managers with experience only in SOEs and planned economy management contexts undoubtedly lack market-economy-attuned management skills and habits. The speed with which China's leadership has moved to create a joint stock economy, privatize under-performing SOEs, and pivot from planning and administering China's economic miracle to regulating it, suggests that it is unrealistic to assume that foreign companies will have long-term advantages because of the weak business management skills of the Chinese.[39]

Sea Turtles Spawn Economically and Scientifically

Mainland Chinese who have gone abroad are called "sea turtles." Their impact on the development of Chinese business, science, and technology, and on China's rate of economic development in the future will be cumulatively more profound than some observers may envisage. Deng Xiaoping was once asked whether he was hopeful about China's future. His reply was, "Just wait till the...Chinese students return from American universities. That's when real change will come."[40] In 2002–2003, there were 64,000 Mainland Chinese students studying in America.[41] Other Mainland Chinese students were studying in more than 100 countries.[42] In 2002, the total number of Mainland Chinese students studying abroad was reportedly 160,000. Between 1978 and 1998, 21,000 Mainland Chinese earned doctorates in science and engineering in foreign universities constituting 7.5% of the global total. The Mainland Chinese are particularly evident at the doctoral level in science and engineering, which are critical for research, development, and educating more students in China.[43] China's global share of published scientific articles grew from 0.63% to 1.86% to 3.54% in 1986, 1997, and 2001.[44] The Chinese government has several programs to entice such people, both new Ph.D.s and those with foreign corporate and research work experience to return to China. They are the huge human capital that China must bring into participation in sustaining its "economic miracle", and offer America and China a huge group of individuals brought up in Mainland China and educated in America. In 1986 thru 1998, 85% of Mainland Chinese planned to stay in America, and in 1998 48% accepted employment offers in America, but this was down from 88% in 1995. Other estimates indicate that 25% to 30% of the sea turtles are returning home to the land of their birth.[45] The generations of sea turtles that have gone abroad since 1978 are emerging in leadership positions in businesses both inside and outside of China.

The partnership between America and China in business, science, technology, education, and social welfare can help sea turtles find their natural place as "change agents" who can shape the mutual respect and goodwill that China and America's partnership requires. The often-exceptional capabilities and bi-cultural backgrounds equip them to be an important link in the America-China partnership. Sea turtles also have a vital personal interest in seeking to forestall America and China taking the ruinous path of trade war and armed conflict. While contributing much to China upon their return, they are a new influence who would be caught, in many instances, in an invidious position if America and China become enemies rather than friends.

Case Study: William Xin

46

William Xin

William's Xin's life illustrates the changes in China and the untapped talent of China that is "coming on line." He grew up in Northern China, among the approximately 900 million Chinese that are not yet fully participating in China's economic success. Approximately 400 million of the 1.3 billion Chinese in the coastal regions are currently driving China's phenomenal emergence as the world's leading economic superpower. William was one of the 900 million Chinese from the inland regions who are not currently actively participating in China's economic growth.

William was a boy of twelve working on his family's farm in 1979 when China opened diplomatic and trade relations with America. While a student in Northern China in 1989, William traveled to Beijing and emerged as one of the leaders in the Tiananmen Square Anti-Corruption Demonstrations. Afterwards, in America, he set out to learn what China needs to know so he could continue to add value to his country.

William earned Physics and MBA degrees from Yale. His first job in America was doing mathematical modeling for Richard Sandor, who played a leading role in the evolution of the commodities, derivatives, and reinsurance industries. William then worked for a venture capital firm backed by George Soros, Oppenheimer Funds, the Heritage Foundation, and the Kouri family, where he focused on emerging markets and new technology. In that role, William helped in building-up several portfolio companies including China Cement Company, which produced over 600,000 tons of cement annually.

William moved on to learn more. He took a job as Chief Operating Officer at Premier Heart Inc., a medical equipment research and development company. Then, to gain more knowledge, experience, and judgment, William co-founded the Cheetah Global Financial Group, where he led mergers and acquisition projects.

William did this in preparation for creating BchinaB Inc., a profitable company he founded with offices in New York and China. *The Wall Street Journal*, in a page-1 March 12th, 2002, article dubbed William a "budding plastics tycoon" in making supply chains more efficient in China. With these experiences, William returned to the venture capital sector.

In 1996, William was elected the Chairman of the Board of the Independent Federation of Chinese Students and Scholars, which had over 40,000 MA and PhD student members in North America.

At least 10,000 of these sea turtles have now returned to China. In 2003, William became the first fellow of the China Bermuda Society, which assists mainland Chinese companies becoming multinational companies.

Executive Talent Absorption

China will need 75,000 globally-capable executives in the next five years, but had less than 5000 in 2005. Chinese companies are energetically recruiting mid-level and senior executives away from leading multinational companies in China. In 2000, locals made up just 20% to 30% of managers recruited in China, but today that figure is 60% to 70%. Chinese companies are cherry-picking the best talent among Mainland Chinese executives working with multinationals, offering higher salaries, stock options, and the opportunity to make a greater contribution and take more responsibility. The Chinese talent is attracted because they find there are more important things they can do for a Chinese company than with a multinational. For example, the president of Shanda Interactive Entertainment, a NASDAQ-listed Chinese company, was head of Microsoft's Chinese operations. Lenovo's head of corporate communications came from Ogilvy & Mather. Huawai, Haier, China Netcom, and Brilliance China have recruited from McKinsey, A.T. Kearney, and Boston Consulting Group. Chinese companies are looking for talent overseas.[47]

Training Employees

Americans should not underestimate China's growing business management's adaptability and capability. For example, Chinese manufacturers' on-time delivery rate is reportedly 99%, compared to 96% for U.S. manufacturers; 98% meet specifications on the first try, compared to 97% for U.S. manufacturers; and 53% of Chinese manufacturers offer training to workers compared to 35% of U.S. manufacturers.[48]

The Hypocrisy of American Capitalism Claiming That China Has an "Unfair Advantage"

America's political and business leaders can not credibly take the view that Chinese companies are somehow "unfair competitors." Such a claim is hypocritical for several reasons. First, they did not complain when American multinationals enjoyed huge competitive advantages in the 20th century. American domestic and foreign policy does what it can to give American companies competing globally what many foreign companies view as "unfair competitive advantages." For example, Yasheng Huang's analysis of foreign direct investment in China in *Selling China*[49] sets out the Chinese government's economic development policy of giving foreign companies unfair competitive advantages over Mainland Chinese entrepreneurs and companies in the process of giving SOEs unfair competitive advantages. Secondly, American state power has fostered what many observers might characterize as "unfair competitive advantages" for American companies (i.e., CNOOC's bid for Unocal). Thirdly, America and American companies cannot win friends and influence people in the court of international opinion by taking the position that capitalism is good for America but "unfair" if capitalism also gives China a competitive advantage. Fourthly, capitalism glories in "unfair competitive advantages." They are what capitalists seek. American multinationals do not recoil in horror when they find they have "unfair advantages" in global markets.

Hypocrisy is not an impressive or effective means of persuasion. Hypocrisy is counter-productive. American politicians and companies complaining that a Chinese company becoming a multinational has an "unfair advantage" is a position that reduces American policy to being one purely of power rather than also of principle. Power that is not based on principle is ultimately based on force rather than persuasion. Force degrades rapidly.[50]

American politicians and companies complain that Chinese companies seeking to invest in America, as American companies have invested in China, complain because they are weak. Weak players should not use force as a key strategy alone. Force is useful as a stick, but where is the carrot? If there is no carrot, no "you scratch my back and I'll scratch yours," American policies of containment will degrade. "Do unto others what you would have them do unto you." The inherent weaknesses of "the force of American containment policies toward China" are that it generates opposition, is only effective temporarily, and damages American interests. Collaboration generates little or less opposition, and instead of degrading rapidly, can grow exponentially. Principle is ultimately more resilient than force or hypocrisy.[51] The capitalist market principles and rule of law that America's political system is based on are among America's greatest national assets and sources of moral authority.

Fifthly, even if American political and business leaders take a containment approach, China is going to pursue its emergence from poverty, just as America has. There are many other countries and companies that will engage in business with China. If America decides to continue on a path of containment towards China, it will travel in the wrong direction.

If You Can't Beat them, Join Them: A Win-Win Rather than Zero-Sum-Game Strategy

As we have seen, CNOOC's superior access to and low or nil cost of capital is an illustration of one of China's Socialist Market Economy Capitalism's advantages. Since American companies like Chevron cannot compete with the access and cost of capital that many Chinese companies going global have, they could choose to enter into genuine global joint ventures. Chinese companies are currently struggling to learn how to be successful multinational companies. The evoking of American state power to block higher bids for American companies can degrade very rapidly as zero-sum-game strategies often do. Instead of Chinese companies investing in and becoming part of American genuine global joint ventures, as Legend and IBM did in 2005 to form Lenovo, Chinese companies will work with companies that are not American. Containment is a lose-lose zero-sum-game strategy for dealing with the emergence of "Mega Multinational" companies in the coming years.

Alignment Opportunity: A New American and Chinese Collaborative Approach in Science and Technology

American political and business leaders who focus on foreigners adopting American technology often overlook that foreigners in many instances helped create such technology. After the attacks of September 11, 2001, America's openness to such foreigners has severely changed. There are instances of very gifted foreigners being denied the opportunity to study and work in America.[52] With this change, American political leaders have undermined America's historic success in attracting the world's best and brightest. Many observers are indicating profound concern at the ramifications for the development and competitiveness of America. China has done just the opposite. It has sought to attract as much foreign scientific, technological, and management talent as possible, and succeeded.

As we have seen, the many Chinese who have been educated in America since 1979 facilitate American and Chinese collaboration. *Business Week* has suggested that China's rapid rise in science could make it a valuable ally of America's in breakthrough research.[53]

China's newly built Shanghai's Institute for Antibodies is quiet. No researchers yet toil amid the recently installed rows of DNA, mass spectrometers, and other state of the art scientific tools. But the 100 Ph.D. researchers and 2,000 technicians and other staffers will be developing cancer treatments at the new $60 million facility in Shanghai's Zhangjiang Hi-Tech Park. "Everything is brand-new here," says Guo, 50, a professor of oncology and immunology at University of Nebraska's Eppley Institute who splits his time between the U.S. and China. "The equipment is much better than my lab in the U.S." Researchers with U.S. experience like Guo are helping to power a remarkable surge in Chinese science. Zhangjiang Hi-Tech Park has become a hotbed of new biotechnology research facilities. Eight government run labs, including the Shanghai Transgenic Research Center, are located in the park, which is also home to 34 local, and multinational drug makers. Roche Holdings Ltd. opened a research and development center nearby last year. And Chinese government spending on R&D is on the rise. It has more than tripled since 1998, and the number of scientific papers from Chinese researchers has more than doubled in that time … if current trends continue, … by 2010 China will produce more science and engineering Ph.D.s than the U.S. …

Experts increasingly see the change of a win-win result from the combination of Chinese and American research might. That is one of the motivations for Wise Young, director of the W.M. Keck Center for Collaborative Neuroscience at Rutgers University, when he decided to set up a network of 17 clinical centers in China and train researchers to test new therapies Born in Hong Kong, Young is a leader in the search for spinal-cord injury cures … Young's clinical centers could help China become a leader in important new areas such as stem cell and nerve regeneration. They could also offer a way for Western companies to get their own treatments to market more quickly. Young says, "Costs for conducting clinical trials in China is about one-fourth of those in the U.S." And while China is previously known for poorly regulating clinical trials, the government is beefing up standards in a bid to attract more Western companies to test their drugs there.

Beijing is also working hard to lure American-educated Chinese scientists back to the Mainland. One way of doing that is hiring returnees, such as Han Jie, 48, a University of Utah Ph.D. in materials science and engineering, to run government institutes. Han worked for IBM and for NASA's Ames Center for Nanotechnology before becoming director of premier Chinese nanotech lab, the National Engineering Research Center for Nanotechnology in Shanghai.... "In the U.S., we try to build up technology for the future, but in China, I try to build technology that can be used today," Han says.

No doubt, some Chinese scientists will wind up becoming world-beaters, challenging their counterparts in the U.S. What is important is that researchers from both countries also expand their efforts at collaboration. That will pay off for all.[54]

The Organization for Economic Cooperation and Development produced the graphs, over, comparing the number of researchers and research and development expenditures in 2003 of America, the European Union, Japan, and China. If you compare the population of the other three with China's and extrapolate out a few years, the number of researchers, costs of research in China, and amounts available to China to spend on research and development will dwarf the others. Remember China has been participating in world trade only since 1978, and currently uses only 30% of its 1.3 billion people.

Year by year, decade by decade, more and more of China's "intellectual capital" or population will be given the new opportunity to participate and be brought "online" in the global economy. China has many more competitive advantages in the 21st century's Knowledge Revolution and Globalization 3.0 than it had during the formulative twenty-five years, from 1978 to 2003, in China's economic, scientific, and technological reform and development.

RESEARCHERS 2003 [55]

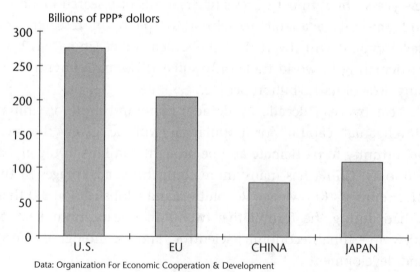

MILLIONS

Data: Organization For Economic Cooperation & Development

Gross Domestic Expenditure On R&D 2003

Billions of PPP* dollors

Data: Organization For Economic Cooperation & Development

Case Study: American and Chinese Collaboration in a Genuine Global Joint Venture Expediting the Commercialization of Plasma Energy

There may be an opportunity to significantly enhance a major new Chinese government program pioneering the commercialization of a new electricity source from plasma energy technology. The development of plasma energy technology is an example of combining American, Russian, and Chinese resources. In 1958, the United States government declassified research regarding plasma energy, developed in the Manhattan Project's creation of atomic bombs. Russia, under President Putin, recently also declassified information regarding plasma energy research. This declassified information involves an attempt to find a new source of cheap electricity. Existing research by an American company, GAT, Princeton University, MIT, and the University of Texas has proven the scientific potential of the plasma technology. However, commercializing plasma energy technology is not a priority for GAT or America at this time. American energy companies are focused on profits from existing technology, and the commercialization of plasma energy will take many years.

Commercializing plasma energy would be advantageous to China. The Chinese government has recently committed US$10 billion for a plasma energy program, which involves many of China's leading experts in the plasma, super-computing, laser, and other technology fields. However, to expedite the creation of a plasma energy demonstration plant, a budget of US $20 billion, assigning a larger team of Chinese researchers, and further funding will be required to move to the full commercialization of this technology.

The project applies American and Russian research developed in part by GAT, which was then funded by the United States Department of Energy, and private investors such as Tri

Alpha, a venture capital firm in Irvine, California. The project could be expedited and enhanced significantly if the owners of GAT sold all or part of GAT to American and Chinese investors. This could help establish an important new template in which the Chinese government uses its commitment to new energy and pollution-control technology to assist such Chinese and American joint ventures and international capital markets to fund the commercialization of plasma energy technology. Another benefit could be to increase the "brain power" collaboration and links between American and Chinese universities and research centers.[56]

Case Study: China and America's Space Programs

America's current space program is less ambitious than the space program China is pursuing. China announced that early in the 21st century it intends to send a manned mission to the moon. America's so-far unique achievement of sending and returning Americans from the moon was a spectacle all of mankind had to hold in awe. This was a declaration of equality with America. It could be mutually beneficial for America and China to collaborate rather than compete in the exploration of space. This could be a signature gesture for the American and Chinese partnership in the 21st century. Certainly, the combined effort would be more than the sum of its parts. Why reinvent what America has done? Why not enrich, and expand the horizon of what mankind can achieve?

14

The Reform of America and China's Intellectual Property Piracy

Overview

This chapter examines the development of the concept of "intellectual property" and notes that in the 19th century, America was a leading intellectual property rights pirate. America did not move to protect intellectual property rights until its economic and technological prowess reached the point where it was advantageous for America to do so. China is following in America's footsteps, or intellectual property privacy boots. Now, early in the 21st century, China is incrementally moving in what may be as short as a ten-year process towards recognizing and protecting intellectual property rights. Because China's economic rise is faster than America's economic rise in the 17th to late 20th centuries, the recognition and protecting of intellectual property rights will likely occur faster in the evolution of capitalism in China than it did in the emergence of capitalism in America.

The Absorption of Ideas or "Intellectual Property": When Is Learning Stealing?

It is ironic that the infringement of intellectual property rights is one of the major issues that America and Europe have with China today. When China made the ancient discoveries discussed in chapter 13, America was unsettled by Europeans, and Europeans were living in more primitive conditions than the Chinese. Such complaints do not take into account many important points:

1. Europe and America did not compensate China for the scientific and technological contributions absorbed in their economic progress that was substantially based on Chinese discoveries.

2. Europe and America obtained at no cost the Chinese discoveries. Human beings learn and share "ideas."

3. The reason no royalties or fees were paid to China for the "intellectual property" discovered by China is that, at the time the discoveries and inventions were made, China, Europe, and America did not have a system of law that recognized property rights in ideas, discoveries, and inventions, just as China lacks a system enforcing intellectual property rights at this time.

4. It is ironic to accuse China of "stealing" or "pirating" foreign "intellectual property," as China only recently began the initial steps in the process of legally recognizing property rights for any entity other than the state.

5. The Chinese assimilating foreign "intellectual property" today without paying for it did not grow up in a "Rights Society" in which private property is a quintessential principle.

6. From a historical perspective, foreigners could be viewed as paying China with today's "ideas" or "intellectual

property" for the "ideas" (intellectual property) China gave them in the past.

7. China's "absorption of foreign intellectual property" is an example of foreigners seeking to impose their laws, to their advantage, on China. From China's Pre-Rule of Law perspective, China is "learning" (not "stealing") about "ideas" (not "intellectual property").

8. This illustrates the contrast between the Rights Society concept of "stealing intellectual property" and the Pre-Rule of Law perspective of the "absorption of ideas".

9. For China to be a respected and accepted partner in global trade, it has to improve its regime of intellectual property protection. It is doing so.

10. China may also benefit from introducing and enforcing intellectual property rights, because doing so promotes Chinese discovery, invention, and innovation. It is such property rights and their protection that assisted in producing the major technological leaps achieved by the West.

Towards a Better Understanding of the Interaction of "Rights Society" and "Permission Society" Mindsets

The above ten points illustrate how it is useful to see issues (like "stealing intellectual property") from both the "Rights Society" and the "Permission Society" perspectives simultaneously. If two societies have different moral codes, how do you judge them? When two societies that have different ways of seeing and doing things have to work together, neither should mindlessly project or impose their mindset and way of doing things and hold the other summarily responsible for "bad behavior" or "bad character." A more mature and sophisticated approach is needed in the partnership of America and China.

A Prediction Regarding China's Future Protection of Intellectual Property Rights

It is important for Americans to realize and acknowledge that America was a leading pirate of intellectual property rights. Oded Shenkar notes:

> China is not the first nation to openly violate intellectual property rights (IPR). It may come as a surprise to many Americans, but the United States, who today leads a global effort to curb IPR violations, was itself a major violator during the nineteenth century...Charles Dickens'...royalty demands were rebuffed by U.S. publishers of the time. When American publishers infringed on the rights of British authors, however, there was not much else that could be copyrighted. The situation today is vastly different. According to the International Intellectual Property Alliance (IIPA), the core U.S. copyright industries accounted for 3.24 percent of U.S. GDP in 2001, to $535.1 billion. From 1997 to 2001, these industries grew at a rate of seven percent annually, more than twice that of the economy as a whole. Employment in this segment grew nearly three times faster than in the national economy and now accounts for 4.7 million U.S. jobs [in 2005]. Exports reached $88.97 billion. From 1977 to 2001, these industries grew at a rate of seven percent annually, more than twice that of the economy as a whole. Employment in this segment grew nearly three times faster than in the national economy, more than for the aircraft or automotives sectors. Other industries, from pharmaceuticals to electronics, are heavily reliant on property rights to protect huge development costs and brand building expenditure, as are service providers. IPR underlie the lead of the United States, and to a lesser extent Japan, the European Union (EU), and other developed economies, in technology-intensive industries of the future. IPR protection is a key element in all free market economies, underpinning the incentive to innovate, develop, invest, and produce. Violations are easier to commit, however: "Digitized" products can be downloaded

off the Internet, and disc production machines can be had for a fraction of their price a decade ago. In today's global environment, IPR infringements show up not only as local market losses but also as worldwide forfeiture of revenue and reputation.

The American precedent may yet be followed by China. Compliance and eventual championship of IPR by the United States came after its legal system had matured and its laws became enforceable. However, compliance and vigorous defense did not come about until America emerged as a major producer of copyrighted knowledge, with more to lose from IPR infringement than to gain from evading those rights. China, too, may become a defender of IPR in due course, but this will not occur until its firms have become technology leaders... In the meantime, China continues to get a free ride on the technology and reputation of legitimate, mostly foreign manufacturers, which is tolerate, often supported, and at times, even orchestrated by Chinese authorities, especially at the local level.[1]

Shenkar also notes:

ABC news recently estimated the losses suffered in China by foreign firms [from IPR infringement] at $20 billion annually. Two out of five foreign manufacturers are losing more than 20% of their local revenue, which for a company like Procter & Gamble, amounts to $150 million a year. In some categories, fakes have now taken over from the original as market leaders. Many imitations are of dubious quality ... others are made surprisingly well and have garnered admiration from brand owners, in some cases even prompting joint ventures with the offenders.[2]

The chart and graphs, over, contain data on intellectual property infringement losses and the types of patents granted to Chinese and non-Chinese in 2001.

Yesterday's intellectual property pirates become today's zealous proponents of intellectual property rights enforcement.

Estimated piracy losses in China for Digital Products, 1990–2003 Millions USD

INDUSTRY	1999		2000		2001		2002		2003	
	loss	level	loss	level	loss	level	loss	level	loss	level
MOTION PICTURE	120	90%	120	90%	160	88%	168	91%	178	95%
RECORD & MUSIC	70	90%	70	93%	47	90%	48	90%	286	90%
BUSINESS SOFTWARE APPLICATIONS	437.2	91%	765.1	94%	1140	92%	1637.3	92%	1593.3*	93%*
ENTERTAINMENT SOFTWARE	1382.5	95%	NA	99%	455	92%	NA	96%	568.2	96%
BOOKS	128	NA	130	NA	130	NA	40	NA	40	NA
TOTALs	NA		1893.3		1933		1085.1		2137.7	

3

*2002 figures

Source: International intellectual property alliance; People's Republic of China

Types of Patents Granted to Chinese (2001)

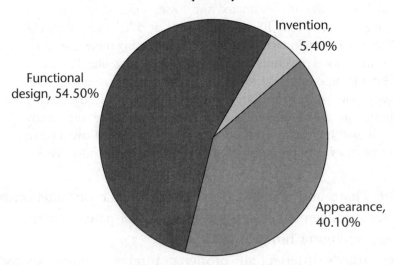

Invention, 5.40%

Functional design, 54.50%

Appearance, 40.10%

Source: National Bureau of Statistics and Ministry of S&T, 2002–2003

Types of Patents Granted to Foreigners (2001)

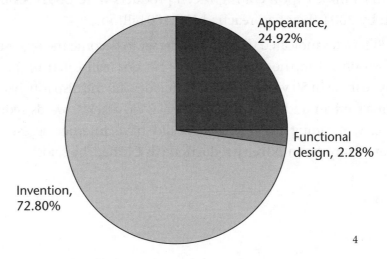

Appearance, 24.92%

Functional design, 2.28%

Invention, 72.80%

4

Source: National Bureau of Statistics and Ministry of S&T, 2002–2003

On January 27, 2006, America and China traded barbs over China's failure to respond to America's request for details about China's efforts to combat intellectual property piracy. In 2005, Americans claimed a third of all new technology patent applications. The growth rates of patent applications in America and China in 2005 were 3.8% and 43.7% respectively in 2005.[5]

On January 28, 2006, Bill Gates commented at the World Economic Forum that beating software piracy in China and getting compliance up to American and European levels would take ten years. He stated, "But, as long as there is year-by-year progress, it holds a great opportunity in terms of scale, which helps us do more, and it's a great place where we have people helping us." He indicated that sales of Microsoft's products went up every year in China and he was optimistic that China would come around to licensing compliance as Taiwan and South Korea had done.[6] China's exports of high-tech products are growing. In 1998 Chinese exports of high-tech products were US$20.2 billion, and by 2004 they had reached US$160 billion.

Bill Gates indicated that China was set to become the biggest user of broadband in the world stating, "No one will catch up [except] maybe India in 50 years." He stated that despite the disparity between China's urban and rural areas, China is on track towards reducing poverty, meaning more people would have Internet access. "The greatest surprise in poverty reduction…is China," he said.[7]

15

Establishing America and China's Committed Partnership

Overview

This chapter examines how the committed partnership of America and China can be established, "the hostile observer" phenomena, and the application of Game Theory's most successful "Generous Tit-For-Tat Strategy" to America and China's relationship.

A 21st Century America & China Partnership

Over 480 of America's biggest companies have made large investments in China, focusing on the competitive advantages China offers them, and on making money rather than amassing majority-rule electoral victories. The stakes for America and American companies in the choice between collaboration or confrontation with China and Chinese companies are very high. Zero-sum-game strategic American responses to China's rapidly deploying economic power will accelerate and exacerbate America's losses in economic competitiveness and growth while China's economic competitiveness and growth rates increase.

They are not helpful to America or China. American business leaders more readily grasp the futility of an American government containment policy towards China than many of America's political leaders do today.

As we have seen, China may transition into a "Rights Society" if it suits the needs of China's leaders and people to do so. But America could transition into a "Permission Society" if popular support for democratic processes, institutions, and rights diminish as American power is dwarfed by China's economy. It is hoped that America and China will increasingly understand, respect, and trust their differences as China's economy grows. Friends are more useful than foes.

Pessimists will say, "Sooner or later, something will go wrong. No nation has risen peacefully to preeminence. Two such powerful countries with such different systems of government and so much national arrogance must confront each other in armed conflict. Once such conflict starts, war will erupt."

Optimists will say "Human beings who want to, can find solutions to problems that human beings create." We are optimists. The futility of a war between America and China is a new reality that China's and America's leaders must mutually see. Our fate is in the hands of America and China's leaders, whoever they may be. Their ability to "get along" could falter. Our fate is also ultimately in the hands of the American and Chinese people. Public opinion shaped by national pride, anger, paranoia, and a myriad of ingredients in human conduct will determine our fate.

Some Americans Are "Friends of China"

Some Americans are what the Chinese refer to as "friends of China." The more Americans understand of the worldview, hardships, relentless drive, and capabilities of the Chinese people, and the goals of the Chinese government, the more mutual respect in The China Game is engendered. America's containment policy is the key problem. President Hu is offering to collaborate with President Bush and American political leaders in seeking win-win responses to the inevitable problems in the relationship. Hopefully, American political and business leaders will accept that a paradigm shift is occurring and that a mindset change is essential, and become "friends of China." Unless the logic and empirical evidence presented in this book are wrong, that is the only smart choice for Americans.

A 2005 survey reported the following attitude distributions in America regarding China[1]:

Impressions of China 2

	General Public	Opinion Leaders	Congressional Staffers	Business Leaders	Chinese-Americans
Very Favorable	9%	15%	1%	17%	29%
Somewhat Favorable	50%	48%	18%	46%	46%
Favorable	59%	63%	19%	63%	75%
Somewhat Unfavorable	26%	28%	63%	29%	17%
Unfavorable	35%	37%	79%	35%	23%
Very Unfavorable	9%	9%	16%	6%	6%
Not Sure	6%	0%	2%	1%	3%

Note that congressional staffers are much more hostile to China than the other groups in the survey. Congressional staffers are at the vortex of the focus of various pressure groups hostile to China for economic or ideological reasons.[3] Such pressure groups' impact must be recognized. Peace and prosperity could be undone by the freedom of democracy. The issue we focus on is not whether China will become an American-style democracy. The real issues are: Will America remain a democracy? And will American Majority-Rule Democracy be able to avoid conflict with China's Consensus Democracy? Is democracy sustainable in America or China in the 21st century?

Is America Politically Capable of Choosing to Collaborate with China?

Is America politically capable of choosing to collaborate with China? The answer to that question is a fascinating test of human nature and wisdom. The Chinese government and people currently want peace with America. There is some anti-American rhetoric in Chinese government publications, and without careful stewardship, nationalism could mutate into confrontational attitudes towards America. However, peace is essential to sustaining China's prosperity. America's leadership and people must also want peace with China. That is the challenge America's political and business leaders face as China moves forward economically. The size and scope of China's economic, intellectual, scientific and technological growth make collaboration America's pragmatic choice. Within the framework of a genuine global partnership, America and China will share prosperity and peace.

As we have seen, the Bush Administration deals with President Hu Jintao and the Chinese government with a zero-sum-game mindset and strategies. The implementation and resiliency even in failure of such a mindset and strategies can be explained, in part, by America's democratic institutions and decision-making processes. They enable 50.0001% of Americans or less to impose their domestic and foreign policy perspectives and choices on America, China, and the world. American domestic and foreign policy can bet against the success of China's 21st century domestic and foreign policy. American capitalism can seek to contain capitalism with Chinese characteristics. American companies can compete rather than collaborate with Chinese companies.

The Chinese Consensus Democracy's institutions and decision-making processes, examined in Chapters 4, 5, and 6, are more supportive to pragmatic rather than ideologically driven policy design and implementation.

The American Neo-Con Reality

George Soros, in *The Bubble Of American Supremacy*,[4] has warned that there is an American foreign policy agenda that endangers America's national security, democracy, and openness as a society:

> The underlying principles of this agenda can be summed up as follows: International relations are relations of power, not law; power prevails and law legitimizes what prevails. The United States is unquestionably the dominant power in the post-Cold War world; it is therefore in a position to impose its views, interests, and values on the world. The world would benefit from adopting American values because the American model has demonstrated its superiority...However, the United States failed to use the full potential of its power. This has to be corrected. The United States must assert its supremacy in the world.
>
> This view of foreign policy is part of a comprehensive ideology customarily referred to as neo-conservatism, but I prefer to describe it as a crude form of social Darwinism. I call it crude because it ignores the role of cooperation in the survival of the fittest and puts all the emphasis on competition.[5]

Soros presents a different vision for America:

> The United States is the only country that can take the lead in addressing problems that require collective action: preserving the peace, assuring economic progress, protecting the environment, and so on. Fighting terrorism and controlling weapons of mass destruction also fall into this category.

The United States cannot do whatever it wants, but nothing much can be done in the way of international cooperation without the leadership or at least active participation of our nation. The United States has a greater degree of discretion in deciding what shape the world should take than anybody else. The other countries have to respond to U.S. policy, but we can choose the policy to which others have to respond. This imposes a unique responsibility on the United States: Our nation must concern itself with the well being of the world. We will be the greatest beneficiaries if we do.[6]

Soros notes:

With the advance of technology, humanity has greatly increased its power over nature. Without similar advances in the ability to manage this power, humanity is now fully capable of destroying itself and its environment unless it develops better methods of protecting common interests. It is incumbent on the United States to take the lead in that endeavor. The proliferation of nuclear weapons poses a specific danger, but other threats, particularly environmental, also lurk. Civilizations have been destroyed long before nuclear bombs were invented."[7]

The Road to Continued Success

Overwhelming success is one of the greatest threats to the overwhelming success of the Chinese government's social, economic, scientific, and technological nation-building. If America's economic competitiveness and growth stalls, the negative political reactions in America, and America's massive military resources and post September 11, 2001 military aggressiveness makes a scenario of America and China slipping from trade war, to Cold War, o tarmed conflict probable.

As we have seen, every leader of China since 1949, including Mao Zedong, recognized that a strategic partnership and friendship with America was China's best option. But that option was not offered by America. America's Cold War made that strategic partnership and friendship impossible. Today, nearly sixty years after the Chinese Revolution in 1949, China is a rapidly emerging capitalist mega-superpower, and capitalism with Chinese characteristics has become a critical supporting mechanism for American capitalism. China's "capitalist revolution" is redefining the world. The shared capitalist ethos and economies of China and America theoretically facilitate the creation of a strategic partnership.

In the real world, the rapprochement implemented by President Hu Jintao on April 15, 2006, with the Kuomintang and other parties in Taiwan, indicates the Chinese government realistically assesses how it can preserve peace with America and demonstrates that the "right spirit" and shared capitalism can overcome deep historical hostilities. The Chinese government's policy of rapprochement to the Kuomintang was deliberately signaled six days before the meeting of Presidents Hu and Bush at the White House. The Chinese government is moving unilaterally to eliminate the risks of war with America over Taiwan. This is a very smart move that opens the way for major, sustainable progress with America. The Chinese government's unilateral move in the rapprochement with Taiwan reflects a win-win-oriented mindset.

The Zero-Sum-Game Strategic Road for America in the 21st Century

As we have seen, the implementation and resiliency, even in failure, of America's zero-sum-game mindset and strategies can be explained, in part, by America's majority rule-style democratic institutions and decision-making processes. The Chinese consensus democracy's institutions and decision-making processes currently are more supportive to pragmatic rather than ideo-logically-driven policy design and implementation.

In response to requests from the Bush Administration in 2005 that the Chinese government increase consumer demand within China, and to CNOOC jingoism, the Chinese government is reducing its economic dependence on exports to America. The Chinese government can do that by increasing consumer spending in China, through its control of China's banking system and China's 35% annual national savings rate. At the same time, there is increasing concern among observers of the American economy that America's spendthrift finances could trigger a precipitous drop in the value of the American dollar by as much as 30% against other currencies.

The Reality That China's Consensus Democracy Has Advantages and New Obligations

The Chinese government, as President Hu's visit to Washington State on April 19, 2006, illustrated, is signaling its "China wants to be America's strategic partner" hopes to America's business leaders. The need of American business and their leaders for good relations with China has not yet transmuted into America's abandonment of the containment attitude and approach to China's rapidly increasing economic power. But both the Democratic and Republican parties must embrace a new strategic partnership with China.

China's government, people, and culture currently are better suited to understanding that The China Game can only be won by China if America also wins. The Chinese style of "Consensus Democracy" processes makes us optimistic that China can contribute it's "win" to the "win-win" solution that is needed.

To do so, the Chinese government and people will have to accept America as an "insider" to whom obligations of loyalty and fidelity are owed. Fortunately, there is nothing more that the

Chinese people yearn for than friendship and knowledge of America. As we have seen, China's leaders and people admire and respect America.

The leadership challenge America's political and business leaders must solve is to produce leaders who understand that America can only prosper if China prospers. We are confident that America will succeed in meeting this challenge. It is more difficult to be optimistic about America's sustained ability to find and use the "win-win" strategies for shared peace and prosperity except within the new framework of a committed genuine global partnership with China.

We believe that the genius of America, a land of immigrants, ideals, and innovation, will find the framework and insights needed for America's prosperity. Americans are profoundly idealistic people. America was itself impossible. Few imagined exactly how a civilization like America could be the enduring reality that it is. The Chinese geniunely respect the genius of American idealism and the "right spirit" often seen in the history of the American people. Tolerance of the opinions and respect of the rights of others are the essence of the innovative genius of the idealism and pragmatism in the American Constitution.

America's leaders and people must stretch again to find the road to success, and preserve America's defining characteristics of opportunity, idealism and fairness. Now, united by capitalism and a yearning for a better life, America and China must share leadership in the world "in a more perfect union."

We recognize and accept the genius of the American Constitution. We also recognize and accept the genius of China's governing institutions and processes. Americans must respect China's success and right to self-determination if it wishes America's interests and needs to be respected. Americans wishing to profit from the growth of China's economic power must accept China's different culture and decision-making process and the economic power they are producing.

It is dangerously naïve and bellicose for Americans to base American foreign and domestic policy on the insistence that China abandon its traditions and culture because America's way of doing things is inherently superior in the minds of Americans. How will this conflict and competition of civilizations be resolved without military conflict? The characteristics of such a problem define what characteristics its solution must have. Since The China Game involves the fundamental problem of the rival powers of capitalist civilizations, the solution must make America and China allies rather than rivals. With that insight, it becomes clear that the interaction of China and America in business will prompt China to move incrementally from a "Pre-Rule Of Law" to a "Rule Of Law" system that over time integrates with America's.

China's 5000-year-old civilization and recent history leads the Chinese government and people to abhor chaos.[8] The Chinese government has demonstrated that it can produce unimagined economic prosperity. That achievement sustains and validates China's "Permission Society" way of doing things. The incremental but major reform policies under Deng Xiaoping, Jiang Zemin, and Hu Jintao demonstrate that a "Permission Society" can thrive economically while a "Pre-Rule Of Law" system." The incremental introduction of new laws will be implemented in a gradual Chinese "Permission Society" way rather than America's revolutionary "Big Bang" creation of the beginning of a "Rights Society" in 1776.

China's tradition of consensus-based decision-making processes is culturally enforced. Laws can be changed, but culture, particularly a 5000-year-old culture in the soul of the Chinese people, cannot be changed as quickly as laws can be written on paper. The Communist Revolution and China's history under

Mao Zedong show that China's feudal and philosophic traditions, like Confucianism, can be suppressed only temporarily.

The leadership of Deng Xiaoping and his successors reaffirm that capitalism is also a part of Chinese culture and that China has a genius for it. But, it is "capitalism with Chinese characteristics."

Since China's systems protect both China's economic sovereignty and growth, they are not going to disappear quickly. America cannot successfully dictate what the Chinese should do. Persuasion rather than force is the only viable strategy that might win tThe China Game for America and American companies. It is the only way America's "Rights Society" and China's "Permission Society" can co-exist peacefully long enough to meld together. It is difficult to persuade a Chinese that the features of their culture that are essential for their prosperity must give way to the features of American culture that are essential to American prosperity.

It is much easier to persuade Chinese to respect America's ideals and needs, if Americans respect Chinese ideals and needs. People with different ideas and needs can sort out problems, and work and prosper together. As President Kennedy said: "... our problems are man made, therefore they can be solved by man."[9]

We hope that American and Chinese political and business leaders and public opinion will support making The China Game work for both nations. If they do, the "Human Experiment" will not fail in ours or our children's lifetimes. That is our shared responsibility. Are we equal to our responsibility?

The "Hostile Observer" Impact on American Policy Making

Observers who look at China with hostility seem to use the following logic: China is different, therefore, China must be weak or wrong; China is not weak, therefore, China is wrong. Or they simply assume: China has to be like "us."

Four important points need to be recognized about the "hostile observer" phenomena. First, American domestic and foreign policy affecting China is being shaped by "hostile observer comments." American human rights and trade and business pressure groups with narrow focuses have achieved a highly lever-aged impact on American political decision makers. Secondly, the "hostile observer comments" may be counterproductive in per-suading the Chinese government to act as the hostile observers insist they must. Thirdly, the combination of "hostile observer comments" dominating Western publications and media, the effectiveness of pressure-group-driven America domestic foreign policy, and hostile observer commentaries' counterproductiveness are volatile ingredients in a formula for confrontation, conflict, and catastrophe. Containment through trade embargos escalating to trade war may be designed to or inadvertently create a destabi-lizing military build-up. In such a dangerous context, one crisis or another, such as between China and Taiwan, can get armed conflict started and America and China could blunder into "unre-stricted war."

America's Slide into Trade War with China

America's Treasury Secretary, Hank Paulson, is leading America's zero-sum-game strategy with China. Mr. Paulson's views, discussed in Chapter 7 of our business strategy book, *America and China's New Economic Partnership* illustrate an American approach that seeks to achieve foreign penetration and control of China's financial system, which is not aligned with China's growing economic power.

The New York Times commented:

> Treasury Secretary Henry M. Paulson Jr. plans a new drive to press Beijing [China] to open its financial systems ... [and] has spent his first weeks in office seeking to assert control within the administration over international economic issues, focusing in particular on developing a plan to confront China's growing economic clout, officials say.[10]

In August 2007, Treasury Secretary Paulson stressed the importance of the economic relationship of America and China.[11] But, partly due to Mr. Paulson's policy goals, America is on a slippery slope towards trade war with China. Mr. Paulson's win-win strategy pursues a win for American economic interest and a win for America's national security interests and a lose-lose outcome for China.

In 2005, a bipartisan group of 67 out of 100 U.S. senators indicated that if China did not revalue its currency, they would impose a 27.5% tariff on goods from China coming into America. A tariff regime above 15% would have a dangerous impact on the Chinese government's ability to sustain the economic growth and manage the reforms that provide the productivity and social stability of China. In March 2006, Senators Schumer and Graham, the sponsors of the bill to impose the 27.5% tariff, reportedly "... started to inch away from their misguided attempt to club China for its currency policies. "[12] However, in August 2006, Senators Schumer and Graham reportedly promised to put their bill threatening punitive tariffs on Chinese goods if China did not revalue its currency, to a vote in the Senate by September 30, 2006.[13]

China's annual GDP growth rate accelerated to 11% in 2006, which Treasury Secretary Paulson characterizes as "overheated." China's leaders are concerned about aspects of the overheating in housing costs, which they are addressing. But China's leaders are reluctant to allow the exchange rate on Chinese currency to increase suddenly. Increasing the exchange rate might have a myriad of consequences difficult or impossible to control. These include possible loss of export income, increased unemployment, and social unrest.[14] America could, through aggressive domestic and foreign policy moves, create a less stable, angry China, with a less cooperative Chinese government.

Treasury Secretary Paulson, with great publicity, has committed himself to obtaining concessions that other American Treasury Secretaries could not obtain from China to revalue its currency, open its financial system to foreigners, reduce its exports to America, fully open its economy to foreigners, and stimulate Chinese domestic spending in its consumer economy.

Mr. Paulson is "reinforcing his reach as Treasury Secretary" within the White House, and moving to coordinate American government departments involved in China matters, and to persuade other countries that the problem of Chinese trade surpluses can be solved with global cooperation.[15] There are concerns in Congress regarding what is seen as China's military build-up, and lack of cooperation with America on political issues such as Iran, North Korea, and The Sudan. Fears in Congress also focus on America's current account deficit of $800 billion in 2005, which is seen as a danger to America's solvency and employment levels, and the risk that China might suddenly reduce its US$300 billion-or-more investment in United States government debt, which constitutes at least 8% of the publicly held total.[16] There are also concerns that America's role as a leading exporting country is slipping and that China will surpass it in export totals.[17] America became the world's largest exporter in the 1990s, but lost that position to Germany in 2002. In 2006, China's exports were only 10% lower than America's.

The New York Times commented:

> By 2003, Chinese exports had expanded to 60 percent of the American total [exports], and in 2005 the figure hit 84 percent. With June figures now reported by all major countries, Chinese exports amounted to 90 percent of the United States total in the first half of this year.
>
> In most export products, Chinese companies compete with other Asian concerns, not with American or European ones, in large part because of the widely different wage rates. That makes it unlikely that a substantial Chinese revaluation would in and of itself do much to stimulate American exports. Conceivably, however, by making Chinese citizens feel richer, and by cutting prices of goods imported to China, it might stimulate demand for products from the United States and other countries.
>
> But the immediate effect of such a revaluation might be to propel the dollar value of Chinese exports up, enabling it to pass the United States in terms of export value, and perhaps setting off demands in Washington for even more action.[18]

The American Government's Unaligned Response to China's Economic Success

As the head of Goldman Sachs and as Treasury Secretary, Hank Paulson is pressing China to allow greater appreciation of it's currency as a means of "dealing with China's own economic challenges."[19] During a CNBC interview Mr. Paulson stated:

> One thing clearly Chinese leaders have to be very careful about is making sure they don't have an economy that overheats. When you are talking about imbalances in China, there's no doubt that in the short term they need to show much more flexibility on the renminbi.[20]

Mr. Paulson distinguished the "longer term" objective of a renminbi "traded in a competitive open marketplace." He stated:

"We need their financial system to be open, and open to competition. China needs to make the transition from an export-driven economy to one that consumes more." He urged China to improve its enforcement of intellectual property rights, arguing that this was also in China's best interest. "They are not going to be able to move from being a low-cost manufacturer to moving up the value-added chain until they have an enforcement regime that protects intellectual property" Mr. Paulson stated.[21]

The Reality That the American Government and People Save Too Little and Spend Too Much

Timothy Adams, while Undersecretary of the Treasury, articulated the core realities that cause America's problems with China. The trade gap with China is a function of the disparity between low spending and higher savings in China versus a low savings rate and high consumer spending in America. Adams recognizes that whatever happens to currency exchange rates, that fundamental disjunction will not change quickly or easily.[22] The American Undersecretary of the Treasury commented:

> People used to have the notion that the U.S. could simply go into its closet, turn some dials and levers and all this will go away. I think we have disabused people of the notion that that is possible.[23]

The Reality of America Hypocrisy in American Demands of China and CNOOC Jingoism

In the aftermath of the American government blocking CNOOC's acquisition of Unocal, Mr. Paulson has no moral authority in asking that the Chinese government respond to his view that "We need their financial system to be open, and open to competition. China needs to make the transition from an export-driven economy to one that consumes more." or his view that "... they need to show much more flexibility on the renminbi." Mr. Paulson's approach, unaligned with China's well-being, combines demands, threats, and unconvincing appeals to what he sees or pretends is in China's self-interests.

American demands that the Chinese government open China to foreign competition and currency speculation attacks that would destabilize China's economy, reform program, and people cannot be granted in the time frame Treasury Secretary Paulson seeks. The threats are that China will not succeed economically. The appeals are to what Americans see as China's self-interest, which serves Americans' goals.

American demands, threats, and appeals to self-interest are unconvincing to the Chinese government, in part, because there is little desire shown by the American government to align China and America's success. The unaligned or zero-sum-game mindset sees China as a dangerous economic competitor encroaching on American economic well-being, challenging America's foreign policies, which and may challenge America militarily.

Hopefully, few political leaders in China or America want armed conflict between the two capitalist superpowers. But, "accidental war" or "inevitable war" are a risk if America persists in a containment policy that has been the key feature of American policy toward China since 1949. The cumulative impact of America's strategies, the hostile observer commentaries in the media, and the pressure group effectiveness with American political leaders, are more dangerous to America's economic and national security interests than most observers realize.

Another danger to be noted is that "Amerocentric" or "Sinocentric" thinking can blind both sides to problems in The China Game. "Hostile observer" hectoring misshapes the American domestic and foreign policy debate and partially discredits the persuasiveness of the valid points contained in the "hostile observer" comments. Put another way, a friend can offer useful advice to a friend, which coming from an enemy seems insulting.

China Is Currently Using a Generous Response to America's Zero-Sum Mindset and Strategies

China is incrementally but rapidly proceeding with the globalization of its economy. As part of its strategy, the Chinese government has formed economic links with many countries and is promoting a "win-win" approach and rhetoric with each.

The American administrations's traditional zero-sum-based domestic and foreign policy could become increasingly aggressive in its reaction to China's emerging global economic power. A "win-win" approach would be a major shift in American attitudes and policy. It is likely that, through inattention or political excesses, America will move along the containment, trade war, Cold War, "accidental" or "inevitable" armed conflict path.

The contrast between China and America's emerging trade war rhetoric is one of the two most important features of "The China Game." The other is the relentless and accelerating growth rates of China's economy and competitive advantages. The seeds the government and people planted in the 1979–2006 reforms will grow faster than widely foreseen in the unprecedented opportunities provided by China's huge and talented population in the Knowledge Revolution throughout Economy and Globalization 3.0.

An increasingly aggressive American zero-sum-game approach would force China into a zero-sum reaction. America's zero-sum-game containment strategy has not worked. But it may be reiterated and fail repeatedly.

America's Majority-Rule Democracy makes it likely that one or more administrations and Congresses will disasterously choose or be forced to follow the zero-sum path by American pressure groups, public opinion, or a crisis or series of crises.

America has another destabilizing disadvantage in The China Game. Americans are losing jobs and America has a large trade deficit with China. More and more of America's economic, intellectual, scientific, technological, and other competitive disadvantages are becoming self-evident to the American people and American political and business leaders. Long-term, it appears that America's competitiveness and standard of living will weaken as China's increases. America's human capital is so much smaller than China's. America will have declining competitive advantages relative to China in the Knowledge Revolution and Globalization 3.0. These factors suggest that the political leaders in America will choose or be forced to follow increasingly confrontational and bolder zero-sum strategies. America is a powerful and proud player accustomed to winning, that is steadily losing and weakening. Americans resent and cannot accept that.

The Chinese government has several advantages. China's leadership's self-interest in retaining power by preserving economic growth and stability encourages it to pursue a "win-win" path. The Chinese government's greatest challenge is that "win-win" rhetoric and zero-sum behavior are inconsistent. If the Chinese government uses both "win-win" rhetoric and behavior, China will have enormous moral authority. If China's requirements for economic growth and social stability do not conflict with aligning its "win-win" rhetoric with "win-win" behavior, its government may have the option of choosing to remain on a "win-win" path because China does not have universal adult suffrage. China's leadership, working with all the tools and controls of China's Permission Society and Consensus Democracy, will be better able to avoid causing The China Game to end in mutual disaster.

The Chinese government's two greatest weaknesses are America's composite of weaknesses and the fact that China cannot win The China Game if America loses it. America does not have the capacity to win without China's help. If China has the desire and capability to enable America to win, China can win.

As we have seen, in China's culture, the more powerful person owes customary duties of benevolence to weaker persons, and China's leaders can only "win" in The China Game if they help America win. It is outcome-determinative, therefore, that China's leaders must recognize this and make it happen. The greatest cultural challenge that China's leaders have is that its culture also has social norms calling for "insiders" to be treated fairly. China's culture has norms that permit and encourage taking advantage of "outsiders." Foreigners are "outsiders." But, we are confident that this cultural challenge will not prevent the innovative pragmatism of China's leaders from helping America to win to the extent they can without seriously harming China.

Game Theory and Elite Accomodation

This is not a book about game theory. However, the results of research in game theory clarify the complex relationship between the world's current and emerging superpowers.

John Von Neumann was one of the pioneers of game theory. He was a mathematician and pioneer of the electronic digital computer and was involved in the creation of the atomic bomb in the Manhattan Project. From the mid-1920s through the 1940s, Von Neumann amused himself with an investigation into the mathematical structure of poker and other games. He realized that mathematics, through game theory, could be applied to economics, politics, foreign policy, and other areas. In 1944 Von Neumann and Princeton economist Oskar Morgenstein published *The Theory of Games and Economic Behavior*.[24]

Game theory is the study of conflict between thoughtful and potentially deceitful opponents. That may sound like psychology, but in game theory the players are assumed to be perfectly rational. Human beings' perceptions of reality, decision-making, and behavior are not always rational, let alone perfectly rational. Game theory is a branch of mathematical logic that is applied to the real conflicts among not-always-rational humans. But the contemplation of human interaction in the context of mathematical logic can be clarifying. Take the example of the relationship of America and China. It becomes clear from a game theory perspective that if either nation uses zero-sum-game strategies, neither can win.

Readers who disagree must come up with a scenario where one of the two superpowers can win while the other loses. If such a scenario is not credible or likely, then readers *must accept* that America and China must both ensure that it and the other nation win. Reducing the fog of life to propositions of mathematical logic can help people do a better job of trying to be rational.

The Search for Nash Equilibrium for America and China

In game theory, Nash Equilibrium occurs if there is a set of strategies with the property that no player can benefit by changing strategy while the other players keep their strategies unchanged. That set of strategies and the corresponding payoffs constitute the Nash Equilibrium.[25] The thesis of our work is that such equilibrium can only be created and sustained in an overt, committed, genuine partnership between America and China.

Game Theory's Generous Tit-for-Tat Game Strategy

Martin Kowak, Robert May, and Karl Sigmund, in *The Arithmetic's of Mutual Help*,[26] report research in game theory that is relevant to the harmful effects of selfish rational behavior and its socially and self-destructive consequences:

Two parties can strike a mutually profitable bargain, but each could gain still more by withholding its contribution. In modern society, an enormous apparatus of law and enforcement makes the temptation to cheat resistible. But how can reciprocal altruism work in the absence of those authoritarian institutions.... This is a difficult question best answered by first considering simple, idealized systems.[27]

In game theory, a metaphor known as "the Prisoners' Dilemma" is used, in which two prisoners are asked whether the other committed a crime; their level of punishment depends on whether both or neither indicates the other's guilt. If both choose to cooperate faithfully they each get a reward of three points. If they do not cooperate, they get one point each. But if one cooperates and the other defects, the defector gets five points and the other nothing. The prisoners' decisions highlight a difference between what is best from an individual's point of view and that of a collective point of view. This conflict endangers almost every form of cooperation, including trade. The reward for cooperation is higher than the punishment for mutual defection, but a one-sided defection yields a temptation of a greater reward, leaving the exploited cooperator with a loser's payoff. This implies that the best move is always to defect, irrespective of the opposing player's move. The logic leads inexorably to mutual defection.[28]

In the relationship of America and China, as in the Prisoners' Dilemma, there are two players. Kowak, May, and Sigmund comment:

In many societies, the same two individuals interact not just once but frequently. Each participant will think twice about defecting if this move makes the other player defect on the next occasion. So the strategy in repeated games can change in response to what happened in previous rounds.... There is no hard and fast recipe for playing the repeated Prisoners' Dilemma. Success will depend on the other player's strategy, which one does not know before hand. A strategy that does well in certain environments fails miserably in others. In the late 1970s, the political scientist Robert Axelrod ... conducted round robin tournaments of the repeated Prisioners' Dilemma on his computer. The contestants—programs submitted by colleagues—were quite sophisticated, but it turned out that the simplest entry ultimately won. This strategy is aptly called Tit-for-Tat. It starts with a cooperative response and then always repeats the opposing players previous move. Remarkably, a player applying Tit-for-Tat is never ahead at any stage of the repeated game, being always late to defect. The Tit-for-Tat player can nonetheless win the whole tournament, because the Prisoners' Dilemma is not a zero-sum game; it is possible to make points without taking them away from others. By its transparency Tit-for-Tat frequently persuades opponents that it pays to cooperate. In Alxelrod's tournaments the Tit-for-Tat strategy (entered by the game theorist, Anatol Rapoport) elicited many rewarding rounds of cooperation, whereas other players, among themselves, were apt to get bogged down in long runs of defection. ...Tit-for-Tat shaped a more congenial environment. The strategies that ruthlessly exploited cooperators succeeded only in depleting their own resources.[29]

Kowak, May and Sigmund performed computer simulations with an extended set of strategies that based their next move on the result of the previous round rather than just the opponent's previous move (as in Tit-for-Tat):

In spite of the rich diversity displayed in these chronicles, they lead us invariably to some simple, clear results. The first is that the average payoff in the population can change suddenly. Most of the time, either almost all members of the population cooperate, or almost all defect. The transitions between these two regimes are usually rare and abrupt ... we found that later in the run, quiescent periods tended to last longer. And there was a definite trend toward cooperation. The longer the system was allowed to evolve, the greater the likelihood for a cooperative regime to blossom. But the threat of a collapse always remained.

Cooperative populations are sometimes dominated by a strategy called Generous Tit-for-Tat, a variant that on random occasions will offer cooperation in response to defection.... A society of Generous Tit-for-Tat players does not discriminate against unconditional cooperators.... *One can safely conclude that the emergence and persistence of cooperative behavior are not at all unlikely, provided the participants meet repeatedly, recognize one another and remember the outcomes of past encounters.*

...Throughout the evolutionary history of life, cooperation among smaller units leads to the emergence of more complex structures ... our models, as crude as they are, illustrate how cooperation might arise and be maintained in real biological systems. Sophisticated creatures may be drawn to follow strategies that encourage cooperation because of repeated interaction among individuals who can recognize and remember one another.... In the course of evolution, there appears to have been ample opportunity for operation to have assisted everything from humans to molecules.[30] (Emphasis added)

Sophisticated organisms, such as America and China, may be drawn to follow strategies that encourage cooperation because of repeated interaction in the context of the negotiated rules of procedure, structured along Generous Tit-for-Tat Strategy,[31] so that selfish moves by one party do not automatically produce a selfish response. But repeated selfish responses deprive both parties of the benefit of selfish responses.

The point we focus on is simple. In the relationship between America and China, the only way either can win a 21st century "unrestricted war" is to eschew armed conflict in dispute resolution. This book focuses American and Chinese attention on the need for and essential features of new policies of collaboration that must be put in place in a mutually beneficial partnership. Whether America and China's decision-makers choose to design and operate such a partnership will determine whether America and China succeed or fail as civilizations.

16

Will America and China Choose to Succeed or Fail?

Overview

This chapter examines the reality that if the world's biggest pollution producers, America and China, do not collaborate to correct environmental damage, they will create ecological catastrophe that will end their civilizations.

Nations Choose To Succeed Or Fail

Jared Diamond's *Collapse: How Societies Choose To Fail Or Succeed*[1] examines four ways societies fail:

1. A society may fail to anticipate a problem before it actually arrives.

2. When the problem does arrive, the society may fail to perceive it.

3. When the society perceives the problem, they may fail to even try to solve it.

4. A society may try to solve the problem, but may not succeed.

2

3

The Bush Administration argued that the science on global warming is too "uncertain" to justify anything more than a voluntary effort to deal with it. It is clear from these photographs of the North Pole region in 1979 and 2003 that the polar ice cap is getting smaller.

Diamond highlights his students' amazement after hearing an explanation of why Easter Island's society and other societies failed:

> ...the apparently simple question which most puzzled my students was one whose actual complexity hadn't sunk into me before: how on earth could a society make such an obviously disastrous decision as to cut down all the trees on which it depended? For every other society... my students raised essentially the same question.... My students wondered whether—if there are still people left alive a hundred years from now—those people in the next century would be astonished about our blindness today as we are about the blindness of the Easter Islanders. This question of why societies end up destroying themselves through disastrous decisions astonishes not only my UCLA undergraduates but also professional historians and archaeologists.4

5

"My students wondered whether if there are still people left alive a hundred years from now—those people in the next century would be astonished about our blindness today as we are about the blindness of the Easter Islanders."

Jared Diamond

Diamond addresses why societies fail even to attempt to solve a problem once it has been recognized:

> Many of the reasons for such failure fall under the heading of what economists and other social scientists term "rational behavior," arising from the clashes of interest of people. That is, some people may reason correctly that they can advance their own interests by behavior harmful to other people. Scientists term such behavior "rational" precisely because it employs correct reasoning, even though it may be morally reprehensible. The perpetrators know that they will often get away with their bad behavior, especially if there is no law against it or if the law isn't effectively enforced. They feel safe because the perpetrators are typically concentrated (few in number) and highly motivated by the prospect of reaping big, certain, and immediate profits, while the losses are spread over a large number of individuals. That gives the losers little motivation to go to the hassle of fighting back, because each loser loses only a little and would receive only small, uncertain, distant profits even from successfully undoing the minority's grab. Examples include so-called perverse subsidies: the large sums of money that governments pay to support industries that might be uneconomic without the subsidies.... A frequent type of rational bad behavior is "good for me, bad for you and for everybody else"—to put it bluntly, "selfish."[6]

The Reality of Global Pollution and Climate Change

The geophysical problems man or nature or both create may rapidly become as dangerous as the geopolitical problems in the relationship of America and China. Global warming threatens America and China's economies, public health, and survival. Satellite pictures taken in 1979 and 2003 show the rapid diminution of the icecap at the North Pole. Collaboration is essential to deal successfully with America and China's contributions to climate change.

Some observers assert that:

> All but the most diehard neoconservatives have accepted the reality of the issue which looks set to dominate the global political climate for some time to come. Climate change is a fact, it's accelerating, and something needs to be done about it in order to avoid potentially catastrophic consequences.[7]

The Bush Administration has argued that the science on global warming is too "uncertain" to justify anything more than a voluntary effort to deal with it. President Bush has advanced many reasons for not pressing for strong controls on greenhouse gas emissions from vehicles, power plants, and other industrial sources, such as that the American federal government has no authority to regulate greenhouse gases.[8] The Supreme Court of the United States has agreed to decide whether America's Environmental Protection Agency has the authority under the Clean Air Act to regulate carbon dioxide and other greenhouse gases. The Bush Administration argues that the Act only mentions carbon dioxide in passing, and that if Congress had been truly worried about global warming it would have given the gases that cause it more emphasis and instructed the E.P.A. to take aggressive steps to control them, as it did with sulfur dioxide and other pollutants.[9]

Bjorn Lomborg, author of *The Skeptical Environmentalist*,[10] had eight of the world's top economists from various political stripes evaluate the world's problems and the costs and efficiencies of dealing with each, and produce a prioritized list of those most deserving money. They largely agreed because "the numbers were just so compelling: $1 spent preventing HIV/AIDs would result in about $40 of social benefits, so the economists put it at the top of the list (followed by malnutrition, free trade and malaria). In contrast $1 spent to abate global warming would result in only about 2 to 25 cents worth of good; so that project dropped to the bottom.... Most people, average people, when faced with these clear choices, *would* pick the $40-of-good projects over the others—that is *rational* ... 'We need to get the policy makers on board, the ones who are dealing with the world's problems.' And therein lies the rub. Political figures... are political. Not rational."[11]

Core Values, Rational Behavior, and Realism

Pollution and climate change caused by mankind involves the question of whether mankind is intelligent enough to continue to exist. Global warming and climate change are a leadership challenge for America and China's political leaders.

Some observers assert that focusing on energy efficiency and pollution reduction will protect the earth's climate and make business and consumers richer.[12] Those rewards to self-interest may be inadequate motivators. Persons or nations addicted to a survival-threatening way of living often need help to ameliorate or end their self-harming behavior. A committed successful partnership of America and China could help each overcome its own unsustainable self-indulgence.

Jared Diamond focuses on why "rational behavior" has often been beyond the capability of human societies. He discusses the problem of the commons, i.e., fish stocks, where it is rational for all fishermen to prevent fishing from eliminating the existence of fish, and at the same time it is rational for individual fishermen to catch as much as they can while there are fish to catch. This type of problem in relation to pollution is one that a committed and successful partnership of America and China can address better than the status quo. But, there are real limits to how "rational" human beings can be said to be. Jared Diamond notes:

> A further conflict of interest involving rational behavior arises when the interest of the decision-making elite in power clash with the interest of the rest of society. Especially

if the elite can insulate themselves from the consequences of their actions, they are likely to do things that profit themselves regardless of whether those actions hurt everybody else. Such clashes ... are becoming increasingly frequent in the modern U.S., where rich people tend to live within their gated compounds and to drink bottled water.... Throughout recorded history, actions or inactions by self-absorbed kings, chiefs, and politicians have been a regular cause of societal collapses.... Conversely, failures to solve perceived problems because of conflicts of interest between the elite and the masses are much less likely in societies where the elite cannot insulate themselves from the consequences of their actions.[13]

Diamond focuses on another key problem:

It is painfully difficult to decide whether to abandon some of one's core values when they seem to be becoming incompatible with survival.... Perhaps a crux of success or failure as a society is to know which core values to hold onto, and which ones to discard and replace with new values, when times change.... Societies and individuals that succeed may be those that have the courage to take those difficult decisions, and that have the luck to win their gambles.[14]

The Reality that Man-made Degradation of the Earth Threatens Man's Existence

Even if the science on global warming or the intention of Congress in passing The Clean Air Act is "uncertain," global warming and climate change are occurring. An authoritative study of the biological relationships vital to maintaining life has found disturbing evidence of man-made degradation. *The Millennium Ecosystem Assessment* that involved 22 national science academies from around the world and 1,300 leading scientists from 95 countries, concluded that the earth stands on the cusp of disaster and people should no longer take it for granted that their children or grand-children will survive in the environmentally degraded world of the 21st century.[15] The report found that 15 of 24 ecosystems vital for life on earth have been seriously degraded or used unsustainably. The report identifies six potential "tipping points" that could abruptly change things for the worse, with little hope of recovery on a human timescale.[16]

The report found that the earth had been substantially "reengineered" in the last 50 years by the pressure put on it's natural resources by the growing demands of a larger human population, which is predicted to increase by 50% in the 21st century. Between 1960 and 2000, the world population doubled from 3 to 6 billion, the global economy increased more than 600%, the production of food and supply of drinking water increased more than 200%, and the consumption of timber products increased by more than 50%. The report found that the rate of various plants and animals becoming extinct is 1000 times higher than natural, background levels.[17]

Dr. Walter Reid, the leader of the report's core authors, warned that unless the international community took decisive action, the future looked bleak for the next generation. He stated:

> ...the assessment shows that the future really is in our hands. We can reverse the degradation of many ecosystem services over the next 50 years, but the changes in policy and practice required are substantial and not currently underway.[18]

Al Gore's *An Inconvenient Truth*[19] addresses climate change and global warming and what we can do about it. Some scientists believe that there is a chance that, if all nations took all necessary action, the damage caused to the earth's ecosystem might improve in 5 years, but it may take 100 years.[20] In any event, the need for a genuine committed partnership of America and China to protect themselves and humanity is essential.

For decades, popular skepticism in America, fueled by energy companies, about climatological science stood in the way of addressing the problems. A Time/ABC/Stanford University poll found that 85% of respondents agree that global warming probably is happening, 87% believe that government should either encourage or require lowering of power-plant emissions, and 85% think something should be done to get cars to use less gasoline.[21]

The Kyoto Protocol on climate change did not slow the growth of pollution damage by America or China. America did not sign it and developing countries such as China are not required under the protocol to make cuts in carbon emissions. China and America are desperate for energy to fuel economic expansion and despite investments in renewable energy it is thought by some observers that much of their energy will have to come from coal.[22] There is a widespread feeling in the developing world that the developed nations, led by America, which grew rich by freely spewing pollution, should take most of the responsibility for climate change and pay the developing world for the privilege of continuing to pollute. Sunita Narain, director of the Center for Science and Environment in New Delhi, says: "Our sense is that, first and foremost, the U.S. needs to reduce its emissions.... It is unacceptable and immoral that the U.S. does not take the lead on climate change."[23] The current American Administration rejected the Kyoto Treaty partly because developing countries were exempt from emission cuts. This disagreement has impeded climate change efforts.

However, *Time* reports:

> ...that is beginning to change—and some of the push is coming from Beijing. For most of the recent Montreal climate conference, the U.S. resisted any serious discussion of what should be done after Kyoto expires. But several developing countries, including China as a quiet but present force supported further talks and helped break down U.S. opposition.

"At the moment, China seems more interested in engaging on this issue internationally than the U.S. does," says Elliot Diringer, director of international strategies for the Pew Center on Global Climate Change.

That's because China and India increasingly see climate-change policy as a way to address some of their immediate problems—such as energy shortages and local environmental ills—while getting the international community to help foot the bill. China and India are extremely energy inefficient. China uses three times as much energy as the U.S. to produce $1 of economic input....

One source of funding is the Clean Development Mechanism, a part of the Kyoto Protocol that allows developed countries to sponsor greenhouse-cutting change for carbon credits that can be used for meeting emission targets. Those don't require any technological break through. A 2003 study by the consulting firm CRA International found that if China and India invested fully in technology already in use in the U.S., the total carbon savings by 2012 would be comparable to what could be achieved if every country under the Kyoto Protocol actually met its targets.

But that window of opportunity is closing rapidly. Every step forward that these countries take today (such as China's move to make its auto-emission regulations stricter than the U.S.'s) risks being swamped by growth tomorrow (for example, China could have 140 million cars on the road by 2020. What China and India really need to ensure green development is what the world needs: a broadly accepted post Kyoto pact that is strict enough to make it economically worthwhile to eliminate carbon emissions. Though actual cuts are off the table for now, Beijing and New Delhi seem willing to discuss softer targets, such as lowering carbon intensity. But they feel that Washington must take the lead. "It is possible for these countries to achieve the growth they deserve without wrecking the climate," says Diringer. "They just can't do it on their own." It has to go through the U.S.

Maybe we can begin by living a bit more like the average Chinese or Indian—before they start living like us.[24]

Jared Diamond states:

> China's achievement of First World standards will approximately double the entire world's human resource use and environmental impact. But it is doubtful whether the world's current human resource use and impact can be sustained. Something has to give way. That is the strongest reason why China's problems automatically become the world's problems.[25]
>
> China's leaders used to believe that humans can and should conquer nature, that environmental damage was a problem affecting only capitalist societies, and that socialist societies were immune to it. Now, facing overwhelming signs of China's own severe environmental problems, they know better.[26]

Zhang Lijun, Vice-Minister of the State Environmental Protection Administration, a senior Chinese government environmental regulator, has warned that China's already serious levels of pollution could grow by 400% or 500% over the next 15 years if its rapid increases in electricity consumption and automobile use continue. Zhang Lijun stated "China isn't able to withstand such a heavy burden of pollution" and needs to greatly tighten its standards.[27] China could easily surpass America as the largest emitter of greenhouse gases believed to contribute to global warming. China's "... pace of economic growth has great economic and environmental implications," says John Beale of the U.S. Environmental Protection Agency.[28]

The International Energy Agency forecasts that the increase in greenhouse gas emissions from 2000 to 2030 from China alone will nearly equal the increase from the entire industrialized world.[29] China's total electricity demand will rise an estimated 2,600 gigawats by 2050, which is the equivalent of adding four 300-megawat power plants every week for the next 45 years. But "anything you want to do about clean energy is easier to do [in China] from the outset...every time they add a power plant or factory, they can add one cleaner and better than before," says David Moslowitz, an energy consultant who advised Chinese officials.[30] "China and India have to demonstrate to other countries that it is possible to develop in a sustainable way.... We cannot fail," says Yang Fuqiang, vice president of the Energy Foundation in Beijing.[31]

China's booming economy may make it the world's largest greenhouse-gas emitter as early as 2020. Professor Li Zheng, the director of The Tsinghua-BP Clean Energy Research and Education Center, opened in 2003, is trying to turn China's massive coal reserves into clean-burning gas so that coal-fired power plants can be shut down. The center's most promising project is a new technology called polygeneration, by which coal is converted into a cleaner gaseous fuel that can generate electricity and be processed into a petroleum substitute, which may reduce China's carbon emissions and dependency on imported oil. Li Zheng says, "China is motivated to develop this technology."[32]

The Win-Win Collaboration of America and China in Energy Creation and Pollution Abatement

America and China must make the same hard choices. Will American and Chinese political leaders co-ordinate their work on achieving sustainable energy sources and the amelioration of pollution? Or are they going to fail through ignorance, inability to act, choosing to fail, or because they are unable to prevent the collapse of their interdependent ecosystems and economies? Neither civilization can continue to exist without the committed, urgently needed help of the other. New energy and pollution mitigation technologies must be developed and deployed quickly by both nations. Former President Clinton stated "If we don't do it, it will eventually impose severe restraints on economic growth and conflict is more likely."[33] Developing leading-edge technologies together will assist both nations facing the same unsustainable oil consumption demands and environmental threats to their civilizations' survival. Failure of either to do so is a "lose-lose" scenario for both nations and the human species.

17

Can Mankind Solve Problems Caused by Mankind?

Overview

This concluding chapter examines further why America and China's leaders need to create a committed, genuine partnership in order to institutionalize win-win geopolitical and economic problem solving that achieves greater likelihood of sustainable reciprocal rewards than ad hoc zero-sum-game strategies can.

Can Man-made Problems be Solved?

Prior to 1945, human beings frequently sought to change the opinions and behavior of others by attacking them. It is not prudent today for America or China to give free rein to their xenophobia and intolerance of each other's prosperity and systems of governance.

Although it was involved in a long, global Cold War confrontation with the Soviet Union, suddenly for thirteen days in October 1962, America found itself on the verge of nuclear war. Soviet missiles that could strike America with five minutes' warning were discovered to be within days of becoming opera-

For thirteen days in October 1962, President Kennedy sought a way to avoid the escalation of imminent armed conflict into nuclear war with the Soviet Union. How often will two superpowers in confrontations be capable of avoiding armed conflict? Which road will America choose: collaboration or containment?

This is a photograph of an expanded meeting of the Chinese Politburo following the military action in Tiananmen Square to build onsensus for Jiang Zemin's elevation to general secretary of the Chinese Communist Party, June 19–21, 1989. Jiang Zemin is seated right center. Which road will China take in the future?

tional in Cuba. As we have seen, President Kennedy's advisors initially recommended an air strike followed by an invasion of Cuba. Since these options almost certainly would have escalated into nuclear war, Kennedy chose instead to blockade Cuba. This strategy had the drawback of not destroying the missiles before they could become operational. But Kennedy realized that to solve America's problems of removing the missiles and avoiding nuclear war, he had to give Secretary Khrushchev a solution to the Soviet Union's problems of how to remove the missiles and protect Cuba.

Kennedy's advisors' initial approach can be characterized as a zero-sum-game strategy that entailed a win-lose mindset and a lose-lose result. The blockade strategy was an attempt to obtain time to find a win-win strategy that would remove the missiles, ensure that America did not try again to invade Cuba, and avoid nuclear war. Fortunately, a win-win strategy was found and used, and worked. Leadership and luck prevailed in that sudden crisis. The ideological and geopolitical competition between America and the Soviet Union later ended with the latter's collapse. More than forty-five years have passed. Leaders change and memories fade.

China now challenges America with the vigor of capitalism. How can America and China's political leaders find win-win solutions to China's challenge to America's status and standard of living? If they do, how will win-win strategies be sustainable?

Humanity's future prosperity and peace will be determined by two small groups of American and Chinese political leaders. All of us are fallible human beings operating in decision-making systems of infinite complexity that no human being can fully understand or control. Three points arise from these realities.

First, since the context is so complex, volatile, and important, the process in which America and China's political leaders struggle to find opportunities for their respective societies and solutions for their societies' problems cannot prudently be left to ad hoc zero-sum-game strategies. The problem of the co-existence of the world's greatest superpower and the world's emerging mega super-power can only be prudently addressed in the context of an overt, committed partnership between them.

Secondly, America and China's business leaders cannot leave the fate of their enterprises to the complexities of political leaders' agendas and abilities. These business leaders must initiate and sustain genuine global joint ventures applying and improving upon the 2004 IBM + Legend = Lenovo deal template that aligns American companies' strategies with China's economic development strategies.

Thirdly, the American people must understand and come to accept that China has the same right of self-determination as America, and that containment and a zero-sum-game domestic and foreign policy is ultimately a road that leads to the collapse of America and China's civilizations. American political and business leaders will not be able, even when they wish they could, to pursue a win-win-driven approach unless the American people understand and accept the sacrifices that are needed to reform America's economy and preserve its democratic institutions. Unless the American people understand and accept the necessity of win-win strategies, Americans will sooner or later select political leaders who cannot make the relationship between America and China work peacefully.

A new mindset is critical to America's choice of the road to success or failure. The wisdom, integrity, and moral authority of the American leaders and people and the genius of their way of doing things is being tested by the genius of the Chinese leaders and their people's way of doing things. The prosperous and peaceful coexistence of America and China constitutes the cut-ting- or melding-edge of the evolution of human societies.

Can America and China co-exist in The Age of Species Lethal Weapons? Can our generation and our children's and grand-children's meet the tests of intelligence and character that the evolution of the Human Experiment confronts and enlightens us with?

The 21st century is a "capitalist century." The 20th century was one of ideological struggle for the hearts and minds of humanity. Capitalism won. Now religious, cultural, resource, and scientific challenges define the 21st century. The 20th century's Cold War and armed conflict struggles are not suitable in the context of American and Chinese capitalism. America and China must define a new geopolitical and foreign policy realism suited to peace and prosperity.

Which road shall we choose? In other words, who are we? What is our potential? What is our fate? We must look forward a hundred years as we struggle with the opportunities and dangers of today. What kind of a world do we want? Will we invest ourselves in a zero-sum world that cannot work in The Age of Species Lethal Weapons? Collaboration and a win-win approach might work. If it is not made to work by human innovation and ingenuity, the American and Chinese civilizations and the Human Experiment will fail before our eyes.

John F. Kennedy, immediately after his assertion that mankind's problems are caused by man and therefore can be solved by man, made another amazing statement on June 10, 1963, which evidences his comprehension of the real opportunity of mankind rather than the minutia of our daily problems:

> "Man can be as big as he wants. No problem in human destiny is beyond human beings. Man's reason and spirit often solved the seemingly unsolvable—and we believe they can again."[4]

President Kennedy avoided a nuclear war on his watch. President Nixon opened America's relationship with China. That helped enable Deng Xiaoping to open China. Jiang Zemin, with his Three Represents and other efforts, has passed the responsibility for China to another generation of leaders. Who will be the leaders of China and America tomorrow and each tomorrow after that? Will they be able to solve the problems in the relationship of America and China? Only establishing and maintaining the institution of the partnership of America and China will enable American and Chinese leaders to discover solutions to the "inevitable" tensions of two superpowers. America and China need partnership in the 21st century to avoid the foreseeable and unforeseeable errors of men. Institutions civilize human beings, and enable them to better understand who they are and who they wish to become. Institutions can sometimes be wiser than individual leaders can. All men are fallible. We must help each other.

Foreign policy "realism" in the 21st century requires institutionalizing a win-win framework rather than a zero-sum-game approach to the economic and national security issues facing America and China. If both countries are not publicly committed to the partnership, how will they co-exist? The lose-lose character of war creates a basis for mutual respect. But America and China must find a new relationship that can help ameliorate the conflicts that will arise as China's economic power grows. Can a consensus between opposites like America and China be found which will provide peace and security?

Human Nature and the Moral Authority of Zero-Sum-Game and Win-Win Strategies

Americans and Chinese share an inclination to demand fairness but to try to exploit others in zero-sum games. A person or nation's "self-interest" is difficult for them to predict.

If self-interest is not a prudent guide, is morality? If a nation is immoral or amoral and does only what its leaders perceive to be in its immediate self-interest, the nation will generate significant conflict with others. Such a zero-sum approach is self-defeating in the circumstances of the 21st century.

America's systems are based on the concept of a reciprocal tolerance of the rights and opinions of others. But America is falling short of its ideals and in respecting the rights and opinions of others. China is evolving economically and politically towards a "democracy with Chinese characteristics." Will America respect the rights and needs of China to proceed at its own steady, incremental pace, and in its own way in defining China's future? Can China respect America's rights if America does not respect China's?

China is thriving and is unlikely to accept what America views as the innate correctness of America's way of doing things. If America bases its foreign policy on the intolerant assertion that Majority-Rule Democracy is the universal best practice, problems will arise. War, the ultimate zero-sum-game in the 21st century, has been the means of settling such issues. And American-style Majority-Rule Democracy may, in fact, be a more unstable way of doing things for China than China's tradition and culture of Consensus Democracy.

"Moral authority" is the common denominator in the Global Village. It arises from our innate respect for persons and nations that find the courage to be consistent with their own ideals and ideas, even when it is costly, dangerous, and difficult. "Do unto others as you would have them do unto you," when manifested in a nation's domestic and foreign policy give that nation moral authority. "Do as I say, not as I do" is not an impressive assertion. Hypocrisy is at the heart of the challenge America and China share. Do they currently have the power of moral authority in the positions they wish to impose on each other?

A lasting partnership will require that candor, kindness, and moral authority be among its revitalizing strengths. Moral authority is powerfully amplified when combined with what the Chinese enshrine as "the right spirit," which Americans enshrine as idealism, altruism, fairness, intellectual honesty, creativity, kindness, and candor. These are powerful collaborative and problem-solving tools. As we will show in the case studies presented in *China Business New Strategies: Chinese and American Companies as Global Partners*, foreigners doing business with China who show candor and respond to the needs and goals of the Chinese can communicate and work effectively across very different cultures and ways of doing things.

Appendix

The following chronology appeared in Geert Bekaert, Campbell R. Harvey, and Christian Lundblad's paper "Financial Openers and the Chinese Growth Experience. April 13, 2006.

A Chronology of Economic, Political, and Financial Events in China

Date	Event
March 14, '85	Regulations governing the establishment of foreign joint ventures in Shanghai Province were relaxed.[IMF]
March 15, '85	China and India signed a three-year agreement to develop economic and trade relations; the accord provided for encouraging joint ventures, the creation of consultancy services, the exchange of economic, trade, and technical delegations, and participation.[IMF]
March 26, '85	The Foreign Economic Contract Law was adopted.[IMF]
April 1, '85	The Chinese Patent Law, enacted in 1984, came into effect. The Ministry of Petroleum and Industry announced that foreign oil companies would be allowed to participate in exploration and development of oil and gas reserves in nine provinces and one autonomous region.[IFC]
April 2, '85	The State Council introduced a regulation on the control of foreign banks and joint venture banks in special economic zones.[IMF]
August 22, '85	China approved establishment of the first foreign branch bank office in the country since 1949. Hong Kong and Shanghai Banking Corporation (a foreign commercial bank) announced a plan to begin branch operations in Shenzhen on Oct.5, 1985.[IMF]

A CHRONOLOGY OF ECONOMIC, POLITICAL AND FINANCIAL EVENTS IN CHINA

Date	Event
November 6, '85	China and Libya signed a protocol aimed at consolidating bilateral cooperation between the two countries.[IMF]
December 3, '85	A joint venture bank was opened in Xiamen with the Panin Group of Hong Kong.[IMF]
February 5, '87	Provisional regulations were approved permitting financial institutions and enterprises with sources of foreign exchange income to guarantee foreign exchange obligations of other debtors.[IMF]
August 27, '87	Provisional regulations were issued on a new system requiring the timely registration of external borrowing with the SAEC.[IMF]
April 13, '88	The National People's Congress adopted a new Chinese-foreign cooperative joint ventures law.[IMF]
February 17, '89	All foreign commercial borrowing required the approval of the PBC and is to be channeled through one of ten domestic entities. The short-term debt of each entity may not exceed 20% of the entity's total debt, and short-term borrowing is to be used only for working capital purposes.[IMF]
March 6, '89	The SAEC announced procedures governing Chinese direct investment abroad, which required government and SAEC approval, a deposit of 5% of the investment to secure repatriation of dividends and other income from the investment, and repatriation of earnings within six months.[IMF]
April 4, '90	The State would not nationalize joint ventures, simplified the approval procedures for new foreign investment enterprises, and extended the management rights of foreigners.[IMF]
May 14, '90	The Shanghai City Government announced plans for the development of the Pudong New Area, offering foreign

A Chronology of Economic, Political and Financial Events in China

Date	Event
	joint ventures tax incentives similar to those available in the special economic zones.[IMF]
May 19, '90	The State Council issued regulations for the sale and transfer of land use rights in cities and towns to encourage foreign investor to plan long-term investment.[IMF]
November 26, '90	The Shanghai Securities Exchange reopened. It had been closed since December 8, 1941.[DT]
April 9, '91	The State Council adopted the Law Concerning the Income Tax of Foreign-Funded Enterprises and Foreign Enterprises and eliminated a 10% tax imposed on distributed profits remitted abroad by the foreign investors in foreign-funded enterprises.[IMF]
April 26, '91	The limit of daily price fluctuations increases from 0.5% to 1%.[GK]
June 3, '91	The stamp tax was decreased from 0.6% to 0.3%.[GK]
July 3, '91	Shenzhen opened the country's second exchange.[DT]
September 26, '91	"Regulations on Borrowing Overseas of Commercial Loans by Resident Institutions" and "Rules on Foreign Exchange Guarantee by Resident Institutions in China" were issued.[IMF]
1991	Shenzhen opened the country's second exchange.[DT] The B share came into existence. B shares can be owned by foreigners only, but they are afforded the same right of ownership as A shares,which are reserved for Chinese nationals. In China, a share entitles the owner to a dividend distribution, but not to a right to influence the operations of the company.[CSRC]
March '92	The policy on foreign trade and investment was further liberalized, opening a large number of island and border areas to such activities.[IMF]

A Chronology of Economic, Political and Financial Events in China

Date	Event
May 21, '92	Free stock price through free trading (less control of price formation). Shanghai index increases from 617 to 1266 on this day.[GK]
October 26, '92	China Securities Regulatory Commission begins.[GK]
1993	The introduction of the Insider Trading Laws.[BD]
May '93	Interim regulations were issued governing the activities of domestic investors, but there is no law explicitly covering the presence or activities of foreign firms. Foreign securities firms may establish respresentative offices, but they cannot establish respresentative offices, but they cannot establish local branches or subsidiaries. They can only purchase seats to broker B shares (dominated in RMB but must be purchased with foreign currency, issued by Chinese companies for sale exclusively to non-Chinese). Foreign firms can not underwrite local securities issues or act as dealers or brokers in RMB dominated securities.[DT]
July 1 '93	ADR effective date. (Company = SINOPEC SHANGHAI PETROCHEMICAL COMPANY LIMITED, Exchange = NYSE).[BNY]
August 6 '93	A common order-driven market for A shares on Shanghai Stock Exchange was introduced. (Buy and sell orders compete for the best price. Throughout the trading session, customer orders are continuously matched according to price and time priorities.)[GK]
1994	The Chinese government converted four "specialized" banks into "commercial" banks by transferring their responsibilities for making noncommercial loans to three newly established "policy" banks. The first PRC's central and commercial banking laws was passed to allowed new, non-state-owned banks to set up business.[DT]
1994	The People's Bank of China (PBOC) issued new supervisory

A Chronology of Economic, Political and Financial Events in China

Date	Event
	guidelines requiring all banks to apply new credit control procedures designed to bring China in line with the risk-weighted capital adequacy established in the Basle Agreement. It also got approval to undertake a special US$32 billion bond issue to re-capitalize the state-owned commercial banks and enable then to meet the 8% capital-adequacy ration of the Basle Agreement.[DT]
May 21, '92	Announcement of the 'Four No' rule. Chairman of CSRC announced that RMB 5.5 billion new shares are not allowed to be traded on stock exchanges within half a year; the transaction tax for stocks would not be levied in 1994.[IFC]
June 15, '94	Prohibition of illegal futures trading.[GK]
January '95	Real interest rates turned positive as inflation has been squeezed out of the economy.[DT]
January 3, '95	Initiate T+1 trading procedure. Stocks bought in one day could not be sold until the next day. This reduces intraday trading.[GK]
March, '95	Exports surged by 62% over last year, increasing trade surplus by $7 billion.[IFC]
May 17, '95	Stopped futures trading on Treasury bonds. CSRC concerned the futures was attracting too much speculative money. On that day, the stock market surges 31%.[GK]
May '95	The central bank increased the subsidy rate on bank deposits from 11.47% to 12.27%.[IFC]
June 20, '95	Commercial banks banned from entering stock or trust business.[GK]
July, '95	A new commercial bank law went into effect.[IFC]
August '95	Inflation rate had decreased to 14.5% from 27% in October 1994.[IFC]

A CHRONOLOGY OF ECONOMIC, POLITICAL AND FINANCIAL EVENTS IN CHINA

Date	Event
November '95	China launched its first national inter-bank market linking 30 short-term credit offices across China into a single computer network.[IFC]
March '96	China carried out three rounds of military exercise across the Taiwan Straits, clouding the relationship between two countries.[IFC]
August '96	The government removed the authority of local city governments to manage the Shanghai and Shenzhen stock exchanges.[IFC]
September '96	The Shanghai city government cut the income tax rate of Shanghai based companies to 15% from 33%.[IFC]
September 25, '96	The regulation of External Guarantees Provided by Domestic Entities was passed, allowing for the provision of guarantees by authorized financial institutions and non-financial legal entities that have foreign exchange receipts.[IMF]
October 3, '96	Decreases in commissions for stock and fund transactions.[GK]
October '96	The CSRC issued a circular prohibiting Chinese from opening up stock trading accounts in the name of their work units.[IFC]
November 14, '96	Central Bank of China prohibits that bank loans can be used to invest in stocks.[GK]
December 16, '96	The CSRC tightened restrictions on Chinese residents opening B-share accounts, which are reserved for foreign investors. A new regulation that will limit the maximum daily change to 10% was imposed.[IFC]
February 19, '97	Paramount Chinese leader Deng Xiaoping died at age 92.[IFC]

A Chronology of Economic, Political and Financial Events in China

Date	Event
April '97	Government agreed to extend the preferential 15% corporate tax rate for nine of 25 H-share stocks for another year.[IFC]
May '97	The CSRC decided to retroactively boost the annual ceiling on new shares issued for 1996 by 50%. China's State Council opted to raise the stamp tax on stock trading to 0.5% from 0.4%.[IFC]
June 6, '97	Central Bank prohibits assets owned or controlled by banks from being used to purchase stocks.[GK]
July 1, '97	Hong Kong was handed over to China.[IFC]
November '97	Securities Commission promulgated rules for establishing mutual funds.[IFC]
January 1, '98	Regulations for issuing bonds denominated in foreign currency by domestic institutions were issued. (Controls on credit operations) (1) The implementation by laws of regulations for external guarantees by domestic institutions were issued. (2) Forward LCs with a maturity exceeding 90 days and less than 365 days have been included in the category of short-term credit, while those exceeding one year have been included in the category of medium- and long-term international commercial loans. (3) External borrowing regulations were changed.[IMF]
February '98	Three-month interbank rates in Hong Kong drop to 7.143%, the lowest level since previous October.[IFC]
March '98	The consumer price index fell 1.9%, marking the fifth straight monthly decline.[IFC]
April '98	S&P revised Chinese foreign currency rating from stable to negative.[IFC]
May '98	The government banned all activities of direct sales companies such as Amway and Avon.[SP]

A Chronology of Economic, Political and Financial Events in China

Date	Event
June 12, '98	Weak Japanese yen forces Chinese exports to see its first decline in 22 month. The government cuts the stock trading tax to 0.4% from 0.5%.[IFC]
July 1, '98	China cut bank lending rates on July 1 by 1.12%. The Japan Rating and Investment Information downgraded China's sovereign rating to A+ from AA–.[IFC]
July '98	Catastrophic floods along the Yangtze River, the country's worst since 1954. It is speculated that Beijing may devalue its currency because of a weaker Japanese yen and slower domestic growth.[IFC]
July 8, '98	(Controls on credit operations) Enterprises are barred from advance prepayment of debt.[IMF]
September '98	The central bank has ordered all companies to repatriate foreign currency held overseas without authorization by October 1. On September 7, the HKSE instituted a "tick rule" for short-sellers.[IFC]
October '98	China closed the 18-year-old GITIC (the Guangdong International Trust and Investment Corp) on October 6, after the company missed an $8.75 million payment on a bond.[IFC]
December '98	China's first securities law was passed on December 29. Under the law, brokers are banned from using client funds to finance their own operations and foreigners may not buy A-shares.[IFC]
January '99	More than 70 companies in Shenzhen and at least 63 companies in Shanghai announced that they would report a net loss for 1998.[IFC]

A CHRONOLOGY OF ECONOMIC, POLITICAL AND FINANCIAL EVENTS IN CHINA

Date	Event
April '99	The government decides to allow cash-strapped brokerages to tap funds from the interbank market and state debt repurchase market. Measures that exempt foreign companies from 3 percent of local income tax are adopted by Beijing Municipal Government.[SP]
May '99	The stamp duty on B-share trading was cut to 0.3% from 0.4% this month.[IFC]
June '99	The People's Bank of China announced it would cut rates on deposits by an average of 0.75%.[IFC]
July '99	The tension in the Taiwan Straits was raised by a speech of President Lee Teng Hui that scraps the "one China" policy.[IFC]
July 15 '99	(Controls on credit operations) Some controls on renminbi loans to FFEs under foreign exchange liens or guarantees were eased.[TMF]
September 8, '99	CSRC allows SOEs and all listed companies to issue shares and trade stocks.[GK]
September 8, '99	China plans to allow more banks and hi-tech private firms to tap the stock market for financing.[IFC]
October '99	The government imposed 20% tax on bank deposit interest income and other market initiatives. Beijing allowed two state firms to sell state-owned shares and permitted certain share buybacks for Chinese B- and H-shares.[IFC]
November '99	The Tracker Fund, representing part of the Hong Kong Special Administrative Region government's HK$208 billion (US$27 billion) share portfolio, was listed. The Stock Exchange of Hong Kong launched the Growth Enterprise Market (GEM) for small-cap and high-tech firms, creating an out-flow of foreign liquidity from the Mainland B-share market to the Hong Kong GEM market.[IFC]

A Chronology of Economic, Political and Financial Events in China

Date	Event
April 2000	The China Securities Regulatory Commission (CSRC) allowed state and listed firms to purchase domestic IPOs without restrictions on the size of these stakes.[IFC]
June 2000	China Unicom Ltd. became the third-largest IPO in the world.[IFC]
June 2000	The Chinese government decided to delay the set up of a NASDAQ-style market for high-growth companies and announced the launch of its first mutual fund to be advised by foreign fund companies. Beijing formally approved the merger of the A-share markets of the Shanghai and Shenzhen exchanges.[IFC]
October 2000	The government announced a planned interest rate reform and published regulations on the opening of the telecommunications sector. China Petroleum & Chemical Corp.'s IPO became the fifth largest in the world for the year.[IFC]
2001	The crackdown on share price manipulation by the China Securities Regulatory Commission rekindled investor concerns about China's volatile stock market.[IFC]
February 22, 2001	The opening of the B-share market to domestic investors boosted the markets. Domestic investors could only invest with existing foreign currency deposits.[IFC]
May, 2001	China cut interest rates on its foreign currency deposits, following U.S.'s rate cuts.[IFC]
June 1, 2001	Domestic investors now invest in B shares with new foreign currency deposits.[PW]
2001	During the third quarter, the government cracks down on illegal bank loans to stock market speculators and its practice of selling of shares to finance pension obligations.[IFC]

A Chronology of Economic, Political and Financial Events in China

Date	Event
July, 2001	China Mobile and China Unicom, the two leading telecommunications companies, saw share prices plunge on investor fears about market growth potential and profit margins.[IFC]
September 17, 2001	WTO successfully concludes negotiations on China's entry.[WTO]
September 19, 2001	Rules relaxed for purchasing foreign exchange for advance repayments of certain debt.[PW]
October 19, 2001	The government suspended the sale of state-owned shares.[IFC]
November 16, 2001	Stamp tax decreases from 0.3% to 0.2%.[GK]
December, 2001	New regulations were announced to tighten delisting rules. A major international rating agency upgraded China's sovereign rating.[IFC]
December, 11 2001	China's accession to the WTO which included promises to open their markets to international competition.[WTO]
January 29, 2002	The regulations governing foreign banks and financial institutions were issued by the People's Bank of China yesterday and are to take effect on 1 February, replacing the five sets of regulations in force since 1996.[IFC]
Febuary, 2002	US President George W. Bush visits, on the 30th anniversary of President Nixon's visit to China (at the time, the first visit by a U.S. president).[IFC]
March, 12, 2002	The government announced a plan to ease restrictions limiting foreign investors to minority stakes in port infrastructure projects and approved foreign investment in urban pipeline projects for gas, heating and water as part of the revised Industrial Catalogue for Foreign Investment, due to come into effect on 1 April 2002.[WMA]
July, 2002	The US says China is modernizing its military to make possible a forcible reunification with Taiwan. Beijing says its policy remains defensive.[IFC]

A CHRONOLOGY OF ECONOMIC, POLITICAL AND FINANCIAL EVENTS IN CHINA

Date	Event
October 9, 2002	China is to let private and foreign investors buy controlling stakes in domestically listed firms for the first time.[IFC]
November 4, 2002	The authorities have announced that foreign companies will be allowed to buy shares in listed Chinese companies.[IFC]
November 5, 2002	The Chinese Securities Regulatory Commission (CSRC) and China's central bank (PBOC) issued the Temporary Measures for Investment in Domestic Securities by Qualified Foreign Institutional Investors (the "QFII Regulation"), effective December 1, 2002. A monumental piece of legislation which, for the first time in history, permits foreign investors to directly invest and trade in publicly listed domestic securities. The historic regulation, released on the eve of the opening of the 16th Communist Party Congress, covers: (i) the eligibility standards of a Qualified Foreign Institutional Investor (a "QFII"), (ii) the foreign exchange aspect of the transactions, including the qualification and operation of the depositary banks and the management of the special QFII accounts at such banks, and (iii) control of the investment transactions per se.[RP]
November 5, 2002	Definition of Qualified Foreign Institutional Investor. 1) Funds (at least five years of operating history, more than US$10 billion under management); 2) Insurance companies (at least 30 years of operating history, more than US$10 billion under management); 3) Securities firms (at least 30 years of operating history, more than US$10 billion under management 4) Commericial banks (total assets ranked in top 100 globally and more than US$10 billion under management).[RP]
November 15, 2002	Vice-President Hu Jintao is named head of the ruling Communist Party, replacing Jiang Zemin, the outgoing president. Jiang is re-elected head of the influential Central Military Commission, which oversees the armed forces.[IFC]

A Chronology of Economic, Political and Financial Events in China

Date	Event
December 3, 2002	China went back on its plan to allow foreign investors into the country's bond market as the registration process for Qualified Foreign Institutional Investors (QFIIs) opened. QFIIs allowed to invest in A shares, subject to regulations.[IFC]
December, 2002	The seven-year Rmb60bn (US$7.25bn) bond sale completed. The bond was oversubscribed by 22 times on generous terms offered by the Ministry of Finance.[WMA]
March, 2003	National People's Congress elected Hu Jintao as president. He replaced Jiang Zemin, who stepped down after 10 years in the post.[IFC]
March, 2003	A new rural land reform in China, extending land-use rights to 30 years, should provide a significant boost to the rural economy by encouraging new investment and providing a source of capital.[IFC]
March, 2003	China and Hong Kong were hit by the pneumonia-like SARS virus, which was thought to have originated in Guangdong province in November 2002. Strict quarantine measures were enforced to stop the disease spreading.[WMA]
April, 2003	New rules on mergers and acquisitions were issued as China seeks to facilitate M&A activity and boost inward investment.[WMA]
May 27, 2003	Two foreign brokers were granted the right to trade in renmimbi denominated securities for the first time, marking a milestone in the development of China's capital market.[IFC]
June, 2003	Sluice gates on Three Gorges dam closed to allow reservoir to fill up. Construction of $25 billion project displaced almost one million people to make way for world's largest hydroelectric scheme.[BBC]

A CHRONOLOGY OF ECONOMIC, POLITICAL AND FINANCIAL EVENTS IN CHINA

Date	Event
June, 2003	China and India reached de facto agreement over status of Tibet and Sikkim in landmark cross-border trade agreement.[IFC]
June, 2003	Standard and Poors estimates that Chinese banks need US$500bn bail-out.[WMA]
July, 2003	Some 500,000 people march in Hong Kong against Article 23, a controversial anti-subversion bill. Two key Hong Kong government officials resign. The government shelves the bill.[IFC]
August, 2003	The Chinese government announced to reduce the size of the country's armed force by 200,000 by 2005.[IFC]
September, 2003	Wu Bangguo, the Standing Committee chairman of the National People's Congress (NPC), has confirmed that exchange rate policy would continue to focus on renmimbi (RMB) stability, but asserted that a shift to market-based determination remained the government's ultimate goal.[IFC]
December 2, 2003	Authorities in China assert no change in Foreign Exchange Policy.
January, 2004	Ceiling for foreign investment in a Chinese bank was raised from 20% to 25%. Any single foreign bank's share was raised from 15% to 20%.[PW]
January, 2004	The Chinese government has dipped into its US$400bn foreign exchange reserves in order to recapitalize two of the 'Big Four' state-owned banks, in a move to accelerate reform in the country's ailing financial sector.[WMA]
January, 2004	The World Bank's private-sector division—the International Finance Corporation (IFC)—has announced that it intends to double its investment in China, up to US$500m by 2006.[IFC]

A CHRONOLOGY OF ECONOMIC, POLITICAL AND FINANCIAL EVENTS IN CHINA

Date	Event
February 2, 2004	The country's State Council has issued new investment guidelines for listed companies, clearing the way for greater capital investment and brokerage opportunities. The plan calls for the establishment of a multi-layered capital market system, consisting of a main board market and a secondary one for venture capital projects and corporate bond/futures products.[WMA]
January 2004	The International Finance Corp (IFC) arm of the World Bank confirmed today that it has committed US$2m to the Chinese mortgage market.[IFC]
2004	Qualified foreign institutional investors (QFII) allowed to invest in A shares.[PW]
March 2004	The US government has filed its first official suit against China under the auspices of the World Trade Organization (WTO), claiming that a tax on semi-conductors gives domestic exporters unfair advantage. The suit underlines the US's increasingly hard line stance over bilateral trade, the iniquities of which are embodied in the US's trade deficit with China, which ballooned to US$124bn in 2003.[WMA]
April 26, 2004	Legislators rule out direct elections for Hong Kong leader in 2007.[IFC]
May 16, 2004	Liu Mingkang, head of the China Banking Regulatory Commission, said that China's banks should use the firms and people whose bad debts are destabilizing the banking system.[IFC]
June 1, 2004	China's banking regulator has ordered tighter scrutiny of bank lending as part of a government campaign against reckless investment.[IFC]
June 14, 2004	China's Premier Wen Jiabao has stressed the need for local officials to implement policies designed to cool down China's overheating economy.[BBC]

A Chronology of Economic, Political and Financial Events in China

Year	Regulations on Foreign Investors
1998	Restrictions: Foreign investors can only hold Class B shares. Investment amounts must be registered separately with each exchange. Holdings of more than 5% of total issued shares of a company must be reported to the People's Bank of China.
	Taxation: Rules on capital gains tax are being finalized. Dividends are untaxed. 0.30% stamp duty, 0.50% value transaction fee, 0.10% registration fee. $8 per transaction clearing fee with a custodian bank, and $4 without a custodian bank, $20 depository.
1999	Restrictions: Same. All settlements and income receipts are in USD or HKD, without repatriation difficulty.
	Taxation: No capital gains tax. Dividend income is subject to 20% withholding tax applied at the registration company on the portion of dividends above the PBoC's (the central bank) one-year RMB certificate of deposit rate for the same period.[B]
2000	Restrictions: Requirements on foreign-exchange balancing and domestic sales ratios were eliminated.
2001	Restrictions: Foreign-funded firms who wish to list on the Shanghai and Shenzhen stock exchanges must have operated in China for 3 years, give details of all foreign shareholders with more than 5% of the firm's stock.
	Taxation: 30% national corporate tax, 3% local corporate tax, 33% capital gains tax.
2002	Restrictions: 1. Foreign bank branches must have at least US$72.5 million in operating capital, and they will be able to conduct foreign and domestic currency business. Wholly foreign-owned banks and Sino-foreign joint venture banks must maintain a minimum registered capital of US$120.8 million, 60% of which must be held in local currency and 40% in hard currencies. 2. Non-bank financial institutions, wholly foreign-owned and joint venture firms, are required to have a minimum registered capital of US$84.6 million.

A Chronology of Economic, Political and Financial Events in China

Year	Regulations on Foreign Investors
2004	Qualified foreign institutional investors (QFII) allowed to invest in A shares with the following conditions: (a) five years of investment experience and 30 years for insurance companies plus they must manage at least $10 billion in assets and no accounting irregularities over the past three years; (b) bank must be in top 100 of assets under management in world; (c) minimum paid up capital for insurance company or a securities firm of $1 billion; (d) maximum ownership of any company listed in Shanghai or Shenzhen stock exchange is 10% and for any company it cannot exceed 20%; (e) QFII must use local banks and local securities firms. Special renminbi accounts must be set up. (f) Closed-end QFII cannot remit capital until three years have passed from initial investment. Other QFII can remit capital after year. Closed-end QFII cannot remit more than 20% of capital at a time and the minimum time between installments is one month. Other QFII also cannot remit more than 20% of the capital at any time. In this case, the minimum time between remittances is three months.[PW]

References

IFC	International Finance Corporation, *Factbook* (various years).
IMF	International Monetary Fund, *Annual Report of Exchange Arrangements and Exchange Restrictions*, 1980–2000.
DT	Department of Treasury, *National Treatment Study*.
BD	Utpal Bhattacharya and Hazem Daouk, *The World Price of Insider Trading, Journal of Finance*, 2002.
GK	Lei Gao and Gerhard Kling, Regulatory Changes and Market Liquidity in Chinese Stock Markets, *Emerging Markets Review*, 2006.
CSRC	China Securities Regulatory Commission website.
BNY	Bank of New York website.
SP	Standard and Poors website.
BBC	British Broadcasting System, UK Edition.
WMA	World Market Research Centre, *World Market Analysis*.
PW	Eswar Prasad and Shang-Jin Wei, Capital Flows in China, 2005.
RP	Roger Peng, China Releases Temporary Measures for Investment, Morrison and Foerster, November 2002.
B	Bridge, *The Bridge Handbook of World Stock, Derivative & Commodity Exchanges*, 2000.
WTO	World Trade Organization, http://www.wto.org/English/thewto_e/countries_e/china_e.htm

Endnotes

Summary

1. Andrew Nathan, "Present at the Stagnation," *Foreign Affairs*, July/August 2006, p. 177.

2. Gordon Chang, *The Coming Collapse of China*, Random House, 2001

3. Bruce Gilley, *China's Democratic Future*, Columbia University Press, 2004; also see Edward Friedman & Barrett McCormick, eds., *What If China Doesn't Democratize? Implications For War And Peace*, East Gate Books, 2000; and Suisheng Zhao, ed., *China And Democracy: Reconsidering the Prospects for a Democratic China*, Routledge, 2000.

4. Andrew Nathan and Bruce Gilley, *China's New Rulers: The Secret Files*, New York Review Of Books, 2006.

5. Minxin Pei, *China's Trapped Transition: The Limits of Developmental Autocracy*, Harvard University Press, 2006.

6. James Mann, *The China Fantasy: How Our Leaders Explain Away Chinese Repression*, Penguin Group 2007.

7. William Hutton, *The Writing on the Wall: Why We Must Embrace China as a Partner or Enemy*, Free Press, 2006.

8. Susan L. Shirk, *China: Fragile Superpower*, Oxford University Press, 2007.

9. C. Fred Bergsten, Bates Gill, Nicholas R. Lardy, Derick I. Mitchell, *The Balance Sheet China: What the World Needs to Know About the Emerging Superpower*, Public Affairs, 2006.

10. See for example Constantine C. Menges, *China: The Gathering Threat*, Nelson Current, 2005; and Jeb Babbin and Edward Timperlake, *Showdown: Why China Wants War With The United States*, Regency Publishing, Inc., 2006.

11. Edward Friedman and Barrett McCormack, Eds. *What If China Does Not Democratize? Implications For War And Peace*, East Gate Books, 2000.

12. See BBC Videos, *The Nazis: A Warning From History*, 1997.

13. See Denis Twitchett, Michael Loewe & John Fairbank, *The Cambridge History Of China*, Cambridge University Press, 1986; and Kenneth Hammond, *From Yao To Mao: 5000 Years Of Chinese History*, The Teaching Company, 2004.

14. See John Dean, *Conservatives Without Conscience*, Yale University Press, 2006; and John Lukas, *Democracy And Populism: Fear And Hatred*, Yale University Press, 2005.

15. One way of paraphrasing Godel's Incompleteness Theorem is that human beings are working with finite minds in infinity and can neither identify all the information required to make decisions and even if they could, the human mind is not capable of processing it all. Another way of paraphrasing the fundamental concept is that all human beings are just guessing about everything. Godel showed in mathematics that within a rigidly logical system such as Bertrand Russell and Alfred North Whitehead had developed for arithmetic, propositions can be formulated that are undecidable or indemonstrable with the axioms of the system. That is, within the system, there exist certain clear-cut statements that can never be proved or disproved. Hence, one cannot, using the usual methods, be certain that the axioms of arithmetic will not lead to contradictions. It appears to foredoom hope of mathematical certitude through use of the obvious methods. Perhaps doomed also, as a result, is the ideal of science devising a set of axioms from which all phenomena of the external world can be deduced. See *www.miskanoic.org*

Chapter 1. Elite Accommodation of America and China

1. The Theory Of Elite Accommodation developed out of a study of Belgian politics. Three principal interest groups dominated in Belgium: the business community, the labor movement, and the Church. The leaders of each group collaborated, while engaging in rhetoric required to sustain their positions as the leaders of each interest groups. They shared two common problems, the need to remain leaders of their groups, and the need to keep Belgium functioning. The latter need was predominant. The leaders of each interest group collaborated in order to solve the country's problems. The leaders of each interest group created the politics of consensus, while they maintained the manageability of their faction of society. One leader would in effect say to the others, "I am going to attack you rhetorically, but that is not going to affect my true regard for and relationship with you". "Yes, I know," the others would say, "I feel the same way." The pragmatism of the Theory Of Elite Accommodation lends itself to the development of the America and Chinese partnership in the 21st century. But the rhetoric of conflict is counter-productive.

2. Thomas S. Kuhn, *The Structure of Scientific Revolutions*, University Of Chicago Press, 1996.

3. See Robert Kennedy, *Thirteen Days*, W.W. Norton & Company, 1973.

Chapter 2. America and China on the Road to Success or Failure Together

1. See Martin A. Nowak, Robert M. May and Karl Sigmund, "The Arithmetics of Mutual Help," *Scientific American*, June 1995, pp. 76–81.

2. See Zhwng Bijian, "Peacefully Rising to Great Power Status," *Foreign Affairs*, September/October 2005, pp. 18–25.

3. Wang Jisi, "China's Search for Stability With America," *Foreign Affairs*, September/October 2005, pp. 39–48.

4. Ted Fishman, *China Inc.*, Simon & Schuster, 2005, p. 17.

5. Richard J. Newman, "China's Turn," *U.S. News & World Report*, June 20, 2005, p. 42.

6. *Business Week*, August 22/29, 2005, p. 58.

Chapter 3. How America and China Can Win Together

1. See Edward Steichen, *The Family Of Man*, Harry N. Abrams, Reissue edition, 1996.

2. Another major relationship in the 21st century is that of Islamic fundamentalist with moderate Islamic and Western democratic civilizations. That relationship is much more challenging than the relationship between America and China, the leading developed and the leading developing nations in the 21st century, with their shared commitments to capitalism. Success in the less challenging relationship between America and China will assist in finding success in the more challenging Islamic and non-Islamic societies' relationship.

3. See John Milligan-Whyte, *The Age Of Species Lethal Weapons Vs. Moral Authority: The Case For The Manhattan II Project* to be published in 2008.

4. Conversation with Ambassador Paul Bremer.

5. John Lukas, *Democracy and Populism: Fear and Hatred*, Yale University Press, 2005.

6. Ibid.

7. Kishore Mahbubani, *Beyond The Age Of Innocence: Rebuilding Trust Between America And The Rest Of The World*, BBS Public Affairs, 2005.

8. Noam Chomsky, Failed States: The Abuse of Power and the Assault on Democracy, Metropolitan Books, Henry Holt & Company, 2006.

9. George Soros, *The Bubble of American Supremacy*, W.W. Norton, 2004.

10. Farrar Straus & Giroux, 2005.

11. Friedman, ibid., p. 10.

12. Ibid.

13. Dow Jones Newswire, "Chinese Pres, PM Use New Year To Vow Help For Rural Poor," *The Wall Street Journal Online*, January 29, 2006.

Chapter 4. China's Capitalism Is Redefining the Competitiveness and Wealth of Nations

1. China Statistics Bureau, Local Annual Report, 2003.

2. Pete Engardio, "Emerging Giants," *Business Week*, July 30, 2006, p. 49.

3. China Statistics Bureau, Local Annual Report, 2003.

4. Kenishi Ohmae, *The Next Global Stage Challenges And Opportunities In Our Borderless World*, Wharton School Publishing, 2005, p. 89.

5. Gongmeng Chen, "A Smart and Sustainable Growth Model for China's Economy in the Following 20 years: Innovation and Venture Capital," presentation at World Economic Forum China Summit 2004.

6. Ohmae, ibid., p. 89.

7. People's Bank Of China.

8. Ted Fishman, *China Inc*, Simon & Schuster, 2005, p. 11.

9. Ibid.

10. Ohmae, ibid., p. 90.

11. Richard McGregor, "Beijing May Intervene As Investment in Cities Rises Sharply," *Financial Times*, June 16, 2006, p. 2.

12. James Areddy, "China Warns Its Banks to Curb Lending As Money Supply Rises," *The Wall Street Journal*, June 15, 2006, p. A2.

13. "China's Economy," *Financial Times*, June 16, 2006, p. 12.

14. "Industrial Output In China Grew 17.9% Despite Cooling Steps," *Wall Street Journal*, June 15, 2006, p. A 8.

15. "Foreign Reserves Rise To a High in Japan on Gains in the Euro," *Wall Street Journal*, June 8, 2006, p. A13.

16. Jennifer Hughes, "Foreign inflows to US dip sharply," *Financial Times*, June 16, 2006, p. 24.

17. Steve Johnson, "Greenback loses more ground," *Financial Times*, June 16, 2006, p. 22.

18. *Business Week*, August 22/29, 2005, p. 57.

19. Bruce Einhorn, "No Peasant Left Behind," *Business Week*, August 22/29, 2005, p. 102.

20. Fred Vogelstien, "How Intel Got Inside," *Fortune*, October 4, 2004, p. 127, 132.

21. Ibid.

22. Ibid.

23. *Business Week*, August 22/29, 2005, p. 56.

24. See L. J. Brahm, "Zhu Rongji's Managed Marketization of the Chinese Economy," P.M.C. Mar and F. Richter ed, *China, Enabling A New Era Of Changes*, World Economic Forum, 2002.

25. Chee and West, ibid., p. 1.

26. Free Press, 1998.

27. Ohmae, ibid., pp. 45–9.

28. Ohmae, ibid., pp. 53–54.

29. Ibid., p. 54.

30. Mar & Richter, "Mapping China's Future: What Scenarios, What Strategies?" Mar & Richter, *China Enabling An Era Of Change*, John Wiley & Sons, 2003, p. 14.

31. See "Behind the mask" *The Economist*, March 18, 2005.

32. Kenichi Ohmae, ibid., p. 17.

33. *Business Week*, August 22/29, 2005.

34. Clay Chandler, "Inside The New China," *Fortune*, October 4, 2004, p. 85, 86.

35. Ming Zeng and Peter J. Williamson, The Hidden Dragons, *Harvard Business Review*, October 2003, p. 92.

36. ffice of the U.S. Trade Representative Website *http://ustr.gov/Document* Library/Fact Sheets/2004/America's Trade with China.html.

37. *CIA World Fact Book* 2004.

38. Goldman Sachs, *China Business Post*, Feb. 2004.

39. Mar & Richter, *China Enabling An Era Of Changes*, John Wiley & Sons (Asia) Pte Ltd, 2003, p. 217.

40. Kenneth Lieberthal & Geoffrey Lieberthal, "The Great Transition," *Harvard Business Review*, October 2003, p. 71-3.

41. "Behind the mask," *The Economist*, March 18, 2004.

42. Ibid.

43. See Kuln, *Scientific Revolutions*, University Of Chicago Press, 1996.

44. Leiberthal & Leiberthal, ibid.

45. Fishman, ibid., p. 10.

46. Fishman, ibid., p. 12.

47. Fishman, ibid.

48. "China sees economy growing at 9.2% in 2005," China View, *www.chinaview.cn* September 26, 2005.

49. Kieth Bradsher, "China's President Says Economy Rose 10.2% in Quarter," *The New York Times*, April 17, 2006, p. C2.

50. Richard McGregor, "Chinese growth at fastest pace for decade," *Financial Times*, July 19, 2006, p. 1.

51. Mark Thirlwill, *Shaking the World? China and the World Economy*, Lowy Institute, August 2005, p. 2.

52. Ibid., pp. 2–3.

53. Fishman, ibid., p. 9.

54. Fishman, ibid., p. 298.

55. Lester Thurow, *Fortune Favors The Bold*, Harper Business, 2003, p. 285.

56. Thurow, ibid., p. 183.

57. *Business Week*, August 22/29, 2005, pp. 54–55.

58. Ibid.

59. Thirlwill, ibid., p. 4.

60. "China to double per capita GDP of 2000 by 2010," *China View*, *www.chinaview.cn*, October 11, 2005.

61. "Special Message by Huang Ju". World Economic Forum Knowledge Navigator

62. Fishman, ibid., p. 7.

63. James Murdoch, "The New Millennium: China In The Connected World," in Laurence J. Brahm ed *China's Century The awakening of the Next Economic Powerhouse*, John Wiley & Sons (Asia) Pte Ltd, 2001, p. 374 at p. 375.

64. Kenichi Ohmae, ibid., p. 129.

65. *Business Week*, August 22/29, 2005.

66. Peter Yip, "How The Internet Will Shape China," Laurence Brahm, *China's Century*, p. 329.

67. Hal R. Varian, "A Plug for the Unplugged $100 Laptop Computer for Developing Nations," *The New York Times*, February 9, 2006, p. C3.

68. The Chinese constitution was only amended recently to enshrine property rights. The economic growth prior to that could be attributed to the emphasis on the efficient use of the social resources rather than property rights.

69. Fishman, ibid., p. 50.

70. Jeffrey D. Sachs, *The End Of Poverty*, The Penguin Press, 2005.

71. Kenichi Ohmae, ibid., pp. 40–41.

72. Ibid., p. 42.

73. John Stuttard, *The New Silk Road, Secrets of Business Success In China Today*, John Wiley & Sons, 2002, p. 37.

74. Andrew Nathan, "Present at the Stagnation," *Foreign Affairs*, July/August 2006, p. 177.

75. Hernando de Soto, *The Mystery of Capital: Why Capitalism Triumphs In The West And Fails Everywhere Else*, Basic Books, 2000.

76. Ibid., pp. 40–44.

77. *Business Week*, August 22/29, 2005, p. 75.

78. Frederik Blafour, "The State's Long Apron Strings," *Business Week*, August 22/29, 2005, p. 74.

79. Ibid.

80. Donald N. Sull, *Made In China: What Western Managers Can Learn From Trailblazing Chinese Entrepreneurs*, Harvard Business School Press, 2005.

81. Laurence Brahm, "Zhu Rongji's 'Managed Marketization' of the Chinese Economy," *China Enabling An Era Of Changes*, Mar & Richter, John Wily & Sons (Asia) Pte Ltd, 2003, pp. 71–74.

82. Hernando de Soto, ibid., pp. 5–7.

83. Farrar Straus & Giroux, 2005.

84. Ibid., p. 11.

85. Ibid., pp. 11–36.

86. Ibid., p. 35.

87. Geoffrey Colvin, "America Isn't Ready," *Fortune*, August 1, 2005, p. 70 at p. 77.

88. Ibid., p. 36.

89. See "The Dark Side of China's Rise," *Foreign Policy*, March/April 2006, p. 32 and Minxin Pei, *China's Trapped Transition: The Limits of Developmental Autocracy*, Cambridge: Harvard University Press, 2006.

90. Minxin Pei, "The Dark Side of China's Rise," *Foreign Policy*, March/April 2006, pp. 32–38.

Chapter 5. China is a Successful Permission Society, Consensus Democracy and Pre-Rule of Law System

1. Mure Dickie, "Hu Savours success of his escape from 'bad elements'," *Financial Times*, September 21, 2004, p. 16.

2. See John Milligan-Whyte, *The Age Of Species Lethal Weapons Vs. Moral Authority: The Case For The Manhattan II Project* to be published in 2008.

3. Chee & West, ibid., pp. 64–5.

4. Brahm, ibid., p. 213.

5. Ibid., p. 216.

6. Ibid.

7. Ibid.

8. See also Business Week, August 22/29, 2005.

9. Pete Engardio, "Emerging Giants", *Business Week,* July 31, 2006, p. 45.

10. Sources: CIA World Fact Book 2002 and 2004: The Economist Pocket World in Figures; World Development Indicators CD-ROM; *Financial Times.*

11. See Yasheng Huang, *Selling China*, Cambridge University Press, 2003.

12. Huang, ibid.

13. Ibid., pp. 308–350.

14. Xinhau News Agency, October 16, 2004.

15. Terrence Barnett, Country Head, Novartis China, quoted in Stuttard, ibid., p. 75.

16. Laurence Brahm, *China's Century*, John Wiley & Sons Pte Ltd, 2001, pp. 58–59.

17. Even an early and sophisticated leader among non-Chinese globally dominant companies doing business in China, Flour Corporation, indicated that it has trouble making money in China in 2004. For a review of the failures of foreign companies' strategies in China, see Joe Studwell, *The China Dream—The Quest For The Last Great Untapped Market On Earth*, Grove Atlantic Press, 2003.

18. Haley, Haley & Tan, *The Chinese Tao Of Business*, 2004, p. 237.

19. Haley, Haley & Tan, ibid.

20. Ibid., pp. 219–33.

21. Fan Gang, "Reform and Development: The Dual Transformation of China," *China Enabling An Era Of Reforms*, Mar & Richter, John Wiley & Sons, 2003, pp. 33–34.

22. Xiao Yang, "A New Chapter in Constructing China's Legal System," Laurence Brahm, *China's Century*, John Wiley & Sons (Asia) Ltd, 2001, pp. 219–233.

23. Sean Wilentz, *The Rise Of American Democracy*, W.W. Norton, 2005.

24. Ibid., from the notes on the cover flaps.

25. Vincent Wilson Jr., *The Book Of Great American Documents*, American History Research Associates, 1967, p. 4.

26. Quoted ibid., p. 27.

27. Ibid.

28. Noam Chomsky, *Failed States: The Abuse of Power and the Assault on Democracy*, Metropolitan Books, Henry Holt & Company, 2006.

29. Haley, Haley & Tan, Ibid., p. 14.

30. Haley, Haley & Tan, Ibid., pp. 9–10.

31. Stuttard, ibid.

32. Stuttard, ibid.

33. Julius Bar, ibid., p. 12.

34. C. Wright Mills, *The Power Elite*, Oxford University Press, 1956, 2000, pp. 3–4.

35. Ibid., p. 13.

36. See C. Wright Mills, Ibid.

37. Noam Chomsky, *Failed States: The Abuse of Power and the Assault on Democracy*, Metropolitan Books, Henry Holt & Company, 2006.

38. Ibid., p.28.

39. "The rich, the poor and the growing gap between them," *The Economist*, June 17, 2006, p. 29.

40. Minxin Pei, "The Dark Side Of China's Rise," *Foreign Policy*, March/April 2006.

41. Hu Angang and Guo Yong, "Administrative Monopoly, Corruption, and China's Economic Transformation," Richter & Mar, Ibid., p. 97.

42. Ibid.

43. Lester Thurow, *Fortune Favors The Bold*, Harper Business, 2003, p. 187.

44. "Atomised," *The Economist*, June 3, 2006, p.37.

45. Richard McGregor, "China cracks down on land sale corruption," *Financial Times*, June 25, 2006, p. 2.

46. "Atomised," Ibid.

47. Fredrick Balfour, "The Starter Home Is A Nonstarter," *Business Week*, June 19, 2006, p. 49.

48. Richard McGregor, "Hu urges party to remain progressive," *Financial Times*, July 1, 2006, p. 4.

49. Joseph Kahn, "China's Leader Pushes Doctrine While Warning of Corruption, *The New York Times*, July 1, 2006, p. A4.

50. Minxin Pei, Ibid.

51. Ibid.

52. Julius Bar, Ibid., pp. 11–2.

53. For insightful commentaries see Hope & Lau, ibid., p. 3 and Laurence J. Brahm, "Zhu Rongji's Managed Marketization of the Chinese Economy," in Pamela C.M. Mar & Frank-Jurgen Richter, *China Enabling A New Era of Changes*, John Wiley & Sons (Asia) Pte Ltd, 2003, p. 71.

54. Hope & Lau, Ibid., p. 6.

55. Ibid., p. 10.

56. Hope & Lau, Ibid., p. 4.

57. Ibid., p. 3.

58. Hope & Lau, Ibid., p. 5.

59. *Documents Of The 16th Congress Of The Chinese Communist Party Of China*, Foreign Language Press, 2002.

60. Hope & Lau, ibid., p. 16.

61. Haley, Haley & Tan, ibid.

62. Dexter Roberts & Michael Arndt, "Its Getting Hotter In The East," *Business Week*, August 22/29, 2005, p. 78.

63. Ibid.

64. See "Short Term Results: The Litmus Test For Success In China," Rick Yan, *Harvard Business Review*, September-October 1998, pp. 61–75.

65. Donald J. Lewis, "Governance In China: The Present And Future Tense," *China's Century: The Emergence Of A New Economic Powerhouse*, Laurence Brahm ed., John Wiley & Sons, 2001, p. 240.

66. Carolyn Blackman, *Negotiating China, Case Studies And Strategies*, Allen & Unwin, 1997, pp. 39–41.

67. Haley, Haley & Tan, ibid., pp. 70–1.

68. Ibid., pp. 14–5.

69. Huang, ibid., p. xvi.

70. Fan Gang, "Reform and Development: The Dual-Transformation of China, *China Enabling An Era Of Changes*, John Wiley & Sons, 2003, p. 38.

71. Xiao Yang, "A New Chapter In Constructing China's Legal System," Laurence Brahm, *China's Century*, pp. 219–31.

72. Ibid., pp. 219–33.

Chapter 6. Why China Is Emerging from Hunger

1. Xinhua, China Daily.com, November 10, 2006.

2. Andrew Browne, "China Drew Over $60 Billion In Foreign Investment In 2005, January 14, 2006, *Wall Street Journal Online*.

3. Julius Bar, Ibid., p. 67.

4. Huang.

5. Julius Bar, ibid., p. 11.

6. Julius Bar, Ibid,

7. Julius Bar, *Tempted by the Dragon-Swiss companies in China,* p. 1.

8. See C.B MacPherson, *The Real World Of Democracy,* University Of Toronto Press.

9. See "Broken China," Gary Shilling, *Forbes,* May, 12, 2003.

10. Oded Shenkar.

11. Yasheng Huang, *Selling China,* Cambridge University Press, 2003.

12. Lester Thurow, *Fortune Favors The Bold,* Harper Business, 2003, p. 207.

13. Ibid.

14. Ibid.

15. *China Economic Quarterly,* 2003.

16. *The Economist,* July 2nd–8th, 2005, pp. 54–6.

17. Gary Skilling, *Forbes,* May 12, 2003,

18. Skilling, ibid.

19. *The Economist,* ibid.

20. Oded Shenkar, *The Chinese Century,* Wharton School Publication, 2005, pp. 47–9.

21. Henry Sender, "Meet China Inc: Topping Japan Inc of 1980," *Wall Street Journal Online,* June 24, 2005.

22. Chee & West, ibid., p. 14.

23. Ibid.

24. See Gordon Chang, *The Coming Collapse of China,* New York, Random House, 2001.

25. Chee & West, ibid., pp. 14–5.

26. Ibid.

27. Ibid., pp. 4–8.

28. Yasheng Huang, *Selling China,* ibid., p. 308.

29. Ibid.

30. Ibid., pp. 308–350.

31. Huang, *Selling China,* ibid., pp. 335–36.

32. "Behind the mask," *The Economist,* March 18, 2004.

33. Jeffrey D. Sachs, *The End Of Poverty,* The Penguin Press, 2005.

34. Ibid.

35. Jeffrey D, Sachs, ibid., p. 154.

36. Chee & West, ibid., p. 15.

37. Jeffrey D. Sachs, ibid., p. 169.

38. Julius Baer, ibid., p. 8.

39. Fishman, ibid., p. 101.

40. Peter Yip, "How The Internet Will Shape China," Laurence Brahm, *China's Century*, John Wiley & Sons, 2001, p. 327.

41. Chee & West, ibid., p. 6.

42. Harold Chee and Chris West, *Myths About Doing Business In China*, ibid., p. 11.

43. Mar & Richter, *China Enabling An Era Of Change*, ibid., pp. 3–4.

44. Julius Bar, *Tempted by the dragon—Swiss companies in China*, p. 1.

45. See Fan Gang, "Reform and Development: The Dual Transformation of China," Mar & Richter ed, *China Enabling A New Era Of Changes*, ibid., pp. 33–47.

46. *New Silk Road*, ibid., p. 2.

47. *New Silk Road*, ibid., p. 3.

48. Ibid.

49. Fan Gang, "Reform and Development: The Dual Transformation of China," *China Enabling An Era Of Changes*, Mar & Richter, John Wiley & Sons Ltd, 2003, p. 37.

50. James J. Shiro, *The New Silk Road Secrets of Business Success in China Today*, John Wiley & Sons, 2000, p. x.

51. Mar & Richter, ibid., p. 16.

52. Yasheng Huang, ibid., pp. 8–9.

53. Mar & Richter, ibid.

54. Ministry of Commerce of People's Republic of China; China Trade Remedy Information, *www.cacs.gov.cn* (http://gb.chinabroadcast.cn/3821/2004/10/15/762@329260.htm)

55. Nicholas Hope and Lawrence Lau, "China's Transition to the Market: Status and Challenges" Working Paper No. 210, Stanford Center For International Development, 2004, p. 2.

56. The U.S. Trade Representative's annual report: *http://www.ustr.gov/assets/Document_Library/Reports_Publications/2004/2004_Trade_Policy_Agenda/asset_upload_file440_4757.pdf*; the report indicates that 60% of U.S. imports from China are consumer goods. That would imply a value of $83.9 billion for consumer-

goods imports from China, which translates that about 31% of all consumer goods purchased in the U.S. come from China. In addition, the authors did a survey at stores in Boston. At Macy's, of 16 items picked up randomly, seven were made in China (44%); at Wal-Mart, of 12 items picked up randomly, four were from China (33%). These are unscientific surveys with many limitations.

57. Mel Fong, Peter Wonacott & Timothy Aeppel, "Chinese Manufacturers Are Closing Quality Gap," *Wall Street Journal*, Thursday October 13, 2004, p. A17.

58. Peter Barkto, former Chairman of EBS and former CEO of Forexster Ltd.

59. Ambassador Chen, UN Undersecretary General, China's former Ambassador to the United Nations.

60. The People's Bank Of China.

61. "Foreign Investors Bought More U.S. Securities In June, *Wall Street Journal Online*, August 15, 2005.

62. Ibid., pp. 157–162.

63. Jeffrey D, Sachs, ibid., pp. 157–162.

64. Ibid., pp. 153–4.

65. W.W. Norton & Co., 2002.

66. Ibid., pp. 206–8.

67. Huang, ibid., p. 310.

68. Sachs, ibid.

69. Mahbubani, ibid., p. 77.

70. Ibid.

71. "Behind the mask," *The Economist*, March 18, 2004.

72. New York Book Review Books, 2002, pp. 4–5.

73. Ibid., pp. 7–8.

74. Ibid., pp. 4–5.

75. Ibid.

76. Andrew Nathan & Bruce Gilley, *China's New Leaders: The Secret Files*, New York Review Of Books, 2002. pp. 3–12.

77. C.B. MacPhearson, *The Real World Of Democracy*, Oxford University Press, 1966.

78. *On Democracy*, Yale Bene Book, 2000: *Democracy And Its Critics*, Yale University Press, 1989.

79. *How Democratic Is The American Constitution*, Yale University Press, 2001.

80. Ibid.

81. *Who Governs? Democracy And Power In An American City*, Yale University Press, 1963.

82. See for example Noam Chomsky, ibid.

83. Laura D'Andrea Tyson, "A Stronger Yuan Helps China," *Business Week*, October 31, 2005, p. 114.

84. See www.Forexster.com.

Chapter 7. Can America Peacefully Accept China's Peaceful Rise?

1. Professor Marshall Meyer, Wharton School, quoted in Richard, J. Newman, "The Rise of a New Power," *US News & World Report*, June 10, 2005, p. 41.

2. f there is a set of strategies with the property that no player can benefit by changing strategy while the other players keep their strategies unchanged, then that set of strategies and the corresponding payoffs constitute "Nash Equilibrium". See Roger McCain, *Game Theory: A Non-technical Introduction to the Analysis of Strategy*, South-Western College Publication, 2003.

3. Some estimates put China's population at 1.5 billion due to an estimated 200 million migrant workers not included in China's census. See Ted Fishman, *China Inc*, Simon & Schuster, 2005, p. 6.

4. Jim Rogers quoted in Laurence J. Brahm, *China's Century*, John Wiley & Sons, 2001.

5. "Behind the mask," *The Economist*, March 18, 2005.

6. Michael Porter, *The Competitive Advantage Of Nations*, Free Press, 1998, does not analyze China in analyzing the competitive advantage of nations.

7. Mar & Richter, *China Enabling An Era Of Changes*, John Wiley & Sons (Asia) Pte Ltd, 2003, p. 217.

8. Joseph S. Nye, *The Paradox Of American Power*, Oxford University Press, 2002, p. 22.

9. Ibid., p. 18.

10. Ibid., p. 21.

11. Ibid., p. 22.

12. Ibid., pp. 18–19.

13. Edward Friedman and Barrett McCormack, eds. *What If China Does Not Democratize? Implications For War And Peace*, East Gate Books, 2000.

14. Joseph Rebello, and Elizabeth Price, "Greenspan Warns Against Raising Tariffs On China," *Wall Street Journal Online*, June 24, 2005.

15. *The Economist*, September 3rd–9th, 2005.

16. Peoples Bank Of China, April 2005.

17. Dow Jones Newswire, "Net Foreign Buys Of US Securities $87.4 billion In July, *Wall Street Journal Online*, September 16, 2005.

18. Ted Fishman, ibid., p. 265.

19. Ibid., pp. 102–3.

20. Mark Daniell, "China In A World Of Risk," *China's Century: The Awakening Of The Next Economic Powerhouse*, Laurence Brahm, ed., John Wiley & Sons (Asia) Ltd., 2001, p. 102.

21. "Powell: China not military threat to US," *Xinhua News Agency*, June 14, 2005.

22. Ibid.

23. Richard N. Haass, "What to Do About China," *U.S. News & World Reports*, June 20, 2005, p. 52.

24. Laurence Brahm, *China's Century*, John Wiley & Sons, 2001, p. 66.

25. In July 1944, Mao Zedong said to Siwei Xie, an American military observer, that China can and should cooperate with America on both economic and political issues. www.news.xinhuanet.com.

26. Mike Wallace: 60 Minutes interview with Jiang Zemin, quoted in Brahm, *ibid.*, p. 64.

27. Ibid.

28. "President Hu's American visit serves common good," China View, *http://news. xinhuanet.com*, August 26, 2005.

29. Rebecca Blumenstein, "Hu Will Press Bush On Energy Deals," *Wall Street Journal Online*, August 25, 2005.

30. China, US have more common interests than differences, China View, *http://news.xinhuanet.com*, July 1, 2005.

31. Speech by Chinese President Hu Jintao at Yale University, April 21, 2006, pp. 2–3.

32. Henry Kissinger, China: Containment Won't Work, *Washington Post*, June 13, 2005, p. A19.

33. Ibid.

34. Brahm, ibid., p. 63.

35. Brahm, ibid., p. 63.

36. See Noam Chomsky, *Failed States: The Abuse Of Power and the Assault on Democracy*, Metropolitan Books, Henry Holt & Company, 2006; and Kishore Mahbubari, *Beyond The Age Of Innocence Rebuilding Trust Between America And The World*, BBS Public Affairs, 2005.

37. Ibid.

38. David E. Sanger, "An Old Presidential Predicament: China Proves Tough To Influence," *The New York Times*, April 21, 2006, p. A15.

39. Joseph Kahn, "In Private Candor From China, An Overture to Promote A Thaw," *The New York Times*, April 21, 2006, p. 1.

40. Joseph Kahn, "Bush and Hu Vow New Cooperation," *The New York Times*, Friday April 21, 2006, p. A1.

41. David Sanger, ibid.

42. Anna Fifield and Stephen Fidler, "Pyongyang succeeds in ratcheting up tension but falls short of mastering missile technology," *Financial Times*, July 6, 2006, p. 3.

43. Joseph Kahn, "In Private Candor From China, An Overture to Promote a Thaw," *The New York Times*, April 17, 2006, p. 1.

44. Ibid.

45. Joseph Kahn, "China's Leader, in Seattle, Tells U.S. Not to Dwell on Divisive Issues," *The New York Times*, April 20, 2006, p. A6.

46. Joseph Kahn, "Bush and Hu Vow New Cooperation," *The New York Times*, Friday April 21, 2006, p. A1.

47. Fredrick Kempe, "U.S. Attempts to Coach China on New World Role," *The Wall Street Journal*, April 18, 2006, p. A8.

48. Ibid., April 21, 2006.

49. "The Unexpected Shout of Dissent," The New York Times, April 21, 2006, p. A15.

50. Ibid.

51. "No Charges For Woman Who Heckled Chinese Leader, *The New York Times*, June 22, 2006, p. A21.

52. Joseph Kahn, "In Hu's Visit to the U.S., Small Gaffes May Overshadow Small Gains," *The New York Times*, April 22, 2006, p. A8.

53. David Sanger, ibid.

54. *Beijing Review*, April 27, 2006, p. 6.

55. Neil King Jr, "As China Boosts Defense Budget, U.S. Military Hedges Its Bets," *Wall Street Journal*, April 20, 2006, p. A1.

56. Ibid.

57. Ibid.

58. Neil King Jr. "As China Boosts Defense Budget, U.S. Military Hedges Its Bets," *Wall Street Journal*, April 20, 2006, p. A1.

59. James Harkin, "Jumping the gun," *Financial Times*, April 22, 2006, p. W6.

60. Jeb Babbin and Edward Timperlake, *Showdown: Why China Wants War With The United States*, Regency Publishing, Inc, 2006.

61. Ibid.

62. G.P. Putnam's Sons, 2004.

63. G.P. Putnam's Sons, 2005.

64. Kishore Mahbubani, *Beyond The Age Of Innocence: Rebuilding Trust Between America And The World*, BBS Public Affairs, 2005, p. 31.

65. Ibid.

66. Victor Mallet, "Rumsfeld softens tone over China's military," *Financial Times*, June 5, 2006, p. 4.

67. *Document Of The 16th National Congress Of The Communist Party Of China*, Foreign Languages Press, 2002.

68. Richard McGregor and Caroline Daniel, "Bush urges Hu to speed up reforms," *Financial Times*, April 21, 2006, p. 1.

69. James Dean and Jay Solomon, "Business Gives Hu a Thumbs-up But Washington Is More Muted," *Wall Street Journal*, April 22, 2006, p. A1.

70. Ibid., p. 9.

71. Neil King Jr, Christopher Cooper & Rebecca Blumenstein, "Lunch, Not Dinner: U.S. China Remain At Odds Over Trip," *Wall Street Journal Online*, August 31, 2005.

72. Speech by Chinese President Hu Jintao at Yale University, April 21, 2006, pp. 9–10.

73. Ibid.

74. Chen Wen "Let's Talk About Trade," *Beijing Review*, April 27, 2006, p. 18.

75. Ibid.

76. Ibid.

77. Ibid.

78. Ibid., p. 19.

79. Keith Bradsher, "Besieged Taiwan Leader Sets Deal on China Flights," *The New York Times*, June 15, 2006, p. A13.

80. Katherine Heller and Mure Dickie, "Air link progress for China and Taiwan, *Financial Times*, June 15, 2006, p. 4.

81. Katherin Hille, "Taiwan to loosen trade restrictions with China, *Financial Times*, August 2, 2006, p. 3.

82. Quoted in John B. Stuttard, *The New Silk Road, Secrets of Business Success in China Today*, 2000, John Wiley & Sons, p. 37.

83. Speech by Chinese President Hu Jintao at Yale University, April 21, 2006, pp. 4–6.

84. Frances Williams, "UN watchdog rebukes US over rights," *Financial Times*, July 29/30, 2006, p. 4.

85. Noam Chomsky, *Failed States: The Abuse Of Power and the Assault on Democracy*, Metropolitan Books, Henry Holt & Company, 2006.

86. Richard J. Newman, *ibid.*, p. 42.

87. China Trade Increases 23.3% in 2005, Continuing Boom," *Wall Street Journal Online*, January 10, 2006.

88. People's Representative Bank Of China.

Chapter 8. Leadership Failure and American Resentment and Fear of China

1. *The Economist*, September 3rd–9th, 2005, p. 25.

2. Regency Publishing, Inc., 2006.

3. Mark Daniell, "China In A World Of Risk," *China's Century: The Awakening Of A New Economic Powerhouse*, Laurence Brahm ed., John Wiley & Sons, 2001, p. 102.

4. Ibid., p. 103.

5. Ibid.

6. Ibid.

7. Joseph Kahn, "In Private Candor From China, An Overture to Promote a Thaw," *The New York Times*, April 17, 2006, p. 1.

8. Joseph S. Nye Jr, *The Paradox Of American Power*, Oxford University Press, 2002.

9. China is often referred to as "The Middle Kingdom" with God and the rest of the world above and below it.

10. Ibid. p. 19.

11. Joseph S. Nye Jr, ibid., pp. 19–20.

12. Shenkar, ibid., pp. 153–56.

13. Ibid., p. 156.

14. Ibid.

15. Geoffrey Colvin, "America Isn't Ready." *Fortune*, August 1, 2005, pp. 70–1.

16. John Stuttard, ibid., pp. 70–1.

17. Geoffrey Colvin, Ibid., p. 70.

18. Ibid.

19. Mahbubani, ibid., pp. 22–3.

20. Ibid., pp. 25–7.

21. Ibid., pp. 30–1.

22. Ibid., p. 72.

23. Kishore Mahbubani, *Beyond The Age Of Innocence: Rebuilding Trust Between America And The World*, 2005.

24. Oded Shenkar, *The Chinese Century*, Wharton School Publication, 2005, pp. 142–43.

25. See Lester Thurow, *Fortune Favors The Bold*, Harper Business, 2003.

26. Fan Gang, "Reform and Development: The Dual-Transformation Of China," Mar & Richter, *China Enabling An Era Of Change*, ibid., p. 38.

Chapter 9. Conflict or Collaboration Among the Elite Capitalist Superpowers

1. Ibid.

2. See Bruce Elnhorn, "Huawei: More Than A Local Hero, *Business Week*, October 11, 2004, p. 180.

3. See Bernard Simon, "Minmetals in exclusive talks to by Noranda," *Financial Times*, September 24, 2004.

4. Russell Flannary, "Getting With The Drill," *Fortune*, April 18, 2005, p. 88.

5. Dan Blumenthal and Phillip Swagel, "Chinese Oil Drill," *The Wall Street Journal*, June 8, 2006, p. A18.

6. Ibid.

7. "How Dare They Use Our Oil," *The New York Times*, April 20, 2006, p. A26.

8. David Zwing and Bi Jianbai, "China's Global Hunt For Energy," *Foreign Affairs*, September/October 2005, p. 25 at p. 28.

9. Owl Books, Henry Holt and Company, 2004.

10. Oil Reserves, The Economist, June 24, 2006, p. 114.

11. Ibid.

12. *The Wall Street Journal*, April 19, 2006, p. A8.

13. David Zwing and Bi Jianbai, "China's Global Hunt For Energy," *Foreign Affairs*, September/October 2005, p. 25 at p. 28.

14. Michael T. Klare, *Blood And Oil The Dangers And Consequences Of America's Growing Dependency On Imported Oil*, ibid., p. 166.

15. Ibid., p. 14.

16. Michael J. Klare, *Blood And Oil:The Dangerous Consequences Of America's Dependence On Imported Oil*, Owl Books, Henry Holt And Company, 2004, p. 19.

17. David Zweig and Bi Jianbai, "China's Global Hunt for Energy," *Foreign Affairs*, September/October 2005, pp. 36–8.

18. *The Economist*, ibid.

19. Matt Pottinger, Jason Singer and Martha Linebaugh, "Cnnoc Outside Director Courtis Stalled Earlier Bid For Unocal Despite Goldman Funding Pledge," *Wall Street Journal Online*, June 24, 2005.

20. *The Economist*, ibid.

21. Dow Jones News Wires, "China Investment Not A Threat To America— Ex-Pres Clinton" *Wall Street Journal Online*, September 10, 2005.

22. "China Paranoia," *Wall Street Journal*, August 3, 2005, p. A10.

23. Ibid.

24. Peter Wonacott, "China Eases Shortage At Gasoline Stations," *Wall Street Journal Online*, August 19, 2005.

25. "Feeding the Dragon: The Middle East, Oil and the Chinese Boom, *World Economic Forum Knowledge Navigator*.

26. Ibid.

27. Matt Pottinger, "CNOOC Stock Arcs to New High, Lack of Unocal Strain Cheers Investors, But Problems Linger," *Wall Street Journal Online*, August 15, 2005.

28. John Larkin, "India And China To Forge an Energy Tie," *Wall Street Journal Online*, August 18, 2005.

29. Ibid.

30. India-China: Blueprint for a Win-Win Relationship, China Business Summit 2004.

31. Stephanie Kirchgaessner, "Congress closer to law on vetting foreign deals," *Financial Times*, June 16, 2006, p. 6.

32. "Schumer Drops Opposition To Trade Nominee," *Wall Street Journal*, June 8, 2006, p. B6.

33. Ibid.

34. Ibid.

35. Ibid.

36. Jason Singer, "CNPC clears a hurdle to buy PetroKazakhstan," *Wall Street Journal Online*, October 17, 2005.

37. Nisha Gopanla and Aries Poon, "CNOOC Considers Offer For Canadian Firm," *The Wall Street Journal Online, January* 13, 2006.

38. "Husky and CNOOC Find Natural Gas Off China Coast," *Wall Street Journal*, June 16, 2006. p. A9.

39. Associated Press, "Russia, China Launch Joint Military Exercise," *Wall Street Journal Online*, August 17, 2005.

40. Gregory L White, Shai Oster, "China Puts Energy at Top Of Agenda for Putin Visit," *Wall Street Journal Online*, March 20, 2006.

41. Associated Press, "Russia, China strengthen ties for 'multipolar' world," *The Bermuda Royal Gazette*, March 23, 2006, p. 10.

42. Reuters, "Pragmatism, not love, draws Russia and China closer," *The Bermuda Royal Gazette*, March 24, 2006, p. 18.

43. Steven Kirchgaesner, "China's oil scramble does not damage US," *Financial Times*, February 8, 2006, p. 6.

44. Gregory White and Shai Oser, "China Puts Energy at Top Of Agenda for Putin Visit," *The Wall Street Journal Online*, March 20, 2006.

45. AP, "Putin commits to gas supplies for China," *The Royal Gazette*, March 22, 2006, p. 64.

46. Joanna Chung, "China and India eye Rosneft," *Financial Times*, June 15, 2006, p. 19.

47. David White, "China's quest for commodities leads to Africa," *Financial Times*, June 20, 2006, p. 1.

48. Andrew Yeh, "China ventures on rocky roads to trade with Africa," *Financial Times*, June 20, 2006, p. 2.

49. Ibid.

50. "China's African Affair," *Financial Times*, June 26, 2006, p. 14.

51. Ibid.

52. Ibid.

53. Ibid.

54. Kate Linebaugh and Shai Oster, CNOOC pays $2.27 Billion For Nigerian Oil, Gas Stake," *Wall Street Journal Online*, January 10, 2006.

55. John Reed, "China and S Africa in nuclear deal," *Financial Times*, June 21, 2006, p. 7.

56. Gordon Fairclough, "Iran Lobbies China, Russia To help Curb U.S.," *Wall Street Journal*, June 16, 2006. p. A4.

57. Ibid.

Geoff Dryer and Richard McGregor, "Opposition to US inspires 'Nato of the east," *Financial Times*, June 22, 2006, p. 4.

58. Steven Weisman, "U.S. Rejects Direct Talks With Iran but Keeps Meeting With Europe, China and Russia," *New York Times*, May 25, 2006, p. A6. and Daniel Dombey, Edward Alden and Gareth Smyth, "Bush frustrated by Iran's slow nuclear response," *Financial Times*, June 22, 2006, p. 2.

59. Daniel Dombey and Edward Alden, "Bush tries to repair battered US image," *Financial Times*, June 22, 2006, p. 1.

60. Daniel Dombey and Edward Alden, "Common enemy speeds transatlantic thaw," *Financial Times*, June 22, 2006, p. 2.

61. Ibid.

62. Ibid.

63. Ibid.

64. Dennis Berman & Mark Heinzl, "Canada Welcomes China's Cash," *Wall Street Journal*, July 15, 2005, p. C1.

65. Ibid.

66. In conversations with John Milligan-Whyte on May 21, 2006.

67. Oded Shenkar, *The Chinese Century*, Wharton School Publishing, 2005, p. 138.

68. Ibid., p. 175.

69. Ibid., p. 137.

70. George Melloan, "Hu Jintao Meets Bill Gates," *The Wall Street Journal*, April 18, 2006, p. A19.

71. Information provided by President Zhang Liyong, President of COSCO America.

Chapter 10. America and China are Currently Economic Partners

1. *Business Week*, August 22/29, 2005.

2. Ibid.

3. Ted Fishman, ibid., p. 8.

4. Frances Guerrera, "GE to shift output from US," *Financial Times*, July 27, 2006, p. 27.

5. Geoffrey Colvin, "America Isn't Ready," *Fortune*, August 1, 2005, 70 at p. 72.

6. Mar & Richter, *China Enabling An Era Of Changes*, ibid., p. 218.

7. See Ted Fishman, *China Inc*, Simon & Schuster, 2005.

8. Ibid., p. 254.

9. Ibid., p. 256.

10. Ibid., p. 258.

11. Ibid., pp. 253–58.

12. Ibid., p. 72.

13. "What America Must Do To Compete With China and India," *Business Week*, August 22/29, 2005, p. 144.

14. Ibid.

15. Ibid.

16. Ted C. Fishman, "How China Will Change Your Business," *Inc.*, March 2005, p. 77.

17. James Areddy, Mary Kissel, Andrew Browne & Michael Phillips, "China Lets Yuan Price vs. Dollar, Easing Trade Tensions Slightly," *Wall Street Journal Online*, July 22, 2005.

18. John Bussey, "The Two-Percent Solution," *Wall Street Journal Online*, July 21, 2005.

19. Tim Annett & David Gaffen, "FAQ: China's Yuan Revaluation," *Wall Street Journal On Line*, July 22, 2005.

20. James Areddy, Mary Kissel, Andrew Browne & Michael Phillips, "China Lets Yuan Price vs. Dollar, Easing Trade Tensions Slightly," *Wall Street Journal Online*, July 22, 2005.

21. Ibid., p. 259.

22. Ibid., p. 261.

23. Andrew Browne, "Currency Reserves Held by Beijing Continue to Swell," *Wall Street Journal Online* January 16, 2006.

24. Ted Fishman, ibid., pp. 264–65.

25. Ted Fishman, ibid., p. 265. It is not clear how Ted Fishman arrived at that number. According to the US National Debt Clock on the Internet, each American citizen's share of the debt is US$ 26,667.06. Multiplying that figure by an average number of persons per household, say 2.63, produces an amount of $ 70,134.37 per household. If the $ 473, 456 estimate is multiplied times 97 million American households, it produces a sum of US$ 46 trillion.

26. Deborah Solomon and John McKinnon, "Bush Would Boost Defense, Security In Budget Plan," *Wall Street Journal*, February 7, 2006, p. 1.

27. People's Bank Of China, April 2005.

28. *The Economist*, September 24th–30th, 2005, p. 15.

29. Ibid., p. 26.

Chapter 11. The Partnership Solution to America's Trade Deficits with China

1. "Behind the mask," *The Economist*, March 18, 2004.

2. Julius Bar, "Tempted by the dragon," 2005.

3. Victoria Ruan,"Beijing Says 2005 Trade Surplus May Not Warrant Revaluing Yuan," January 14,2006, *Wall Street Journal Online*.

4. "China Trade Grew 23.3% In 2005, Continuing Boom," *Wall Street Journal Online*, January 10, 2005.

5. Thirlwell, ibid.

6. Thirlwell, ibid.

7. Dow Jones News Wire, "China logs growth in retail sales and industrial-export shipments," *Wall Street Journal Online*, October 25, 2005.

8. Mark Thirlwell, S*haking The World? China And The World Economy*, Lowy Institute For International Policy, August 2005, p. 6.

9. Thirwell, ibid., pp. 9–10.

10. *Business Week*, August 22/29, 2005, p. 57.

11. Thirlwell, ibid., pp. 5–7.

12. Haley, Haley & Tan, *The Tao Of Chinese Business*, John Wiley & Sons, (Asia) Pte Ltd, 2003, p. 198.

13. Ibid.

14. Ibid.

15. Chee & West, ibid., p. 13.

16. Thirlwell, ibid., p. 8.

17. Ted Fishman, *China Inc*, Simon & Schuster, 2005, p. 263.

18. "China's GDP is forecast to grow by 9.4% this year before slowing," *Wall Street Journal Online*, October 17, 2005.

19. Timothy Aeppel, "U.S. Group Sees China Trade Gap Widening in 2005," *Wall Street Journal Online*, August 31, 2005.

20. Ibid.

21. Andrew W. Browne, "China Trade Surplus Drops, Welcome Sign For U.S. Talks," *Wall Street Journal Online*, October 12, 2005.

22. *Business Week*, August 22/29, 2005.

23. Thirlwell, ibid.

24. "Does The Future Belong To China?" *Newsweek*, May 9, 2005, p. 28.

25. Richard J. Newman, "The Rise Of A New Power," *US News & World Report*, June 10, 2005, p. 40.

26. Jason Dean, "China's Hu Visit to US in April," January 24, 2006, *Wall Street Journal Online*.

27. *The Economist*, September 3rd–9th, 2005, p. 44.

28. *The Economist*, ibid.

29. Martin Wolf, "Why Washington and Beijing need strong global institutions," *Financial Times*, April 19, 2006, p. 13.

30. Ibid.

31. Ibid.

32. Ibid.

33. Ibid.

34. Julius Bar, ibid., p. 7.

35. "Behind the mask," *The Economist*, March 18, 2005.

36. *Business Week*, August 22/29, 2005, p. 57.

37. Oded Shenkar, *China's Century*, Wharton Publications, 2005.

38. Thirlwell, ibid., p. 5.

39. Keniche Ohmae, *The Next Global Stage*, Wharton School Publications, 2005, p. 101.

40. Ibid., p. 150.

41. John Frisbe, "Sino-American trade needs a bilateral framework," *Financial Times*, April 20, 2006, p. 13.

42. *Business Week*, August 22/29, 2005.

43. Joseph Kahn, "In Private Candor From China, An Overture To Promote A Thaw," *The New York Times*, April 17, 2006, p. 1.

44. Henry Pulizzi "UPDATE: China Hu: Trade Frictions With US Are 'Inevitable," *Wall Street Journal Online*, September 13, 2005.

45. Neil King Jr, "Hu Tells Bush China Will Work On U.S. Concerns," *Wall Street Journal Online*, September 14, 2005.

46. Jane Lanhee Lee and Nisha Gopalan, "Chinese Airlines to Buy 42 Jets From Boeing in $5.04 Billion Deal," *Wall Street Journal Online*, August 8, 2005.

47. Horizon Group Survey, www.horizon-china.com.

48. Neil King Jr. & James Areddy, "U.S. Urges Chinese To Save Less, Buy More," *Wall Street Journal Online*, October 14, 2005.

49. Joseph Kahn, "In Private Candor From China, An Overture to Promote a Thaw," *The New York Times*, April 21, 2006, p. A1.

50. Martin Crutsinger, "Trade deficit hits record $68.5 billion in January," *Bermuda Royal Gazette*, March 10, 2006, p. 28.

51. Neil King Jr. & Mei Fong, "Snow Signals Faith In China Reform," *Wall Street Journal Online*, October 17, 2005.

Chapter 12. Will America Choose 1.3 Billion Chinese Friends or Enemies?

1. Kishore Mahbubani, *Beyond The Age Of Innocence*, BBS Public Affairs, 2005. Joseph Nye Jr, *The Paradox Of American Power*, Oxford University Press, 2003.

2. Lester Thurow, *Fortune Favors The Bold*, Harper Business, 2003.

3. Plato, *The Republic*, Everyman's Library, 1993.

4. Mahbubani, ibid.

5. Mahbubani, ibid., p. 95.

6. Ibid., pp. 121–123.

7. Menges, ibid., pp. xv–xvii.

8. Menges, ibid., p. 151.

9. Menges, ibid., p. 152.

10. Ibid.

11. Ibid., p. 156.

12. Ibid., p. 155.

13. Ibid., p. 154.

14. Mahbubani, ibid., p. 101.

15. Mahbubani, ibid., pp. 123–25.

16. Jared Diamond, *Guns, Steel & Germs: The Fates Of Human Societies*, W.W. Norton, 1999.

17. Fishman, ibid., p. 181.

18. Fishman, ibid., p. 8.

19. Fishman, ibid.

20. Geoffrey Colvin, ibid., p. 72.

21. Mark Landler, "Few Answers From China at Economic Forum," *New York Times*, Sunday January 30, 2005, p. 2.

22. Friedman, ibid., p. 310.

23. Ibid.

24. See Novak, May & Sigmund, ibid; and Bertrand Russell, *The History Of Western Philosophy*, Touchstone, 1999, Chapter XVI.

25. "Does The Future Belong To China," *Newsweek*, May 19, 2005, pp. 25–47 at p. 28.

Chapter 13. China's Past and Future Scientific and Technology Contributions to America

1. Ibid., pp. 24–25.

2. Gavin Menzies, 1421: *The Year China Discovered America*, Harper, 2002, back cover.

3. Robert Temple, *The Genius Of China 3000 years of Science, Discovery and Invention*, Prion, 1999.

4. Ibid., pp. 9–12.

5. Ibid., pp. 4–5.

6. Ibid., p. 181.

7. Ibid.

8. See Buderi and Huang, *Guanxi: Microsoft, China, and Bill Gates's Plan to Win the Road Ahead*, Simon & Schuster, 2006.

9. Ibid., p. 73.

10. Ibid.

11. Quoted in Laurence Brahm, *China's Century*, pp 318–19.

12. Ibid., p. 318.

13. Ibid.

14. Wu Jichuan, "The Development Of The Information And Network Technology Industry Of China," Laurence Brahm, *China's Century*, John Wiley & Sons (Asia) Pte, 2000, p. 325.

15. Ibid., p. 325.

16. Ibid., p. 323.

17. Peter Yip, "How The Internet Will Shape China," Laurence Brahm, ibid., p. 327.

18. *Business Week*, August 22/29, 2005, p. 31.

19. Ibid.

20. Title of 2005 Venture Capital Forum on April 6, 2005, Beijing.

21. *The Economist*, "China: Something New," August 5, 2006, p. 38.

22. Lester Thurow, ibid.

23. Joseph Needham & Robert K. G. Temple, *The Genius Of China: 3000 Years Of Science Discovery and Invention*, Prion Books, 1998.

24. David Stipp, "Can China Overtake The U.S. In Science?" *Fortune*, October 4, 2004, pp. 187–8.

25. Bruce Elnhorn, *Business Week*, October 11, 2004, p. 181.

26. Vogelstein, ibid., p. 136.

27. Geoffrey Colvin, "America Isn't Ready," *Fortune*, August 1, 2005, p. 70 at p. 77.

28. Ibid., p. 72.

29. Michael Lewis, *The New New Thing: A Silicon Valley Story*, W.W. Norton & Company; 1999.

30. Kathy Chen & Jason Dean, "Low Costs, Plentiful Talent Make China a Global Magnet for R&D," *Wall Street Journal Online*, March 13, 2006.

31. Santiago Perez, "Davos Interview: Dow Chemical Eyes China's Human Capital," *Wall Street Journal Online*, January 30, 2006.

32. Ibid.

33. Ming Zeng & Peter Williamson, "The Hidden Dragons," *Harvard Business Review*, October 2003, pp. 95–7.

34. Mara Hvistendahl, "What Happens When Science Is Made In China?" *Seed*, October/November 2005, p. 58.

35. China Electronic Equipment Solicitation Center: http://www.cec.gov.cn/info/zt/20020916/index.jsp.

36. Geoffrey Clovin, "America Isn't Ready," *Fortune Magazine*, August 1, 2005.

37. David Stipp, "Can China Overtake The U.S. In Science?," *Fortune*, October 4, 2004, p. 187, 194.

38. Kenneth Lieberthal & Geoffrey Lieberthal, "The Great Transition," *Harvard Business Review*, October 2003, p. 73.

39. "Stealing Managers From The Big Boys," *Business Week*, September 26, 2005, pp. 54–5.

40. Mahbubani, ibid., p. 21.

41. Oded Shenkar, *The Chinese Century*, Wharton School Publishing, 2005, p. 5.

42. Ibid., p. 74.

43. Ibid., p. 75.

44. Ibid., p. 76.

45. Ibid.

46. *Wall Street Journal*, March 11, 2002, p. 1.

47. Ibid.

48. Mei Fong, Peter Wonacott & Timothy Aeppel, ibid.

49. Ibid.

50. See Bertrand Russell, *The History Of Western Philosophy*, Simon & Schuster, 1945, Chapter XXV on Friedrich Nietzsche, p. 760.

51. See Kovak, May & Sigmund, "The Arithmetic Of Mutual Assistance," *Scientific American*, June 1995, pp. 76–81.

52. David Heenan, *Flight Capital The Alarming Exodus Of America's Best And Brightest*, Davis Black Publishing, 2005.

53. Bruce Einhorn and John Carry, "A New Lab Partner For The U.S.?," *Business Week*, August 22/29, 2005 p. 116 see www.businessweek.com/go/china–india/

54. Ibid.

55. *Business Week*, August 22/29, 2005.

56. These proposals can be explored with John Milligan-Whyte, of Milligan-Whyte & Smith Consulting Ltd., *jmw@mws.bm* and Dr. Robert Budny, Principal Research Physicist, Off-site Research Department, Plasma Physics Laboratory, Princeton University *bundny@princeton.edu.*

Chapter 14. The Reform of America and China's Intellectual Property Piracy

1. Oded Shenkar, *The Chinese Century*, Wharton School Publishing, 2005, pp. 82–3.

2. Ibid., pp. 83–4.

3. Oded Shenkar, ibid., p. 71.

4. Ibid., p. 70.

5. Fareed Zakaria, "How Long Will America Lead The World," *Newsweek*, June 16, 2006, p. 45.

6. Davos News Tracker, January 28, 2006.

7. Ibid.

Chapter 15. Establishing America and China's Committed Partnership

1. "American Attitudes Toward China: Committee Of 100 Survey," *Committee Of 100 Bridges*, Summer 2005, p. 1.

2. Ibid.

3. Ibid., p. 6.

4. George Soros, *The Bubble Of American Supremacy*, W.W. Norton, 2004.

5. Ibid., pp. 3–4.

6. Ibid., p. 30.

7. Ibid., p. 80.

8. Fan Gang, "Reform and Development: The Dual-Transformation of China," Mar & Richter, ibid., p. 46.

9. John F. Kennedy, Commencement Address at American University, Washington, D.C. June 10, 1963.

10. Weisman, ibid., p. C2.

11. Floyd Norris, "There's More Than the Currency Advantage Behind China's Export Surge," *The New York Times*, August 12, 2006 p. C3.

12. *The New York Times*, "Mr. Schumer Goes To China," March 17, 2006.

13. Krishna Guha, "Paulson urges more renminbi flexibility," *Financial Times*, August 12, p. 4.

14. Steven Weisman, "Paulson Reinforces His Reach As Treasury Secretary," *The New York Times*, August 10, 2006, p. C1.

15. Ibid.

16. Ibid.

17. Floyd Norris, ibid.

18. Ibid.

19. Ibid.

20. Ibid.

21. Ibid.

22. Weisman, ibid.

23. Ibid.

24. See William Powndstone, *Prisoner's Dilemma: Jon Von Neumann, Game Theory And The Puzzle Of The Bomb*, First Anchor Books, 1993.

25. See Roger McCain, *Game Theory: A Non-technical Introduction to the Analysis of Strategy*, South Western College Publications, 2003.

26. Kowak, May & Sigmund, "The Arithmetics Of Mutual Help," *Scientific American*, June 1995, pp. 76–81.

27. Ibid p. 77.

28. Ibid.

29. Ibid., pp. 78–9.

30. Ibid., p. 81.

31. See Richard Dawkins, *The Selfish Gene*, Oxford University Press, 1976, pp. 203–233; and David P. Barash, *The Survival Game: How Game Theory Explains The Biology Of Cooperation*, Owl Books, Henry Holt and Company, 2003, pp. 67–120; James Miller, *Game Theory At Work: How To Use Game Theory To Outthink And Out Maneuver Your Competition*, McGraw-Hill, 2003, pp. 115–150: Michel Shermer, *The*

Science Of Good & Evil: Why People Cheat, Gossip, Care, Share, and Follow the Golden Rule, Owl book, Henry Holt and Company, 2004.

Chapter 16. Will America and China Choose to Succeed or Fail?

1. Jared Diamond, *Collapse: How Societies Choose To Fail Or Succeed*, Viking Penguin, 2005.

2. Against the tide," *IQ Insider Quarterly*, Autumn 2005, p. 38.

3. Ibid.

4. Ibid., pp. 419–20.

5. Ibid.

6. Ibid., p. 427.

7. Ibid., p. 36.

8. Editorial, *The New York Times*, July 8, 2006, p. A12.

9. Ibid.

10. Cambridge University Press, 2001.

11. Kimberley A. Strassel, "Get Your Priorities Right," *The Wall Street Journal*, July 8–9, 2006, p. A10/.

12. See Amory Lovins, "More Profit With Less Carbon," *Scientific American*, September 2005, pp. 74–83.

13. Ibid., pp. 430–31.

14. Ibid., pp. 433–34.

15. Steve Connor, "The State of the World? It is on the Brink of Disaster," *The Independent*, March 30, 2005.

16. Ibid.

17. Ibid.

18. Ibid.

19. Rodale, 2006.

20. Greg Holland, National Center For Atmospheric Research, gholland@ucar.edu.

21. Jeffrey Kluger, "The Tipping Point," *Time Magazine*, April 3, 2006, p. 35.

22. Bryan Walsh, "The Impact of Asia's Giants: How China and India could save the world—or destroy it," *Time Magazine*, April 3, 2006, p. 59.

23. Ibid.

24. Ibid., p. 62.

25. Jared Diamond, ibid., p. 373.

26. Ibid., p. 373.

27. Andrew Batson, "China warns pollution will grow with economy," *Wall Street Journal Online*, October 25, 2005.

28. Ibid.

29. Bryan Walsh, "The Impact of Asia's Giants: How China and India could save the planet—or destroy it," *Time Magazine*, April 3, 2006, p. 61.

30. Ibid.

31. Ibid.

32. Bryan Walsh, "Clean Power For China," *Time Magazine*, April 3, 2006, p. 59.

33. Dow Jones News Wire, "China Investment Not A Threat To America—Ex-Pres Clinton," *Wall Street Journal Online*, September 10, 2005.

Chapter 17. Can Mankind Solve Problems Caused by Mankind?

1. Robert Kennedy, *Thirteen Days*, W.W. Norton & Co, 1973.

2. Inhaul New Agency.

3. Published in Robert Lawrence Kuhn, *The Man Who Changed China The Life And Legacy Of Jiang Zemin*, Crown Publishers, 2004.

4. John F. Kennedy, Commencement Address at American University, Washington D.C., June 10, 1963.